Praise for Previous Edition

"This autobiography deserves to be placed next to Victor Klemperer's *I Will Bear Witness* as a vivid account of the Nazi years. In plain and lucid language Angress recounts the gradual disillusionment of a Jewish schoolboy in Berlin after 1933. No less strikingly portrayed is his experience as an American soldier in the Second World War, parachuted into France on D-Day, wounded in battle, and shocked at the liberation of concentration camps. Readers, whether professional historians or not, will find in these pages the unforgettable depiction of a turbulent life."

—Allan Mitchell,
   Professor Emeritus of History
   University of California, San Diego.

"This is an extraordinary memoir, self-ironic and humane, dealing with one of the darkest chapters of twentieth century history. A Jewish historian of Germany recounts his privileged childhood in Berlin, his flight to exile in the United States, and his experiences as a soldier in the liberation of Europe. In a lively style, these recollections recreate a lost Jewish-German world, destroyed by Nazi racism, while reaffirming a deep commitment to rational inquiry and personal forgiveness."

—Konrad H. Jarausch,
   Lurcy Professor of European Civilization in the Department
   of History, University of North Carolina, Chapel Hill.

D1569651

WITNESS TO THE STORM

Witness to the Storm

A JEWISH JOURNEY
FROM NAZI BERLIN TO
THE 82ND AIRBORNE,
1920–1945

Werner T. Angress

INDIANA UNIVERSITY PRESS

This book is a publication of

Indiana University Press
Office of Scholarly Publishing
Herman B Wells Library 350
1320 East 10th Street
Bloomington, Indiana 47405 USA

iupress.indiana.edu

The paper used in this publication meets the minimum
requirements of the American National Standard
for Information Sciences—Permanence of Paper for
Printed Library Materials, ANSI Z39.48-1992.

Manufactured in the United States of America

LCCN: 2012908730
ISBN 978-0-253-03912-5 (hardcover)
ISBN 978-0-253-03913-2 (paperback)
ISBN 978-0-253-03914-9 (ebook)

1 2 3 4 5   24 23 22 21 20 19

To my deceased parents,
Ernst and Henny Angress,
dedicated in loving memory

Contents

Acknowledgments.. X

Foreword... XI

Personal Notes... XII

CHAPTER 1
Family Life in Berlin, 1920–1936.. 1

CHAPTER 2
Early Childhood and School Days... 31

CHAPTER 3
The Youth Movement... 97

CHAPTER 4
Gross Breesen Training Farm for Emigrants, 1936–1937......... 128

CHAPTER 5
The Road into Exile, 1937–1939.. 160

CHAPTER 6
United States—Hyde Farmlands, 1939–1941......................... 201

CHAPTER 7
Service in the Army and War... 227

CHAPTER 8
From the Battle of the Bulge to the
End of the War, 1944–1945... 293

Epilogue... 328

APPENDIX 1
Diary covering jump on Normandy (June 6, 1944) through
time in Prisoner of War camp (June 15–27, 1944)................. 333

APPENDIX 2
Travel Authorization into Holland
by Major General Gavin, November 21, 1944....................... 344

APPENDIX 3
Article from *Richmond Times-Dispatch*, June 4, 1945........... 345

Acknowledgments

I would probably never have written these childhood memories if my four children (especially), my two brothers, as well as several friends had not repeatedly asked for them. I have confined myself to the first, formative twenty-five years of my life because I cannot imagine that many readers are interested in my academic career. But I grew up during the years of the Weimar Republic and the twelve years that the "Thousand Year [German] Empire" lasted, which included the war years from 1939 to 1945. It seemed important to me to communicate my experiences as a "Zeitzeuge," or contemporary witness, to this period in history.

A number of friends were kind enough to help me while I worked on the manuscript, and then later, after I had a draft, to make corrections and suggest changes. So I would first like to thank Trude Maurer for reading section by section and carefully correcting the manuscript. Helpful suggestions came from a number of friends: Gisela Bittner, Ernst Cramer, Silvia Diekmann, Dagmar von Doetinchem, Astrid Eckert, Elma Gaasbeek, Christine Granger, Konrad H. Jarausch, Gabriele Krebs, Gabriele Jonelat-Krüschet, Cornelia R. Levine, Michael Maurer, Rita Röhr, Katherine Rürup, Andrea Schultz, Angelika Tramitz and Werner Warmbrunn. Also, Claudia Angress, Wolfgang Benz, Andrea Brill, Belinda Cooper, Angelika Kipp and Fred and Sally Tubach took an active interest. Finally, last but not least, I want to thank the Kampe family in particular for their efforts: Angelika and Jonas for their comments and Norbert for his assistance in getting the manuscript ready for publication.
— *Werner T. Angress*
Berlin, 2005

Foreword

This memoir was originally published in German in 2005.* Tom Angress always planned to make an English version available to his relatives and friends, and he worked on a translation during the last years of his life. After his death in 2010, our family decided to publish the English edition in the United States, and we collaborated on its preparation. Tom would have liked how the family worked together on this project, either directly, by contributing time and funds, or by clearing away other work connected with his estate so that a group could focus on the book.

A few of the ways family and other loved ones participated: by organizing the historical photographs and appendices (including the diary Tom kept during his jump on Normandy and brief stay in a German P.O.W. camp); by going through the copyedits to check that Tom's distinctive voice had not been lost; by asking Tom, before his death, and others afterwards, to answer questions raised by the copyeditor (because none of us is familiar with paratrooper protocol, or knows what it was like to be part of a Jewish youth group under the Nazis); by brainstorming about a title and subtitle for the English edition; and by translating a few pieces (frontmatter, mostly), that Tom hadn't tackled himself.

We did this out of love, but also because we believe that this volume will be interesting and valuable to readers who never knew him.

We thank Helen Robinson for her thoughtful and elegant design and Kay Robin Alexander for her deep generosity (for proofing the text, and going far beyond her initial pledge to just read through the manuscript). We are grateful to Alex Martin for beautifully copyediting this edition and for suggesting that the family add a foreword. Alex said that he developed affection for Tom, whom he never met or spoke to, through working on this text. He started referring to Tom as "the Zeitzeuge" (contemporary witness), which is how Tom described himself in the German acknowledgments. That is, really, the point of this book: to share what he witnessed and the part he played.

— *Tom Angress's children*
United States, 2012

*...immer etwas abseits: Jugenderinnerungen eines jüdischen Berliners 1920–1945 (Berlin: Edition Hentrich).

Personal Notes

One of the gifts of my father's memoirs was the portrait it provided me of a grandfather I'd never met. My father's increasing closeness to his father as he grew older mirrored my own maturing relationship to my father over the years. His absorption of Ernst Angress' beloved Prussian values—"Be honest and straightforward, and behave toward others in a way your parents would be proud of"—was reflected in my adoption of those same values, two generations removed. My father lost the companionship of his father at seventeen. I was luckier; I enjoyed his company for over half a century.

—*Percy Angress* (one of Tom's sons)

Once, when I visited my father in Germany, he took me to a Berlin public library. We both loved Wim Wenders' movie, *Wings of Desire*, and he knew I'd be moved to see the library that in the film was filled with angels leaning tenderly over the library patrons, whispering in their ears. After reading this memoir, I thought again of that scene, because he was in danger in many ways during his life, but something kept him safe. He speaks candidly, in the memoir, about his mistakes and struggles with his flaws—the Nazis were one tremendous danger he faced, and another threat was his own darkness—but he managed so often to approach the world with kindness, courage, humor, and decency. Maybe angels leaned over him.

—*Miriam Angress* (one of Tom's daughters)

WITNESS TO THE STORM

CHAPTER I

Family Life in Berlin, 1920–1936

In early 1990, only a few months after the Wall came down and not long after my return from almost fifty years in the United States, I went back for the first time to where the private clinic had stood, at Genthiner Strasse 12, Berlin. I was born in this clinic in June 1920. It was destroyed during the Second World War, and now another building stands in its place. To the right and left and across the street are now large furniture stores, which make Genthiner Strasse look quite different than at the time of my birth. It was strange to see the place where I was born. As a historian I noted that the clinic had been near Bendlerstrasse, today Stauffenbergstrasse, where everything went wrong on July 20, 1944 [the date of the failed attempt to assassinate Hitler via a bomb in Lieutenant Colonel von Stauffenberg's briefcase].

Of three brothers, I was the only one born in a hospital. My two younger brothers—Fritz Peter, born on April 14, 1923, and Hans Herbert, born on April 14, 1928—were both delivered at home, probably even on the same dining room table. Their common birthday was no accident. My mother thought it would be easier on her through the years to have one birthday party for both sons, so she had her doctor help out a bit.

Until she died at age ninety-two, my mother assured me that my childhood was very happy until January 30, 1933. And if one compares it to the fate of many others, she may have been right. I often perceived things differently, however. As a child I was occasionally reproached for being reserved and, worse, for not being a "family person." This was true, but there were, of course, reasons for it.

We were a large, complex family, which often caused confusion in my young mind. Not that the family was in any way exceptional. Like

Thank-you card: "For the expression of your kind regards shown on the occasion of the birth of our son Werner we express our sincere thanks. Ernst Angress and wife, Henny née Kiefer." Berlin—Schöneberg Rosenheimerstrasse 31, July 1920.

many German Jews at the time, both my parents came from the Jewish petit bourgeoisie of the nineteenth century that had slowly advanced to solid middle class. Of course, they would have liked to belong to the educated middle class and strove for that position. But my family never reached that goal, partly for financial reasons. School education ended with the tenth grade, three years earlier than today and with no *Abitur*, or final examination. Instead Germans either finished school with an exam called the *Mittlere Reife*, or we could volunteer for one year of military service. The education of my maternal grandfather, the only one of my grandparents with real intellectual interests, thus also ended at this level. I am the first of my family to have attended a university, but not in Germany and without having obtained a German high school diploma.

This Jewish family in Berlin—very bourgeois, very Prussian—was representative of many other Jews who lived in Berlin during the Weimar era. During the Third Reich they were all persecuted, driven out, and murdered, under the watching eyes of the educated German middle class that was "lucky" enough to be "Aryan," often approving of what was happening, at the least indifferent, and sometimes participating. For this reason, and not because of any interest in genealogy, I would like to describe my family in more detail here.

The name "Angress" was fairly common in Upper Silesia, especially in the region of Gleiwitz, as I saw in the deportation lists of the National

LEFT: *Werner Angress, three years old.* RIGHT: *My father, Ernst Angress, with us three sons in summer 1928. Left, Fritz Peter; right, me, Werner Karl; Hans Herbert is in our father's arms.*

Socialist period. My father said we didn't come from Upper Silesia, however, but rather from either Kleve, near the Dutch border, or Danzig (Gdánsk). He wasn't sure which. As I was able to ascertain later, there was no family by the name of Angress in Kleve. Whether or not there were or are Angresses in Danzig I don't know, as I've never been there.

Like his father before him, Papa was a native of Berlin. Born on August 5, 1883, at Jerusalemer Strasse 42, Papa grew up in the heart of the city, between Hausvogteiplatz and Spittelmarkt, the traditional garment district. Grandfather Isaac Angress was a businessman and worked in the clothing industry. My paternal grandparents were strict, observant Jews, and my grandmother kept a kosher household. During the first thirty years of his life my father ate only kosher food. Isaac and Amalie Angress had four children: Hanna, Rosa, Käthe, and Ernst, my father, their youngest child and only son.

I never met Grandfather Angress, but from the tone of a remark

Papa once made about him, I concluded that their relationship wasn't good. That remark (whose precise content I don't remember) is all Papa ever said to me about his father. He got along better with his mother, and I got to know her before she died in the mid-1920s. Her maiden name was Trepp and she came from Fulda, where the Trepp family is documented back to the second half of the fifteenth century. The Jüdenhaus an der Trepp [Jew house above the stairs], the ancestral seat of the family, which in its five-hundred-year history had produced rabbis and many doctors, was torn down in the 1960s.

My grandmother Angress I saw rarely and briefly. She lived with her oldest daughter, Tante Hanna, in the Tiergarten district on Holsteiner Ufer. I remember a hunched-over, almost blind old lady who groped her way around the apartment. When we went to visit, my father would lovingly administer her eyedrops. When she died and was buried at Weissensee I was only seven years old, and my parents thought I was too young to attend the funeral. Her death didn't affect me; the fact that my father wore a black crepe band around his left arm for a year struck me as peculiar, but I didn't ask questions.

For the first fifteen years of my life my father was above all a figure of authority. He was of medium height and muscular but slim. At the age of twenty his hair began to fall out, and by the time he became my father at the age of thirty-seven, he was completely bald. Until the beginning of the 1920s he wore a beard. His eyes were light blue, and when I look in the mirror, my father's eyes look back at me. He liked to smoke cigars, and of course he always wore a dark suit, a stiff collar, and a tie to work. He had a salaried position at the private Berlin bank Königsberger and Lichtenhein, which in my childhood had its offices on the ground floor of Französische Strasse 60–61. He had begun at that bank as an apprentice at the turn of the century, and at the end of the First World War he became the *Prokurist*, a leading executive who, as the owners' representative, has the right to sign financial contracts. In 1932 he took over the bank, or what was left of it after the stock market crash of 1929 and the ensuing Depression. Moritz Lichtenhein had, according to rumor, taken his own life in July 1930. Leo Königsberger had retired at the end of 1930, and Dr. Werner Lichtenhein, the son of Moritz and his successor, left the bank in March 1932 and went abroad with his wife.

My father's two elderly bosses were something quite special in my mind, because, on the one hand, they were always spoken of at home in an unusually respectful tone of voice, and, on the other hand, I always had to be dressed in my Sunday best when my parents took me along to visit them. I detested Sunday clothes like the plague. I remember only Leo Königsberger clearly. He was a tall man, at least from my perspective at the time, had a very deep voice, and resembled President Paul von Hindenburg to an amazing degree. He was kind, polite, and always seemed a bit absent. When he visited us, which didn't happen often, he brought small gifts, mostly a kind of chocolate that I didn't much like—I ate only chocolate with nuts—and of course I had to thank him for it nonetheless. I don't believe that Moritz Lichtenhein ever visited us at home, but he had us over to his villa in Nikolassee/Wannsee now and then. Their property radiated wealth, from the wrought iron entrance gate to the magnificent huge lawns.

Every weekday morning I saw Papa for only a moment in my parents' bedroom, where I dutifully gave him and my mother a hasty kiss before I raced off to school, since I was usually late. Normally he didn't come home until we children had eaten dinner, and so on weekdays I didn't see much of him. On Saturdays he got home from work in the early afternoon, but then his friends came to play cards, or he went to one of their homes. We only saw each other on Sundays, but in the afternoons he often worked at the enormous dark desk in his study or went somewhere with my mother. After lunch, however, the family did take the obligatory Sunday walk, weather permitting. We walked down the streets of Westend, where we lived from 1923 to 1932, and I was horribly bored. Papa and Mutti walked in front, and Fritz and I followed, both wearing the same coats, the same shirts and short pants, the same black berets. He and I didn't have much to say to each other back then. He was three years younger and developed quite slowly. Being somewhat plump, he had picked up the nickname "Möpschen" [Little Pug Nose]. He learned to speak quite late, but quickly made up for it. When he grew up he became a good-looking, very athletic young man. Together with my mother and our youngest brother, Hans, he survived the war in Holland in hiding. After the end of the war both of my brothers went to the United States, where they still live today, in California, and we get together regularly.

I look back on this phase of my early childhood, approximately from my sixth to my twelfth year, with some discomfort. I hated the Sunday walks, hated the clothes that my mother chose and bought for me, and hated having to greet adult visitors to our home (who for the most part meant little to me) with a kiss and a bow, after which I was usually sent to my room. Mutti surely knew how annoying all this was to me, but convention was more important. Papa most likely didn't waste a thought on the matter.

My father was a conscientious German businessman and at home he took care of all our finances. He demanded precise accounting of expenditures from his wife and children and didn't tolerate wasting money. He could be quite stingy when it came to little things. I had to go to him whenever I wanted to buy something for which my meager allowance didn't suffice (when I was fifteen it still amounted to only one mark a week). We children found it humiliating to have to, first, beg for every penny and then afterward give a precise accounting of how these pennies were spent. But for Papa it was the principle of the thing. He wanted to keep us from spending money on *schuschkes* [junk]—one of the few Yiddish expressions that was tolerated at our house—and so he tried to teach us the value of money by not giving us much of it, especially since we didn't yet earn any ourselves.

At the time we children weren't conscious of the fact that we were quite well off materially; we lived in a comfortable home, wore good clothes, went on trips with our parents, and had a servant girl and a cook who took care of our daily needs. It wasn't until years later during my agricultural training at the Gross Breesen farm, when I was seen as one of the *KJs* or *Kapitalistenjungen* [capitalist boys] by my comrades from less- prosperous social classes, that I began to think about it. At that time I also realized that my father was very generous when it came to basic matters. Not only did he make sure that his wife and three sons lacked none of the essentials; he also financially supported three relatives he wasn't very close to: my maternal grandfather, Max Kiefer; Tante Emma, my mother's aunt; and a cousin of my mother's, Didi, whom I loved very much (both my grandfather Kiefer and Tante Emma had lost their savings in the inflation of the early 1920s). But during the early years of my childhood I didn't see this generosity, and instead was annoyed at how tightfisted Papa was with me. That is why, whenever possible, I let my mother covertly finance the pleasures that were otherwise "withheld" from me. For example, I was dying to have a blank cartridge pistol, which I needed like a hole in the head. Mutti finally gave me the money for this purchase and then had to doctor her household bookkeeping to cover it up. But she was an expert at that.

My father lived in full accord with traditional Prussian virtues, the most important of which were honor and a sense of duty. In 1935 my father hired one of the leaders of the youth movement I belonged to to work in his business, and I learned from him what a conscientious businessman Papa was. He was still firmly anchored in the business tradition of the nineteenth century in which he was raised. Although he expressed reservations about some of the characteristics labeled in my youth as "Prussian," it was clear that he highly esteemed the old Prussian virtues, and in business matters Prussian principles were his own. I must have been ten or eleven years old the evening that I asked him what it meant to be a Prussian (I was sitting in the tub and by chance he had stuck his head into the bathroom). I got a concise explanation of the essential Prussian virtues—honor, responsibility, thrift, and so on—and then, to my astonishment and delight, he sang a song I had never heard before: "I am a Prussian / you know my colors / the black and white flag waving before me." In short, we three sons were urged from early childhood on to be honest and straightforward and always to behave toward other people in a way our father could be proud of.

Several years later, when we were living in Lichterfelde, I asked him if he had served on the front during the war. The reason for my question was that I would have loved to be able to portray my father as a frontline soldier to my classmates, most of whom were in the Jungvolk or even the Hitler Youth (the former was a version for young boys of the latter [the Hitlerjugend], a National Socialist organization founded in 1933). He gave me a curt negative answer, then added that after two years of service at a military base in Jüterbog he had been discharged as unfit for war service (he was chronically hard of hearing as a result of a severe childhood cold) and sent home. I decided to get to the bottom of the story and one day snuck into his study and rummaged around in his desk. From the military ID card he kept in one of the drawers I discovered that he had volunteered several times to go to the front but that each time he was classed *g.v.*, that is, *garnisonsverwendungsfähig* [only useful on a military base]. I never brought it up again, but was, as a "German nationalist," as I considered myself at the time, secretly proud of him for trying so hard to get to the front. Today this is incomprehensible, because the Zeitgeist that gave me those ideas is fortunately long dead. So is my father, killed with Prussian efficiency at Auschwitz on January 19, 1943.

My mother was born Henny Kiefer in 1892, also in Berlin, where

RIGHT: *My parents with my aunt and uncle Rosa and Arthur Simonsohn at the Tegernsee, May 1922.* BELOW: *My mother, Henny Angress, née Kiefer, around 1934.*

she spent part of her childhood living directly above the Thalia Theater. She was twenty-seven years old in 1919 when she married my father, then thirty-six, and she remained a good-looking woman well into old age—she died in 1985, shortly before her ninety-third birthday. She wore her brown hair cut short, had dark brown eyes, and was always concerned about appearing slim, so that she wore a corset her entire life. As a ten-year-old boy I sometimes had to help her lace the thing, which was always terribly embarrassing to me. She was vivacious and enjoyed life to the full up until the end. She was a survivor, a fact she proved as a young woman during the First World War and even more substantially during the Second.

My uncles and aunts always said that Henny was happy-go-lucky, and this was certainly true. I can still see her in our apartment on Hessenallee sitting at the grand piano singing Schubert songs, and at parties, which my parents liked to give until 1933, Mutti in a dirndl dancing the "go-home-folks polka" with Papa, who wore a red scarf around his neck, like a Parisian *apache*. The dining room had been cleared out for dancing, and the guests, already in their coats and hats, stood along the walls and applauded.

Mutti's character was much more complex than this picture suggests, however.

First of all, she always insisted on being well dressed and having her hair nicely done. Before I started school in 1926 and afterward during the various short school vacations (during the long summer vacation we routinely traveled), I spent a lot of time with my mother on Tauentzienstrasse, usually at KaDeWe (Kaufhaus des Westens), one of the largest and most luxurious Berlin department stores. Just getting off the underground train at Wittenbergplatz station put me in a bad mood. I knew that I would now have to spend one or two dreadfully boring hours in the ladies' department of KaDeWe. Since my parents knew one of the Jandorfs, who were the owners of the department store until Hermann Tietz took it over in 1926, my mother was given a 20 percent discount on everything she bought there. That didn't change after the KaDeWe changed owners.

And so I sat around there what seemed to me an eternity, watching Mutti try on clothes. Although my father closely examined the daily household expenditures, he was generous when it came to his wife's wardrobe because of his deep love for her. He might get upset about dinner ingredients that had cost too much, but he was simply incapable of denying his *Schneckchen* [Little Snail] one or two hundred marks for a dress, skirt, or sweater. My annoyance increased considerably (and I was a very moody child who eternally pouted) when, after shopping at the KaDeWe, we sometimes went to Arnold Müller's, where the Europa Center is today. Arnold Müller's was a children's clothing store where I was usually provided with pants or shirts that I was ashamed to be seen running around in. The clothing there was expensive and, I found, pompous-looking and often uncomfortable. But there was no mercy, and silk shirts and pants that ended just above the knee were, after agonizing fittings, bought for me. On top of all that I had to say "thank you." Since Mutti knew very well what I thought of shopping at Arnold Müller's, she treated me beforehand to a piece of pastry at the KaDeWe restaurant.

Our mother fully intended to make our childhood years pleasant and even, as far as possible, luxurious, but the shopping mania connected to this was distasteful to my brothers as well as me. Even more questionable was Mutti's attitude toward us children. This remained ambivalent until the end of her life. She wanted to make our childhood as happy as possible—but with a minimum of participation on her part. Isn't that what nannies were for? So, until my thirteenth birthday, when I gradually began to emancipate myself from my parents, my brothers and I were left to a series of domestic servants who changed over the years, and some of whom I really liked. But with one significant exception, Didi, these servants were no substitute for a mother who mainly pursued her own interests and whose displays of affection toward us were sporadic. She, of course, wanted to be loved. "Won't you give me a kiss?" she often requested, or demanded, and I complied, but mechanically and apparently sometimes with a look on my face as if I had been asked to drink vinegar. I just wasn't a nice child. But maybe I was also reacting to the uncertainty I felt about the love only now and then shown to me by my mother.

She could also be very loving in certain situations, which became apparent especially when we were sick. Then she cared for us with touching devotion and zeal. Before the war she was engaged to a doctor, who died in 1916 from an infection contracted in a field hospital at the front (his gravestone is in the war section of the Jewish cemetery at Weissensee). Mutti would have liked to become a doctor herself. But that wasn't possible for various reasons, especially since she finished school without a diploma. So she must have realized her youthful dreams at least partly in her enthusiastic care of her sons when we were sick. Our pediatrician, Dr. Willy Wolff, who would hurry over at any time of the day or night my parents called, had passed on to her some medical knowledge, especially how to apply bandages and what remedies to use for childhood illnesses. The result was my mother's touching, eager, bustling activity when one of us was ill. Wet neck and chest compresses inspired especial loathing in me, but I received them regardless of how much I protested. Once she gave me surgical alcohol instead of cough medicine. Another time, when I had twisted out one of my loose baby teeth, causing some bleeding, she poured half a bottle of iodine down my throat, so that I threw up like crazy.

Probably her biggest challenge came in the summer of 1930, when all three of us brothers came down with the whooping cough and had to stay home for six weeks. Instead of leaving this bout of nursing to the servants, she rolled up her sleeves and did it herself, just as she took part in the monthly major housecleaning and also personally directed each of our many moves to a new apartment. In general, she was much more receptive to our wishes, practical problems, and, above all, friendships than our father was. Thus our home was always open to my friends from the youth movement, and when my poor father came home from the office in the evening he sometimes found a battalion of adolescents bivouacked in my room and sometimes even in the hallway.

But all these positive aspects of my relationship with my mother were countered by some very negative ones. In addition to her sporadic care of my brothers and me, she had a nervous hand, you could say, so that whenever something about us didn't meet her approval, we got slapped, and not lightly. This could be occasioned by a trifle, but it was guaranteed in the case of contradiction. The older I became, the more I resented these chastisements. When I was almost fifteen, after another slap, I rode my bike to my father's office and told him that I was sick and tired of this treatment and that I thus planned to go to Paris to live with an older friend who had moved there, an escape that was pure fantasy on my part. He promised to talk to my mother, which he did, and the slapping stopped. That must have been the first personal talk I had with my father.

Finally, and this weighed most heavily on me, Mutti tried to invade my private sphere. She wanted to know the contents of all mail my brothers and I received, and although my correspondence at that time was quite superficial and harmless, I didn't see why I should have to tell her what was in it. Nor was she above secretly opening a letter addressed to me. And so I hid from her, as well as I could, my poetic outpourings, short stories, and of course letters, in which endeavor my almost illegible handwriting helped.

She also tried to check on my friendships, which at the time were almost exclusively with boys. If I told her about someone I wanted to invite over, she put me through the third degree: What was the father's profession? Did the family have a telephone? Where did they live? and so on. My reaction, especially after the beginning of puberty, was to give as little information as possible and to be very reserved, which of course only solidified the wall already separating us. Only when I left home in early 1936 to go to Silesia for agricultural training at Gross Breesen did the physical distance begin to bring me emotionally closer to both my parents. As is evident in our correspondence from 1936 to December 1941 (which is still in my possession), this became increasingly true after late 1939, when I emigrated to the United States while my parents and brothers remained in Holland.

During one of my annual visits to Berlin in the mid-1980s I went with my cousin Ilse and her son Kai to the Jewish cemetery at Weissensee, in East Berlin, to look for the grave of our grandfather, Max Kiefer. Ilse, who had survived the Third Reich in Berlin as the daughter of a "privileged mixed marriage," said the grave had disappeared and probably been destroyed, but we decided to look for it anyway. So the three of us crossed through the checkpoint, I as an American going through in a special line, and for the first time in my life I went to that cemetery. It was a sad sight: graves overgrown with weeds, gravestones fallen down, neglect everywhere we looked. Nonetheless, Kurt Tucholsky's poem "In Weissensee" occurred to me:

> There where fire clay factories stand—deep motors sound.
> There you can see a graveyard with walls around.
> Each has his world here, a field.
> And each such field is called something like O or I ...
> They came here from their beds, from cellars, cars, toilets,
> and some from Charité Hospital to Weissensee, to Weissensee ...

"The Kiefers are in field E5," the friendly gatekeeper told us, and the three of us set out to find field E5. We discovered a wilderness. It was almost beautiful. Kai dove into the thicket, pulled and tugged at vines, weeds, young trees, and finally called out, "Here it is!" My cousin and I breathed a sigh of relief: we had at last found our grandfather.

I know a little more about the family history of this grandfather than about my father's side. Surprisingly, the Kiefers come from the region of Upper Silesia, where the Angresses were supposed to come from but apparently didn't. The few available documents show that my great-great-grandfather, the distiller Berl (later Bertold) Kiefer and his wife, Friederike Wolf, born in 1793 or 1794, had a son on November 14, 1819, in Peiskretscham, Silesia, whom they named Joseph. In another document, however, his name is Julius. Today Peiskretscham is in Poland and called Pyskowice. It is a little west of the triangle formed by towns known formerly in German as Tarnowitz, Gleiwitz, and Beuthen. Friederike Wolf's family wasn't originally Jewish, but she became Jewish as a result of her marriage to Berl Kiefer. That is the opinion of my "Aryan" Onkel Kurt, the father of my cousin Ilse and the husband of Tante Margot, one of my mother's younger sisters. During the Nazi period Onkel Kurt tried, by focused research in genealogy, to weaken the Jewish ancestry of his wife as much as possible, and Friederike Wolf with her un-Jewish first name seemed a good line to trace. Today neither claim can be proved. Sometime or other Friederike Wolf became Jewish, because it says so on the birth certificate of her son, Joseph, alias Julius, Kiefer and also on the certificate of her death (January 7, 1869, in Breslau [now Wrocław, Poland]). In any case, a resigned Onkel Kurt wrote in the margin of his research findings, "Aryan ancestry not proved."

Joseph/Julius was the second of six children, three boys and three girls, and became a businessman. In Paris in 1866, at the age of forty-seven, he married one Johanne Caroline Heil, born in Danzig on June 24, 1843, and was christened as a Protestant on July 16, 1843. Her parents were the tailor journeyman Karl Leopold Heil and his wife, Auguste, née Schauroth. Thus my great-grandmother was undoubtedly born as a Christian. But she also became Jewish in the end. When, however, isn't revealed by the documents. When Joseph/Julius and Johanne got married in France (probably because they could have a civil ceremony there, which wasn't possible in Prussia until 1875, and because the church wedding of a Jew and a Christian was also not allowed at that time) my grandfather Max Oskar Friedrich Kiefer, who was born in Berlin, was already three years old, and thus an illegitimate child. It wasn't until October 26, 1870, after Joseph/Julius had declared himself to be the father, that he became legitimate. Grosspapa and his two younger brothers, Bismarck (!) and Julius (Meier), who was born illegitimate and remained illegitimate, were all christened as Protestants shortly after their birth. The information I have about them is incomplete, primarily because no one wanted to talk about these things. When I was a little boy, Grosspapa and I once visited Julius Meier and his family, and I had to promise not to mention the visit at home. Why Julius was named Meier when his mother's maiden name was Heil I have never found out. The two daughters, Rosalie and Frieda, were Jewish, but both married Christians and converted to the religion of their husbands.

Grosspapa was the only one in the family who was well educated, although he had only reached the *Obersekunda-Reife*; that is, he only completed the tenth grade in school. Most of what he knew and what he was good at doing, he had taught himself. In addition to reading voraciously all his life and having a beautiful library, he played the violin well and was equally good at drawing and painting. Some of his pictures hung on our walls and also at the Baumgarts', but unfortunately only one survived the war. Grosspapa also wrote humorous poems for specific occasions and published various short stories in the 1920s, a few of which I still have.

Grosspapa grew up in Steglitz. When he had finished school he became a clothier, as did most of my paternal family except for my father, and was employed for years at the company Flatow and Wachsner. Since he designed clothing, he traveled around a lot in Europe, especially to Paris, London, and Vienna, all of which he preferred to Berlin, as he often told me. He loved Paris and Vienna for their tradition of theater and opera as well as their rich artistic atmosphere. He regretted not having become an actor, and it was no accident that he moved from Michaelkirchplatz to Dresdner Strasse, for behind the courtyard of his apartment was the Thalia Theater, where he got together with the actors as often as he could. He was a great admirer of the Austrian Joseph Kainz, whom he painted in various roles. In Grosspapa's family, music and theater were cultivated: they read aloud classical plays and modern ones by Gerhardt Hauptmann and Hermann Sudermann, among others, and each of his three daughters learned to play an instrument.

He must have gotten married around 1890, because my mother was born in April 1892. He chose as a wife Sara Ehrlich, a pretty Jewish woman from a well-to-do family. From what I heard, it was probably less a marriage of love than one of convenience. Before his wedding he had to convert to Judaism, which he did much against his will. At almost thirty years old, he was told he would have to undergo a ritual circumcision, as the Ehrlichs were pious people. According to what he told us grandsons, behind closed doors he gave money to the *mohel* who was supposed to perform the circumcision and told him that he was now circumcised, at least as far as the two of them were concerned. Cash also enabled Grosspapa to escape the *mikwe* [ritual bath], making him Jewish from then on. But he never became a believing or practicing Jew. Once shortly after their wedding he went with my grandmother to the synagogue, where the men and women had to sit separated, the men downstairs and the women upstairs. Having brought along his drawing pad, as he told us grandsons later, he began to draw "interesting Jewish heads." Of course he was thrown out on his ear by the *shammes* [synagogue attendant], and he swore never again to enter a temple. How much of this is true I can't say. My grandfather was an enthusiastic and talented storyteller, but the authenticity of his tales can't be proved. But he wasn't circumcised, and as long as I knew him he didn't go into a synagogue, not even to my or Fritz's bar mitzvah.

Did Grosspapa have anti-Jewish prejudices? Not at all. He was certainly not religious (and I am not either), but he was too intelligent and tactful to be intolerant. When he lived at our house for a while in the early 1930s, I witnessed one of his many confrontations with my mother, his eldest child. Grosspapa played the violin well and especially enjoyed duets. The young violinist Willie Kriegsmann would come visit and play the violin once a week. Grosspapa insisted that he first be given some coffee and cake before the two of them played pieces by Schubert, Beethoven, Haydn, and other composers the whole afternoon long. Willie, a poorly dressed redhead who at the time was probably not much older than thirty, originally came from a former province of the Hapsburg Empire, possibly from Bukovina. Mutti, who found Willie a boor, asked her father that day, clearly irritated as she set the table for coffee, why he had chosen an Eastern Jew to play the violin with. I watched from around the corner, out of sight. Grosspapa answered very calmly that the Eastern Jews might be poor but their hearts were in the right place. They were good people, which was more than could be said for a lot of German Jews.... I tiptoed away, surprised at my grandfather's tolerance. I more or less shared my mother's prejudices about Eastern Jews, although, except for Willie Kriegsmann, I had never met any. My father wasn't entirely free of such prejudices either.

I was never really close to my grandfather—he was too much of an authority figure for me for that—but I nonetheless owe him a great deal. Shortly after I began school in 1926 he sent me the first of a number of carefully handwritten letters, and up until our hasty emigration in October 1937 (he himself remained in Berlin) he always looked after my cultural and intellectual education. Like him, I read a lot, and on my birthday and at Christmas he gave me books that showed his close attention to my taste and interests. When he lived with us for several years he brought along his library and selected books from it that might interest me. And so at the age of eleven or twelve I read, at his instigation, among other things, Mark Twain (of course in German translation), various plays by Friedrich Schiller, and Franz Kugler's *History of Frederick the Great* with the fine illustrations by Adolf Menzel. It was my first step toward the study of German history, to which I would later devote my professional life. In the living-room bookcase, my grandfather's collection now overwhelmed that of my parents. He owned the classics, modern plays,

My grandfather Max Kiefer in Warmbrunn in July 1925.

history books, and the entire Knackfuss edition of great painters. My parents' books—mainly modern novels and biographies of well-known business people—took up only the right-hand corner of the bookcase, and Grosspapa saw to it that I stayed away from that corner. Once he caught me reading Erich Maria Remarque's *All Quiet on the Western Front* and hit me over the head with the book—not because the book is about war but because in it three German soldiers with only boots on and loaves of bread under their arms go to see French girls at night. Of course I finished the book secretly—he couldn't stand watch all the time—and I read other forbidden literature, such as Ernst Gläser's *Vintage 1902* and Upton Sinclair's *Oil!*, also rated X by my grandfather.

Does this mean Grosspapa was a puritanical moralist? Quite the opposite. After Fritz and I learned the facts of life, even we heard about his infidelities during business trips, especially his affair of many years with Miss Martha M., an employee who usually accompanied him on his travels. But we also heard that he never engaged in such escapades in Berlin. A song my father wrote for Grosspapa's seventieth birthday, and had my mother sing at the party, made this quite clear.

Today such occurrences wouldn't raise an eyebrow at all. But during my childhood double standards and hypocrisy were rampant. This darker side is part of the picture of my grandfather that I have carried in my head my whole life, along with his efforts to raise me as an educated person and to teach me honesty, decency, and fairness in dealing with others.

After I emigrated from Holland to the United States at the end of 1939 and worked on a farm in Virginia, Grosspapa and I wrote each other. His letters, which I still have, show not only his great interest in my life, but also his clearness of mind until the end. His final years weren't easy. I had never known him as the prosperous if not rich man he was at the beginning of the 1920s. Like millions of other Germans at the time, he lost all his savings, and in the last years of his life he was a very poor and lonely man. Before we fled Germany, my father took care of him financially, but this allowed him only a very modest allowance, a furnished room, and food from the soup kitchen of the Berlin Jewish congregation. He bore it with dignity and sometimes even with humor.

Grosspapa died on February 6, 1940, before the deportations began, in the Berlin Jewish hospital on Iranische Strasse. Two weeks later he would have turned seventy-seven. His end was marked by the kind of strange circumstances that had accompanied him all his life. Grosspapa had acute sciatica and a brother-in-law of my father's, Onkel Arthur Maass, took him to the Iranische Strasse hospital because, under National Socialist law, only a Jewish hospital could treat him. But when Grosspapa was told to present identification he pulled out his birth certificate, which stated that he was baptized as a Protestant. Since the hospital was allowed to admit only Jews, he had to return home and find a document that identified him as Jewish. He found one, was admitted, and died of a stroke six days later. On an icy day, in the presence of Jewish and non-Jewish relatives, he was buried next to his wife at Weissensee. He was the last one of my family to be buried there.

My mother's two younger sisters were twins, born when she was three years old. In 1895 my grandmother (who died of leukemia in 1912 and was for me only a portrait on an easel in the living room) gave birth to the twins Edith and Margot. They resembled each other so closely that I later had a hard time telling them apart. When Grosspapa announced the good news to his boss, Herr Wachsner, the latter said laconically, "Rather a lot, Herr Kiefer!" [*Etwas reichlich, Herr Kiefer!*]. This sentence became a familiar household expression. I liked both aunts. Edith, Grosspapa's favorite, never married. She worked somewhere in Berlin in an office and lived with a close girlfriend, one of her coworkers, in my grandfather's apartment. Edith contracted tuberculosis at the end of the 1920s and died in November 1931 in spite of an operation performed by the well-known surgeon Ferdinand Sauerbruch. I was eleven years old and not taken to the funeral, but I was home when the wreath that the family ordered for the grave at Weissensee was delivered. It seemed to me enormous. I was standing in the hallway before it, perplexed, when Grosspapa put his arm around my shoulders and began to sob uncontrollably. I had never seen my grandfather cry.

Shortly after the First World War, Tante Margot married Kurt Baumgart, an official of the Reichsversicherungsanstalt (the Empire's social security department). This didn't please my grandfather. Onkel Kurt, whose father had been a *Konsistorialrat* [church council member] in Krotoschin, was the stereotypical Prussian civil servant. According to a mean little saying in the family, every workday at 4:30 p.m. his pen fell from his hand, even if the i wasn't dotted yet. After our speedy emigration in October 1937 I lost contact with the Baumgarts, but I got back in touch with them after the war. We stayed in contact until the death of these two very old and, to me, dear people.

Before that, however, I had found out things that made Onkel Kurt a lot more interesting to me than I could have imagined. One day while I was researching early German communism a photo in a book almost made me fall off my chair. It showed the men of the Garde-Kavallerie-Schützen Division (Cavalry sharpshooter guard division) on January 16, 1919, the day after their murder of the socialists (and antiwar activists) Rosa Luxemburg and Karl Liebknecht. The soldiers were celebrating their "heroic act" at the Eden Hotel, their headquarters at the time. There are only two civilians in the picture, a waitress and Onkel Kurt. When I wrote him to ask about it, he answered that he was on duty that day as an ambulance man for the Wilmersdorfer civic guard (deferred from military service in the war, he had volunteered for the civic guard in 1918) and by chance had walked through the room where the cavalrymen were drinking. One of them encouraged him to get into the group photo, and Onkel Kurt thus became a footnote in the history of Germany after World War I. He assured me that he hadn't participated in the killing; he had only glimpsed Rosa Luxemburg with a guard in the hallway on the way to the toilet and didn't see Liebknecht at all. I have no reason to doubt him, but I don't believe he judged the murders negatively at the time.

When Hitler took power in 1933, the decisive question for Onkel Kurt as for all other "Aryans" then married to Jews was whether to stay married and be punished by the regime or get a divorce. Without hesitation he chose the first alternative. Promptly forced to retire, he struggled until the end of the war, all the while protecting Tante Margot from deportation and death in the gas chamber. Their daughter, my cousin Ilse, was Protestant from birth on, so my aunt and uncle lived in what the Nazi government termed a "privileged mixed marriage." After the war they benefitted from the federal compensation law as victims of National Socialist tyranny and were able, for the first time in their lives, to travel abroad, buy themselves a little Volkswagen, and spend the rest of their days free from financial worries. This is one of the few cases I know of in which fate dealt with persecuted people in a fair and kind way.

Grosspapa's sister-in-law, "Tante" Emma Ehrlich (actually my great-aunt), was his exact opposite. To say the two of them didn't like each other is an understatement. Why the antipathy I have never discovered, but the tension was clearly perceptible even to me at a young age. Tante Emma, the sister of my grandmother Kiefer (the portrait on the easel), was a small, intelligent, and lively woman who never married. Most of her life she was independent and successful. She worked in women's clothing at Menzel and Ehrlich on Markgrafenstrasse, and it was her highest ambition to be "Imperial Clothier," a title she never attained. For that, either the empress or one of the princesses would have had to place orders with her. A few of the ladies of the court did come to Menzel and Ehrlich, but that unfortunately didn't suffice for a golden "Imperial Clothier" sign. Nonetheless, my mother said with great pride, when she was a child Tante Emma had once introduced her to a Frau von Grumme who was shopping at Menzel and

Ehrlich, and whose husband was an aide-de-camp under Kaiser Wilhelm II. And in the glass cupboard in our living room was Mutti's white bridal veil, which, together with her bridal gown, Tante Emma had made from the train of Countess Douglas, also a customer of hers and probably the wife of the Industrial and Free Conservative parliament member Hugo Count of Douglas, who was close to the emperor. When my father heard these stories, he would say softly, *"Mach Schabbes damit"* [Forget it].

Like her brother-in-law (my grandfather), Tante Emma lost her entire savings during the great inflation of the early 1920s and after that was financially dependent on my father. Then, already more than sixty years of age, she was run over by a bicycle, broke her hip, and for the rest of her life limped around with a cane. I knew her mainly from my family's regular visits to the old people's home, which we children enjoyed about as much as the measles. But she was a dear, good woman who was happy to see us, although she didn't really know what to do with us growing boys. Very religious, she fasted on Yom Kippur even in very old age, kept the Sabbath, and attended my bar mitzvah as well as Fritz's. When I last saw her in April 1937 she was small, bent over, and almost deaf. She was leaving the festivities at our apartment late in the evening, one hand gripping tightly to her cane and the other on the arm of an acquaintance who was going to drive her back to the old people's home at Roseneck. Like Grosspapa, she was spared the gas chamber, for she died in the Berlin Jewish hospital before the deportations began. Her grave isn't far from his in Weissensee.

And last but not least on the Kiefer side was my great-aunt Frieda, Grosspapa's youngest sister, who lived at our house for a few months in 1934–35. Tante Frieda was an "afterthought" in the Kiefer family. Like her elder sister, she converted to Christianity after marrying a Protestant, Karl Ernst, a businessman from the Rheinland. Before the First World War she moved with him to Madrid, where Karl built up a large furniture company. As a child I liked to look at a photo in the family album that showed Tante Frieda and Onkel Carlos Ernestos, as he soon started calling himself in Spain, in a small group with King Alfonso XIII. (The photo disappeared with the rest of our belongings when the Gestapo seized our apartment in October 1937.) Having been a monarchist all her life, she didn't have the heart to stay in Madrid after Onkel Carlos died and Spain became a republic. So in 1934, Tante Frieda came back to Hitler's Germany and lived at our house until she found an apartment for herself. In the meantime she had again converted, this time to Catholicism, so now three religions were represented in our family. Tante Frieda survived the Second World War unharmed in Heppenheim, where she lived with a girlfriend, and I visited her a number of times after the war, at the end in the old people's home of a convent, where she died at the age of almost ninety-six.

I would like to end the family saga with the aunts, uncles, and cousins on my father's side. I saw them less often, and we weren't nearly as close as I was to my mother's side of the clan. My father had three elder sisters, all of whom married businessmen. Of these three uncles, only Arthur Simonsohn, Tante Rosa's husband, earned a good living, in the clothing trade. The Simonsohns also had an excellent sense of humor and got along very well with my mother, partly because Onkel Arthur and Mutti were distantly related. The Simonsohns lived at Holsteinische Strasse 24, near Hohenzollerndamm. We took over this apartment in 1936, when they moved into a smaller flat to prepare for their emigration. This is where we were living in October 1937 when we also left Germany, under quite hazardous circumstances.

My Tante Rosa became for my mother a kind of big sister. Mutti, newly married, called her sister-in-law almost daily (at Pfalzburg 29 55— why do I still recall this telephone number?) and complained bitterly that my father demanded a precise accounting of the household money every evening. Once she was short ten cents. "Parsley, dear Henny," her sister-in-law advised. When my mother said she hadn't bought any, Tante Rosa replied, "How would he know that?"

Tante Hanna and Onkel Arthur Maass lived in a much less exclusive part of town, Moabit, on Holsteiner Ufer. Onkel Arthur originally came from Filehne in Posen and earned his meager pay in the men's clothing business, as did his brother-in-law Arthur Simonsohn. But in contrast to "Schim'che," as the latter was sometimes affectionately called, Arthur Maass was not a talented businessman. He was short and unimposing, had flat feet, and looked just like Jews were supposed to look, according to the stereotypes of right-wing and Nazi "literature." I was unfortunately familiar with these as a twelve- and thirteen-year-old, unbeknownst to my parents. But Onkel Arthur Maass never came to visit without bringing me a bar of chocolate, although never the kind I liked. My mother wasn't very fond of this brother-in-law either, but for other reasons. To all family events, whether it was the Friday evening gatherings Papa's relatives took turns hosting, Christmas, or birthdays, he always came with ties or scarves in his pocket, which he tried to peddle to his relatives. Mutti had forbidden him to do this, but he did it anyway. He was simply the family *nebbish* [pitifully inept], as Mutti sometimes called him when she thought I was out of earshot.

Onkel Arthur Maass also had another brother, Leopold, who as a young man had had himself baptized as a Protestant and who was therefore ostracized by the family. I only saw him once, sometime after 1933 on one of the big Jewish holidays, standing lonely and forsaken in a niche at the entrance of the Prinzregentenstrasse synagogue. Before the Nazis seized power he got along by writing political poems for specific occasions, but the political direction apparently didn't much matter to him. I only remember one that he wrote in 1932 for the *Deutschnationale Volkspartei* (German Nationalist Party, which at the time called itself the Vanguard Black-White-Red) for one of the election campaigns:

> *Jump up, march, march into the last fight!*
> *The winner must be black, white, red*
> *For Germany's greatness, for Germany's right*
> *For freedom and work and bread*
> *For the Vanguard Black-White-Red.*

Leopold Maass escaped the Final Solution by emigrating to Shanghai.

Thanks partly to my mother, I saw Onkel Arthur Maass mainly as the incapable person that in many respects he was. But he was also decent, kind, and always somewhat shy. He dearly loved his wife and daughter and cared attentively for his mother-in-law, my almost-blind grandmother Angress, who lived in his apartment until her death. I didn't pay attention to these things at the time. My last memory of him is a short walk we took together in the spring of 1936. We had met in town so that I could pick up his old military coat, which he was giving me for my agricultural training in Gross Breesen. He had served in the war at a supply base, and told me now, punctuated with *oi vay*s, how he once had to ride a team of horses into a pond and was scared to death that he would fall off and drown. I remember being amused and also embarrassed by this. Here finally was an uncle who had served not far from the front, and he had no heroic stories to tell...

The picture that I have in my mind of Tante Hanna is quite faint. Like her husband, she was very shy and often stood around with folded hands, embarrassed. But she loved us children with all her heart. When one of us was sick, she would come visit and inevitably bring a chocolate bar (again always the wrong kind!). Of course, as with all my aunts, I had to kiss her on the cheek when she arrived and left, and I hated it. Her daughter, my much older cousin Gerda, was tougher. She learned tailoring as a very young woman and in 1935 went to Palestine, where she lived until her death. When she died in January 2000 at the age of almost ninety, she was physically frail but mentally in fine shape. Our contact, which had never been frequent, broke off for good after her emigration; we never saw each other again, although I now and then heard from others how she was doing. But her parents, those two decent, always somewhat helpless-looking people who lived their withdrawn lives on Holsteiner Ufer with tile stoves in the rooms, and from whom I never heard an unfriendly word, the Nationalist Socialist state "evacuated," probably in 1942, to the Trawniki forced labor camp in the *Generalgouvernement* (occupied Poland under the Nazis). There they were "lost and missing, presumed dead," as the black commemoration book reports about German Jews who were deported, then murdered.

The youngest of the three Angress sisters, my Tante Käthe, was a few years older than my father. She married Rudolf Levy and moved with him and their daughter, Ilse, to Frankfurt am Main when I was about ten years old. So my memory of that part of the family is even weaker than my memory of the Simonsohns and the Maasses. Onkel Rudolf was also a small-time businessman, employed in an electrical appliance and supply store in Frankfurt and, as with Arthur Maass, his petit bourgeois prevailed. The Levys were also good people through and through, but I didn't know enough at the time to appreciate this, or their modesty and reserve. They also always brought a chocolate bar (and also the wrong kind) for each of us children, although they didn't have much money. Tante Käthe kissed me on the cheek, looked at me lovingly and whispered, *"der Bubi"* [the little boy], even though, as soon as I started to go to school, I had forbidden anyone to use that nickname for me ever again. So I wasn't at all thrilled by the Levys. A few years later, after Kristallnacht (the pogrom night of November 9, 1938), Rudolf and Käthe managed to send Ilse to England to work as a maid. Soon thereafter, the couple was deported from Frankfurt to labor camps in the *Generalgouvernement*. Tante Käthe died in Lodz/Litzmannstadt on May 16, 1942. Onkel Rudolf was "lost and missing, presumed dead."

The person in our household to whom I felt closest was a more distant relative, Didi. That wasn't her name, she was christened Elise, but as a small child I couldn't pronounce this, so she became and remained Didi. She came to our house as a nanny shortly after my birth and stayed eight or nine years. Didi was one of the four children of my great-aunt Rosalie, the elder of Grosspapa Kiefer's two sisters. (Rosalie's three additional children were two sons and a daughter whom her husband had brought to the marriage.) As I've already mentioned, my maternal great-grandfather had his sons christened as Protestants but left his daughters as Jews. Both girls later married Protestants and converted to Christianity. My great-aunt Rosalie married a cardboard manufacturer from Blankenburg in the Harz, Wilhelm Kahlmann, and lived there for many years, until his death. As a child I went to Blankenburg twice, with Didi, naturally. Besides Grossmama, as I called Didi's mother, I have the best memories of the blacksmith, Herr Faupel, because several times he set me on a newly shoed horse and sent us off down the street. I was four or five years old, riding alone and bursting with pride. I never met Didi's father, Wilhelm. He was said to have been a hot-tempered man who was rough with his seven children from two marriages. The two sons from his first marriage became hard-line Nazis.

A strong, masculine-looking woman who tended toward corpulence, Didi was incredibly skilled with her hands. As a teenager she repaired the machines in her father's factory. When she told him she would like to study to become an engineer, her father refused, saying that she was, after all, a woman. When my mother needed a nurse for her firstborn child, she turned to her Blankenburg cousin and suggested that she move to our house in Berlin to "take me over." Thus it was Didi who took care of me the most during the first eight or nine years of my life, telling me stories, singing me songs that she accompanied on the lute, and teaching me very early on not to be a crybaby, to put up with little aches and pains. But she never lectured me, never said that a boy shouldn't behave like this or like that. When she washed off my scraped knee or elbow and disinfected it with iodine, she spoke to me calmly and without raising a scolding finger. Since I trusted her completely and did what she said as I did for nobody else, she toughened me up and taught me to accept and not magnify small accidents.

She was also a wonderful swimmer. I remember how at the public swimming pool in the summer I would climb on her broad back and hang on like a baby monkey with no fear at all as she jumped from the

LEFT: *"Didi" (Lise Kahlmann) in front of her tobacco shop on the Barbarossastrasse with my brother Hans, 1933.* RIGHT: *Hans and Werner in front of Didi's tobacco shop in 1933.*

ten-foot-high diving board. That I didn't know how to swim didn't enter my mind. Once she fished me and another boy out of Teufelssee [Devil's Lake] after we, still not knowing how to swim, had gone out beyond our depth and were nearly drowning.

Not much ever became of Didi professionally. When she left us around 1928, possibly after a conflict with my mother, she got a job as a cashier at KaDeWe, probably with my father's help. Since she was a chain smoker (although she at least put out her cigarettes to change my diapers, as testified by the many burn marks on the window sill next to my changing table) and also suffered from kidney and gall bladder problems, it was torture for her to sit for hours squeezed behind the cash register. My father rescued her from this fate by helping her rent a tobacco shop on Barbarossastrasse, where she became her own best customer. Until our emigration the shop struggled along, and I visited her there often.

Now and then Grosspapa, who lived on Barbarossastrasse starting in 1936, helped out in the shop. Although he and Didi were completely different, they got along well. I remember when my grandfather would be tending the shop and the men of the Sturmabteilung came in and demanded *"drei Trommler!"* [three Drummers], a brand of cigarettes that SA men famously preferred. But since most of them didn't have much money, they usually bought only three or four at a time, which they were handed in a little paper bag. My grandfather, to my eternal horror, would answer their "Heil Hitler" with a mumbled "drei Litter" (a pronunciation of "three liters" that more or less rhymed), but fortunately no one ever noticed.

During the Nazi era Didi stayed in Berlin, as did her brothers and sisters. According to the Nuremberg Laws the four youngest were non-Aryans, since Grossmama Kahlmann and Grosspapa, her older brother, were at least half Jewish. But somehow the Kahlmanns were able to cover this up, since they had a pure Aryan father and their mother had become a Christian when she married. During the war Didi became an air-raid warden and attended to her duties in high-shafted boots on the roof of the building on Fasanenstrasse, where she lived with her younger sister Hilde. Hilde told me after the war that the people in the air-raid cellar were most reassured when Fräulein Kahlmann was up on the roof all alone fighting fire bombs with sand and buckets of water. Once when she wasn't on duty, she and Hilde, who was also almost forty, broke the rules by staying in their room during an especially heavy air raid, instead of going down to the shelter. The younger sister was so frightened she crawled under the bed, and Didi hissed at her, "Hildchen, don't make such a fuss!"

Didi died in the early 1970s in London, where she and Hilde had emigrated after the war. Since my mother also lived there starting in 1947, I always saw Didi when I came from the United States to visit. Until she was sixty-five, Didi worked for a physician's family, where she was appreciated, allowed to have a dog, and even got her driver's license. She bought a second-hand car that she drove wonderfully and on which she made minor repairs herself. In 1969–70, when I was doing research in Europe and lived in London with my wife and three of our four children, I visited Didi regularly. She was retired and lived in a small apartment in Kew Gardens. Each time we met, we talked about the past. Already over seventy, she remained for me the person who had influenced me the most during my early childhood. She had finally quit smoking, but too late: she died of emphysema.

What I remember the most on my father's side of the family is the Friday evenings, when religious Jews usher in and celebrate the Sabbath. We met each week at the home of a different household in the family: the Simonsohns', the Angresses', the Maasses', or the Levys'. Everyone sat around a large table in the dining room as the host blessed the bread and the wine. But it was mainly the dinner afterward that interested those of us in the younger generation. Until I was about ten years old I wasn't taken along to the Friday evenings and thus could only take part once a month when they were held at our house.

Passover, the commemoration of the exodus of the children of Israel from Egypt that sometimes coincides with Easter, was always celebrated at our house. Then the four brothers-in-law—Ernst, the two Arthurs, and Rudolf—sat at the head of the long table, their bodies rocking back and forth as they prayed. When it came to the songs (the song about the little goat and the one with the refrain *"dai daiyeinu* [it would have been enough]," the two Arthurs and Rudolf sang very nicely in chorus, but Papa, hard of hearing, was either far ahead or behind them and caused a musical chaos. We children, sitting at the table with our berets on, found all that extremely funny, but we hid our laughter from the adults. Passover was, next to Christmas, by far the most important family occasion that we celebrated, and we children always looked forward to it immensely. Since my brothers were still too young, I, the youngest child who could express himself verbally, posed the obligatory Four Questions, which begin with *"Ma nishtana halaila hazeh?"* [How does this night differ from all other nights?]. Papa wrote it down for me phonetically, and I learned it by heart anew each year. When I, feeling very important, recited it with intense expression, his pride was obvious.

Naturally there followed a traditional Jewish meal, usually chicken and, most important, matzo ball soup. My older cousins Kurt and Herbert Simonsohn made bets beforehand as to which of them could eat the most matzo balls, until finally my mother ended the competition by informing us that we each would get the same number. We children always sat at the other end of the long table, which on such occasions was set with the fine Rosenthal china. I quietly enjoyed the fact that a cousin of mine by marriage, Rudi Katz, the husband of my cousin Edith Simonsohn, was also put at our end of the table, probably because my mother liked him as little as I did. Rudi was a fat, albeit quite successful, businessman who my mother claimed had married Edith only because with her he got an unpaid secretary. Squirming around at one Seder, I accidentally knocked over his glass of wine. He hissed at me, "Bubi, you're naughty!" I never forgave him, not for thinking I was naughty, which didn't bother me at all, but for calling me "Bubi [little boy]." Once he proudly told us about an evening when he and Edith were at home having dinner and he rang the bell for the servant girl. When the girl appeared he told her to fetch and climb the stepladder. When she was standing at the top of it, quite perplexed, he asked her, "Do you see the salt?" My mother wasn't impressed: "That's how you make people anti-Semitic [*Risches*]!"

Of course the Kiefer side of the family was also invited to the Jewish family celebrations, especially Passover. The Kiefers included Grosspapa, Tante Edith, later Tante Frieda, and occasionally also Kurt and Margot Baumgart along with Kurt's sister Adele, called "Abbela," an old maid and primary school teacher who, after the Nazis seized power, kept an altar at home with a swastika flag and pictures of Hitler and other Nazi leaders. She came to our family evenings until 1935, but her presence made political discussions impossible.

As hard as it may be to imagine, at least among religious Jews (which my parents considered us to be), each year we also celebrated Christmas and Easter. And we were by no means alone in this. Many German Jews of the time had been doing the same since the Empire, and few of them gave it much thought. Many German Jews back then claimed, often with more embarrassment than veracity, that they celebrated these occasions only for the sake of the Christian household staff. We observed Christmas because my mother grew up celebrating it as a holiday, and she wanted her children to experience it, too. My father, who loved my mother very much, consented.

So at the end of November I went out looking for an Advent calendar, with the little windows that you open, one each day, until Christmas. On the last Sunday of Advent the whole Angress family was involved in buying a suitable Christmas tree, "suitable" meaning that it had to be symmetrical and tall enough to reach almost to the ceiling, but not so tall that the silver star wouldn't fit on top. Each of us was allowed to make suggestions as to which tree to buy, but Papa always had the last word. After it had been bought, dragged into the apartment, and freed of the strings restraining its branches, it was screwed onto the wooden stand we stored in the cellar. But the tree wasn't decorated until Christmas Eve, and it was our parents who did that, while we were sent out on the street for a few hours, with or without a servant girl. Reichskanzlerplatz was usually freezing cold, and we couldn't return until about four in the afternoon. As soon as we came in we were sent to our room to wait until we were called for the distribution of the gifts. In the meantime the whole family (usually disrespectfully called *Mischpoche* by Grosspapa) had arrived and gathered in the dining room, where the tree stood.

As soon as my parents had lit the candles on the branches—and our tree was always decorated entirely with white candles, white icicles, and white plastic snowballs—we children were called in. But before we could rush to the tree and get our gifts and plates of sweets (*bunte Teller*), I as the eldest son had to recite a Christmas poem. After Didi's departure, the poem was always chosen by whatever nanny happened to be with us at the time. Printed booklets for this purpose could be bought at any newspaper stand. My parents gave strict instructions beforehand that the poem couldn't contain any references to Christian traditions. But once, on Hessenallee, there was a mishap. I stood there, nervous and trembling, before the gathered relatives, some of whom (especially Tante Rosa) viewed this "goyish" celebration with thinly disguised disapproval, and began to recite: "Imagine, I've seen the Christ child today." Despite the rising murmurs around me, I continued on, desperately, to the bitter end. Looking up, I saw red faces, and my cousin Kurt Simonsohn hurried to the piano in the next room and laid into the keys, singing loudly, "Shield and protection in storm and whirlwind / to you we sing a song of rejoicing"—the Hasmonean or Chanukah song.

In 1935, the year of the Nuremberg Laws, the family celebrations came to an end. It became increasingly awkward to bring together the Jewish and the non-Jewish parts of the family. Tante Adele B. was the first to disappear from the scene. The Levys had already been in Frankfurt for five years and no longer came to visit, supposedly for financial reasons. The two Simonsohn children, Kurt and Edith, together with her husband, the fat and disagreeable Rudi Katz, left Berlin around this time and emigrated via Paris to Brazil, sending for their parents afterward. Thus all of the Simonsohns survived the Nazi era, since Herbert Simonsohn, a second cousin, was able to emigrate to South Africa soon after getting married. But after the war the only one I saw again was Edith, whom I met twice at my mother's in London. I lost sight of the others, not unusual in those times. Gerda Maass went to Palestine. Of the younger generation, only we three Angress boys and Ilse Levy were still in Germany in 1935.

If I had had any idea of the horrible fate that awaited some members of my family, would I have been nicer to them? I look back sadly at the relatively few things I had in common with my aunts and uncles, of whom only the memory has remained. My mother's remark that "Werner is not a family person" was only too justified, unfortunately. I can't change it today, but I regret it. I only felt real love for Didi. With all the others—whether aunts, uncles, cousins, or even Grosspapa—I was reserved and kept my distance. It would be too simplistic to blame this all on my (then completely unconscious) distaste for the bourgeois milieu in which I grew up. It was more likely my character that caused me, from early childhood on, to set limits and barriers and keep my distance. Besides that, I was egocentric, even egotistical. I always tried to get my way, and I wasn't very pleasant when I didn't succeed. Maybe it would have been different if I had been born into a more peaceful time. As a mature person I might have gotten to know and understand my relatives better. But as a friend said to me recently, "You can't live in the subjunctive." The circumstances of the times prevented renewed acquaintance. Instead our quite ordinary family was scattered to the winds, and those who didn't escape in time were murdered as "racially inferior subhumans" and "enemies of the German people."

Bayerischer Platz around 1909.

CHAPTER 2

Early Childhood and School Days

I'm maybe three years old, or even a little younger, and lying in my bed staring spellbound at the ceiling, where some frustrated Michelangelo has painted two little pictures. One is near the window, where bars have been installed for my safety, and the other one is near the door. I don't remember what they looked like anymore, but I do recall that I liked to look at them before my mother, Didi, or the maid turned out the light in the evening. I don't have precise memories of those very early years in Schöneberg. What remains are fleeting impressions, like snapshots projected on the wall by a magic lantern. Some feelings they provoke are pleasant, others rather painful.

My room was on the second floor at Rosenheimer Strasse 31, in the part of Schöneberg that satirists, and not only anti-Semitic ones, back then called *die jüdische Schweiz* [Jewish Switzerland]. But there was another part of Berlin with a lot of Jews, the *Scheunenviertel* [shantytown] in the city center, where the Eastern Jews lived. They were mostly immigrants from Poland, who, with their black caftans, curled sidelocks, and caps, provoked feelings of sympathy as well as aversion among assimilated German Jews like my family. I visited that part of Berlin for the first time in the early 1980s. At that time there were hardly any Jews left there. The fact that I never went there when I was young was something that my Israeli colleague, Avraham Barkai, who grew up in the *Scheunenviertel*, liked to rub in. Living in the western part of town, I was never exposed to his world, although it was only a half-hour subway ride away from where we lived.

One of my earliest impressions of the Rosenheimerstrasse is the great inflation of 1923. As a three-year-old I naturally didn't understand

Bayerischer Platz around 1920.

what was going on, but I remember certain occurrences. My parents talked constantly about money, which, as I found out later, had become almost worthless. My father often came home in the evening with a huge sack of bank notes, emptied it out onto the floor of our small living room, and instructed my mother to go shopping first thing in the morning and buy whatever she could find, because by noon the money might be worth nothing again. Sacks full of sugar, potatoes, and flour piled up against the walls of the narrow hallway, as if we were about to face a famine. Mutti bought our family silver at that time—heaven only knows how she managed that—and succeeded in saving the treasure throughout the Nazi period, our hasty emigration, and the Second World War, including living illegally in Holland. Later I hated that damned silver, because it had survived, so to speak, but my father had not. Mutti divided it among my brothers and me, but I soon got rid of my share of it.

We lived on Rosenheimer Strasse until shortly after the birth of my brother Fritz in April 1923. The street was connected in my mind to the Bayerischer Platz and the area surrounding it. The Platz is where I threw my first tantrum and got spanked for it by Mutti, who intended to "cure" me. If anything, the spanking had the opposite effect. Then there were little things, like the routine walks with Tante Emma, before her accident.

Bayerischer Platz around 1925.

I liked to go see the chicken coop next to a pub on Martin Luther Strasse with its half dozen hens and a rooster. My childless aunt took care of me with great devotion. She also participated in the attempts to feed "Bubi" (as I was still called). I was a picky eater and spit out a lot of what they tried to shovel into me. I still haven't forgotten that trying routine. I sat on Didi's lap in my little room at noon, pinned between her strong thighs, in front of the plate containing what I was supposed to consume. The routine went like this: "One spoon for Mutti, one spoon for Papa," and so on, but I turned my head sideways and spat. Then Didi called for help, at which point Mutti and often Tante Emma appeared. My aunt sat down at the piano in the living room and played children's songs, and my mother danced in front of me, sometimes even with castanets, like Salome for King Herod. It was all in vain, but this torture was applied again and again. Dr. Willi Wolff, our pediatrician from Münchener Strasse, had, in fact, advised my mother to leave me alone, that when I got hungry I would eat. But she couldn't stand watching me "starve." When I was six years old, Mutti, Didi, brother Fritz, and I went to St. Ulrich (today Ortisei) in South Tyrol, also on Dr. Wolff's advice, where we spent the summer at eight hundred meters altitude. There I ended my hunger strike and since have eaten more or less whatever is set before me.

By that time we were no longer living on Rosenheimerstrasse, but at Klaus Groth Strasse 7, in Westend. Not long after Fritz's birth, when we needed more room, we moved there and took over the first-floor apartment of the Jandorfs, who were part-owners of KaDeWe. We also had use of the garden, which seemed to me at the time quite large. (When I saw it again in 1950, it appeared tiny.) This period in Westend, which included the "golden middle years" of the Weimar Republic, was the only really financially carefree time in my parents' lives. Papa had become first *Prokurist* at "K and L," as we called the Königsberger and Lichtenhein Bank, and every morning except Sunday Herr Müller, the chauffeur of the company limousine, pulled up before our house to pick up Papa. The two directors were already sitting in the car. I liked to accompany my father to the car to shake hands with his bosses and Herr Müller and bow politely, as I was supposed to, before they drove off and I had the street mostly to myself.

The house next door was a huge villa in which Herr Meier, a banker, lived with his wife, their daughter Irene, and their domestic staff. Today it is classified as a historic monument and occupied by several families. The Meiers were Jews, too. I saw Herr Meier and his wife rarely and briefly, and they left no impression on me. But I was friends with "Irenchen." She was a year or two older than I, and in order to visit each other we had made a hole in the wire fence that separated our two yards. Irenchen lived under the watchful eye of "Frolli," her nanny, who also directed Irene's birthday parties with an iron hand. There were always very nice prizes for the winner of *Topfschlagen* ("Hit the Pot," a game in which a blindfolded child bangs around the floor with a wooden spoon looking for an overturned pot concealing a prize, while the other children call out "cold!" "warm!" "hot!"), and the food was fantastic. This wasn't just prosperity, this was wealth. Herr Meier's chauffeur taught me how to ride a bike, for which my father paid him. Later, after a short stay in Amsterdam, where I was invited to her first wedding, Irene went to the United States and lived in Los Angeles. My mother used to visit her there in the 1960s. Irene told me that Frolli and the chauffeur became enthusiastic Nazis in the 1930s, which didn't surprise me.

Although in Westend I had one childhood illness after another, our yard there with its flower beds and fruit trees (all gone today) and the ivy-covered wall next to which we ate our meals in the summer seem to me in retrospect almost a paradise. Didi was still with us then, and together we found lots of animals, which we housed in the cellar and which, strangely, always disappeared after a few days. Today I know that Mutti made sure the hedgehogs, grass snakes, frogs, rabbits, and other such animals never stayed long in our house. As she later confessed to me, either she found them disgusting or they made too much of a mess. I could also play games such as hopscotch in the street. (Did we call it *Himmel und Hölle* or *Himmel und Erde* ["Heaven and Hell" or "Heaven and Earth"]?) Aside from the limousines of Herr Müller and Herr Meier, hardly any cars drove down Klaus Groth Strasse. The ice man, Bolle with milk, the vegetable seller, all came with horse-drawn carts, and as a little boy I loved to climb up to the box seat, take the reins, and say "giddyap" to make the horse pull me to the next house, although the horse would have gone anyway and probably paid little attention to me.

The complexities of my birthdays began with the guest list. Of course the children of my parents' friends were always invited, as were the cousins my age, whether I liked them or not. But my parents were the ones who decided who came, not I. Until I started school, only the children of family and friends attended, including Irene Meier, of course. The afternoons of my first birthday parties I endured like rain showers in April. I was an unpleasant host who, for example, took gifts away from his guests if they happened to take them off the gift table to have a closer look or, God forbid, play with them. They might break them!

In 1926, when I wasn't quite six years old, I began school. The Twenty-Seventh *Gemeindeschule* [Community School] was on Kastanienallee. It had opened in 1909, the year of Haley's Comet, a picture of which could, and still can, be seen on the wall of the main building. The first day of school was a bad one. Instead of Didi, as I had hoped, Mutti took me. She left me in the classroom of Herr Meier (no relation to the banker), the teacher who was to instruct and look after us for the coming four years. I headed for one of the seats, wishing I were invisible. Herr Meier wrote down information in his class register as I, thoroughly embarrassed, told him that I was "of the Mosaic confession" (Jewish) and that my father's profession was bank *Prokurist*. Papa had patiently taught me these words the evening before, until I was able to repeat them without difficulty. I wasn't sure what they meant.

Suddenly I noticed that someone in the seat behind me was waving his arm wildly over my head in order to get Herr Meier's attention. When he finally succeeded, he pointed at me and announced loudly that I had soiled my pants and that it stank. I must have turned red with shame. Herr

Meier came down from his lectern, leaned over me, pulled my collar back, and sniffed. Letting my collar go, he told the boy behind me that he must have made a mistake, that I hadn't soiled my pants at all. Not much later, my "accuser" and I developed a friendship that lasted for six years. Lorenz Eitner came from Vienna and was a Catholic. In 1932 he went with his parents to South Carolina, where his father opened a furniture factory. When Hitler came to power a year later, the Eitners decided to stay in the United States, although as "Aryans" they had no reason to fear the Nazis. Lorenz, whom I met again briefly in New York in 1954, became a renowned art historian and taught for many years at Stanford University.

My first four years of school were pleasant and without problems, thanks mainly to Herr Meier. A widower, he had a teenage daughter, lived on Krumme Strasse, and was probably a Social Democrat. But above all he was a human being rather than a drillmaster. He was patient, concerned with our development, imaginative in his teaching, and he very rarely punished us. When he did find punishment necessary, he only hit us symbolically with what he called his *Zischer* ["whizzer"]. I was lucky that he was my teacher, because I could have had someone like Herr Müller, a redheaded tyrant who taught one of the higher grades and made us tremble when he monitored recess. One day after recess I was returning to our classroom. We had to go up the stairs in rows of three and were only allowed to step out of this military-style formation when we arrived in the hallway of our classroom. As so often, I was walking along daydreaming, climbing the spiral staircase as the fourth person in a row of three. On the landing of the second floor a hand suddenly grabbed my collar—Herr Müller. He pulled me behind his broad back and looked for further victims. I began crying, sure I was going to get a real beating this time, not just a *Zischer*. Herr Müller was a first-class sadist.

But then a miracle happened: someone else grabbed me, this time very gently by the arm, and pulled me up the spiral staircase to the next floor and our classroom, into which I immediately fled. We didn't say a word to each other. This older student, a complete stranger to me, was probably dying to get back at Herr Müller. He had discovered me, miserable crying thing, and decided to kidnap me from the claws of my tormenter. I didn't even have time to thank him. This little episode happened more than seventy years ago, but the feelings of helplessness, fear, and unbelievable relief are just as vivid to me today as they were then.

The composition of my class mirrored the social structure of

Westend in the mid-1920s. The majority of us came from the middle class, a few from the upper middle class, but there were also some poor boys. No girls attended our school, of course: only private schools were co-ed. Back then it was still possible to tell the social class of the parents by the clothes their children wore. At first it surprised me to see classmates in patched pants or shirts. There was nothing of the sort at our house. Worn-out or torn clothes landed at the Salvation Army, which my mother thought a great deal of, or in the box of cleaning rags. As usual, Didi explained it to me, saying many poor people couldn't afford new clothes. That was a revelation to me, since I had never seen real poverty. In the affluent Westend where I grew up, there were hardly any poor people, and the few I met at primary school were outsiders.

What I didn't notice at the time, because it didn't interest me, was the relatively large number of Jewish students in school. A lot of Jews lived in Westend then, but many sent their children to private Jewish schools, such as the Goldschmidt or Kaliski School, because they assumed that these schools would prepare their children better for later studies than the normal public schools could. Maybe that was occasionally the case, but I met a lot of former private school students in *Gymnasium* [high school] and didn't notice much difference.

My two best friends from primary school weren't Jews. The first was Lorenz Eitner and the second was Dieter Delschau. One evening at home during my first year of school, the doorbell rang. I was already in bed, rattling off my evening prayer. As usual, an adult was with me— Didi, my father, Mutti, I don't remember who. I heard the front door open and someone ask in a high boy's voice if he could play with Werner. It was Dieter Delschau. Of course he was told I was in bed, which I found horribly embarrassing. But he was allowed to come into my room. When one of my parents asked him whether he always walked around in winter in short pants and shirt sleeves, he simply said, "Yes."

Dieter and I remained good friends for the four years of primary school. Unfortunately, in fifth grade he went to another *Gymnasium* than I. He was just as tall (or, rather, short) as I was, slim, sinewy, strong, and could run incredibly fast. I was a good sprinter, too, and we often made use of this talent, because we had only silly pranks on our minds and often had to leave the scene in a hurry. We especially liked to throw stink bombs, which was not at all appreciated at the United Pommeranian Dairy branch on Reichsstrasse. But they never caught us. You could buy the bombs, which were about the size of a piece of candy, for a few pennies at any drugstore.

The Delschaus lived on Reichskanzlerplatz (today's Theodor Heuss Platz) on the corner of Reichsstrasse and Lindenallee above a "colonial" grocery store, on the door of which often hung a dead deer, hare, or pheasant. Dieter's father was an engineer and had built the Wannsee bridge, if I remember correctly. His mother was a wonderful woman who went around at Dieter's yearly birthday party, to which I was always invited, with a huge pitcher of lemonade, calling out in her singsong voice, "*Wer will noch mal, wer hat noch nicht?*" ("Who wants more, who doesn't have any?" or, more literally, "Who wants to again, who hasn't yet?") She once told us that she had worked in a field hospital as a nurse during the war and had gone from bed to bed with a chamber pot asking these two questions. Dieter also had two older brothers, but they ignored us little kids. They didn't notice when we once secretly borrowed their air rifle and shot at the windows across the street, where, Dieter assured me, the people were on vacation. The clinking of the window panes was music to our ears.

Once I started school I was allowed to invite my friends to my birthday party myself. The guest list was then inspected by my mother, always with the question, "Are their parents in the phone book?" If they had a telephone, the invitation was approved. If the parents weren't in the phone book (much thinner in those days than it is today), there were two possibilities: either they had an unlisted number and were consequently very important people (I never knew any children from such circles) or they were poor and couldn't afford a telephone (which in the mid-1920s applied to most of Berlin's population). Once, for example, I wanted to invite a classmate whose father was a shoemaker. Mutti immediately exercised her right of veto, upon which I turned to my father. He thought it over for a moment and decided, "You know, Henny, he can actually invite whomever he wants." And so the boy came to my birthday party, where he probably felt like a fish out of water.

During my last two years of primary school we lived at Hessenallee 3. We moved there after the birth of my brother Hans in April 1928, into a newly built apartment that still smelled of wet cement. It was larger than the apartment on Klaus Groth Strasse and extremely expensive, so, after a year had gone by and the Depression had set in, my father went with a tenant delegation to the landlord to plead for a reduction in rent. I don't know if they succeeded, but three years later, in 1932, we moved to an apartment in Lichterfelde that was just as large as the one on Hessenallee but much less expensive. Our landlord on Hessenallee was a Mr. Herwarth von Bittenfeld, who lived around the corner on Bayernallee. My parents found him fair and cooperative, a man you could talk to. Perhaps for that reason he had to put up with occasional appeals from tenants. Once new tenants brought in bedbugs, which had supposedly laid eggs in their baggage during the move. A delegation of tenants showed up at the landlord's door, each carrying a jar of squashed bugs. The exterminator came right away. Shortly after Hitler took power, when we had already moved to Lichterfelde, my father ran into Mr. Herwarth von Bittenfeld by chance somewhere in town, and the baron told him in a low voice that he had been shocked recently to discover that he had a Jewish grandmother. My father consoled him by saying that he himself had two Jewish grandmothers. This story may actually be true: my father, unlike Grosspapa, rarely told fibs. The fact that the Herwarth von Bittenfeld family wasn't completely *judenrein* [free of Jews] is well known today.

In the course of my first sixteen years (that is, prior to our emigration in October 1937) we moved four times. Before we moved into a new apartment, an interior designer, Herr Radunsky, was called to take care of furnishing the new lodgings. My parents accepted his suggestions, which were expensive but good. On moving day Fritz and I were sent to friends' houses after school; Hans, until the last move to Holsteinische Strasse, was too little for that. My father went to work at the bank, and my mother and the two servants set up the new apartment. The movers, who to my eternal amazement never dropped my mother's grand piano as they carried it up and down the stairs, were given beer and, I imagine, generous tips, so there was never any friction, not even during the last move in early 1936, during the Nazi period. When my father came home in the evening, he looked over our new home in silence, striding from room to room, my mother watching his inspection with confidence. Then he usually announced radiantly, "Schneckchen, once again you've done a wonderful job"—although occasionally he added, "I would put this armchair over there." That was the extent of my father's participation in our moves.

During our years on Hessenallee, from mid-1928 to mid-1932, the worsening global economic crisis and the political situation in Germany didn't prevent us from enjoying our lives. There were a lot of social activities, because my parents liked to have company, and they could easily entertain with the help of the cook and the nanny. I always found it exciting when the long dining room table was set with the Rosenthal china; the pretty wine glasses; the starched, pressed, and folded damask napkins; and of course the family silver. Once when I was looking for something in the sideboard and broke a saucer, I got a slap from my mother and a lecture from my father about how I had no business digging around in the sideboard. Curious as I was, it was disappointing not being allowed to be present at the social evenings. For that I had to be an "adult." In the meantime, after about the age of ten, I was allowed to attend the family Friday evenings. But these differed considerably from the dinners designed for my father's colleagues and business friends and their wives, although occasionally other family members also came. Since my brother Fritz and I were sent to bed before the guests' arrival—although we usually had to return in our pajamas to say goodnight to them—we crept out of our room, which was strictly forbidden, and eavesdropped at one of the dining room doors.

Sometimes we took revenge for being excluded from these social events. Once, for example, we got into the hall closet and sewed together the guests' coat sleeves. Another time, before the guests arrived, I filled the sugar bowl with salt. Onkel Arthur Maass was the first and only one to serve himself from the sugar bowl (he spit out his "sugar" violently). Since this was the brother-in-law who tried to sell ties to guests, my mother let me off with a mild reprimand. Finally, we sometimes sneaked into the dining room after the guests had left and drank what remained in all the wineglasses.

Almost all the guests belonged to the upper middle class. Some of the gentlemen were addressed as *Herr Doktor* (as one calls attorneys in Germany), though none had gone beyond the study of law and actually practiced. Instead, they earned their money in banking and especially on the stock market. A number of them were relatives of one of the directors of the Königsberger and Lichtenhein bank. Of course I only knew them from a distance, which was alright with me, since I found most of them self-satisfied, too loud, and too "bourgeois," a word unknown to me at the time. To us they were adults, guests who patted us on the head in a friendly way, held out their cheeks to be kissed if they were women, and brought us small gifts. Otherwise they paid no attention to us. And so I rejected these people, most of whom were doubtless decent and kind, because their world wasn't my world. My parents, who had no titles, were proud of their "educated" connections.

What was the makeup of these groups that frequented our house? Was my family an example of the often-cited German-Jewish symbiosis? My parents had a few Christian friends and acquaintances, particularly among my father's card-playing and bowling pals, and of course there was the non-Jewish part of our family. Now and then Willi Kollo, the son of the operetta composer Walter Kollo and the father of René, the well-known tenor, stopped by our house. Willi was a friend of Didi's younger sister Hilde for a while, so he turned up now and then, also with chocolate for us children, but he didn't normally come to the dinners. Otherwise my parents' circle of friends and acquaintances was for the most part Jewish. As a result, after Hitler became chancellor on January 30, 1933, the adults in my family didn't lose many friends at first. We children, for whom it was much easier to make non-Jewish friends, suffered in this respect much greater losses.

In 1930 I transferred from elementary school to the Herder Realgymnasium on Bayernallee and started the fifth grade (the beginning grade of *Gymnasium*). To my great relief I was exempted from the entrance examination, since I had good grades. It was hard for me to leave Herr Meier, but I figured I would continue to have nice teachers. In addition, some of my classmates were also going to the Herder school, among them Lorenz Eitner. Today I still have a (probably incomplete) list of my classmates in my head, as reeled off each morning by the first-period teacher: Abendrot, Angress, Apfelbaum, Aschheim, Berg, Böhme, Eitner, Engelmann, Fuhrmann, Goller, Grombach, Guttmann, Hirsch, Hoffmann I, Hoffmann II, Jäger, Jaretzki, Kindermann, Knopf, Landsberg, Lehmann, Lindenheim, Löwald, Marx, Mecklenburg, Meyer, Mielke, Pauly, Rautenberg, Renner, Schulz, Wenderoth, and Zilm. Of these, at least thirteen were Jewish or of Jewish descent. There was no separation of Jews and non-Jews after class. In the two years that I went to the Herder Gymnasium I only heard one anti-Semitic remark. Friendships between Jewish and non-Jewish boys were common, and my friend Klaus Löwald assured me that it remained that way until he left the school in 1938.

I can only remember a few of the teachers. Most were colorless figures or became such. There was "Vater" Timm, a man with a long Santa Claus beard and a soft, even-timbred voice. I believe he taught biology. If one of us whispered to a neighbor or attracted his attention in any way, he hurried down from his lectern and poked the transgressor as hard as he could under his right shoulder bone with the stiffened fingers of his right hand, murmuring, "Don't, boy: you'll have to write a penalty composition." No one escaped the punishment.

Then there was Herr Heilbronn, possibly the only Jewish teacher on the faculty. The various Jewish religion teachers with whom we were blessed, all boring, came only once a week to teach religion and taught at other schools the rest of the week. Herr Heilbronn taught German, had imagination, and knew how to hold our attention. I especially loved his readings on the last day of school. Even before Grosspapa recommended Mark Twain to me, Herr Heilbronn had read us parts of *Tom Sawyer*, Rudyard Kipling's *The Jungle Book*, and other classics. Sometimes in the winter when he was the monitor outside on the courtyard during the long recess, he was the only teacher who would be hit from behind with snowballs (although anti-Semitism was much less virulent at Herder Gymnasium than at many other German schools, we certainly had some anti-Semitic students and teachers). But he had a friend among the other teachers. Herr Elendt, who had lost an eye in the war, taught geography. I still see him standing with his pointer before a big map of Germany and intoning the names of the territories taken from Germany by the Treaty of Versailles: "Alsace-Lorraine! Eupen-Malmédy! North Schleswig! Danzig! The Polish Corridor! Memel Land! Upper Silesia! Hultschiner Ländchen!" Each name he accompanied with a loud rap of the pointer on the map. And yet this man turned out to be our Jewish teacher's protector. Every time Herr Heilbronn had to supervise recess, Herr Elendt was standing at a window somewhere, and as soon as the first snowballs began to fly, he shot into the schoolyard, grabbed one or two of the snowball throwers, and screamed at the others. Then Herr Heilbronn could continue his supervision undisturbed. These two vastly dissimilar men had been hired around the same time and had become friends. What happened to Heilbronn after 1933? And Elendt?

Three other teachers—Schlenker, Eder, and Schlunke—were much less colorful. Schlenker taught French, the first foreign language at our reformed *Realgymnasium*, and he never let us forget that he was an *Oberstudienrat* [senior teacher]. His first *dictée* I still know by heart today, but I will spare the reader. Eder—I forget what subject he taught— had frozen all his toes in the war. They had to be amputated, and consequently he walked somewhat unsteadily. Schlunke taught history, but what period he bored us with I have forgotten.

Those Westend years were our last easygoing years of play, the last when we children of Jewish families were able to move about freely. We could choose friends of our age without worrying about whether they were Catholic, Protestant, or Jewish, and we could go on adventures with them on foot or bicycle. We loved to play Indians on empty lots on Hessenallee and Preussenallee. Our inspiration came from books by Karl May (a German writer famous for his stories set in the U.S. Far West). I had been devouring his novels since the age of eight or nine, having become acquainted with the three volumes of *Winnetou* at one of the summer camps Fritz and I attended. I insisted on being Chief Donnerwort and behaved like him. Since I had also been introduced to the *Nibelungenlied* by the book *Deutsche Heldensagen* [*Heroic German Legends*], I loved to play Hagen von Tronje and "thrust" my "saber" (a sharpened broomstick) between the shoulder blades of Siegfried (hapless Fritz).

I was always the one to decide who played which role. I wasn't a nice child and I tyrannized Fritz, whom I also made the object of my Karl May fantasies. I am very ashamed to recall the day that I tied his hands and feet together, like Old Shatterhand had done to a villain in one of the novels. I gagged him, shoved him under the bed, and forgot about him, because a friend had come to pick me up. The nanny finally discovered Fritz by chance after hearing strange noises coming from our room. Of course it was all child's play, but for my brother it was torture. We also liked to throw stink bombs and firecrackers into the stores on Reichstrasse, and bags of water from our balcony onto unsuspecting passersby, scoring some bull's-eyes, then ducking out of sight behind the geranium boxes. We once started a wonderful fire in a big sewer pipe at the edge of the Grunewald neighborhood, then ran to the next street to laugh at the puzzled residents poking around in the smoking street drains. All this was part of our carefree prepubescence before the Nazis came to power.

While we were living on Hessenallee I began to take an interest in politics. At home this topic was generally not talked about in front of the children. "You don't understand that yet," "You're much too young for that," and "Politics are dirty" were the explanations we got from our parents. The first time I heard anything about politics was from my father shortly after we had moved to Hessenallee. Not far away, on our street, was an empty lot where I liked to play with my friends and where we dug deep caves, of course without using wood or any other material to hold them up, to my father's horror when he discovered it. My father saw me with a flag one morning as I was about to leave our apartment for this "playground." My flag consisted of an old broomstick onto which I had nailed a red rag. Where did I think I was going with "that thing there"? He refused to let me go out into the street with this "communist flag." When I asked who the communists were he informed me that they were people who would take away one coat from anyone who had two coats, for example. Since I hated to wear a coat (I don't even own one anymore), I quite approved of such a principle, but I kept my mouth shut and promised him I wouldn't go out in the street with the flag until our seamstress, Fräulein Berta, had sewn a white cross on it. A few days later I headed out into the field with my Swiss flag. This was my introduction to politics.

A further source of information for me about politics was our neighbors on the opposite landing, the Grüns. "Onkel" Walter Grün was a big, loud Bavarian man from Munich, and not Jewish. He was the only adult on Hessenallee who knew how to get along with us children, and now and then he took his son Peter, Fritz, and me into the Grunewald forest and played Indians with us. His wife, "Tante" Else, came from Nuremberg and was of Jewish origin. We and the Grüns had moved onto the fourth floor of the new building at the same time, and our two families became friends. This friendship lasted until their deaths in the 1960s and 1970s in London, where they had emigrated in 1931 for business and not political reasons. The Grüns were usually part of social events at our apartment, whether my parents had one of their big dinners or invited only a few guests. I soon found out that politics was the subject of conversation at all of these gatherings, because the raised voices penetrated into our bedroom. The most piercing voice was that of Tante Else, a leftist. She was very dear to me all of her life, but I never understood her salon communism, which she stuck to until her death in the spring of 1970. My father had voted for the German People's Party [*Deutsche Volkspartei*] since the 1920s because he thought a great deal of Gustav Stresemann (the party's chairman until his death in 1929), so the conversations were very energetic. Papa had begun with the German Democratic Party after the war, but I don't know how he voted during the Empire. These discussions didn't hurt the friendship between our two families, but since they were so loud, we children sneaked into the hall to hear what was going on. So I learned about the politics of the Weimar Republic through the keyhole, so to speak.

I also learned a few things about German politics from Lorenz Eitner, who was slightly older, but none of this allowed me to completely understand the political views of my parents. When at lunchtime one Sunday, an Election Day in 1930 or 1931, I asked them for whom they had voted, my father dismissed my question, invoking the secrecy of the ballot. My mother ignored this objection and said she had voted for the Center Party. My father, she added, had voted for the German People's Party. During all the Weimar years my mother refused to hang the black, red, and gold flag of the Republic from the window, because she had grown up with the former black, white, and red imperial flag. And my father followed her lead on this point. In 1933, on my initiative (!), we bought a black, white, and red flag and hung it from the balcony of our Lichterfelde apartment on every national holiday that the National Socialist government decreed. After the death of President Hindenburg my father finally put an end to this nonsense.

One day in the summer of 1930, in our living room on Hessenallee, I asked my parents what "evacuation of the Rhineland" meant. I had seen the headlines on the newsstand outside. Once again I got a lesson on politics from my father, this time about the shameful Versailles treaty. After more than ten years of Allied occupation, he said, a first step had been taken to restore Germany's honor: the foreign troops were finally leaving the Rhineland. Then Mutti sat down at the grand piano, holding her head high, and the three of us sang proudly, "Deutschland, Deutschland über alles!" Thirteen years later my father was killed at Auschwitz. Since then I shudder when I hear the expression "German honor."

Though my friend Lorenz was hardly an expert on politics, he had picked up a lot more from his parents than I had from mine, and I profited from his knowledge. One morning we were standing before the locked school doors waiting for the caretaker to open them. Suddenly for no apparent reason Lorenz snapped to attention, raised his hand in the Hitler salute and called out, "Wake up, Germany, Hitler is making coffee!" Not all that funny, but it was the first time I saw the "German salute." Lorenz also took me along one day shortly before the Reichstag [parliament] election of 1930 to remove stickers of the National Socialist Party from the house walls. One read, "Comrades, clean up / you've put it off long enough / give the big shots a kick in the pants / fight together with us for the Third Reich / Heil Hitler!" We went around Reichskanzlerplatz and down part of Kaiserdamm and took down all the stickers we were able to reach. Finally—and this was his idea too—we took some worthless old iron coins from the war or from the inflation that I had gathered somehow and made a call from a phone booth on Reichskanzlerplatz to the Nazi newspaper *Der Angriff*. Lorenz, whose voice was already deeper than mine, asked to speak to an editor. When someone answered, he shouted obscenities into the receiver and hung up. He had to explain to me the political position of *Der Angriff* and who Dr. Goebbels was. I am still surprised today at how much Lorenz already knew. His parents, Viennese Catholics, apparently weren't afraid of introducing contemporary politics to their oldest child. There was a little epilogue to our prank. When I got home that day my grandfather was there, and I told him about our heroic deeds. But instead of praising me for fighting against National Socialism, he scolded me for using worthless coins in the phone booth: "You cheated the post office!" (It was also the telephone company.) The word he used for "cheated" was *bescheissen* [shit on], and hearing him use such language shocked me.

Aside from Lorenz, whom I played with several afternoons a week (the Eitners lived on Fürstenplatz, almost directly opposite the Herder Realgymnasium), no one at school taught me anything about politics. The topic came up in class once, and it wasn't raised by the teacher. One of our Jewish classmates, a boy named Theo Meyer, had, with his asthmatic voice, told each class at the beginning of the year that his name was "Meyer mit e-ypsilon" [Meyer with a y]. And so we called him that, this disagreeable, overweight, rich banker's son who lived in a villa in Grunewald, from which he was brought to school every morning by a chauffeur in a limousine. In late April 1931, "Meyer mit e-ypsilon" stood up, waved his arm, and, once he got the teacher's attention, declared, panting, that he wasn't allowed to come to school on May 1. When the teacher asked him why, he answered that the communists were going to be on the rampage that day, and it would be too dangerous for him. This was the only time that politics penetrated our classroom at the Herder Realgymnasium. The topic surely came up more often later, but by then I was no longer there.

Thanks to my parents' tendency to shield us children from unpleasant and controversial facts, it isn't surprising that I only perceived the Great Depression from a distance. My parents didn't explain to me at the time why Papa was no longer the *Prokurist*, but instead had been made director of a now much smaller Königsberger and Lichtenhein bank. Of the city of Berlin I only saw the socially "tranquil" neighborhoods, and never the parts of town where the workers lived, stood in unemployment lines, and starved. I didn't see my first tenement houses, with their dark inner courtyards, until I was in Kreuzberg on a visit to Berlin after the Second World War. I once went to Alexanderplatz briefly with my mother, but I only remember this because I had heard of "Alex" (as Berliners call this large public square in the center of the city) from the saying, "You go with your hand over Alexanderplatz" (meaning, you take a crazy detour). As far as I was concerned, the northern and eastern parts of Berlin could have been in Siberia.

Of course, I wondered why so many people were begging for money; why young people, usually part-time students, played music on the streets for tips; and why often elderly organ-grinders played in the courtyards and sang songs like "*Waldeslu-u-ust*" [Forest Delight] and "*Das einz'ge was ich noch auf Erden hab / das ist die Rasenbank am Elterngrab*" [The only thing I have left on earth / is the grassy mound at my parents' grave], often horribly out of tune. And then they walked through the crowd with their hats in hand. I was allowed to toss down from the kitchen window a bit of change wrapped in newspaper and accept those poor people's thanks. When I went with my mother to Tauentzienstrasse or somewhere else to shop, she sometimes handed me a coin for a beggar. As a child I didn't notice the long lines in front of the unemployment offices. I know that even in Westend I sometimes saw groups of men in their prime wearing torn clothes standing around on the street, smoking and talking for hours. But that was all. No one explained to me that it hadn't always been this way or why the men were standing around. At ten or eleven years old, I didn't worry about it.

But one thing left an impression on me that I haven't forgotten. Southwest of Karolingerplatz in Westend, north of Eichkamp, was a large, empty sandlot. There whole families had settled. No longer able to pay their rent, they had been evicted with their few belongings. Some of them had dug themselves little caves, covering the floors and walls with newspaper and the flat "roofs" with whatever they could find. I liked to play on Karolingerplatz with a classmate of mine who lived nearby. We, being curious, sometimes went to the "colony" and talked to its inhabitants. Decades later, when I first saw Bertoldt Brecht's film *Kuhle Wampe*, the portrait of the homeless people seemed almost idyllic to me in comparison to the caves that I had seen on the other side of Karolingerplatz.

Once we witnessed a theft there. We had just been talking with an older man when, from nowhere, two or three teenagers appeared in front of his cave, grabbed his little cart, and took off with it. The man ran after them almost crying, and we pursued them with him, but they paid no attention to his pleas or to the insults we yelled at them. After we finally lost sight of them, we tried in vain to console him. He returned to his improvised home, and we went to the nearest police station, somewhere near the Kaiserdamm. But when we reported the theft, the police laughed at us and sent us away. They were apparently not interested in thefts committed against the poorest of the poor, especially when the accusation came from kids like us.

It wasn't by chance that I, then ten or eleven, went to the police in that situation. My parents had impressed upon me that the police were "guardians of the law," that we could always turn to a policeman, and that he would protect children at all times. I didn't know the now-common slang term *Bullen* (more pejorative than "cops"). Such language was used in working-class neighborhoods, where I never went. The Prussian police were respected, especially by the people in the western part of Berlin. If they read that the brave *Schupos* were battling the Reds and the Browns in the northern and eastern parts of town and were holding them in check, then good citizens felt safe. The decision by the parents of "Meyer mit e-ypsilon" to keep him home from school on May Day might seem a little paranoid, but it wasn't atypical behavior for people who lived in the western parts of town.

At the time I believed that I had a special connection to the Berlin police. My parents had met the vice president of the police department, Dr. Bernhard Weiss, whom the entire political right wing, not just the Nazis, called "Isidor" (considered then to be a typical Jewish name). He was a distant relative of one of the K and L directors. One day Mutti told me proudly that she, with "Vice Weiss" as a partner, had won first prize in a bottle dance at a big party. Another day my mother and I met Vice Weiss's daughter Hildchen in front of the police station at Sophie Charlotte Platz. She was almost the same age as I. I was convinced that we were indeed very closely connected to the police. This impression was strengthened by the fact that during the years when Herr Müller still drove the two directors and Papa to the bank on Französischer Strasse, they stopped at the Brandenburg Gate just before Christmas every year and each gave the traffic policeman on duty a gift. The policeman accepted the presents with a salute and added them to the pile gathering at his feet. I was taken along once or twice for this annual ritual and even allowed to hand over the gifts. But when I told my father one day that I had asked a *Schupo* standing at

Reichskanzlerplatz to pass on my greetings to Herr Weiss, he was annoyed and told me to refrain from such familiarities in the future.

Yes, we were brought up very "Prussian"—at least Papa and I were. How could we have dreamed that only a few years later the police we so admired would look on as National Socialist thugs beat Jews on the streets? How could we have believed that on July 13, 1943, Police Reserve Battalion 101 would shoot fifteen hundred Jews in the town of Jozefów, one hundred kilometers south of Lublin, only one example among many murders of this sort.

Sometime in the spring or early summer of 1932, it became clear that our days in Westend were numbered. The economic crisis had worsened markedly, and we could no longer afford the rent in Hessenallee. After my father had taken over the direction of K and L (in school I subsequently had to say simply that my father was a banker), he was no longer picked up by Herr Müller but took the subway to town (we said "town" when we were talking about the city center). The bank couldn't afford a company car anymore, Herr Müller became a taxi driver, and my parents drove around with him looking for an apartment. Fritz and I went along and were thrilled by every apartment we looked at. My mother was attracted to the showy suburbs—Zehlendorf, Wannsee, Nikolassee, Babelsberg, Nowawes—but they were too far from my father's work, and surely too expensive as well, so we ended up in Lichterfelde-West, at Unter den Eichen 115 on Asternplatz, where we lived until the beginning of 1936.

In 1989, when I was living again in my birthplace, Berlin, after almost a half a century in the United States, I took the train one day to the Botanischer Garten station. The station hadn't changed much. Before I went upstairs, I stood around a little on the platform, and all of a sudden I was twelve or thirteen again. We boys of the seventh or maybe eighth grade of the Lichterfelder Realgymnasium (the high school today called the Goethe Oberschule) on Drakestrasse were on a class trip into town. When the train came and the group I was part of noisily shoved its way in, I heard the voice of my main enemy in our class, "Arndte" Glaubitz, saying behind me, "Take it easy, boys, no non-Aryan rushing!" And with this closer-than-life memory I was back in the Lichterfelde of the early 1930s, where I experienced the end of the Weimar Republic and the early years of the Third Reich, and where I first encountered anti-Semitism as a fact of life. These were also the years when I joined the Jewish youth movement and when puberty hit me. The latter was almost worse than the Nazis.

Shortly after our move from Hessenallee to Unter den Eichen I got pleurisy and had to spend several weeks in bed. This gave me plenty of time to think, and my spirits were quite low. The move had cut me off from my beloved Westend, and it was very difficult to get together with my friends there. The idea of showing up at a new school as a complete stranger and several weeks late frightened me. Mutti had already registered me there, and a student I didn't know delivered to our house the homework that the teachers had assigned.

The new apartment, which overlooked Berlin's botanical garden, was just as spacious as the previous one, but what I enjoyed the most after my recovery was the inner courtyard, which we hadn't had at Hessenallee. There was a long wooden beam for beating rugs which we could climb onto, a sandbox, and a hazelnut tree that really belonged to the neighboring lot but that Fritz and I plundered every fall. Once again the landlord was a Prussian baron, Richard Nikolaus Eugen Freiherr von Lyncker, a close relative of Moritz Freiherr von Lyncker, the former head of the Prussian war ministry and adjutant general to Emperor Wilhelm II. Herr von Lyncker, a tall man with a grating commander's voice, was quite aware of his proud family tradition; in his living room hung the portraits of at least thirty relatives in uniform. Papa joked that he only had us move into buildings that belonged to Prussian nobility. My father and the baron, such different men, came to have frequent lively discussions based on their common interest in finance and politics. For some reason I never fathomed, Herr von Lyncker had continual financial problems. His car, which had surely seen better days, stayed in the garage as long as we lived there, because he lacked the money for gas and upkeep. But I still liked to look at it now and then, because the doors sported the baronial crown.

The Lynckers—that is, the baron, his wife Ditha, and their daughter Ursula—lived in the apartment above ours, and since his wife had a wooden leg, we had to get used to the thudding above our heads as she attended to her household chores. Herr von Lyncker was a cooperative and well-meaning landlord, but that didn't help the tenants much in a practical way. When my mother asked him about something that needed repair, his raspy reply, in his thick Berlin accent was always, "It will all be taken care of, ma'am, it'll all be taken care of." Nothing was taken care of, and Papa paid for the repairs. The origin of his raspy voice wasn't only military: he had bad asthma, and the superintendent, Herr Weppner, every month lugged several large tanks of oxygen up the stairs, which the baron needed in case of an attack.

It was mainly the influence of our landlord that accounted for my father's political drift to the right. After having voted for the German People's Party for years, Papa switched to the German Nationalists for the various elections of 1932, because, as the baron assured him, only that party could keep the Nazis out of the government. In exchange for this political counsel, so to speak, the landlord had Papa advise him financially, but unfortunately this didn't help him much. But as long as we lived on Unter den Eichen, thus until the beginning of 1936, Herr von Lyncker's behavior toward us, the only Jews in the building, never changed. He remained charming, gallantly kissing my mother's hand and, when repairs were necessary, promising us everything under the sun. He never made us feel that we as tenants were in any way undesirable. The Third Reich also has his death to answer for. Quite late in the war, when he was nearly seventy and very ill with asthma, the baron was conscripted into military service and ordered to Paris, from which he never returned. Whether he suffocated because there was no oxygen tank available or whether he was somehow involved in the failed plot to assassinate Hitler, I never found out.

The tenants under us, the Gerickes, had a daughter my age, Ricarda. Besides her, the Lynckers' daughter Ursula, whom we greeted with a nod when we met on the stairs, and the youngest daughter of the superintendent, Ilse Weppner, there were no other children in the building. Ricarda, who matured early, suggested one day in our apartment that we play doctor. The malady that she proposed was appendicitis, and I was to be the doctor, she the patient. We chased my brother Fritz out of the bedroom, since the patient couldn't be disturbed. I examined the patient thoroughly, following her instructions, without the slightest idea of what I was doing. The facts of life hadn't been explained to me yet; that came when I was fourteen. But I didn't feel quite right in what we were doing, and when she suggested we change roles, I declined, and she, pouting, went downstairs. I only mention this because I, completely naive, had agreed to do something that could have been very dangerous for us. Ricarda's father was a leader of German Christians group and a member of the National Socialist Party. Immediately after Hitler took power, the swastika flag waved from the Gerickes' balcony. The criminalization of *Rassenschande* (literally "racial disgrace," the Nazi term for sexual relations with a non-

Aryan) was still a thing of the future, but I can imagine Herr Gericke's reaction to our game—as a father and as a Nazi—if he had found out about it. Fortunately Ricarda kept her mouth shut. At the end of the war, she went to the United States with an American G.I.

We had little contact with the other tenants, and the only one I remember is the vegetable seller "Paule," who lived in one of the two basement apartments with a huge German shepherd and his very old mother. Paul was a Communist and let everyone know it: us children and anyone else who was hanging around in the courtyard, including the superintendent's son Rudi, who remained his friend even after joining the *Sturmabteilung* (SA, the political fighting troops of the National Socialist Party) in 1932. After Hitler became chancellor in January 1933, Paul finally stopped talking about his politics, but I don't think he changed his position. In the other basement apartment lived the superintendent Herr Weppner with his wife, their son Rudi, and their daughter Ilse. A second, older daughter came to visit now and then and told me once, when I was paying one of my occasional visits to the superintendent's apartment, that she worked for a Jewish company, Goldschmidt, where they were glad to have her and where she enjoyed working. She said this with a sideways glance at her family. Rudi was about twenty years old at the time and wore the "bonbon," the Nazi symbol, on his lapel. After 1933 I saw him only in uniform. Rudi's profession was "unemployed." That was understandable, it being 1932 and the height of the Great Depression. But he remained unemployed, even after the Führer created jobs building the Autobahn and airports, preparing the country for war. In 1950, when I returned to Berlin for the first time since our flight in October 1937, Rudi was in "the West" (West Germany) and unemployed, in spite of the nascent "economic miracle."

Sometimes when we children were playing in the courtyard, Rudi joined us and taught us, among other things, how an SA man would tie up an adversary hand and foot. I can still do it today. He knew that we were Jews, as everybody in the building did, although it isn't clear to me how they found out. We didn't trumpet it from the windows. When I once asked Rudi if he wouldn't get in trouble for associating with us, he said that we were "white Jews." Back then I had no idea what that expression meant, but I assumed it meant something positive. "Old Weppner," the superintendent and Rudi's father, was likewise already in the Party by 1932. Now and then he chatted with Grosspapa, who lived with us for a while after 1933, about art and literature. He knew some Greek and Latin, too, and Grosspapa was impressed. Something must have gone wrong in the course of Herr Weppner's life, for he became a superintendent and remained one until the end of his days. Looking back, it amazes me that these early and dedicated Nazis had such a relaxed relationship with us, a Jewish family. We never heard an unfriendly remark, not to mention a threatening one.

But after the beginning of the Third Reich some gradual changes became perceptible under the smooth surface of our relations. Shortly after we moved into the building, my mother proposed to the parents of little Ilse, who was then about nine years old and anemic, that she eat with us once a week to improve her health a bit, as Mutti put it. The Weppners could have taken this the wrong way, but they didn't seem insulted. The superintendent didn't earn much money, after all. My mother's gesture helped the superintendent's family to make themselves increasingly at home in our apartment. Strange as it may sound, with the beginning of Nazi rule our relationship with them became closer. For we had a good radio, and the Weppners had no radio at all. And so they appeared, usually only father and son but sometimes Frau Weppner as well, in a disarmingly matter-of-fact way whenever the Führer broadcast one of his unending speeches. They made themselves at home in our living room, applauded now and then, and didn't budge as long as Hitler's strident voice was to be heard over the airwaves. Of course my parents never dared raise an objection, and as long as we lived on Unter den Eichen we listened to Hitler's speeches, in which we were not very interested, in the company of the superintendent's family.

But why did the Weppners come to our apartment and not go, for example, to that of the Gericke family, who as good National Socialists also listened to the voice of their master? For one, Mutti had clasped Ilse to her non-Aryan breast and thus apparently given the rest of the family the impression that they, too, were welcome at any time. The Weppners also knew that as Jews we couldn't refuse their "visits." And they weren't alone in this way of thinking. Sometime after Hitler became chancellor, Frau Gericke, Ricarda's mother, who had never spoken a word to any of us, asked if she could now and then play the grand piano in our living room. Naturally Mutti couldn't refuse this request, so Frau Gericke occasionally appeared in our apartment in the afternoon to play folk songs. In this way it was made clear to us, albeit indirectly, that we as Jews had to bow to our neighbors' wishes, whether it suited us or not—and these were people who were not antagonistic toward us. A few years later such nuances would disappear, but we were no longer in the country then.

When I returned to Berlin in 1950, I went to look at our old building on Unter den Eichen. The courtyard looked much smaller than I remembered. The bar on which we dried our rugs was gone, and so was the sandbox. Suddenly a voice I recognized called out, "What are you nosing around here for? What do you want?" I went to the window of the superintendent's apartment. "Don't you recognize me, Herr Weppner?" The old man ran out of his apartment and hugged me, crying and praising God that I was still alive. His daughter Ilse, a nurse during the war, had died of pneumonia after jumping into the water to save a drowning person during an air raid in the winter of 1944–45. Rudi was in the West and unemployed. I soon left—too many ghosts!

In 1933 and 1934, I began to realize that I was entering not just a new part of town but the beginning of a new phase in my life. My existence to that point had been very protected and mostly limited to Neu-Westend: Reichsstrasse, Preussenallee, and a bit of Grunewald. Occasionally, with "Onkel" Walter Grün and his son Peter, we got as far as Schildhorn. I had good friends at school, my grades weren't exceptional, but, up until I finished sixth grade and left, they were good enough, and our parents tried to keep anything unpleasant away from us, especially politics. What is more, Westend was a relatively new, open-minded part of town, and relations between Jewish children and our non-Jewish classmates and their parents were unproblematic. People knew that Dr. Joseph Goebbels lived above a delicatessen on Reichskanzlerplatz—his stepson Harald Quandt attended Herder Gymnasium after I left—and that Hermann Göring's apartment was in a building on the corner of Kaiserdamm, but they didn't make a to-do about it. Emil Jannings, the famous movie actor, who lived at Reichsstrasse 3, and the boxer Max Schmeling's mother, who lived across the street and whom I once talked into giving me an autographed photo of her son, were much more interesting to us children.

And then came Lichterfelde, with its beautiful avenues under old trees and its often defiant-looking single-family homes of retired officers, senior teachers, and high civil servants, many of them retired, giving that section of town a much more conservative aura than Westend had ever had. That was intensified by the street names commemorating Prussia's past glory: Roonstrasse, Moltkestrasse, Manteuffelstrasse, and also Gardeschützenweg, which I went down on my way to school. There were very few Jews in Lichterfelde. Aside from "Mutter" Grosser, the mother-in-law of "Onkel Schorsch" Silberstein, our dentist and my father's best friend, we didn't know any. The nearest synagogue was on Prinzregentenstrasse in Wilmersdorf, where my bar mitzvah was held in December 1933, six months late.

When I finally went to my new school for the first time in early 1932, I was shocked. I was wearing a parka, short pants naturally, and I mounted the stairs to the seventh grade classroom full of apprehension. Class hadn't begun yet, and when I walked in I was soon surrounded by a group of curious boys. "Are you the new student?" I nodded. Then one of them, "Arndte" Glaubitz, who during the coming four years would try to make my life at school as hard as he could, asked, "Are you the Jew?" I nodded again. "Go stand by the wall," Arndte commanded, "or you'll get lynched." I didn't take it literally but went to the wall, turned my back to it, and waited for the teacher's arrival. The seventh-grade homeroom teacher, Dr. Walter Muchall, called "der kleine Muck" ["Little Muck," from a fairy tale about a dwarf by Wilhelm Hauff], asked me if I was Angress. He consulted his class list, where in the "Religion" column the designation *mos.*—for *mosaisch* ["of Moses"]—had been entered next to my name. He then had me take a seat in the front row, because, as my mother had apparently told him, I was nearsighted. Next to me was "Schmidtchen," a frail, sickly boy who asked me in a whisper whether I was a "Sozi." I had no idea what that meant but nodded to end his whispering, upon which he informed me that he was a Nazi. A sour look from "der kleine Muck" ended the conversation. That was, for me, the beginning of four years of gradual isolation, occasional hostilities, and almost daily small (and sometimes not so small) humiliations. But the brutal treatment that many other Jewish children had to suffer I was spared.

The fact that I was a Jew affected my relationships with my classmates from the first day on. Most of them were from conservative families. There was also a group of children from petit bourgeois families who, although they weren't conservative, brought anti-Semitism with them from home. Schmidtchen as well as Arndte, whose father was a switchman for the Stadtbahn, Berlin's urban railway, belonged to this group. For most of my classmates, Jews were fairy-tale creatures they had never met personally but had heard about, mostly nothing good. When I appeared in the seventh grade from someplace outside of Lichterfelde, I caused confusion.

Although I had known for years that I was "different," I often wondered in what way. After all, I didn't correspond to the stereotypes of a Jewish boy, which were well-known even to me. I was blond with blue eyes. Although not very tall, I was slim and athletic. So I didn't look "Jewish." I didn't talk with my hands, didn't have flat feet, didn't have a "Jewish accent," didn't smell of garlic, and was certainly not a coward. In addition, I got consistently good grades in German and gymnastics, whereas my grades in the "typical Jewish" subjects like geometry, algebra, physics, and chemistry fluctuated between D and F. From the seventh grade on I barely managed to get promoted to the next grade, and from the eighth grade until I finished school, every February I received a "blue letter," in which my parents were informed that I would have to repeat the grade if my performance didn't improve drastically by Easter. And yet I remained a Jew, and not one school day passed when I could forget it.

Not long after starting school at Lichterfelder Realgymnasium, one of my classmates, possibly Schmidtchen, told me that there was a second Jew at the school. His name was Teppich, and he was regularly beaten up by his classmates. I never did meet this mysterious "fellow believer," but neither did I make any attempts to do so. Why should I, just because he also was a Jewish student? Soon I heard that he had left the school. Half a century later, at the beginning of the 1980s, I attended a conference of the *Liga für Menschenrechte* [League of Human Rights] on Mehringdamm in Berlin together with the Berlin journalist Marianne Regensburger, an old friend of mine from my time at Gross Breesen. As we walked into the lecture hall she said, "Wait a moment, I want to tell Teppich something quick." "Teppich?" I said excitedly and told her to ask him if he had attended Lichterfelder Realgymnasium. A couple of minutes later Fritz Teppich, an heir to the Kempinski hotel fortune and a professional leftist, ran over to me and shouted, "Yes, and I was the only Jew there!" "No, you weren't," I replied. "I was the second one and stayed a lot longer than you did." But we were both wrong. According to the files in the Berlin *Pädagogisches Zentrum* [Education Center], in 1935–36, my last year of school, there were actually three Jews there. But I didn't know the third one either.

When I look back today to my Lichterfelder days from a distance of more than sixty years, I don't see them as hell on earth, but they certainly weren't pleasant. It helped a great deal that I had transferred to the new school in 1932, for when the Nazis came to power the school had already gotten used to my presence, though with definite limits. The way my classmates treated me changed only minimally. From the beginning I was simply ignored by most of my fellow students. They looked past me or over my head, which wasn't hard, since I was one of the shortest in the class. I probably never even spoke with some of them. Then there were those who behaved toward me the same way they behaved toward their other classmates. They weren't my friends, but at recess they let me play with them, they spoke to me in a normal way and didn't make any insulting remarks. But they never invited me to their homes, although they often visited each other.

Only one invited me over, Hansjürgen Lehmann, a boy my height who lived around the corner from us at Lilienstrasse 2 (the building was later bombed). Since we went to school the same way, by bike starting in the eighth grade, we met every morning at Asternplatz and rode to Drakestrasse together. Hansjürgen soon invited me over to his house, and I met his parents and his younger brother, Ulfi. His father worked at the Reichsbank and was extremely reserved, not only with me but with his family as well. His mother was open-minded, of Huguenot descent, and always friendly to me. One Sunday in 1933 I spent the day with the Lehmann family out on a rowboat. Herr Lehmann rowed while the rest of us sat comfortably. On a bridge above us a group of Hitler Youth went by, yelling raucously, and Frau Lehmann said, "They apparently don't have anything better to do." I am sure the remark was directed at me. After a while Hansjürgen joined the Jungvolk (a subdivision of the Hitler Youth for boys between ten and fourteen), became a squad leader, and wore a uniform, but our friendship continued. Early in 1936, shortly before I left school, he broke his arm and couldn't ride his bike to school. We agreed that I would take him to school and back home again on the bar of my bike whenever our slightly differing class schedules permitted. As thanks he gave me a book that I still have today. The dedication reads, "To my true friend Werner, Hansjürgen." A few years ago we found each other again, now old men, and both of us enjoy our revived friendship.

Another boy I got along well with was Wolfgang Sauer, but we weren't as close as Hansjürgen and I were. After the war Wolfgang became a well-known German historian who was my successor at the University of California, Berkeley, in 1963. He too joined the Jungvolk in 1933 and became a squad leader. He continued to give me little pen drawings now and then, mostly about the period of the Prussian King Frederick II. He was quite good at drawing. He also gave me an imperial war flag [*Reichskriegsflagge*], which I hung over my bed, much to my parents' annoyance. The flag disappeared only after bugs nested behind it and an exterminator had to be called. One day during recess in the schoolyard Wolfgang asked me if I wanted to join his squad. I answered that it wasn't possible for me as a non-Aryan, but Wolfgang said no one had to know about that. I enthusiastically told my father about it in the evening, whereupon I got a long lecture about honor and self-respect and such things. I dejectedly reported this to Wolfgang the next day, and he told me, likewise dejectedly, that his group leader had forbidden him to take me into his squad.

I met Wolfgang again in the early 1960s at a conference in the United States. We were sitting in a bar, and I reminded him of our school days together. To my great surprise he said he didn't believe he ever knew me. He remembered all of our teachers and many of our classmates, especially one who had Jewish relatives, something Wolfgang said he was the only one to know (in fact, I knew it, too). But me, the only Jew in our class, to whom he had always been respectful and friendly, he had banned from his memory. He died in Berkeley in 1992.

And then there were my aristocratic classmates. Although later I taught German history every other year in the United States and naturally talked about German, and especially Prussian, nobility, my personal acquaintance with this former ruling class was limited to a few encounters. I would have liked to belong to the nobility, and I didn't hide this fact. "Werner *von* Angress" didn't sound bad, I thought, and I could see myself sitting high on a horse at the head of a regiment riding into some battle. I was fascinated by my aristocratic classmates, especially the ones in my class at Lichterfelder Realgymnasium. Already earlier, at Herder Gymnasium, we had in our class a young aristocrat, Holger von Höslin. Holger, who came from Munich where his father worked as a conductor or musician, if I remember correctly, was the stereotypical poor aristocrat. There the boy sat in threadbare clothes in the first row and had to listen to the mean things his classmates, ten or eleven years old, said to him. But Holger was a quiet, modest person, someone who could only be called a good boy. He never stepped on anyone's toes, and I am still ashamed today when I think of how I sang the "Holger song" along with the others, to the tune of the "Toreador" aria from *Carmen*:

> *Into the laundry, Holger von Höslin,*
> *Dirt on your breast, want to get clean.*

No, washing wasn't his strong point, which we could sometimes see from the ring on his neck above his shirt collar. But that was mainly because of his poverty. Later, when I read about Hanno's friend Count Kai Mölln in Thomas Mann's *Buddenbrooks*, I thought of Holger, although Kai was much more robust.

At Lichterfelder Realgymnasium I had three aristocratic classmates. Of the three, the faintest in my memory is Günter Werner Eberhand Robert von Mantey. He was one of those who treated me as if I actually existed, and during recess we sometimes played tag or did "horseback fighting" in the schoolyard, always in a small group that included my friend Hansjürgen. Günter's group, all of them already in the Jungvolk, protected me in the schoolyard one day, forming a ring around me and then energetically defending me from a surprise attack by Hitler Youth fanatics in the parallel class. The attackers learned their lesson and didn't make another attempt. (Harrassment by this group of Hitler Youth was a principal reason Teppich left the school.) Günter, the first lieutenant of his division staff, was killed near Stalingrad on January 23, 1943.

I remember Bär Burkhard Alexander Adalbert Schilling von Cannstatt a little more clearly because he was the poorest in physical education in our class. He was a short, thin boy who just couldn't do an upwind circle on the horizontal bar, who hung from the rings like a sack of potatoes and was just as bad on the parallel bars and the vaulting horse. But this was just one side of him that stuck in my memory, and by no means the most important. He and also his older brother, who was in the grade above us and whom I saw only occasionally, were completely immune to National Socialist thinking. Burkhard, extremely intelligent, didn't have a high opinion of the Nazis. That was apparent from the way he behaved toward me; that is, he was always friendly, polite, helpful, unbiased, and natural. After I left school I lost track of him, as I did of almost all of my classmates, but I know that he studied medicine after the war, married a South American woman, and still lives abroad.

The third *Junker* [aristocrat] was Franz Heinrich ("Heiner") Adolf Karl Otto Ferdinand von Rosenberg. His father had supposedly been a military aide of Emperor Wilhelm II. When I met Heiner, he belonged to a conservative monarchist group of the German youth movement—the Scharnhorstjugend, I believe. Like all other organized groups, his was taken over by the Jungvolk, and by 1935 at the latest Heiner was a squad leader in the Jungvolk as well as the best student in our class. I secretly envied and admired him for these two positions. Once during a class outing he and I had a long conversation. It must have been shortly after the announcement of the Nuremberg Laws in September 1935. On the day of the outing I was seething, and I talked about the injustice of the regime in their treatment of us Jews, including those who had risked their lives for the *Vaterland* in the (First) World War. I can still see us, walking side by side on a sandy path of the Grunewald, me talking, Heiner staring straight ahead. After I had vented my feelings, we walked on in silence for a while. Then Heiner, who was a little taller than I was, looked down at me from the side and said, "Yes, I understand; but Germany comes first." And that was that. I often copied his algebra and geometry homework, which he never refused me. The fact that I finished school in 1936 with Ds instead of Fs in those two subjects I owe entirely to his generosity. But I couldn't offer him anything in exchange.

Heiner and I had an old chemistry teacher who had retired from teaching in a girls' school and was substituting at Lichterfelder for half a year. This was in early 1936, shortly before I left school. The man's name I have long since forgotten, but not his lack of talent as a teacher and his anti-Semitism, of which he made a display. The others in the class disliked him as much as I did, but for a different reason: they found him boring. The man taught us nothing and even gave the impression that he wanted to have as little to do with chemistry as possible. Instead, he tried to teach us *Rassenkunde*, "the science of race," although we heard enough about that in biology class. Being nearsighted, I always sat in the front row, though I was just as unfamiliar to him as my classmates were. One day, as he was going on once again about racial characteristics, he pointed at me and announced, "This boy has a well-formed Dinaric head, just like our Reich Propaganda Minister Dr. Goebbels." For a few seconds the class seemed to hold its breath, and then a burst of laughter broke out. The man had succeeded in promoting the sole Jew in the class to an "Aryan" (which the "Dinaric race" was, according to H. F. K. Günther's *Rassenkunde des deutschen Volkes*). Involuntarily declaring Jewish students to be Aryan in this way wasn't unusual, as various autobiographies of German Jews of the time show. The chemistry teacher looked quite perplexed, but to my great relief no one explained his error to him.

Shortly before the end of the tenth grade, the class decided it had had enough of this chemistry teacher. Who thought up the plan, I didn't and don't know. It was arranged that each of us would come to class the next day with a pocketful of dried peas or lentils, which, when the signal was given, we would throw at the blackboard. It was the first period of the school day, from eight to nine o'clock. The lights were still on in the classroom, and the old codger stood at the board, for a change writing some chemical formulas. Suddenly someone said softly, "Now!" and we all grabbed the contents of our pockets and threw it at the board. It sounded as if it were hailing. The man turned around, horrified, and stared at us as if we were ghosts. The whole floor was covered with peas and lentils; some had even lodged in the teacher's thin white hair. At that moment, but only at that moment, I felt sorry for him. Without a word he walked out of the classroom, and we never saw him again. The last few weeks of the term another teacher taught us chemistry.

As one might expect, this was only the first act. Shortly after the chemistry teacher fled from the classroom, our homeroom teacher, Dr. Martin Lampel, whom we called "Fatzke" [Dandy], and who taught us English for better or for worse, burst in. Not exactly young anymore either, he had white hair and walked slightly bent over. One Sunday morning I saw him from the window trotting by our house, at Unter den Eichen 115, with the National Socialist faculty union. He was 100 percent Nazi and for that reason an exception among the older teachers of our school, who were almost all members of the German Nationalist Party. When he erupted into our classroom, Fatzke looked at the floor, then at us, then at the floor again. His hands on his hips, he asked, "W-h-o did it?" From the quantity of projectiles lying on the floor, it was obvious that most of the class must have participated in the attack. As I write this, I can still feel the profound silence that reigned in the room. And then Heiner stood up, slowly and unperturbed, as was his wont, and said, "I did." Then—and the devil only knows what bit me, probably the fact that I admired Heiner greatly and was impressed by him—I stood up and said, "I did, too." Now the spell was broken. Fatzke ignored the A student and, foaming with rage, seethed at me, "You, of all people, YOU have to do something like that." He didn't need to say anything more; his "You, of all people" spoke volumes. The rest of the class sat there as if mute. I couldn't see the expression on Heiner's face, since he was standing to my left in front of the window. But I could imagine his disdainful grin directed at the collective cowardice of our classmates. Fatzke talked to himself for a while, apparently at a loss what to do.

If I had been the only one to stand up, it would have all been very simple. He would have gone to the principal, Dr. Schmidt, who under the circumstances would have had no choice but to expel me from school, although he wouldn't have enjoyed doing it. But the other culprit was the best student in the class, of old Prussian nobility, and a squad leader in the Jungvolk. Finally, his voice almost failing, Fatzke delivered his judgment. We were both sentenced to three hours of detention, and he noted it in the records. He said he would dictate a task for us. Heiner and I sat out our three hours in calm resignation, and Fatzke kept an eye on us from the rostrum, having to stay after school with us. Heiner von Rosenberg didn't survive the war. He fell on July 21, 1941, as a lieutenant in Grenadier Regiment 9 near Mogilev on the Dnieper, not quite two months after his twenty-first birthday.

The more I remember of my school days in Lichterfelde, the more pronounced is my memory of isolation during the period from 1932 to Easter 1936, when I left school. I was indeed lucky that my classmates didn't tease me, insult me, or beat me up, as happened to some of my Jewish friends at other schools; some of them were even driven from school. But I was nonetheless reminded almost daily in one way or another that I was different, that I was a Jew and therefore only tolerated. I say this without any self-pity, now or then. It was simply the way things were.

Anti-Semitism, not necessarily always directed at me personally, was noticeable on many occasions at school even before Hitler was appointed chancellor. It reared its head especially during class outings, which I came to hate. As we walked through the Grunewald, or sometimes marched in formation, I often heard around me anti-Semitic comments. I tried to walk next to classmates who weren't in the habit of making such remarks. Sometimes, when such a conversation was starting near us, Hansjürgen would try to distract me by talking loudly and intensely. The songs were the worst. Even before 1933 people felt safe enough in the woods to let their anti-Semitic feelings loose. Although the Republic still existed in 1932—in the not-so-safe keeping of the monarchist chancellor Franz von Papen—by then those on the far right didn't respect or fear it anymore. On the contrary, they sang:

> *Up with the bigwigs,*
> *Up with the bigwigs,*
> *Up with the bigwigs onto the lamppost!*
> *Let the dogs hang,*

Let the dogs hang,
Let the dogs hang till they fall down.
Blood, blood, blood, blood, blood
shall flow as rain and hail so thick,
We shit on the freedom
of the Jewish Republic.

Or:

Two Jews were once bathing in the Nile,
The first one was eaten by a crocodile.
And when it eyed the second one,
It puked the first one out again.

There was a second version of that one:

Two Jews were once bathing in a river,
since even pigs sometimes have to bathe.
The first one, he drowned;
the other one, we hope he did, too.

While these ditties were being sung, our homeroom teacher, at the time "der kleine Muck," strolled among us smiling with pleasure, pretending not to hear a word.

And then there was this one:

There was once a young trench soldier,
Oh, this was his destiny:
He had to leave wife and child,
Had to leave them rapidly... .
When the trench soldier steps into the enemy'sfire,
Yes, then he's in good spirits,
But when Jewish blood spurts from his knife,
Then he's feeling doubly fine.

To my classmates' credit let it be said that they spared me this song, even after the Nazi seizure of power. It is interesting that no one I've asked in Germany today, at least no one of my generation, seems to have ever heard this song. My brothers and I heard it often starting in the fall of 1933, always on Sunday morning, when our parents were still asleep. From our window we observed as Adolf Hitler's SS bodyguards, whose quarters were the former cadet school around the corner from Lichterfelder Realgymnasium, marched by, singing. My brothers hummed along softly, so as not to wake our parents, until I told them to stop. They found it funny.

My unmistakable enemy in my class was Arndte. Short, stocky, and after January 30, 1933, always in Hitler Youth uniform, at recess he usually had a cigarette in his mouth. He was older than most of us, having flunked one or two grades. He'd had it in for me since the first day I stepped into the classroom. Aside from the anti-Semitism that he undoubtedly brought with him from home, I never really understood his attitude, especially since there were days when he talked to me the way he did to anyone else. However, most of the direct verbal attacks I received came from him. One day as we stood in the schoolyard at recess, we were amazed and somewhat frightened to see a thick yellowish-red wall of cloud cover the sun, casting a heavy shadow on everything in the middle of the day. Somewhere nearby, something industrial had gone wrong and caused what we today call pollution. Suddenly I heard Arndte say, as usual not directly to me, but rather casually to no one in particular: "Now they are sulphurating out those who shouldn't be in Germany." Hansjürgen, in Jungvolk uniform, was standing next to me. Furious, he rushed over to Arndte and ordered under his breath, but loud enough for me to hear, "You apologize right now!" Arndte came over to me and apologized. A few other boys watched the exchange but said nothing.

The tension between Arndte and me only became physical once, silently in gym class. The physical education teacher, Max Haase, was a former petty officer in the imperial navy and a decent but completely unimaginative man. He always wore the same patched sweater, but the yarn of the patches didn't match it, so we whispered that Haase's wife must be colorblind. Gym class was boring. We marched back and forth in the gym and, when Haase's whistle sounded, did an about-face. Sometimes we did exercises on the horizontal bar, the vaulting horse, or the parallel bars, but mostly we either climbed ropes or played dodgeball (for which I was always the last one chosen, not because I was a Jew but because I couldn't catch a ball). On this particular day Herr Haase announced a competition. The members of each of the five teams were to climb to the top of the ropes and slide down, one after the other, as long as they could, until only one person was left, and that person would be the winner. We weren't thrilled about this competition. The members of team after team climbed the ropes once or twice and then collapsed to the floor, feigning exhaustion. Then it was the next team's turn to do exactly the same thing.

Haase soon disappeared into his little office, and our contest continued unsupervised. Arndte and I were on the same team, made up of the shortest members of the class. Ours was the last team to climb, and Arndte and I were its final climbers. The rest of the class sat on the floor in front of the ropes and watched us with increasing interest. "Germany against Palestine," I heard somebody whisper loudly, but I continued and didn't look down. How many times we last two Mohicans struggled up again I don't know anymore, but it was at least eight. I was absolutely determined to win, but so was Arndte. I, however, had an advantage: Arndte smoked, and I didn't. Finally he fell in a heap, and I climbed up once more, the victory lap, so to speak. Then the bell signaled the end of the period and we went to our lockers and got dressed. No one mentioned the competition, at least not within my earshot, and Arndte and I acted as if nothing had happened.

January 30, 1933, the day Hitler took power, went by peacefully. As Hansjürgen and I were biking home after school we saw the headlines at a newspaper stand at the Botanical Garden station. The president of the Reich had appointed a coalition government of nationalists with Hitler as chancellor and Papen as vice chancellor. My reaction was typical of a twelve-year-old boy: Wow, this will be interesting! When I got home, I found my father there already, for him unusually early. He and Didi's brother Fritz, who had been working in my father's business for a while, were cracking jokes: Hitler was running back and forth in the state chancery opening all the desk drawers and cabinets. When asked what he was looking for, he answered, "My government program." A flag with a swastika on it, hoisted by Rudi Weppner and his father, was already waving from the roof of our building. But there was no worry or fear in the air at home.

The next day, however, was different. Arndte had thought up something special. When I entered the classroom, I immediately felt the tension in the air. First period was German, taught by der kleine Muck. He would be arriving at any moment. Arndte stood at the rostrum. I can't say whether he had waited for me to arrive or not. In any case, he stretched his short body as tall as he could in his Hitler Youth uniform and instructed the class to shout out when der kleine Muck stepped into the classroom, "Wake up, Germany! Death to the Jews!" I will never forget that moment of waiting. We all sat in our seats straining to hear the approaching footsteps, which didn't come soon. I was already uninterested in religion at the time, but I remember directing a fervent prayer to heaven: "Dear God, let a miracle happen!" And a miracle did happen. The teacher who came into the classroom wasn't der kleine Muck but Dr. Karl Körner, a reserved man who taught algebra. The class immediately jumped to its feet (the obligatory "Heil Hitler" salute was first introduced a few weeks later). After quickly inspecting the class and ordering us to sit down, Körner informed us that Dr. Muchall was seriously ill and that we would have to make do with him, Körner, and practice our algebra. With that he began the lesson with his usual words: "In our last class we …" We heard nothing more from Arndte, and when der kleine Muck took up his teaching again several weeks later, Arndte had abandoned his plan. That bitter cup had passed me by.

During the years in Lichterfelde I only had one fistfight, and that was with Schmidtchen. I've forgotten what he said to make me angry, but I told him to take his glasses off and then punched him. He hit me back, and we continued boxing each other rather half-heartedly, while our classmates stood around us enjoying the spectacle. But nobody interfered, and we ended our fight when we heard the footsteps of the teacher approaching out in the hall. Our classmates' neutrality was no accident. Because of his poor health, Schmidtchen was not a member of any state youth organization. He was also cowardly, which made him unpopular. But he was an Aryan and let everyone, especially me, know that he was in favor of national socialism. One day much later, shortly before I left school, he and I were the last ones in the classroom, all the others being already on their way to the schoolyard. Suddenly Schmidtchen put his arms around me and kissed me on the mouth before I could push him off, and then he ran out the door and down the stairs. Two souls, alas, were dwelling in his breast (as Goethe might have put it).

If my position in relation to my classmates was inconsistent, complicated, and sometimes unpleasant, this was even truer with some of the faculty members. But here the situation was also inconsistent. The school principal, Dr. Wilhelm Schmidt, was a tall, straight German nationalist. He inspected his school regularly. No one knew when and where he would turn up, and when he caught one of us doing something against the rules, he boxed our ears and rebuked us sarcastically. Nonetheless he was generally liked by the students because he was fair, approachable, and had a sense of humor. When the Third Reich befell us, he immediately had hoisted on the school flagpole, instead of the black, red, and gold flag of the Weimar Republic, the black, white, and red one of the former Empire. He "forgot," however, to raise the swastika at the same time, until March 12, 1933, when President Hindenburg's order made this obligatory. Sometime after Hitler became chancellor, my mother went in to speak to him and suggested that it might be better if I transferred to a Jewish school. She hadn't told me beforehand; I only heard about this from her later. Schmidt advised her to let me stay at his school and assured her that nothing would happen to me as long as he was the principal. So I stayed there until the *Mittlere Reife* at the end of the tenth grade.

Wilhelm Schmidt was unfortunately unable to transmit his fairness to his whole faculty. Looking back, it is amazing—or maybe not, considering the behavior of so many educated people during the Nazi period—that grown men, persons of authority, amused themselves by publicly humiliating the only Jewish student in the class. Muchall and Lampel, that is, der kleine Muck and Fatzke, I have already mentioned. The former taught us German in the seventh and eighth grades, and it must have rankled him that I was one of his best students. At the end, under a different teacher, I even finished school with the grade *sehr gut* [very good] for German. Der kleine Muck and Fatzke never made an openly anti-Semitic remark to me, but their malice was apparent in the way they looked at me, and in their sarcastic tone of voice when they talked to me.

I must admit that sometimes I made this very easy for them. For example, one day der kleine Muck asssigned us to learn a poem of our choice by heart for homework. In the course of the next class some of us would be called on to recite our chosen poems. Without asking my parents' advice I took my father's edition of Echtermeyer's *Selection of German Poems* from the bookcase and looked for appropriate verse. My choice was Karl Gerok's *"Ave Caesar, morituri te salutant!,"* an epic poem about the persecution of Christians in ancient Rome. When I was chosen, among others, to recite my poem, I stepped up to face the class, my heart pounding, and recited in a fairly steady voice. After the first few verses my classmates began to show their amusement, but on the face of der kleine Muck was open derision. Today I can understand their amusement when the only Jew in the class stood up and declaimed with pathos:

Hail [Heil] to you, Christ! They who are dying salute you!
Short is the fight, eternal the reward.
O blessed art those who appeal to thy crown
O blessed art those who inherit thy realm [Reich]
Lift up our souls, O Son of God! (verse 9)

When I had finished, the teacher, still grinning, asked me why I had rattled off such a beautiful poem with so little expression in my voice. Not a word about the unfortunate choice of topic. Nonetheless, the class understood. I returned to my seat, my face beet-red.

Two other teachers, in history and music, didn't bother to conceal their anti-Semitism. The history teacher was a war invalid who had lost a leg. His classes were so boring that today I no longer know where he began or ended chronologically. They consisted mostly of the names and dates of rulers and battles. But now and then he made an anti-Semitic remark that had nothing to do with what he was lecturing on at the moment. Once, for example, while talking about a well-known Jewish parliament member during the Empire, he noted that the man's "Jewish nose" was recognizable through three thick layers of cloth. (This stupid remark has stuck in my mind for over sixty years!) When he engaged in such verbal abuse, he never looked at the students but rather leaned back in his chair, addressing the ceiling.

The music teacher was an unusually fat man who looked like Falstaff. He assigned us an opera guide that he had written and that only few of us dared not to buy (I asked my parents for the money and bought it, which still annoys me today), and he loved to have us sing Nazi fighting songs. Since many of these songs had anti-Semitic lyrics, I was always sitting on coals until class ended. Most of my classmates who had been in the Jungvolk or the Hitler Youth since 1933 knew the songs, of course, and when we came to a line that had to do with Jews, some of them looked over at me, while others avoided doing so out of embarrassment. After a while I went to the man and told him I wouldn't sing songs with anti-Semitic content. "You don't have to sing any songs with us at all," he replied. And that was that.

Looking back at the experiences of other Jewish children, the animosities that I encountered at Lichterfelder Realgymnasium seem comparatively moderate. Sooner or later, most Jewish children and teenagers who attended state schools in the 1930s transferred to a Jewish school, which is probably what they were expected to do from the start. But I didn't mention at home whatever offensive incidents occurred at school during the day. This increasing reserve on my part began months before the Nazis seized power. My reserve was easy to maintain, because my parents hardly ever asked about my day at school. What counted with them were my grades, and these became worse and worse after the move from Herder Gymnasium to Lichterfelder Realgymnasium. This also had something to do with puberty, which was slowly beginning to make its appearance. In the summer of 1932 I turned twelve. Although I didn't know what was happening to me physically and emotionally (and nobody seemed interested in enlightening me about it), I gradually withdrew and avoided conflicts with adults whenever possible. I preferred to deal with instances of malice and humiliation by myself.

Frankly, the idea that my parents might send me to a Jewish school frightened me. What did I have against Jewish schools? Before I turn to the problem of reconciling Germanness and Jewishness, I should mention my aversion to what I perceived as the "ghetto mentality" with which Jews in 1933 reacted to Nazi anti-Semitism. The extent to which I completely misapprehended what the future had in store for us requires no further comment.

In hindsight, however, it is astounding how complex my situation at school was at the time, in many respects. So far I have mainly described the occurrences that isolated and often humiliated me. But there were other aspects, and I would now like to go into greater detail about the two most significant. First, I naively found it quite natural that in my daily activities I would behave exactly as my classmates did, and that I would also take part in extracurricular school activities. These two choices were at the time unusual for Jewish children still going to state schools. Second, and perhaps more important, there were also teachers at Lichterfelder Realgymnasium whose consistently courteous behavior toward me somewhat offset the behavior of the Fatzkes and kleine Mucks.

As to the first point, no one in school ever commented about the fact that at the beginning of each class I, like everybody else, raised my arm to give the "German salute" and shout "Heil Hitler." While Jewish students at most state schools weren't allowed to participate in extracurricular school activities and practices, I continued to take part in most of them. In addition, in 1933 and the two following years I went to the Lustgarten rallies on May 1 with classmates who, for some reason, weren't attending with a Jungvolk or Hitler Youth group. Once I even listened from my perch in a tree to Hitler's hoarse introduction and then Goebbels' bell-like voice with his Rheinland accent: "German boys and girls! Once again we are gathered here in the Lustgarten to celebrate the beautiful old German May Day festival." And in early 1934 when the Führer drove with his SA chief of staff Ernst Röhm in an open car to review the SS "Adolf Hitler" bodyguard stationed at the Lichterfelder Kadettenanstalt near my school, I stood with my classmates on the narrow Karwendelstrasse like a guard of honor and saw the two men up close for the first time. (Shortly there-after, Hitler had Röhm killed as part of the Night of the Long Knives.)

And finally, I took part in all the celebrations held in the school auditorium. I remember most clearly the annual Reformation Day and the broadcast of Hindenburg's funeral (Hitler's "Deceased General, Walhalla welcomes you!" didn't yet shock me) and listening to more speeches by the Führer, after which I, the other pupils, and the teachers sang the German national anthem and *"Die Fahne hoch"* [Raise High the Flag], the Nazi anthem. I also went along when the whole class went to the movie theater to see the film *Hitlerjunge Quex*, a compulsory event. Neither my teachers nor my classmates seemed to find anything odd about all of this. Nor did it surprise them that every morning I recited loudly with the rest of the class the following prayer:

> *Dear God, hear our plea,*
> *Let Germany become strong again.*
> *Fill us all with moral energy,*
> *It is the pious who work for the fatherland.*
> *Let good German work succeed*
> *So that we will achieve the Empire anew.*
> *Amen!*

After the Nazis took power I prayed for the Empire's return with special fervor.

As for the courtesy of some of my teachers, most of the faculty lived in Lichterfelde and embodied the conservative atmosphere of that part of town. But although they all surely knew I was Jewish—after all, my religion was designated in the class register as "Mosaic"—this fact didn't seem to interest most of them. Some didn't even make an effort to connect the faces of the individual students with the names in the register.

The teacher read the name out, waited for an answer, and then entered a grade or short comment first in his gradebook and sometime later in the class register. This was the standard operating procedure for our two mathematics teachers, Kurt Rindfleisch and Dr. Karl Körner. Rindfleisch taught geometry, Körner algebra. Herr Rindfleisch had fought at the front during World War I, and on national holidays he wore his Iron Cross First Class. The problems he gave us to solve were often of a military sort: for example, at what angle a mortar must be set up so the grenade will hit a target at a given distance. He had a sense of humor, sometimes joked with us, and always seemed to pity me in a sympathetic way, not because I was Jewish, but because I simply didn't comprehend what he was teaching. I don't remember ever hearing him make a political remark.

Körner was more boring, dry, and interested only in the subject he was teaching. After Hitler became chancellor, whenever Herr Körner walked into the classroom he raised his arm in the "German salute," mounted the rostrum with short quick steps, turned to the class, and said, "Heil Hitler! Sit down!"—all in one breath and in a single gesture. His right arm clapped down like a railroad signal, and class began. Most of the other teachers, instead, examined us carefully after we had stood up upon their entrance—making sure we were holding our right arms at the correct angle—then snappily sounded off the Hitler greeting and gave the order to sit down only after we had answered loudly in chorus. That's how it was to be done. (Even before Hitler's takeover we had to jump up from our seats when the teacher entered and stand stiffly at attention.) Körner and a few other teachers didn't exactly follow this procedure in the expected way; one might assume this was because they didn't particularly care for Herr Hitler.

Then there was the *Oberstudienrat* [senior teacher] Max Naumann. We didn't get to know him until June 1934, when State Youth Day was introduced on Saturdays. All the members of such organizations—Jungvolk, Hitler Youth, and *Bund Deutscher Mädel* [League of German Girls]—spent that day with their organizations and didn't have to go to school. The rest of us were blessed with classes in national politics and paramilitary physical training. Who were "the rest of us"? The physically handicapped, politically questionable, and "racially inferior" (non-Aryan) students. There we sat every Saturday—the "cripples," the potential enemies of the people (whose parents, usually former socialists, didn't send their sons to join the Hitler Youth), and the *Untermenschen* [subhumans] like me—and listened to Nazi doctrine.

The person chosen to dispense it to us was Herr Naumann. He was a quiet gentleman shortly before retirement, refined in all aspects of his behavior, and dignified as a patriarch. He had to give us lost souls lessons in national politics. He began by drawing our attention to the street names in Lichterfelde and explained who Moltke, Manteuffel, Roon, (Empress) Augusta, and others had been. He told us how once, in the entourage of Emperor Wilhelm II, he had taken a trip north to the fjords of Norway, and how gracious and genial His Majesty had been to his guests. Herr Naumann spoke slowly and chose his words carefully, in order to stretch out the lesson, so that he would only very slowly, and if possible too late, arrive at the obligatory teaching material. But finally no more tangents occurred to him, and one Saturday he told us we would now go through the twenty-five points of the program of the National Socialist Party. Although I had never read the program, I knew that it contained anti-Semitic sections and was rather forbidding. But Herr Naumann, contrary to many of our other teachers, knew by name all seven or eight of us sitting there, and he was no Fatzke or kleine Muck. He lingered quite a long time on the first three points, which mostly concerned foreign policy demands by the Party. Then came points four and five, which expressed the Party's anti-Semitism and its corresponding goals, as yet relatively limited. "A person can only be a citizen if he is a member of the people [*Volksgenosse*]. A member of the people can only be someone of German blood," and so on. But Herr Naumann didn't read these. He simply glanced at his notebook with the program in it, then over at me—I remember his look exactly—and said something like, "Now, the next two points are clear and don't need any explanation." After that we spent a good amount of time on the part of the program that dealt with "capitalist exploitation of the economy."

In late 1934 or early 1935 we got a new, much younger physical education teacher. Heinz Kirschke was a member of the SA. His first day with us he wore the uniform of a *Scharführer* or *Oberscharführer*, comparable to an army sergeant. I had a feeling of dread when I saw him heading with determination for the gym teacher's little office next to our locker room. Arndte grinned and said that now I would "get it." At first nothing happened, but gym class changed drastically. We worked hard on the horizontal bar, the vaulting horse, the parallel bars, and the rings. In the schoolyard we practiced relay racing, running one hundred meters, broad jumping, high jumping, and so on. At the end of each gym class our muscles ached. A few weeks after this new enlivening of our physical education, I was summoned to Heinz Kirschke's office. Once again Arndte's eyes followed me, and once again my knees trembled. To my great amazement, the SA man told me that he had been observing me during sports and training and had a positive impression of me. In a little more than a month there would be a gymnastics competition against a school in Steglitz, and there was still a lot of practicing to be done in preparation, especially on the horizontal bar. He was thus appointing me as squad leader and expected me to get my squad into shape, especially little Burkhard Schilling, who always hung like a wet rag on the horizontal bar. I thanked him curtly and left his office. Arndte was waiting outside the door. "I've been appointed squad leader," I said as I walked by. He rushed to the door, knocked, was called in, and shortly afterward came back out with a beet-red face. I can imagine why.

We won the competition against Steglitz in February 1935, and I expected that I would soon have to give up my position as squad leader. Nothing of the sort happened. On the contrary, Kirschke suggested that I begin the necessary training to obtain the Reich youth badge in sports [Reichsjugendabzeichen], which I did. At the end of August 1935 I had passed four of the five tasks, and Kirschke had recorded them in my booklet. But I had trouble with the fifth one, either javelin-throwing or shotput. On September 20 I wrote in my diary, "Afternoon tried javelin-throwing for the Reich youth badge. Broke the spear." One morning at the beginning of January 1936 I read a short notice in the newspaper that from then on Jews weren't allowed to wear the Reich youth sports badge. When I reported this to Kirschke that same day, he cursed under his breath. A few weeks later I left school and went to say goodbye to him at his office. He shut the door and asked me what I planned to do in the future. I told him I had applied for agricultural training at a Jewish training farm and hoped to hear soon that I had been accepted. He nodded, shook my hand, and said something like: "Good. See that you get out of this country as quickly as possible. There is no future for you here. Good luck!" Unbelievable things do happen! Why did he treat me so decently? I don't know. Kirschke died in an accident shortly after I left school.

One of the strangest encounters I had in those days was with Dr. Wilhelm Heise, my tenth-grade German teacher. He was young, and I assumed he was a Nazi. But his very lax "German salute" when he entered the classroom soon made me doubt my assumption. Included in the curriculum for the school year was the writer Theodor Storm, and one day we read his poem about an evening at the seaside, *"Meeresstrand"* ["Seacoast"]. The first verse read:

[The seagull flies to the lagoon,
And dusk begins to descend;
Over the moist sandbanks
The evening glow is mirrored.]
Ans Haff nun fliegt die Möwe,
Und Dämmrung bricht herein;
Über die feuchten Watten
Spiegelt der Abendschein.

One of the students in the class read it out loud, and Heise commented dryly that another poet of the preceding century had treated the same topic in a much more exciting way. Then he recited:

[The young miss stood at the seaside
And sighed long and anxiously.
It moved her so very much,
The sun going down.
Dear Miss, don't you worry!
It's an old and well-known tale;
It goes down here in front
And comes up again from behind.]
Das Fräulein stand am Meere
Und seufzte lang und bang,
Es rührte sie so sehre
Der Sonnenuntergang.
Mein Fräulein! sein Sie munter,
Das ist ein altes Stück;
Hier vorne geht sie unter
Und kehrt von hinten zurück.

I couldn't believe my ears. Grosspapa had shown me Heinrich Heine's poems, and this particular one I'd found so nice and rude that I recognized it right away. But Heine, a Jewish poet, in a German classroom in 1935? Heise didn't name the author of the poem, but I could see from the grins on my classmates' faces that they also knew who had written it. They liked this German teacher so much that no one protested.

We then read Storm's novella *Der Schimmelreiter* [*The Rider on the White Horse*]. After we had worked through the text carefully, Heise asked us one day what we thought of the earl of the dike, Hauke Haien, a character in Storm's tale. Since the students were blathering rather aimlessly, Heise turned the class into a court before which Haien would have to answer to a charge of negligence. He told us the trial would start in a little over a week and began to assign roles. In the class of *der kleine Muck* I would have simply been overlooked, since there were too many students in the class for each of us to get a role. To my amazement Heise chose me as the investigating judge, so I went home and asked Grosspapa what such a judge was supposed to do. My grandfather was enthusiastic about my German teacher's plan and instructed me very carefully. It turned out to be a very interesting process.

One day not long before I left the school, I was heading down to the schoolyard for recess when Heise told me to wait a moment. When we were the only ones left in the room, he asked me how I, as a Jew, was treated by my classmates. He said that I was lucky to be in a relatively decent class. He had some young Jewish friends who had it a lot worse. I was amazed. And then he told me that a few days earlier he had been invited to a meeting of Zionist revisionists, and he was horrified; they were real fascists! My head was spinning. I agreed with him, because I had met a few representatives of *Brit Trumpeldor* (a Zionist youth movement) and I remembered only too well the hymns of praise for one of its founders, Vladimir Jabotinsky, who would become one of the spiritual fathers of Israel's Likud Party. After the war Heise became dean of the school of education at Humboldt University in East Berlin, where he supposedly had many conflicts with the GDR's leadership. I later found out that he was married to a non-Aryan woman. He died in 1949 at the age of fifty-two.

My school days in Germany ended on March 27, 1936. My report card was nothing to be proud of. Although I received As in German and physical education, I also earned many Ds and Fs. But at least I had reached *Mittlere Reife*. I saw no sense in continuing. In contrast to my earlier years of school in Westend, my Lichterfelde years were a fiasco in many respects. My parents were sorely disappointed by the annual "blue letters," my below-average grades, and my obvious aversion to school. A number of factors were responsible and influenced my behavior in general, but they were never seriously discussed at home. First among these factors was the political atmosphere in the country, but especially at school, where I was socially isolated, which hardly increased my interest in learning. I only made an effort in the subjects that interested me and whose teachers didn't exclude me. And, even under the best of circumstances, I had never understood math, physics, or chemistry.

A second reason for my unimpressive performance was that school didn't challenge me. In my 1935 diary, entries like "Morning: school—boring!" appear repeatedly. Our teachers were mostly drill sergeants who only wanted to get through the curriculum and didn't bother to stimulate our interest—or not mine, at least. Fatzke, for instance, had us sing songs like "School is over / oh, what fun, / oh, what fun, / oh, what fun" in English class. Except for English grammar, I learned almost nothing from him. Most of the others—I have already mentioned the few exceptions—weren't much better. The other foreign language classes besides English—that is, French and Latin—as well as algebra, math, physics, chemistry, and so on, were as dry as the Gobi Desert. But it was clearly a plus that the French teacher, Hauke, as well as the mathematics teachers Rindfleisch and Körner weren't Nazis and that they were patient with all of us, including me.

Finally, something important directed my attention away from school, and sometimes away from politics as well. This was the Jewish youth association, which I joined in the fall of 1933 and which occupied me fully for the following three years, much beyond its dissolution in December 1934.

In spite of all the unfortunate aspects, and unlike many Jews my age, I don't look back on my school years only with horror. After all, I had a number of teachers who treated me with respect. And some of my classmates who saw me as more than just a Jew tolerated or even were friendly to me. These factors made my school days bearable until they ended in spring 1936.

On my last day I said goodbye to all the teachers who were kind to me, and of course to the principal, Herr Schmidt, who sincerely wished me all the best for the future. But I also said goodbye to some individual classmates. One of them, Wolfgang Robinow, with whom I had never much to do but who was always friendly to me, beckoned me into the hallway as I was saying farewell to a few classmates in classroom. He whispered in my ear that he was also "non-Aryan," but that nobody except Hansjürgen knew it. I mention this only because our paths continue to cross, although we were never friends. When I was about to go down the stairs and leave the school forever, Arndte suddenly stood before me. Up until that moment I had studiously ignored him. To my great astonishment he reached out for my hand and said that he had often made life hard for me, and that he was sorry for this. He hoped I wouldn't hold it against him. I was completely perplexed and still today can't understand what motivated him to say this to me. We shook hands in an embarrassed way, and a few minutes later the German part of my education lay behind me for good. I can still feel the relief with which I walked out the door, got on my bike, and rode down Drakestrasse toward home. The last thing I could have imagined then was that ten years later I would begin studies at an American university and set out on a three-and-a-half-decade career in research and teaching.

In the process of treating my school days as a separate unit, I have passed over some important questions and developments to which I would now like to return.

In 1932 we began to speak of politics increasingly often at home, and I was gradually included in these discussions. As protected as our homelife was, in Westend and also at the beginning in Lichterfelde, the storms in the world outside couldn't remain completely hidden from my brothers and me. So I asked more and more questions, and my parents tried to answer in a way that I could understand. I saw the signs of the Depression every day—the long lines of unemployed people, the itinerant singers and organ-grinders in the courtyards, the part-time students, the beggars and homeless people—but the causes were unknown to me. Gradually I learned that the economic situation was closely connected to politics. I was only allowed to listen to the radio when my parents had approved the program, but there were newspapers, and they lay on top of the laundry bin in the apartment hallway every morning. Since school started early, I rose before my parents and got into the habit of reading the headlines quickly. When something particularly interested me I read some of the articles, too. So I became a newspaper reader at the age of twelve. Papa subscribed to three: the *Berliner Börsenzeitung* [*Berlin Stock Exchange Times*], the *Berliner Tageblatt* [*Berlin Daily Newspaper*] and the newspaper of the Central Association [*Central-Verein*, or CV] of German Citizens of the Jewish Confession, to which my parents had belonged for many years. We weren't Zionists but assimilated upper-middle-class German Jews, and my father, especially, took his CV membership very seriously. I regretted (but kept this to myself) that he wasn't a member of the *Reichsbund Jüdischer Frontsoldaten* [RJF, the Imperial Association of Jewish Frontline Soldiers]. That wasn't possible, however, since during the First World War his poor health had kept him from getting any closer to the front than the Jüterbog training camp.

I read the newspapers every day, and slowly my political knowledge grew. One of the first political crises that made a lasting impression on me was Papen's *Preußenschlag* [Prussian Coup] on July 20, 1932. Not that I really understood what was going on, or what was at stake. I only knew that a state of emergency had been declared in Berlin that was enforced by a general of the *Reichswehr* (as the German armed forces were known between 1919 and 1933), and that because of this we weren't allowed to go out of the house in the evening. The general's name, Gerd von Rundstedt, I learned only years later, when I was studying German history in the United States. Much more important to me was a telephone call my father received from a relation of one of his former bosses. The caller asked Papa if for a few days he would take in Hildchen Weiss, the daughter of the Berlin police vice president Dr. Bernhard Weiss (the man Goebbels called the "*Vipoprä* Isidor"), who had been arrested by the *Reichswehr*. My father refused this request categorically. This little incident made a profound and negative impression on me, because I saw no reason not to put up Hildchen in our seven-room apartment for a limited time. Papa clearly didn't want to take the risk of lodging the daughter of a high official who had been arrested, although no one would have interpreted our taking in this girl as a political act. It was Mutti who told me about my father's refusal. She didn't share his view of the matter at all, and she didn't conceal this from me, her oldest child. I was increasingly becoming my mother's confidant.

The refusal to take in Hildchen Weiss had a sequel. Years later, when I was teaching at the State University of New York at Stony Brook, I got a telephone call from a student, an extreme leftist for whom I didn't much care, telling me that the campus police were after him and meant to arrest him. Would I put him up for the night in my apartment? My first thought was to refuse, but then I remembered 1932, so he spent the night on a mattress on my living-room floor. (Early the next morning I was awakened by the clacking of my typewriter—my guest was writing a "revolutionary manifesto.")

In early 1933, after Hitler became chancellor, my parents, along with thousands of other German Jews, waited to see what would happen. We certainly weren't living in terror. The general atmosphere was seen, in the words of a common German saying, as "We won't have to eat it as hot as it was cooked." And indeed, for quite a while nothing much changed. To be sure, my situation in school wasn't pleasant, but I put up with it. My mother often came home with political jokes that she had heard during her shopping. Once, for example, the woman who owned the fish store on Asternplatz asked her if she knew what a Hitler herring was. No? Well, the woman said, you take a Bismarck herring, remove its brain, tear its mouth wide open, and there you have your Hitler herring.

Mutti told jokes like that at the beginning—but only until mid-1933—without hesitation in front of us children and our two domestics: the cook Frieda and Erika, a pretty blonde five or six years older than I, who was my little brother Hans' nanny. They both stayed with us until late 1934 or early 1935, and although after a time they began bringing back Nazi newspapers and magazines from their days off, their basic attitude toward us didn't change. Frieda left us to get married, and Erika because she had found a better-paying job. We parted as friends. However, I still feel uncomfortable today when I think that we had servants at all. Even if they seemed to enjoy working for us, it was in many respects crass exploitation. The often-heard (but hard to prove) claim that non-Jewish house personnel liked to work for Jewish families doesn't change a thing. But it is undeniable that after the Nuremberg Laws went into effect in September 1935, many an "Aryan" servant girl, who was no longer allowed to work for Jews because she wasn't at least forty-five years old, kept in contact with her former Jewish employers until they emigrated. During the war some secretly helped "their" families, who had been unable to emigrate, until their deportation.

How did we react to everyday life under the "Third Reich"? Later in the United States, I was often asked why we didn't pack up and leave the country immediately after the Nazis took power in 1933. If we had known what was in store for us, my family and probably the majority of German Jews would have done just that. But of course we didn't know. So during the first three years of the Nazi regime, emigration was unfortunately not a topic of discussion either at our home or at those of our friends. We waited, tried to adjust, hoped the Nazis would change their minds about the Jews, and otherwise went about our daily activities, at work, at home, and at school. In addition, during the Weimar period none of my parents' friends and acquaintances had been politically active, except for voting, so no one was politically "tainted" and thus under pressure to leave the country in 1933. Hitler's becoming chancellor didn't frighten us into thinking about leaving. Papa was reluctant to take his wife and children to a foreign country, where his future would have been uncertain. Only in September 1935 did my parents slowly begin to change their way of thinking, at least in connection with the future of their three sons. As long as the business was doing alright—and until 1937 that was the case—my parents refused to emigrate, in spite of the steadily increasing gravity of the regime's policies toward the Jews.

We also grew accustomed to the changed appearance of the streets. Wherever one went, one saw uniformed men, mostly in shades of brown, but occasionally also brown and black. On weekends columns of SA, SS, Hitler Youth, Jungvolk, and Bund Deutscher Mädel marched in the streets on the outskirts of Berlin. In addition, nonuniformed members of the Party, for example, members of the *Nationalsozialistische Betriebszellenorganisation* (NSBO), sometimes marched sluggishly through town in their civilian clothes on Saturdays. And everywhere the "German greeting," which was usually shouted, and which sounded quite natural in Berlin, because Berliners had always shouted, before as well as after the Nazi period. There were the idiotic signs above the entrances of many shops with the rhyming advice, *"Trittst Du in diesen Laden ein / so soll Dein Gruß 'Heil Hitler' sein"* [When you come into this store, your greeting should be 'Heil Hitler']. And everywhere seas of flags waved on all possible occasions. Thanks to me, we hung a black, white, and red flag (the former imperial flag) on the balcony until August 1934, and I also fastened a pennant with the same colors to my bicycle. Sometime in the summer of 1933, after the German Nationalist Party had "dissolved itself," a friendly elderly gentleman stopped me on the street, pointed at my pennant and advised me in a low voice either to hang a swastika there as well, or to get rid of the black, white, and red one. I removed the pennant. We were never bothered by anyone about the solitary black, white, and red flag on our balcony.

When I heard that the Reichstag [Parliament building] was on fire on February 27, 1933, I wanted to ride my bike into town to watch, but my father wouldn't let me. That March 21, the "Day of Potsdam" (when Hitler inaugurated the new Parliament in the historic Prussian capital, symbolically uniting Nazi and old Prussian Germany), we sat for a long time in the school's auditorium and listened to the broadcast of the ceremony in the Potsdam garrison church. Thereafter we had the rest of the day off from school. In the evening I went together with Erika, the nanny, to Leipziger Strasse to watch the torchlight parade of the different military and party organizations. That time I had my parents' permission. On the collar of my parka I was wearing a steel helmet badge that I had found somewhere. We were standing in the crowd, and I couldn't see anything because I was much too short. Suddenly someone called out in the Berlin accent, "Bring a ladder for the little guy here with the steel helmet, he can't see anything!" Promptly a stepladder was brought out of the house in front of which we were standing; I climbed up and had a clear view. Erika stood below and held onto me and the stepladder.

I was quite pleased with my private platform; before me the uniformed columns of mainly SA men marched by to military music, and my not quite thirteen-year-old patriotic heart beat proudly. After a while another SA column went by, and at the foot of the ladder someone said it was the SA Sturm-5, the company of Horst Wessel (the author of the Nazi anthem, whom Goebbels made into a martyr after Wessel was shot by a Communist). At the head, with a chin strap like the rest of his men, marched a tall lanky man, and from the ongoing commentary of the people below me I learned that this was *Obersturmführer* Fiedler, who had been Wessel's superior. As these SA men marched by, they began to sing:

> *Throw them out, the whole Jewish band,*
> *Throw them out of our fatherland.*
> *Send them back to Jerusalem,*
> *But first chop off their legs,*
> *So they won't come back.*
> *Throw them out, all these Jews of Moses,*
> *Throw them out with their hooked noses.*
> *Send them back to Jerusalem,*
> *So they'll all be together*
> *With their clan of Shem.*

That ruined the rest of the evening for me. The song had the same effect on me as the remarks of Arndte and der kleine Muck at school. I told Erika I was tired, and, after thanking the people again for the ladder, we went home. Of course neither of us said a word about the song to my parents.

Aside from the experiences at school, the first really cold shower I experienced was the "Jew boycott" of April 1, 1933. At first I believed the official explanation that the purpose of the boycott was to ward off foreign propaganda about German atrocities. My parents viewed it differently, and since they couldn't conceal this government action from us, they spoke to us—for the first time, if I remember correctly—quite openly about the Nazis' hatred of us Jews. The first of April was a Saturday, and my father stayed at his office until early afternoon as usual. My mother used the occasion to fight back a bit, which my father would surely have forbidden had he known of it. Near the Botanical Garden railway station there was at the time a sewing goods shop owned by two Jewish women. Contrary to many other Jewish shop owners, these two had decided not to close their store that morning. Mutti had gotten wind of that fact, and so she instructed Fritz and me to go into the shop one after the other and buy some buttons or thread. After that she, together with our little brother Hans, would sabotage the boycott herself as well. And so it happened: with a few coins and my heart pounding, I walked across Asternplatz to the shop, where a bored SA man stood guard outside. He didn't prevent me from going in, and I quickly bought the thread, or whatever it was, and went back home. Then Fritz went in, then Mutti and Hänschen. When my father came home later and Mutti proudly reported our activities to him, he only shook his head.

If I had been older and wiser, maybe the day of the boycott would have opened my eyes. I was convinced that sooner or later the government would recognize what good Germans we Jews were and change its attitude toward us. Since I was also strongly influenced by the continual nationalistic pomp celebrating the "spirit of national awakening," I felt keenly the enthusiasm bordering on fanaticism of my peers for the new "community of the people," making my exclusion from it all the more painful.

Given this attitude, the Jew boycott of April 1 was counterbalanced in my mind by the May Day Lustgarten rally. After attending the event at the Lustgarten in the morning, I went with my parents, brothers, and Grosspapa to the home of Tante Margot and Onkel

My father around 1933.

Kurt Baumgart (Mutti's sister and brother-in-law), who lived on what was then called Dreibundstrasse and today is Dudenstrasse. Their balcony on the corner building looked out on Katzbachstrasse, and from that perch we watched the endless parade of the guilds and other workers' organizations, some of them in their traditional costumes, going down Katzbachstrasse on their way to Tempelhofer Field to listen to Hitler's speech. I was impressed by the scene's apparent harmony and annoyed by the sarcastic remarks Papa and Grosspapa made only occasionally, out of consideration for the non-Jewish family members present.

My still more-or-less uncritical attitude toward the new government increasingly opposed me to my parents. This expressed itself in what today would seem almost ridiculous trifles. For example, one day at table I praised our new rulers for having instituted cheaper tickets for shorter trips on Berlin's public transportation. I wouldn't have to spend as much of my meager allowance to get around town. To my amazement my mother reacted very strongly, accusing me of continually defending "those pigs in high places."

On the other hand, our parents didn't forbid us from bringing home friends in Jungvolk uniform. Fritz had his group of *Pimpf*s (under the National Socialists, equivalent to the Cub Scouts), and my friend Hansjürgen was a particularly welcome guest in my mother's eyes, in spite of his squad leader's uniform with its Führer string tie (called a "monkey swing"). But an adult also visited us, Werner Meier, a nephew of Didi's and thus a distant relative of ours. He had joined the Flieger-SA [Air Force SA] and appeared on our doorstep in uniform, to the astonishment of Herr Weppner, our superintendent. I looked up to Werner and coveted his motorcycle. When he was at our house one evening in December 1935, I confided to him that I wanted to get a motorcycle for myself and that I had already started saving for it. He made me promise not to buy one whose engine was more than two hundred cubic centimeters, since anything bigger was too dangerous. But he surely knew that I would never be able to scrape together the money for such a purchase myself. And yet, in spite of that he showed me that he took me seriously. That was the last time we saw each other. A test pilot for the Luftwaffe during the war, he was killed when his plane crashed in a practice flight.

Month by month our family conflicts became more marked. My father, as I said, was a German patriot and in his whole outlook a Prussian. My mother, who had never forgiven Kaiser Wilhelm II for fleeing to Holland in November 1918, and who pined during the Weimar era for the black, white, and red flag of the Empire, was almost as German in her opinions as Papa. But after January 30, 1933, their patriotism was more and more severely put to the test. The result was a slow evolution in my parents from a patriotic German attitude to a markedly Jewish one. My father had always been a conscientious Jew, but he had made allowances for the times and for the non-Jewish members of our family. Under pressure from the omnipresent and rising anti-Semitism, the Jewish aspects of our lives at home became increasingly emphasized, and the German aspects less and less visible. Of course, I also wasn't immune to the poisoned atmosphere in general and at school in particular. But I imagined that if a person felt German and let others know it, he would sooner or later be recognized as German.

Back then I secretly wrote short stories that I never showed to my parents, and for good reason: they all had the same theme, that the regime would have to recognize in the end that we Jews were Germans. As late as November 1935 I wrote an untitled story on this topic, and I still have the manuscript today. In it I tell how a group of boys from our recently dissolved Jewish youth group, already illegal at the time, came under a "Jewish amnesty" at the outbreak of war against France. I wrote that we were drafted and "allowed" to fight on the front lines but couldn't be promoted. At the end each of us, one after the other, gave his life heroically for our fatherland. Pure kitsch.

In March 1935 I expressed in a poem this inner conflict of being Jewish in Germany during the beginning years of the Nazi regime:

Germany!?!!
Cold blows the wind from the east,
We are sailing on a stormy sea

Once it was ours, our sea!
And now? Woe to us, such woe.
We stand up on a mountain cliff
And look down from on high.
Once we were sons of this land.
And now? Woe to us, such woe.
We know only hate, know only distress
And still love Germany so much—
We know no more justice, only repression.
Our homeland doesn't love us anymore.

But what did it mean to me, being German? I was, after all, still a child when the Nazis came to power, unlike my parents who were born in the nineteenth century and grew up during the Empire. I hadn't thought much about what it meant to be a German. I just took for granted that I was German, a German "of Jewish confession." That is what I learned at home, and at the beginning there was no reason for me to give it a second thought. Only when Hitler's regime defamed Jews as foreign bodies inside the nation, as racially inferior and alien sub-beings, and gradually excluded them step by step, did I have to figure out my identity.

I asked at home how long our family had lived in Germany, but I only got vague answers; nobody had ever thought much about it. I was told that the Angress and Kiefer branches of the family were documented to have been in Germany at least since the beginning of the nineteenth century, but probably much longer. That was enough proof for me: we were Germans, regardless of what the Nazi regime said about it. I confided my thoughts about this in my very first diary starting in January 1935. I kept it, without my parents' knowledge, in a Jungvolk yearbook I had bought that was published under the direction of the *NS-Reichsjugendführung* [National Socialist Youth Administration]. In this diary I wrote, for example, on January 13, 1935, "I believe and certainly hope that the Saar will become German," and noted, on March 16, that the military draft had been reinstated. After this entry I then scribbled the question: "and Jews?"

Many of the snappy sayings printed in the yearbook I underlined heavily in pencil, but I changed the ones with which I didn't agree. On December 31, for example, in the sentence, "Boys, a year is over. Ahead to the new one. Not hours, not days, *life* for the Führer!" I simply replaced the words "the Führer" with "Germany." Interestingly enough, there is no entry in my diary about the decree of the Nuremberg race laws of September 1935. I was too involved with myself and my friends to even notice that event. Of course I hid the diary from my mother's curious eyes, but she wouldn't have been able to read my awful handwriting anyway.

My nationalistic affectations went far beyond any patriotism I ever encountered at home. Where did this fervor come from? And what did "German" mean to me back then? In part, my attitude came from the youth movement that I had joined in the fall of 1933—but only in part. The fact that I joined neither the Zionists nor the *Bund Deutsch-Jüdischer Jugend* [German Jewish Youth Association] but instead became a member of the *Deutsch-Jüdischer Jugendbund Schwarzes Fähnlein, Jungenschaft* [Black Flag German Jewish Youth Association, Boys' Section], which was firmly on the right of assimilated German Jewry, clearly shows my attitude at that time. Put simply, even perhaps oversimply: to me, being German comprised a number of characteristics that I someday hoped to possess. I wanted to be brave, upright, willing to sacrifice, and patriotic.

That most of these ideals were military is not surprising, since my generation grew up with the legends of the First World War. "German heroism," "invincible in the field," and "the stab in the back" at the end of the war are only a few of the nationalistic phrases that we heard repeatedly. It began at home, though in my case only in a limited way, continued at school, and with Hitler's accession to the government became a wave of propaganda that washed over everything. The NSDAP wanted to raise a new generation in a soldierly spirit, because that was what it needed for the planned war. Naturally I and everyone else my age were unaware of this. But there is no doubt that such concepts as heroism and dying for one's country strongly influenced our thinking. The omnipresent uniforms and then, starting in March 1935, the military parades on Unter den Linden; the rough, grating military tone that came to saturate the language of the Third Reich and ultimately dominated everything from radio broadcasts to speeches in the school auditorium—all of these manifestations became everyday for us growing children, and they unfortunately also became our models. The books we read increased the enthusiasm of my generation for soldiers and everything related to them. The experience on the front, glorified by the authors Ernst Jünger, Franz Schauwecker, Werner Beumelburg, and Edwin Erich Dwinger, became the goal we strove for. Some of these books I owned, others I got from my friends. Since my parents weren't acquainted with any of these books, they didn't complain about my reading them.

So there I was with my reverence for German heroism, but it was of little use to me, because I was a Jew. When Hitler took power on January 30, 1933, fate effectively excluded me overnight from everything heroic and German. All of a sudden I was forced to deal with being Jewish.

During the first four years I was in school the religious affiliation of students played a rather secondary role. At first, my father's instructions to me to tell the teacher that I was "of the Mosaic religion" confused me. Then shortly after school began, my mother asked Herr Meier to excuse me from attending Jewish religion class because I was yet too young and immature. Whatever moved my mother to do this remains as mysterious to me today as what Herr Meier must have thought of her request. In any case, during my first two years of school I didn't have to go to Jewish religion classes that a Herr Spieldoch gave once a week for the Jewish children at our school. Instead, a number of times I attended Herr Meier's Protestant religion classes, without official authorization but with Herr Meier's silent assent. I instinctively avoided telling my parents about this, since they surely wouldn't have allowed it. As a result of my occasional presence in the Protestant religion class I became aware for the first time of being "different." I wondered why some of my classmates stared at me, some of them even grinning; I couldn't understand why they seemed so interested in my being there, and it was somewhat embarrassing to me. Whether or not I realized at the time that it had something to do with my belonging to "the Mosaic religion" I can't say today.

Thus I discovered soon after starting school that I was different from my non-Jewish classmates. I already knew from my parents that I was Jewish, but I didn't know what difference that made since no one had explained to me what it meant to be Jewish. Besides, I wasn't curious enough to puzzle about it. Two otherwise insignificant incidents have stuck in my mind that showed me I was different and made me feel uncertain. They happened one shortly after the other, in approximately 1929 or 1930, the first one probably while I was still in primary school. After recess in the schoolyard I was returning to our classroom when a classmate from a very wealthy family named Schaper asked me sneeringly whether it was true that on Yom Kippur (the Day of Atonement, the most important Jewish holiday) Jewish people didn't wash or brush their teeth and therefore stank. I don't know why he asked me, one of ten or more

Jewish students in my grade, especially since I had always avoided talking about my religion with anyone at school. What has remained in my mind is his grinning face and his very elegant clothes for a schoolboy of that time. Confused and probably red-faced I assured him that my parents washed themselves and brushed their teeth on that day as on all other days. He said in that case my folks must be a rare exception.

About a year later, at Herder Gymnasium, once again at the end of recess, I had a very short and quite strange conversation with a boy named Jäger. In contrast to Schaper, Jäger was almost a friend of mine. A few classmates, Jewish and not Jewish, had started a little club, The Club of Merry Four [*Verein der lustigen Vier* or VdlV]. I joined the club and we met at our homes in turn, where we played, talked, and dreamed up pranks. Jäger was one of the club's founders. On that day as I was moving back between the desks on the way to my seat, Jäger, already at his seat, grabbed my sleeve and asked me almost sadly why we had crucified Jesus. Taken aback, I answered that I hadn't crucified Jesus. "Of course not you," he said impatiently, "but your people!" And when I asked what he meant by "my people," he replied, "The Jews, naturally." I don't remember what happened then, if anything. I certainly never talked about this again with Jäger, either at school or at our club meetings, and when I changed schools soon thereafter, I lost track of him. But this little incident made a lasting, visual impression in my mind. So even my "friend" considered me to be different; that was the conclusion I drew.

The whole concept of religion developed only gradually for me, and it did so, ironically, because I became acquainted with various aspects of the Christian faith before I had even the vaguest idea about Jewish traditions. Maybe that was because a few of my relatives were Christians and because I had some non-Jewish friends and acquaintances. But, more important, as a little boy I loved to spend time in the small room of our servant girls who, whether Protestant or Catholic, talked not only about their home, their family, and their teenage years (most of them came to work for us when they were eighteen or nineteen), but also about their religion, usually in connection with Easter and Christmas. Some of them noted with satisfaction that we also celebrated these holidays, although we were Jewish. I remember well, as a very little boy, hunting for Easter eggs or sitting under the Christmas tree, stuffing myself with the goodies from my plate of sweets [*bunter Teller*], but it wasn't until I was nine or ten years old that I took part in the Jewish holidays and Friday evening family celebrations, even when they were held at our house. And because it was always made clear to me at home, I was aware of the fact that the Christian faith wasn't mine, that I was a Jew and therefore didn't really have a right to celebrate Easter and Christmas.

Looking back, I imagine that this confessional balancing act wasn't always easy for my parents, especially for my father, who was quite religious. That was evident, for instance, from such minor daily activities as my evening prayer. In the beginning, when I was three or four, it wasn't complicated: "Dear Lord, make me pious, so that I shall go to Heaven. Amen" [*Lieber Gott, mach mich fromm, dass ich in den Himmel komm, Amen*].

Sometime later I learned another rhyming prayer, probably from one of the usual sources—namely, Didi or one of the servant girls—the first verse of which became my evening prayer: "I am tired, I lie down to rest, / close my little eyes. / Father, let Your eyes / stay over my bed. / Amen" [*Müde bin ich, geh' zur Ruh, / schließe beide Äuglein zu. / Vater, laß die Augen Dein / über meinem Bette sein. / Amen*]. That was fine for quite a while, but one evening when we lived on Klaus Groth Strasse I decided for some reason to add the next verse of the prayer: "If I have done wrong today, / please, dear Lord, don't take heed. / Your grace and Jesus' blood / will make it right again. / Amen" [*Hab ich Unrecht heut' getan / sieh es lieber Gott, nicht an. / Deine Gnad' und Jesu Blut / machen allen Schaden gut. / Amen*]. Since almost always at least one of my parents was there to hear my evening prayer, the second verse caused some consternation. I can still see the niche where my bed was and hear the well-meaning voice of my father, who kindly but firmly corrected me. Thereafter I stuck to the first verse.

A much more important occurrence impressed itself deeply in my memory. It was the summer of 1926. We—that is, my mother, Fritz, Didi, and I—on the advice of the family doctor, had traveled during summer vacation to Ortisei (formerly St. Ulrich) in South Tyrol, as the altitude there would supposedly stimulate my very weak appetite and make a "normal" eater of me (as I have mentioned, it worked). During one of our walks I asked Didi the meaning of the crucifixes with the man hanging on them that stood at so many intersections and on so many roadsides, and which were strange but fascinating to me. Didi, who was born and raised a Protestant but later left the church, told me the story of the suffering of Christ. Her description made a strong impression on me. I don't remember whether she mentioned the role of the Jews in the crucifixion or not. Soon after, on another walk, the two of us were surprised by a sudden thunderstorm and found shelter in a mausoleum in a churchyard. At the entrance to the mausoleum stood two angels—huge to me at the time—carved from stone and wielding swords, and so I learned about the archangels and their meaning in the Bible. Since Didi had only completed elementary school and wasn't especially well-versed in questions of her religion, her explanations were probably quite primitive. But she put feeling into the telling, and because of my love for her, it made a big impression.

A year or two later—I probably wasn't going to Herr Spieldoch's Jewish religion class yet—Fritz and I were sent to summer camp in Schierke in the Harz Mountains, while our parents went on vacation somewhere without us. The camp director was a Dr. Sieben, a pious Protestant woman, as I later found out, who went to church on Sundays and then came and read to the children in the camp from the New Testament. So I was confronted with the story of Christ's sufferings a second time, this time in a more penetrating way than Didi had told it in the Dolomites. Dr. Sieben stressed the role of the Jews, especially of the High Priest and the scribes, in the interrogation and judgment of Christ. Although I am quite sure that I detected no hostility on her part toward the Jewish children in the room, I still didn't feel entirely comfortable. We were all sitting in the small living room—I can still see the eyes of that nice woman looking up at us from the bible—and I know that I disapproved of the Jews' behavior as described by Dr. Siebens' reading from the New Testament.

When at the age of eight, I started going to the weekly Jewish religion classes at school, my lack of clarity regarding my religious identity was by no means resolved. Part of the reason for this was surely the quality of the religion teachers, at least of those I was exposed to up until I left school in the spring of 1936. Their incapacity to adapt to children was only surpassed by their deadly dullness. From Herr Spieldoch to Herr Schimmelmann—and there were some odd ones in between—the weekly Jewish religion class became a hated obligation that I gritted my teeth to get through. We were drilled in Hebrew, without the structure of the language being properly introduced. They made us learn by heart only the most important blessings, especially the ones about bread and wine, and also the confession of faith ("Hear, O Israel, The Lord is our God, the Lord is One"), so that we could recite them in Hebrew. I can still say them today, but I don't remember much else. Besides that, each week we had to read a passage about biblical history in a textbook written by a Herr Auerbach, if my memory serves me correctly. It was about the five books of Moses, trimmed to the intellectual level of children eight to ten. But Herr Auerbach was horribly boring, too. The texts were carefully censored—for Heaven's sake no sex, not even biblical sex! Readings were assigned and the following week we were questioned on the details to see if we had read them. Whether we understood the significance of the passage or whether it stimulated us to ask questions didn't seem to interest anyone.

An introduction into the rich world of the Old Testament didn't come from this musty corner of my childhood but rather from a seamstress who came to our house once a month to mend clothes and bed linens and such. Fräulein Berta Stange was a very small, shy woman who sat behind our old-fashioned Singer sewing machine all day, energetically pedaling and finishing amazing amounts of work. When I came home from school on these days, I had lunch in the kitchen then went straight to the room where Fräulein Berta was working and, sitting on a chair next to her, asked her to tell me a story. Sometimes she first told me of the latest experiences of her grown daughter Cilly. (To my repeated questions of my parents as to why Fräulein Berta, if she had a daughter, wasn't called Frau Berta, I got a satisfactory answer only many years later.) After a while she began at some point in her soft, slightly trembling voice to tell tales or to sing ballads, almost always based on the Old Testament. And thus I was introduced to the stories of my religious tradition by this dear, elderly woman who wasn't Jewish. I sat there in the nearly dark room, lit only by the sewing machine lamp, and listened to her tell and sing to me about Adam and Eve's expulsion from Paradise or David's fight with Goliath. Whatever she told or sang stuck in my mind, while the Jewish religion classes of Spieldoch, Schindler, Schimmelmann, and whoever they all were did not. In fact, religion classes alienated me from my religion more than they brought me closer to it.

In 1933, at the end of my thirteenth year, when I was of an age to follow the commandments, as it is expressed formally, the time came for my bar mitzvah. After that one can be called on to read the Torah at services and, if orthodox, put on phylacteries for morning prayers; one becomes a member of the Jewish community of worshippers with all the accompanying rights and duties. To be bar mitzvahed, however, one has to prepare. Ambitious parents insist that their sons, besides saying the usual blessing, also read aloud from the Old Testament (in Hebrew) the passage pertaining to the week of the bar mitzvah, which is always on the Sabbath. My father had instructed Herr Schimmelmann months in advance to teach me the necessary material for my bar mitzvah. To my father's annoyance and disappointment, when my birthday came in June, I had learned almost nothing. My knowledge of Hebrew wasn't even sufficient for me to read aloud from the Torah the blessing of the day, let alone the passage for the week. So Papa decided to take me to the youngest rabbi in Berlin, Dr. Manfred Swarsenski. This proved to be a good solution. Swarsenski had a sense of humor and knew how to deal with boys like me and get them to learn what they needed to know. When I cautiously hinted at Herr Schimmelmann's incompetence, Swarsenski made a slightly snide pun on the teacher's name.

It wasn't long before I was making progress, although the whole business still went against the grain with me. Probably the main reason I hadn't learned anything from Schimmelmann, even more than the good man's incompetence, was my unconscious reluctance to be bar mitzvahed. Swarsenski, with his kind and charming manner, challenged me in a way that I accepted in spite of myself, and on December 2, 1933, I was ready. With the exception of Grosspapa, the whole family went to the synagogue on Prinzregentenstrasse, I in a tie and dark blue suit, but with short pants, and it all went without a hitch. I recited the blessing loudly and clearly in Hebrew. At home there was a small reception with canapés, wine for the adults, and juice for us children, and in the evening we had a nice dinner together, and Papa and I each gave a short speech. My parents were satisfied with me, and I was glad it was finally over. The gifts most common on such occasions are books, some of which I still own today.

Now I had the right to take my place in the Jewish congregation of Berlin. But I never made use of this right. My parents had bought their seats in the synagogue on Prinzregentenstrasse, and so on major holidays as well as on occasional Friday evenings I had to go with them and then sit on the crack between my parents' chairs, since I didn't have my own seat. After my bar mitzvah my parents redoubled their efforts to make conscientious Jews of my brothers and me. My father was mainly reacting to the mounting anti-Semitic violence and the continually increasing number of anti-Jewish laws. In 1934 we stopped celebrating Christmas at our house. Papa insisted on this. Instead we lit the Chanukah candles for a week and sang the Hasmonean song, "Rock of Ages, let our song / Praise Thy saving power / Thou amidst the raging foes / Wast our sheltering

The day of my bar mitzvah in 1933, on the balcony in Lichterfelde.

tower." But we weren't the only ones who reacted this way. Many Jewish families stopped celebrating Christmas then. The switch from Christmas candles to Chanukah candles was symptomatic. Jewish people began to think about their roots and to act accordingly. And what did I do? Of course I was a good boy, sang along with my family, and accepted my gifts. But on Christmas Eve I fled to Didi, who had put up a Christmas tree in a small room on Barbarossastrasse next to her cigar shop (which was doing poorly). Together with her I secretly celebrated the holiday we had lost at home.

Why did I kick and scream and refuse to accept my being Jewish? Partly because of the brainwashing we were subjected to in school even before the Nazis seized power but also because of the decidedly patriotic stance of the German Jewish youth organization I joined in 1933. But even that can't account for it completely, especially since a good number of my friends in the organization were very consciously Jewish, although they made a show of their German patriotism at the same time. Fritz, who is three years younger than I am, also developed a feeling of Jewish identity that he still has today. But it was different with me. Without a doubt at that time I would have preferred not to have been born a Jew. I'd had that attitude even before the Nazis took over the government. Though I can't say so with certainty, I believe it had something to do with the psychological distance I felt from most of my family. I felt myself to be an outsider, not really belonging either to my family or to the Jewish community. For although I sat between my parents without grumbling when they took me to the services in the synagogue, and though I listened attentively to the sermons by the mostly very old rabbis, my mind then was somewhere else completely, wrangling with the fate that had stamped me as something I didn't want to be.

The only time that I felt something like belonging was during a service on one of the high holidays in September of either 1933 or 1934. The preacher was Manfred Swarsenski, my Swarsenski, whose youthful appearance and behavior was such a pleasant contrast to the prevailing rabbinical senility. (Besides him there were two other young rabbis in Berlin, Joachim Prinz and Max Nussbaum, all three not only excellent speakers but good spiritual advisors, something with which the Jewish community in Berlin was otherwise not richly blessed.) On that day Swarsenski counseled the obviously dejected members of the congregation to practice more restraint. The women shouldn't stroll along the Kurfürstendamm decked in pearls and flashy clothes, and both sexes should be quiet and reserved when they appeared in public. And then, discussing the increasingly difficult situation of German Jews under the Nazi regime, he quoted, to my amazement, the Gospel of Saint Luke: "Forgive them, Father, for they know not what they do." I immediately peered over to the entrance of the synagogue, where two uniformed police officers were sitting on a bench monitoring the service. Their expressions didn't change, and nothing happened afterward. I was proud at that moment to be a member of Swarsenski's congregation.

It wasn't until much later that I was able to comprehend fully how hard it must have been for my parents, especially Papa, to see their eldest son reject everything that was an essential part of their lives. But how could I, a boy in puberty at the time, have freed myself from my own prejudices, which, even though I didn't express them openly, my parents could hardly have failed to notice? They saw my often dismissive glances at the members of the congregation surrounding us on the days when I accompanied them to the synagogue. To me these fellow worshippers had nothing heroic about them, even though some of them were named Siegfried. They were no blond giants, but then neither was I. I would have liked to be huge, blond, and heroic, and I wanted to prove at least that I had heroic, soldierly thoughts and feelings, like my classmates and peers in the Jungvolk and Hitler Youth. When I was fifteen, shortly after the announcement of the Nuremberg race laws, I wrote in my diary: "Friday, September 27, New Year (Jewish New Year). At the synagogue in the evening. I am outside of it all. Germany doesn't want me and I don't want the Jews. OK, I am alone. Who cares." And the next day: "Saturday, September 28. At the synagogue in the morning. My parents want me to become a good Jew. No!" Finally, a week later, on the eve of Yom Kippur: "Sunday, October 6. In the evening I was at synagogue. The same impression as always. I don't belong."

So, despite my parents' efforts, my belonging to the Jewish religion never went beyond external forms and led me to neither religious devotion nor identification with ethnic Jews. In addition to that, it was made clear to me in a variety of different ways, but especially from the *outside* and at a very young age, that my being Jewish separated me from most of my peers. The result was confusion, sadness, and above all resistance to having been born into a religious community that meant nothing to me at the time, but was the reason why I was seen and treated as an outsider, even a pariah. It would be useless for me to say today that I am ashamed of the attitude I held at that time. It is simply the way I was, and years passed before my viewpoint on this question changed. Today I can only say that I deeply regret all of this in retrospect.

Two paths were available for me, and many Jews of my generation took one of them after 1933. In defiance of the Nazi regime I could have joined one of the various Zionist groups, the National Jews, whose right wing, the Revisionists, impressed me a great deal at the time, in spite of my "German nationalist" and non-Zionist views. I was also attracted to Hermann Gerson's *Werkleute*, probably because they came from the former *Jüdische Jugendbund Kameraden* like my own youth organization, *Schwarzes Fähnlein, Jungenschaft*. The other possibility that tempted me was to withdraw from Judaism as soon as I was no longer under my parents' authority. But though I emigrated overseas without my parents before I had come of age, I decided against withdrawing from Judaism and have remained at least nominally Jewish. The main reason I made this choice was that my father was killed at Auschwitz, which I learned shortly after the end of the Second World War.

CHAPTER 3

The Youth Movement

Like almost all the decisions in my life, my joining an organization of the Jewish youth movement was based not on planning but on chance. The only youth organization I knew of then was the Hitler Youth [Hitlerjugend], especially its youngest age group (ten to fourteen), the *Deutsche Jungvolk*. Many of my classmates were members, including Hansjürgen, Heiner, and Wolfgang Sauer, and I suffered greatly at being excluded. One day in late summer of 1933 my father had the crazy idea to sign me up at a Jewish sports club. There I would learn to box, the better to defend myself against Nazi attacks, especially from members of the Hitler Youth. The idea of what would happen to a Jew who physically resisted a uniformed attacker didn't seem to have occurred to him, nor did it to me, of course. A few months later he would have no longer suggested such a move to me, at least not with the reason he had given for it.

So for a brief time I went obediently once a week after school to the Makkabi Jewish sports club where I unenthusiastically boxed around with Jewish boys of my age, not paying much attention to the advice and admonitions of the small and stocky coach who intended to fill us with fervor, and wishing my father had bought me horseback riding lessons instead. After one of the three or four boxing lessons that I took there, a friendly looking boy turned to me in the changing room, introducing himself as "Dreas" (short for Andreas) Carlebach. He asked me if I was a member of any club. I said no. He then gave me a flyer with the title "A Thousand Boys Are Calling You," told me to read it and let him know the next week if I was interested. Thereafter we rode our bikes home, he to Hubertusallee in Grunewald, I to Lichterfelde.

Dreas was a member of the *Schwarzes Fähnlein, Jungenschaft*

[Black Platoon, Boys' Club]. It had originated as part of a larger Jewish youth organization, the Kameraden, *Deutschjüdischer Wanderbund* [Comrades, German Jewish Hiking Movement], which had been founded after the First World War by young assimilated German Jews. At least at the beginning, it was the non-Zionist counterpart to the Zionist *Blau-Weiss* [Blue-White]. Over the years, three factions developed within the Kameraden, which at Pentecost 1932 separated into three independent groups: the Zionist *Werkleute* [Working People], who in April 1934 founded the Hazorea kibbutz in Palestine, which is still in existence today; the *Freie Deutsch-Jüdische Jugend* [Free German Jewish Youth], a radical socialist organization that had to be dissolved in 1933; and Schwarzes Fähnlein, Jungenschaft, which, with a total of fifteen to twenty local groups and four hundred members, was much smaller than the Werkleute and only slightly larger than Freie Deutsch-Jüdische Jugend. So "a thousand boys are calling you" was an exaggeration.

I thought about it for a few days, and the next time I met Dreas at our boxing class I told him I would like to become a member. I had gotten my parents' permission. Two weeks later I was accepted into *Schwarzes Fähnlein, Jungenschaft*, as a *Pimpf*, the equivalent of a Cub Scout. I never did succeed in convincing my parents and their friends and relatives that we weren't called *Schwarzes Fähnchen* [little black flag], and that in the sixteenth and seventeenth centuries a *Fähnlein* was a military organization of about three hundred men. My group called itself the Mohicans and belonged to the Brandenburg district of our organization. There were also the Delawares and other groups named after American Indian tribes, and after a while I got to know boys from these groups as well. My group's leader was Gert Lippmann, who was simultaneously the head of all groups organized within the Brandenburg district. He was then nineteen years old, six years older than I, and from my point of view an adult. He died in Australia in 1999.

What had prompted me to join this youth organization? First of all, I liked Dreas, who had "roped me in [*gekeilt*]," as this procedure was called at the time. A few days later he took me along to a *Heimabend* [group meeting] where I was introduced to Gert Lippmann and the members of the Mohicans and where Dreas asked formally that I be admitted to this "tribe." Very solemnly I was officially inaugurated by being shown the "secret" handshake members used to greet one another (it consisted of using the left hand with the little finger held open). I then was told where to buy my uniform [*Kluft*], what equipment I required to go camping, and when and where I could get my membership card, which ironically speaking was then still issued by the National Socialist *Reichsjugendführung* [Federal Youth Leadership]. When the meeting was over I rode back my bike as if I were riding a horse because I felt like a proud cavalier of the garde du corps. Finally I belonged to a group of boys my age and thus could cope much better with the daily unpleasantness at school. It was a first, if small, step toward obtaining more independence from my parents, for now I entered a world that I didn't share with them. An additional attraction was the fact that I now wore a "uniform"—a dark blue jacket [*Jungenschaftsjacke*] of the type worn by the *Deutsche Jungvolk*, and dark blue shorts no longer than two hands' width above the knee. Finally I shared the ideological components of the group—at least to the extent I then knew what ideological components were. But of prime importance was the fact that my new friends shared with me the idea that we were first and foremost Germans whose religious faith happened to be, "by chance," Jewish. As we then saw it, Germany was our fatherland and would remain our fatherland. For here not only were we born, but also our parents and their parents and so on. Naive as we (and many adults) were then, we firmly believed that all we had to do was prove to the new German government that in all our being, thinking, and actions we were German and would remain German. When the Nazis understood this, they would have to accept us into the broad front of "German renewal."

Of course, we "thousand boys" of the *Schwarzes Fähnlein* (or "SF" as we referred to it) weren't the only Jews in Germany who held this nationalist hope. Until the pronouncement of the Nuremberg racial laws in 1935, the attitude wasn't unusual. The executive boards of several Jewish organizations belonging to the most assimilated segment of German Jewry (of which two-thirds were members of these organizations) sponsored us. We were to them the shining example of a rising generation of German-Jewish patriots who wanted to serve their fatherland if only it would let them. At least during the beginning phase of the Third Reich, many Jewish leaders hoped that the new German rulers might be persuaded to drop their anti-Semitic attitude and measures.

The numerically largest but for us rather uninteresting Jewish organization was the *Centralverein Deutsche Staatsbürger Jüdichen Glaubens* [Central Association of German Citizens of the Jewish Faith], usually referred to by the abbreviation CV. Most of our parents were members, and the weekly *CV Zeitung* printed from time to time kind little articles about us. Of much greater importance to us was the German-Jewish veterans' organization, the Reichsbund Jüdischer Frontsoldaten (RJF), under the leadership of Dr. Leo Löwenstein, who during the First World War had been promoted to the rank of captain in the Bavarian Army. (We loved to recite a verse that circulated among the Jews in Berlin: "*Das Judentum hat kein Unglück allein, es hat auch Hauptmann Löwenstein*" [Jewry doesn't have one misfortune alone, it also has Captain Löwenstein]. Already during the 1920s the RJF had made efforts to convince young Jews not to enter professions that were considered by many Germans as "typically Jewish." And so it happened that the lawyers, businessmen, physicians, and academicians who sat in the executive board of the RJF and determined its policies were saying that "skilled handicraft has a golden basis" [*Handwerk hat einen goldenen Boden*], praising the farming profession and other branches of manual labor, and promoting such professions among young Jews. Their efforts had very limited effect until 1933, when the initiative for such social and professional restructuring fell to the hated Zionists, who throughout Germany and beyond established *Hachsharah* [preparation] camps where Jewish youngsters were trained to become farmers, move to Palestine, and work in kibbuzim. To this the pertinent administrative bodies of the Nazi state gave their blessing.

For the RJF, our *Bund* [movement] proved a useful element in the image of German Jewry it sought to project. Here were German Jewish boys one could proudly present to the state authorities (the girls of the SF's *Mädelschaft* [roughly, Girls' League] were of very little interest to the old warriors of the RJF). Thus we became sort of a front for the type of Jew the RJF wanted to present proudly to the new German rulers: upright, soldierly, good at sports, but above all German to the core. The fact that the Nazis didn't give a damn for our German pride but were merely interested in forcing as many Jews as possible to leave the country by applying constant political pressure occurred to many Jews only very gradually, and to the RJF even more slowly. Thus it happened, to give a few examples, that the *Schild* [Shield], the association's weekly newspaper, reported quite regularly about our activities, frequently with photos; that we marched with a group of RJF veterans to the synagogue on Veterans Day 1934, in uniform and with flags flying; or that during sport festivals on the "Jewish" athletic field in the Grunewald we were cheered on by leading RJF representatives.

A third Jewish organization with which we had contact, without taking it very seriously, was the *Deutsche Vortrupp, Gefolgschaft Deutscher Juden* [roughly, German Vanguard of German Jews], led by Hans-Joachim Schoeps. A studious and liberal religious Jew, he was at the same time, at least until 1934, an admirer of National Socialism and its "seizure of power" in January 1933. Even we found it embarrassing to read his essays, which struck us as schizophrenic. Schoeps considered himself close to us; we didn't share this view. And yet, he and Gert Lippmann occasionally exchanged ideas. Once, while visiting Gert, Schoeps invited me to eat ice cream with him. At his suggestion we met the next day on Unter den Linden beneath the equestrian statue of Frederick the Great and then went to Café Kranzler. I have forgotten what we spoke about. It was the only occasion on which I met with Schoeps.

Finally, the *Verband Nationaldeutscher Juden* [VNJ, Association of German-National Jews] made attempts to get us under its wing, and during the first months of 1933 there was in fact some weak contact between the association and the SF. The leader of the association was the lawyer Dr. Max Naumann, like Löwenstein a former captain in the Bavarian Army. (In Bavaria, unlike most other German states, Jews could become reserve officers.) In contrast to the RJF and the *Deutsche Vortrupp*, the members of the VNJ attempted to ingratiate themselves shamelessly with Germany's new rulers, even ranting in their organ *Der Nationaldeutsche Jude* and during public events against Eastern Jews and Zionists. That outdid everything the RJF and *Deutsche Vortrupp* had ever tried to prove their nationalist enthusiasm. In the Jewish circles of Berlin the VNJ's leader was referred to as "*Raus-mit-uns-Naumann*" [Let's-have-us-kicked-out-Naumann].

However, the general attitude of our *Bund* wasn't determined by adult organizations; we didn't pay much attention to them. To be sure, our leaders on all three levels—group, *Gau*, and *Bund*—oriented themselves to some extent by the adult organization's patriotism and accepted gratefully any assistance that came from this corner of German Jewry. But it didn't go any further. For those of us in the *Bund* who were then thirteen or fourteen years old, these adults belonged to the generation of our parents, with whom our relationships during the beginning of puberty were generally rather tense.

Thus the adult nationalist organizations reinforced our conviction that, if we tried hard enough to prove it to them, the Nazis would sooner or later recognize our fervor for Germany. Beyond this, however, we had very little contact with groups led by our parents' generation.

What really guided and inspired us was a non-Jewish *Bund*, the *Deutsche Jungenschaft* 1/11, generally referred to as the DJ 1/11. Founded on November 1, 1929, the DJ 1/11. became during the early 1930s the model for all Jewish and non-Jewish youth *Bünde*. We wore the same dark blue uniform jacket (*Jungenschaftsjacke*) that the leader of their *Bund*, Tusk (Eberhard Köbel), had designed. (This jacket was ultimately adopted—in black—by the *Deutsche Jungvolk*, which originally had also belonged to the *bündisch* youth before it joined the Hitler Youth in 1931.)

At the time I wasn't particularly interested in historical or organizational questions pertaining to the German youth movement, and most of my friends in the group felt the same way. We were told that the *Bund* had originally developed out of the traditional *Wandervögel* movement of the late 1890s, but this made little impression on us. We thought the old "wander birdies" must have been strange characters because they—boys and girls together!—had roamed through the forests, singing from their songbook, the *Zupfgeigenhansel*, which we rejected as silly. Instead we made up little verses in which we made fun of the *Wandervögel*: "What sort of weather must it be when the old *Wandervögel* are going on hiking trips without freezing their butts off?" [*Was muss das für ein Wetter sein / wenn die alten / Wandervögel auf Fahrt mal geh'n / ohne zu erkalten?*].

Occasionally Gert or other older leaders of our organization told us their memories of the *Kameraden*, but even that didn't give us the feeling that we were part of a tradition. All that really interested us was our own *Stamm* [group] and its activities.

Our *Stamm*, the Mohicans, included twelve to fifteen boys whose ages ranged between thirteen and fifteen. Many of us had nicknames, most of which had developed spontaneously within the group—I got mine at the end of 1933—and when I spoke at home about Antek, Blöo, Knirps, Pudding, Dresch, Sab, or Inch, my parents shook their heads. Many of these nicknames were anything but complimentary. For instance, "Blöo" stood for *blöder Ochse* [stupid ox] and "Dresch" for *Dreckschwein* [dirty pig]. We all bore our nicknames with dignity. Initially my best friend was Dreas, the boy who had gotten me into the group. Later it was Vici—Victor Lewinsohn (who died a few years ago in São Paulo). The majority of the group came from the same social background as I did, the bourgeois Jewish middle class. Antek's father, however, was a shoemaker, and the parents of Sab and Inch were "Eastern Jews." But since the structure of the group was very solid, the social origin made little difference. We met once a week for *Heimabend* [home evenings]. Initially we rotated from one member's home to the next; later, and until the *Bund* was dissolved in December 1934, we met in a garage in Westend's Ahornallee that a "patron" (unknown to me) had put at our disposal, and which we could furnish according to our taste and ability.

From the onset I hoped that in this group of boys my age I would find the acceptance, human warmth, and friendship I had never found in school. And behold, it worked out! Within a very short period of time I was completely devoted to the Mohicans, my life centered on this group, and at home I spoke of virtually nothing else. This initially amused my parents, then worried them, and ultimately annoyed them. In school my grades got worse and worse, and only after a very serious lecture from Gert (at the request of my parents), did I begin trying to improve my grades. Despite this effort I got my first "blue letter" (a warning from the school) in February 1934, and another thereafter every February until 1936, my last year of school.

My attempts to be a perfect *Pimpf* were by no means appreciated by all of my friends (all members of the youth movement ten to fourteen years old were called *Pimpfe*, nomenclature later also used by the Jungvolk, the early age group of the Hitler Youth). I was too eager, volunteering for every task that Gert or any of the other leaders wanted done, and as a result irritated especially my old friend Dreas, to the point of threatening our friendship. "If Gert were to tell you to go and jump off the Funkturm [Berlin's radio tower]," he hissed at me, "you would do it immediately."

I didn't understand his anger. Didn't he know that all I wanted to show everyone was how much it meant to me to belong to the group? And although subsequently during my agricultural training in Gross Breesen I made several very close friendships which in some cases have lasted over half a century, there has been no other community—not even that of Gross Breesen—to which I have felt so closely, naively, and unconditionally affiliated as I did as a thirteen year old to the *Mohikanern*.

A few months after joining the *Bund* my unrestricted willingness to serve and my sense of belonging, which I stated over and over again, were rewarded by the leader of the group, Gert Lippmann, when he formally admitted me to the Mohicans. During one of our weekly meetings, without any previous announcement, Gert solemnly handed me a blue scarf and then fixed a blue cord to the right epaulet of my *Jungenschaftsjacke*. (I still own the scarf. The cord I placed in 1937 on the grave of a Gross Breesen friend, Gustl, who died in an accident there.) In the spring of 1934, while we were on an overnight hike and sitting around a campfire, Gert suddenly appointed me "cornet" (standard-bearer) of our organization's *Gau* Brandenburg.

Perhaps I should state here that "*Gau* Brandenburg" (county or province of Brandenburg) was a bit of an exaggeration. To be sure, the *Bund* had several groups in Berlin, but beyond that there existed to the best of my recollection no additional local groups in *Gau* Brandenburg. Nevertheless, it sounded good. Our flag showed on one side the red eagle of Brandenburg, on the other the SF's logo. I was extremely proud to have been appointed cornet, despite the fact that we had few opportunities to show ourselves with that flag in public. But now I was the one to carry it whenever there was a chance to do so. I always took it home after it had been hung on the wall during the weekly *Heimabende* (literally, "a place to meet") and, conversely, was always ready to jump on my bike with it and the wooden spear to which it was attached and go wherever the flag and I were needed. Secretly I identified myself with Rainer Maria Rilke's Cornet Christoph Rilke, whose "*Weise von Liebe und Tod*" ["Air of Love and Death"] Gert had read to us during a *Heimabend*:

> *Cries: Cornet!*
> *Cantering horses, Prayers, Shouts,*
> *Curses: Cornet! Iron on Iron, Orders and signal;*
> *Silence. Cornet!*
> *And once again: Cornet!*
> *And forward with the thundering Cavalry... .*
> *But the Flag is not there... .*
> *But then she starts to shine, extending herself and*
> *   becoming big and red...*
> *And there the flag flares in the midst of the enemy, and*
> *   they chase after it.*

One could hardly accuse us of lacking romanticism.

Nothing could have shaped us so intensely as did these weekly meetings. After arriving at the meeting place, having parked our bikes outside, we sat down on the ground in a circle and sang for half an hour or longer.

Gert, and occasionally Sab, accompanied us on the guitar from which once-colored ribbons hung, as had been customary during the age of the *Wandervögel*. And what did we sing? Not folk or love songs but ones that dealt with fighting and death: war songs, mercenary songs, songs that glorified violence. Again we drew predominantly on the songs of the *Jungenschaft* DJ 1/11, gathered in *Lieder der Eisbrechermannschaft* [*Songs of the Icebreaker Team*] . But we also didn't neglect the *Sankt Georg Liderbuch deutscher Jugend* [*St. George's Songbook of German Youth*], the musical bible of the *bündische* youth movement during the Weimar Republic.

And there we now sat on the ground in a circle—Angresses, Danielsohns, Lewinsohns, Carlebachs, Lichtensteins, Lippmanns, and whatever their names were—and sang with great enthusiasm and feeling of the heroic deeds of Georg von Frundsberg, leader of Emperor Maximilian's mercenaries during the fifteenth century; of the *gueux* who fought against the Spanish Duke of Alba in the Netherlands; of the Regiment Forcade "which no foe had ever beaten," but whose soldiers the Prussian King Frederick the Great sent to be slaughtered in the Battle of Hochkirch. We moved with the Free Swiss, "*trem trem trem trari dee*," to protect the frontiers; with the French King Francis I into misfortune, and with Radetzk into Italy. We won the war of 1870–71 ("Leipzig-ein-und-Leipzig," as it was called at the time) against Napoleon III: "Sedan, big battle of the nation / your dead casualties are alive! / France's entire imperial force / had to surrender." And in 1914 we went into the Great War: "The happy years of travel which gave us knowledge are over / because we move to Flanders / into bloody battle." Or we stood high on the bridge of a German battleship that was steaming toward England: "Up on the navigating bridge stands the captain, laughing / his looks sweep toward the enemy, / tomorrow will be the big battle." Here, with these belligerent songs, began my first introduction to European history—from the Battle of Pavia to the Battle of Verdun.

But we were not one-sided! Our German nationalism didn't prevent us from admiring other armies. Our choice of songs was politically neutral, as long as they dealt with fighting. This was shown, for instance, by our fascination with Russia. Of course we praised the heroic General Platoff, who "defeated his enemy in every battle." This song was always the highlight of the evening when the Don Cossak choir sang under the direction of its conductor, the anti-Semite Serge Jaroff. Whenever the choir visited in

Berlin during the 1930s many former youth movement members attended, even after their *Bünde* were dissolved by the *Reichsjugendführung*. I also went to one concert, in 1936 or 1937, when the choir sang in Breslau (now Wrocław, Poland). Platoff, who had fought against Napoleon I, was widely admired in the early Nazi period when we sang these songs and went to listen to the choir. In contrast, the "White" (anti-Communist) Admiral Aleksandr Kolchak, who had fought in the Russian civil war of 1918–20, was controversial. So we sang: "Hey, the white waves extinguish red fire / Kolchak is advancing / he liberates the land." But we sang with equal enthusiasm—although only deep in the woods where nobody could hear us—"The waves they are roaring, the storms they are howling, the Red Navy is pushing on. / Forward Communists, let's arm for the final battle, the Red Navy is attacking." We were neither reactionaries nor communists; we simply liked these songs and sang them with what in retrospect seems almost touching neutrality and naiveté. We also liked the song about Cavalry General Budjonny, who was well known in the Red Army that Leon Trotzky created in 1918. It fit so well with its counterpart, a song that glorified the Don-Cossak choir of Serge Jaroff:

> At night hunger haunts our dreams
> In daytime rifle shots crack at the edge of the woods.
> Misery walks next to the columns of prisoners
> And at night in the fog the wolves trot along.
> And yet Russia's sacred eagle still flies
> Mother dear,
> Our heart belongs to you!
> May the Red Army chase us
> Your banner remains shining brightly.

Finally, we didn't deny ourselves the wildest, most nihilistic songs, especially those we found in the songbook of the DJ 1/11. With shining eyes we children of mostly well-to-do Jewish families sang verses like these:

> Beat yourselves and kick yourselves
> You are a bunch of pirates.
> Sell your honor
> Throw away the spear
> And pluck the stars from the sky.

Hoi! We are the wild army
Unafraid of those who face us
And if you curse us and chase us
We just laugh!
Take away your hand
We want no bonds
If you build on us, we are sand
Destroy the country,
Burn the knickknacks
And be a disgrace to the Lord.
Hoi!

The songs that came out of our own ranks and were generally written by our two bards, Tulle (of Breslau) and Oka (of Hannover), were no less belligerent. Our *Bundeslied* [anthem] was titled "*Heertrommel* [Military Drum]":

The military drum sings a song as hard as iron.
The drumstick beats
and orders us into formation.

Yet victory will not radiate from our blue banners
until all of us follow the drum beat.
Many who march with us in step today
were moved to join by the drummer boy.

After the *Schwarzes Fähnlein* was dissolved in December 1934, the *Deutsche Jungvolk* appropriated "*Heertrommel*" with minor changes.

The anthem of our *Gau* Brandenburg didn't sound exactly pacifistic either:

Let's all turn out for the last time
You troops of united blue soldiers.
Hear once again drums and battle cries
Which will prompt us all to fight bravely.
On the flag ahead our eagle flies
An eagle red as hot blood.
He's part of a banner that's black and white.

We are greeting you, homeland, you märkisch
[Brandenburger] world:
Do you hear the signals? Brandenburg, lead on.

And yet, compared to the hymn of our *Gau* Silesia (to which the future historian Walter Laqueur—known as "Lacke"—belonged), that of *Gau* Brandenburg sounded tame:

Comrade, the drums entice us,
We're marching through Silesia …
Comrade, the circle of tents
Awaits you in the woods.
Ignore the heat and the cold
Make use of freedom's short time.
Before us the flags are waving
Behind them all we
of our Gau *stand aligned.*
Silesia is attacking!

This selection should give an idea of our mentality at the time. Everywhere throughout the country the SA, SS, and Gestapo beat and tortured political opponents, Nazi leaders talked about extinguishing the "Jewish pestilence," and we lost ourselves musically and otherwise in heroic fantasies. We didn't even notice what was going on in our world.

Much more important than the *Heimabende* were our *Fahrten*, our periodic journeys into the countryside. Shortly before we traveled to our *Winterlager* [winter camp] in Czechoslovakia, and fairly soon after I had joined the organization, our group went on an overnight trip somewhere in the environs of Berlin, for me the first such experience. Most of the details I can no longer recall. Whether we went by bicycle or took the bikes with us on the train I have forgotten. What I do remember is that I wore my *Kluft* [uniform] and had purchased a backpack (called at the time an *Affe* [monkey]), plus a half-tarpaulin for shelter, a cantine, and so on, everything secondhand although my father nevertheless shook his head at the cost of all this. All I still needed was a sleeping bag. What we call a sleeping bag today may have existed then, but I don't recall ever seeing one. In any case my mother instructed Fräulein Bertha, who came every four weeks to mend our clothes, to sew for me a sleeping bag from an old woolen blanket that must have served some family member during wartime in the field. At the *Heimabend* prior to our overnight *Fahrt* I was shown how to roll the "sleeping bag" into a tarpaulin, which we called a shelter half, and then fasten the giant sausage thus created around the backpack so that everything looked tight and square. And the following Saturday we took off.

I clearly remember the Saturday night that we spent in a hayloft. I slept next to the outside wall underneath a large opening designed for ventilation and froze miserably all night long. The sleeping bag was a dud. I found out subsequently that most of my buddies had taken along two blankets. During future trips I learned never to lie next to an exterior wall and to bury myself in the hay, ignoring the dust that got into my nose. It was naturally clear to me that I couldn't tell any of these little adventures to my parents. They would have never permitted me to go *auf Fahrt* again. I stuck to the principle I had applied for years regarding the happenings at school: The less the parents find out, the better things will be. Thus I only informed my parents about matters I thought they could handle—and that wasn't terribly much. Fortunately I was at that time in good health and never returned sick from our trips.

For me the first important event was the Czech *Winterlager*, which lasted from Christmas 1933 until New Year's 1934, and which we spent at Nieder-Klein-Aupa, a small village on the Czech side of the *Riesengebirge* (Sudeten Mountains), in the so-called Sudetenland. We traveled by train until Schmiedeberg, then hiked for eight kilometers, mostly uphill, through the snowy winter forest to the German-Czech border, where our passports were checked on both sides. Then we proceeded to the farm of Herr Kirschlager, in whose "living room" we slept on straw bags laid on the floor. Above us hung the portrait of Emperor Franz Josef I of Austria-Hungary.

During the winter camp I was given my nickname, which I thoroughly earned. The day after our arrival we decided to go skiing with a few members from *Gau* Silesia, who had joined us and were living in a farmhouse close to where we stayed. I was the only one who was not able to ski. They suggested that I "practice" on a slope behind the house, then left me to my fate. The slope was rather steep and intimidating. But I told myself that one reason why I had come along to this place was to go skiing, so now I would have to learn how to do it. I walked to the edge of the slope and began rather clumsily to put on one of the skis. Suddenly the second one got loose and raced off down the slope. Cursing, I untied the ski I already had put on, pushed the ski poles into the rather deep, crusted snow and placed the ski against the two poles. Then I waded downhill through the snow to retrieve the fugitive and get it back to the top of the slope. When I was nearly at the bottom—about ten minutes later—I saw my ski next to a pile of firewood. I picked it up and began to climb uphill again. This was when I saw the second ski, which I had thought I had well secured, racing downhill toward me. At great speed it passed by me and smashed into the pile of firewood. Its three shattered pieces I added to the pile.

Having no more skis, I was condemned to "daily duty" [*Tagesdienst*] for the duration of our stay. This meant each morning piling up the straw bags on which we slept, keeping the place swept, and, above all, cooking the daily meals. In accordance with the National Socialist currency laws, anyone on vacation abroad could take only ten reichsmarks out of the country. We had been carefully searched for money when we crossed the border. Given the shortage of money our meals were rather monotonous: pea soup, chocolate rice, pea soup, chocolate rice—and always for around twenty people. I stood for hours over the giant, sooty kettle, feeding the ancient stove with wood and stirring, stirring, stirring. And yet there was hardly a day when at least the chocolate rice wasn't burned. I wasn't a popular cook. If no one replaced me, this was only because I had no skis and thus couldn't join the others outside.

One evening in the room where we slept I placed my wet rubber boots in the grate of the stove to dry. The grate was nice and warm, just right for drying the shoes by next morning. Unfortunately, I had forgotten that early each morning Herr Kirschlager tiptoed into the room and loaded new wood into the stove, which soon was blazing hot. The next morning we woke up in a smoke-filled room. Yelling "My shoes!" I rushed to the stove, but my furious buddies screamed at me to open a window first. I tried, but it stuck, and in my haste I broke one of the windowpanes. The smoke rapidly disappeared through the broken window, and was replaced by bitterly cold air.

My last fit of bad luck occurred on New Year's Eve. A few days earlier the flu had broken out, and several boys were in bed with high fevers and sore throats. Since it was planned that shortly before midnight most of the *Bund* would ski downhill with burning torches, the patients were brought to Herr Kirschlager's house, where they could be cared for while the others were away. The one taking care of them was I, the only who had neither skis nor the flu. Good boy that I was, I brought water to those who were moaning with thirst. But that was the limit of my nursing skills. Shortly before midnight I decided I should at least watch my friends' downhill run with their burning torches. This required that I put on my ski boots, which I had set to dry, alongside those of the patients, on a wooden platform built around the stove. I found my boots, grabbed the laces, pulled, and ten pairs of heavy ski boots came thundering down onto the floor. So much for the restorative sleep of my patients, who shot up and stared at me. I also missed the downhill run, which was over by the time I had attended to my patients and their footwear. When somebody told Gert Lippmann the following day about my clumsiness he pointed a finger at me and only said one word: "Töpper!" [Klutz]. With this nickname I have now lived for more than seventy years.

For me, 1934 was the year of the Mohicans. As standard-bearer, I considered it annoying that I had to spend time with activities such as going to classes or doing homework, so my grades grew worse and worse. The only things that mattered to me were the weekend overnight trips, the outings at Easter and Pentecost, and, in the summer of 1934, the big *Reichstreffen*, the national meeting of the entire *Bund* at Krüselin Lake near Thomsdorf in the Uckermark (a region northeast of Berlin).

At this time my first really close friendships developed. Unfortunately, they were accompanied by those painful experiences only puberty can produce. Public schools in Germany during this period were either for boys or girls; co-ed public schools didn't exist. In addition, contact between Jews and Aryans was strictly forbidden. Thus, in contrast to having to stay away from our "Aryan" classmates, we "non-Aryans" couldn't walk after class to the ("Aryan") girls' school nearby and start flirting with the *Mädchen*. Our *Bund* included a *Mädelschaft*, in which Jewish girls were organized just as we were in the *Bund's Jungenschaft*, the boys' league. For some reason I never learned, these two groups were strictly separated and operated independently from each other. Given these circumstances, for us in our male organization who were then deeply engulfed in puberty, everything was preconditioned. The homoerotic atmosphere—which at that time dominated in all youth organizations, ours included—was omnipresent, confusing, and agonizing, particularly for boys like me who hadn't yet been enlightened on sexual matters. (When I was more than sixty, I reproached my mother for never having told me the facts of life. She claimed that she'd tried several times to talk to me about sex but that I'd been so stupid that

Werner Angress ("Töpper") at the Reichstreffen [national meeting of the Bund, a Jewish youth movement] in Thomsdorf, July 1934.

whatever she said had gone in one ear and out the other. And yet I still see the two of us, probably sometime in 1933–34, waiting at Asternplatz for the 20 bus. I asked her where children came from. Mutti looked at me and shouted, "There comes the bus!" And that was that.)

In the end it was to Gert that I entrusted my problem, in the fall of 1934. He told me very matter-of-factly the tale of *la petite différence*. Whatever sexual behavior existed at that time in our organization was rather restrained and limited to occasional mutual masturbation among boys of the same age, at least in our group. But the jealousies thereby awakened, and the frustrations and fears that haunted us, could turn our lives into virtual Hell. If the Devil should show up at my door offering, in return for my soul, to give me back my thirteen- or fourteen-year-old youth, I would kick him out so fast he wouldn't know what hit him.

Nineteen thirty-four was also the year I discovered the beauty of the Mark Brandenburg and the lake region of Mecklenburg. When we went on our frequent overnight camping trips, we took the train, depositing our bicycles in the baggage car or a fourth-class compartment. Somewhere in the region of the campsite we left the train and biked the rest of the way. During vacations we usually stayed longer than one night. Occasionally we biked all the way from Berlin, or traveled by train but without taking our bikes along and then, upon arrival at our station, marched for many hours on the country roads with our heavy backpacks. We might reach our destination as late as midnight, since we couldn't leave Berlin before Saturday noon. Some of us, myself included, had school on Saturday morning and some of the older ones, mostly group leaders like Gert, worked at jobs until noon that day. At times we also left without knowing for certain where we were going.

If we went on longer hikes and didn't want to burden ourselves every night by putting up a tent, we found a farmer on the way who would let us sleep in his barn. If we wanted to stay longer at one place, we looked for a clearing, if possible close to a lake, and there pitched our tents. Each of us carried a shelter half and a blanket that we strung around our backpacks, along with the pegs we needed to pitch the tent. With flash-lights or, if we were lucky, by moonlight, we scrambled on all fours over the twelve shelter halves, buttoned them together, then pulled the whole thing up with a rope. Once we had secured everything with pegs, the big tent stood in front of us, stretched tight and rainproof, shelter for at least twelve of us to sleep in.

Now we could eat. All of us were obligated to take along on our overnights open sandwiches generally prepared by our mothers at home. Water we carried with us in canteens fastened to our belts, like the sol-diers we wanted to be. After sitting in a circle before the entrance of the tent each of us threw his food into the center of the circle, and Gert then distributed it at random. What usually happened was that, instead of the deliciously prepared sandwiches our mothers had made for us, we received a piece of bread covered with jam or similarly lackluster covering. But we had to eat what had been given to us: any exchange of sandwiches with a friend was forbidden. After some of our boys were careless enough to describe this routine at home, their mothers decided thenceforth to pre-pare "simple" sandwiches only—two slices of bread covered with sliced radishes or cucumbers—because their boy wouldn't get the "good sand-wich" in any event. Fortunately, not all mothers were so narrow-minded. Our dinners also had their traditional rites. Before we ate our sandwiches or, if the trips were longer than one night, simple meals cooked on the campfire, we all recited jointly an "eating poem." Here is an example:

As for taste, it's truly sad
People are different.
Chinaman Pipi Wang Hai
Eats each day a rotten egg.
And in Nishny Novgorod
Folks put even salt on bread.
But then, whether black, yellow, or white
What comes out is for all alike.

While singing this we beat in time on our mess kits with our spoons. Let's face it, we were still very young...

After supper we got into our tent and slept, freezing for the most part even though we lay pressed tightly against each other, until the last sentinel of the night woke us up. Keeping watch was part of the game. Each of us chosen by Gert had to sit for two hours during the night in front of the tent, listening and staring into the nocturnal landscape. In 1934, there were very practical reasons to do this. Any sound might indicate the approach of a group of Jungvolk or Hitler Youth, or just a group of our own *Bund*, wanting to surprise us and then join us for a couple of vacation days. Such incursions had to be reported to Gert immediately so he could decide whether we should wait quietly in our sleeping bags or quickly get dressed and prepare ourselves for the coming encounter.

During the day we played sports or skinny-dipped in a lake when no outsiders were around. I have never forgotten the landscape of Mark Brandenburg—the forests of pine interspersed with birch and oak, the sandy paths we negotiated for better or worse on our balloon bicycles— even though subsequently in the United States I encountered landscapes, especially in the West, that I still love today. Around campfires deep in the forest, we sang our songs and, at solstice, jumped through the flames, either alone or hand-in-hand with a friend. We also had to pass ordeals of courage and learn to read a compass and maps. To teach ourselves Morse code we practiced at night with flashlights and whistles.

The high point of our camping experiences was the *Reichstreffen* at Krüselin Lake in the summer of 1934, the first (and last) national meeting of the *Bund*. A farmer, Herr Peters of Thomsdorf, close to the Mecklenburg border, had offered us one of his pastures, and there we moved that summer, the "thousand boys" and the *Mädelschaft*, who pitched their tents some distance away from us. (Once at the lake, as we had undressed to go skinny dipping, one of the girls' leaders appeared on a hill above us, a sight that sent us diving hastily into the water. I can still hear her sarcastic voice, "Do you little rascals really think I've never seen anything like that before?" Then she turned around and disappeared.)

Herr Peters knew who we were. One day when I went with an older comrade to pick up a giant can of milk from his dairy barn, he said in passing that he considered the *Reichserbhof* Law to be a poor joke (the National Socialist regime used this federal inheritance statute to prevent non-Aryans from inheriting land and to confiscate land that wasn't under at least partial Aryan ownership). He was definitely not a Nazi.

During the five days of the *Reichtreffen*, from July 27 to 31, we roamed the giant pasture, held competitions in different sports, swam in the lake, took turns as standard-bearer, sang and ate around the campfire, stood guard at night, and spent considerable time digging underground tunnels to keep our food from spoiling in the heat of the summer. Groups from throughout the country showed up, pitched their tents, and got to know each other. I remember in particular the arrival of a group from Breslau in Silesia. While hiking along the coast of the Baltic Sea prior to the *Reichstreffen*, they had been attacked and badly beaten one night by a gang of Hitler Youth. We watched them limp toward the entrance gate of the pasture, their upper bodies bent forward, soundless, like distraught animals. When we lined up quickly to greet them, their figures grew tight, they stopped limping, and they entered the pasture singing in tight military formation. Many decades later I saw *The Bridge over the River Kwai*, in which Colonel Nicolson (played by Sir Alec Guinness) marches snappily with his badly hurt Tommies into Japanese imprisonment, whistling the "Colonel Bogey March," and couldn't help recalling that strange scene at the *Reichstreffen*.

We couldn't have known that the seeds of the *Bund*'s dissolution had already been sown. To begin with, there were difficulties about the organization's future ideology. The groups located in the south and west of Germany, led by the *Bundesführer*, Paul Yogi Mayer, wanted to place greater emphasis on Jewish elements and used the first evening of the *Reichstreffen*, a Friday, to hold an *Oneg Shabbat* (a celebration to honor the Jewish Sabbath, which lasts from Friday sundown to Saturday sundown). The invitation was declined by Berlin and Breslau, and possibly also by Hamburg and Hannover. As a result there was a split that first evening: at the one end of the pasture gathered those who wanted to worship; they lit Sabbath candles and said their prayers and blessings. Simultaneously, on our side of the pasture, we sat around a huge campfire, singing loudly and inconsiderately about wars, mercenaries, and related themes. Although we *Pimpfe* at first didn't understand what was happening, we soon figured it out. Thus the *Bund* split during the *Reichstreffen*. The majority of the regional groups followed Yogi in separating from the *Schwarzes Fähnlein*, and within the course of a few weeks they founded a *Bund* of their own, the *Blaue Schar* [Blue Troop].

The now much-smaller *Schwarzes Fähnlein* started life on its own. For some crazy reason our district now called itself "Freecorps Brandenburg," which prompted our rivals to sing, "Here comes Lippmann's wild and daring band!" (a parody of an early nineteenth-century military song). We Berliners were proud that Gert, the leader of the Mohicans, was now also leader of the entire organization.

Paul Yogi Mayer of Frankfurt am Main, who led our *Bund* until the fall of 1934, turned ninety in 2002. He lives in London. All his life he has coached and advocated for sports. During the 1980s and 1990s he gave talks in the Federal Republic of Germany about Jewish athletes. A few years ago he was awarded an honorary doctor's degree from Potsdam University, prompting him to write a dissertation about Jews and sport to "justify" his degree. It was only in recent years that we finally got to know each other, having met only very fleetingly in the summer of 1934 during the *Reichstreffen*. Now we two elderly gentlemen see each other occasionally in Berlin or London and talk about the youth movement that left such a strong imprint on both of us, but which we never have glorified nostalgically.[1]

The end of the *Schwarzes Fähnlein* came a few months later. While Yogi's *Blaue Schar* soon joined the *Ring-Bund Jüdischer Jugend* (Ring-Movement of German Jewish Youth, formerly the *Bund Deutsch-Jüdischer Jugend*, or BDJJ)—and stayed there until the *Ring-Bund* was dissolved by the government in 1936, our activities in the SF became increasingly restricted after our return from the *Reichstreffen*. Today we know that the National Socialist regime discouraged all assimilationist Jewish organizations, be they ones for youth or adults, as well as anyone

---

[1] In the summer of 1992, Gert Lippmann—who then spelled his name "Lippman" and lived in Sydney, Australia—and Yogi Mayer both happened to be in Berlin, and the three of us met for dinner one evening at Savignyplatz. During our polite, noncommittal conversation I attempted to take myself back spiritually nearly sixty years to the meeting at Lake Krüselin, but this effort did not succeed.

who continued thinking there was a future for Jews in Germany. Jews like us who so strongly emphasized their being German were "undesirable" by 1934. On the orders of the *Reichsjugendführung* (the National Socialist command of German youth organizations), we stopped wearing the jackets [*Jungenschaftsjacken*] that had led us to be taken for Jungvolk and were given new "uniforms," light-blue jackets and pants, that we liked much less. We were likewise forbidden to carry our flag in public, which made me an unemployed cornet. In addition, Gert was informed shortly after our return from Thomsdorf that henceforth the authorities had to be notified in advance of all *Heimabende* so that the meeting could be observed by a uniformed policeman. We still had the garage in Westend's Ahornallee—decorated by us with pictures, spears, and neckerchiefs—but now we had to wait for a police officer to show up and sit down with us. Given this presence, we became very careful about which songs we sang. The pleasure of the *Heimabende* gave way to anxiety.

In early December, an Aryan former classmate of Gert's, a man who now held a high position in the *Reichsjugendführung*, knocked late one evening at the door of Gert's apartment at Bozener Strasse 10. He informed Gert that the Schwarzes Fähnlein and several other German-nationalistic Jewish youth organizations would be dissolved by the state within days. Taking the initiative ourselves would have political as well as financial advantages. And if, after we had dissolved our organization, we met in small groups, we wouldn't be in violation of the *Reichsjugendführung*'s official dissolution order.

I didn't know anything about this development. At that time I lay in bed with a light flu, very happy that for a few days I wouldn't have to go to school. Late on the afternoon of December 8, when I no longer had a fever, Gert phoned me in Lichterfelde and told me curtly to get on my bike with the spear and flag and come to the headquarters in Ahornallee. Then he hung up. I got dressed and was ready to sneak out the back door when my mother appeared and asked where in God's name I was off to. There was a lively exchange, but I insisted on executing my leader's order. When I got to the garage I discovered that everyone had been waiting for me. No police officer was in sight. We jumped on our bikes and went to one of the lakes—I believe it was Grünewaldsee—at the edge of which we gathered on a small hill in the woods around a hastily lit fire. Meanwhile I had tied the flag to the spear. Gert then let us know briefly that the *Schwarzes Fähnlein* would dissolve itself the next day, December 9, to avoid a dissolution order from the *Reichsjugendführung*. (He didn't tell us then how he had found out about the impending order. I learned this only decades later when I read his memoirs.) He then pulled Ernst von Salomon's autobiographical novel *Die Kadetten* [*The Cadets*] out of his pocket and read us the book's final pages: "The Corps of Cadets no longer exists. Dismissed!" And there we stood in the cold, which we felt despite the fire, and looked sadly at each other. After a brief moment of silence, Gert ordered me to step up to the fire and lower the flag slowly into the flames until it was completely burned. Today this passage reads as if from a tearjerker novel. But for us at the time the self-dissolution of the *Schwarzes Fähnlein* was a decisive event. For the first time we sensed the regime's despotism in our own body, so to speak. We were Jews, and for this reason our *Bund* no longer had a right to exist.

After the *Bund* had dissolved itself our group continued its activities clandestinely for a little more than a year. We continued to go on trips, but in groups of no more than four or five and, of course, without uniforms or a flag. In 1934–35 we traveled in December again to the winter camp in Nieder-Klein-Aupa, and in the summer of 1935 we hiked from Hirschberg to Glatz, slept in our tents, and sat in the evenings around campfires we lit, as in the past, in hidden places in the woods. We continued to meet once a week for *Heimabende*, but now in our homes. It was above all friendship, not so much nostalgia for the dissolved *Bund*, that kept us together. We didn't want to fool the Nazis with our "illegality," as a colleague interpreted the situation many years later. We were still too young to be politically motivated. And yet, occasionally we sang with somewhat self-conscious grins a parody of one of our songs:

> We're marching through the corn fields,
> The flag we left at home.
> Many thousands stand beside us
> Who have been likewise forbidden.
> We called it "The Song of the Naked Men."

At this point one would be justified in asking whether we were so preoccupied with our youth movement that we didn't notice the political changes all around us. Of course, we were perfectly aware of Nazi politics both in daily life and especially through our *bündisch* activities. To begin with, we had to be alert to our environment in public and scrupulously careful not to arouse public attention or get into conflict with any of the Nazis' numerous party organizations. That was true before and after the dissolution of our *Bund*. While the last two years of the Weimar Republic were marked by long unemployment lines, emergency decrees, and political street fighting, after Hitler became chancellor "order" prevailed in the German Reich. This "order" consisted for the most part of men in uniform marching through the city streets with nailed boots, bellowing songs that ranged from the one about the "black-brown" hazelnut girl to the one about the knife that sent Jewish blood spurting. In addition, many German men wore brown or black uniforms and the little Hitler moustache. The subaltern adaptability displayed by so many Germans was staggering.

Faced with this turmoil, we "non-Aryans"—the appellation "racially inferior subhumans" came later—had to try and find our way, not a simple task for us in the Jewish youth movement, who were up to our ears in puberty and nationalists to boot. On the one hand, we admired and envied our "Aryan" companions who were "doing their duty" in the Jungvolk or Hitler Youth. On the other hand, we were excluded, publicly humiliated, and at times even physically threatened. That in 1933 we were already fair game for the Nazis we found out very soon, sooner than our parents did. And yet we continued to go on our night hikes, walking through Berlin wearing a dubious uniform, exposing ourselves to danger that still makes me shudder.

One Saturday in 1933, shortly after I joined the *Bund*, we went on a night hike in the Brandenburg countryside. It had gotten dark, so we looked around for a place to sleep. Gert, looking snappy in his uniform, which at that time still very much resembled the one worn by the Jungvolk, had us stop at a farm located in a village next to the highway on which we had come. He asked the farmer, who was also a bartender in a tavern close by, whether we could spend the night in his barn. The farmer said yes, and Gert led us to the door of the tavern, from which we heard loud voices. In that tavern what must have been more than a hundred Storm Troopers sat around long tables, drinking beer. The local militia was celebrating the weekend. As soon as we were standing in the glare we saw no other choice but to walk calmly between the long tables to the exit on the other side of the room. A rapid retreat would undoubtedly have aroused suspicion and might have prompted some of the Storm Troopers to take physical action. Thus we marched smartly and rather noisily through the room—our shoes had also soles with nails—Storm

Troopers to the right and left of us, in front of us safety in the form of the exit door leading to the barn. One of Hitler's rather tipsy fighters called out: "Now look at these snappy boys! Tough, and dark-looking like Italians." Had I been born a Catholic I would have crossed myself when we made it to the barn.

Another time, during a trip when we wanted to go camping for several days, we walked at night in single file through the forest. The path led to a clearing where a large campfire was burning. When I saw the brown uniforms and the swastika flag, my heart began to pound: this was a camp of Hitler Youth. While we stood there waiting for a word from Gert, we heard one of them yawn loudly and say, "Shit, what a bore this is today. Nothing happens!" We didn't need much imagination to visualize how they would relieve their boredom if they detected us. Gert whispered to the boy next to him an order that was whispered down the line: "Turn around and walk quietly and carefully to the place where we entered the forest." So we did, each of us with one hand on the shoulder of the boy ahead of him, giving the Nazi camp a wide berth. Several kilometers later we felt safe enough to pitch our tents in a clearing where we spent the weekend.

Then there was the day—most likely in the spring of 1934—when I was nearly arrested. As so often in those days I was riding my bike to Gert's apartment in Schöneberg—rather a long trip from Lichterfelde—when shortly after I passed Friedrich- Wilhelm-Platz I saw a Jungvolk boy who was likewise biking and who wore an insignia of his low rank. He passed and then stopped me. What *Verein* [association] did I belong to, he wanted to know. With my heart beating I replied to his question. Didn't I know, he asked, that uniform buttons displaying a lily had been forbidden? I looked at my jacket and saw the lilies, to which up to then I had never paid any attention. The lily on buttons and sometimes on flags was a traditional emblem of the *bündisch* youth movement, whereas the Jungvolk and Hitler Youth wore, naturally, only National Socialist insignia. Well, there we stood next to each other on the street with our bikes. The *Pimpf* was my age and height, but low as it was, his rank in the *Deutsche Jungvolk* set him above me, a mere member of a Jewish *Verein.* I'm not sure the boy even knew that it was a Jewish organization I belonged to. It is much more likely that he assumed I was a member of an outlawed non-Jewish *Bund.*

Be that as it may, he ordered me to follow him; he would take me to his *Bannführer*. The thought that I would have to go to an office of the Hitler Youth, dragged there by a *Jungvolk-Pimpf*, where they would certainly soon find out that it was a Jewish organization I belonged to, terrified me. Suddenly a thought struck me (this happens at times even to thirteen-year-old boys) and I suggested to the little Nazi that we should bike just a little further to my group leader who would be able to explain everything. Amazingly, it worked! The *Pimpf* who had wanted to arrest me merely nodded, and the two of us biked to Bozener Strasse 10, where Gert lived with his mother in a small downstairs apartment. Luckily, Gert was home. He threw me a questioning look as we entered and then walked through the apartment to his room, kicking in the process a small printing machine under a couch, since owning a printing machine could at that time get a Jew into trouble. As soon as he saw Gert, my *Pimpf* stopped acting like a sergeant but repeated, with less assurance, his complaint about the lilies on the buttons of my jacket. Gert listened, then shook his head very gently, almost sadly, and asked: "Don't you know the difference between a lily and a *Klewe*?" The *Pimpf*, looking confused, shook his head. What Gert further said I have forgotten, but the boy disappeared quietly just a little later. As soon as he was gone I turned to Gert, my group and district leader, and asked him what a *Klewe* was. He replied: "I just invented it." We never heard from the little Jungvolk sergeant again.

Other small events of this kind were less dramatic but still potentially dangerous. For instance, one day we rode with a regional train to a little town in Brandenburg. From there we would continue by bike until it was time to camp. Suddenly a small troop of girls from the *Bund Deutscher Mädchen* (the girls' section of the Hitler Youth) entered the compartment and soon began to flirt with us. Tightly pressed against each other, they occupied the seats in front of us and started to sing while grinning at us: "And if one bakes an omelet such as this, / then everything is perfect, / yes, that's the way it is." We remained calm, stared out of the window as if there were something special to be seen, and didn't move. Under "normal" circumstances the natural thing would have been for us to make contact with the girls, tease them a bit, and sing along with them. But we were no longer allowed to do that. Gert, who might have helped us out of this situation, wasn't there because he was riding to our meeting place on his motorcycle, "Balduin." That the girls didn't recognize us as Jews wasn't surprising because they probably only knew the stereotypes circulated by the Nazi press, and none of us looked like that. Fortunately they got off the train a few stations later, looking at us a little contemptuously, not because they had discovered who we really were but because we had reacted to their approaches with embarrassed silence. For today's readers all this may sound a little unreal, even frivolous. There we were, a bunch of Jewish boys living in a world that was hostile to us but still going camping regularly in the countryside around Berlin, showing our faces where we shouldn't, and running the danger of at least getting beaten up.

But while we did feel more and more isolated, we didn't feel seriously endangered. Our identification cards, which showed that we were members of the *Bund Schwarzes Fähnlein*, were legal and issued by the National Socialist *Reichsjugendleitung*. Thus as long as we could legally hold our weekly *Heimabende* and go camping, we didn't give much thought to the dangers (such as the bored group of Hitler Youth we nearly ran into in the woods).

Half a century after the Final Solution, many people will find it difficult to visualize the situation Germany's Jews then faced in any way other than how it has been shown on television (in programs like *Holocaust*) or in films such as *Shoah* and *Schindler's List*. But when we were thirteen and fourteen years old the smokestacks of the extermination camps didn't yet blow smoke. Auschwitz, Sobibor, Treblinka, and other extermination camps didn't even exist yet. The spots where they would subsequently be placed were still for the most part in the republic of Poland, a country with which Hitler in 1934 signed a ten-year nonaggression treaty. To be sure, there had been concentration camps in Germany since 1933, and Jewish and non-Jewish prisoners there were mistreated and occasionally killed. But initially Jews were a small minority in these camps and found themselves arrested because they had been active leftists. The road to Auschwitz was a winding one.[2] In 1933 and 1934 the Nazis began to think about how to get rid of the Jews, all of them, forever. For the time being, however, Jews still had a lot of leeway, despite the professional restrictions, harassment, and humiliations that began in early 1933. We made the best of our situation, not paying much attention to the government's steadily increasing anti-Semitic measures. Only knowing this can one understand why we kept putting ourselves in danger on our camping trips and risking other confrontations, which we considered "adventures."

One day in 1934, coming home from school on my bicycle, I rode

---

[2] Karl A. Schleunes, *The Twisted Road to Auschwitz* (University of Illinois Press, 1970).

to the side entrance of our apartment building on Unter den Eichen in Lichterfelde and found the path blocked by a bunch of Jungvolk boys who obviously knew me and had been waiting for me. So I swung my bicycle pump over my head and rode my good old balloon bike through the surprised little group and into safety. I felt like Karl May's Old Shatterhand, fighting his way through a bunch of hostile Kiowa.

What revealed the brutality and inhumanity of the regime clearly and for the first time was the so-called *Röhm Putsch* of June 30, 1934 (also known as "The Night of the Long Knives"). It was a Saturday, and our organization's Berlin leadership had decided for some unknown reason to use the weekend to drive to Frankfurt an der Oder with a hired truck and truck driver. In Frankfurt we were supposed to "raid" the local headquarters of the *Bund Deutsch-Jüdischer Jugend* [Movement of German Jewish Youth], our rivals, steal their flag, and return with this trophy to Berlin. The day was poorly chosen, but this none of us could have known. We left Berlin in the afternoon and about an hour later we were on the Rüdersdorf Müncheberg highway that led to Frankfurt. A private car passed us in which sat several men in uniform. The car stopped and a leader of the Reich Labor Service got out, signaled us to stop, and yelled the usual question: "What kind of *Verein* are you?"

A brief and whispered conversation ensued between Gert and his friend Harry "Harsch" Schulvater, whose group had joined us for this mission. Then Harsch jumped out of the truck and told the questioner who we were. Harsch had a non-Jewish mother and looked like a typical member of the Hitler Youth—tall, blond, blue eyes—the false Aryan hero. It seemed wiser to send the *Renommiergoy* [one looking and acting like a non-Jew] to talk to the Nazi leader than to let the black-haired Gert do it.

The man who had stopped us ordered the driver to take the truck off the road and not to move it again until the following day. If we didn't, then ... I have forgotten the threat, but a threat it was. And so we sat or stood for the next fourteen hours on a slope about fifty meters from the road and tried to figure out what all of this meant. The non-Jewish driver took off for the nearest village and came back with the news that there was something going on with the SA, but what exactly it was he didn't know. It was the first night in my young life when I didn't sleep a wink. We hadn't brought any blankets or sleeping bags because we had planned to return to Berlin the same night. I was glad that my parents and brothers had gone that weekend to Wannsee, where they had rented a place for the summer vacation. I was to follow them the next day with Erika and Frieda, the cook. Thus my absence that night wasn't noticed by my parents.

After dark we saw from our observation point columns of military trucks driving in the direction of Frankfurt an der Oder, and also in the direction of Breslau; at dusk military silhouettes appeared, wearing steel helmets and holding their rifles between their feet. Where they were headed, and why, we didn't know. Dresch whispered to me that those trucks were probably all *Reichswehr* [German Army], and that this night might in fact spell the end of the Nazi spook. But it wasn't *Reichswehr* that we saw pass on the road, it was SS.

Dead tired, we returned to Berlin the following morning, looking very sheepish. On the roofs of the streets leading into the city were SS men with machine guns. Several street crossings were closed with barbed wire. Nobody bothered about us after we had driven back into the city, returned the truck and its driver, and then parted as unobtrusively as possible. On the way home I saw the headlines in the *Völkischer Beobachter*, the major Nazi newspaper that was being sold in the kiosks: *Putsch*, *Putsch*, and *Putsch* [revolt] again. At that time we really believed that this was truly happening; to quote the anti-Nazi poet Erich Kästner, we "spread that nonsense on our bread." At home Erika told me that she and Frieda had heard shots all night long coming from the nearby former Lichterfelder cadet school where Hitler's elite SS unit, the *Leibstandarte* Adolf Hitler, was stationed. In the evening we read that men of the *Leibstandarte* had shot their former comrades of the SA. Naturally, the word "murder" was never used.

A few days later I had to deliver a letter written by Gert to another Berlin group leader, Gerhardt "Krümel" [bread crumb] Löwenthal, who was five years older than I. Somehow we started talking about the *Röhm Putsch* and he said something like, "Don't you know, Töpper, that this government is a bunch of criminals who don't know what the word *law* really means, who torture and murder people?" His words left a deep impression with me—though they took a while to sink in.

During the *Reichstreffen* at Lake Krüselin a few weeks later, I received an additional lesson. As the first group to arrive at the area reserved for our *Bund*, we had to make a number of preparations before the rest of the association showed up. Gert, who had ridden his motorcycle and had gotten there before us, told us about the murder of the Austrian chancellor, Engelbert Dollfuss, the day before. When we sat down in front of our tent for supper Gert also made it clear that he thought the

Nazi leadership was a bunch of criminals. The murder of Röhm and his fellow leaders and now the assassination of Dollfuss showed this without any doubt. But Gert's comments confused me as much as Krümel's had. How could a government be criminal, especially when it had been appointed by President Hindenburg? And yet, it must have been then that I began to separate in my head the Nazis and Germany. For instance, in the Jungvolk daybook I had selected for making my diary entries in 1935 I struck out Hitler's name and any references to the Führer and in their place penciled in "Germany." Very gradually it began to dawn on me that although the Nazis had introduced the cheaper *Teilstrecken* for Berlin buses (making short trips cheaper than a regular ticket) and planned to lead Germany to new glory, they also committed crimes which the Führer in long and tortuous speeches tried to justify as essential measures for national security. Thus it was the leaders of my *Bund* who made me begin to think. At that time I also began to listen more carefully to my grandfather's "slanderous" comments about the Nazis, which I had up to then internally rejected. And in 1935, at age fifteen, I also finally began to take my father's admonitions seriously.

For a while after the Schwarzes Fähnlein had been officially dissolved, it seemed that nothing had changed. But this appearance was deceptive. Gert left for Paris where his great-uncle Heinrich Stahl, a leader of Berlin's Jewish community, had gotten him a position with the local branch of the Victoria Insurance Company. Our group was now without a leader. We had to organize everything by ourselves, and even though Antek, who was slightly older than the rest of us, tried very hard to take Gert's place, things were no longer the same. In March 1935 we suffered another disappointment when Hitler reintroduced the national service law for the armed forces. It contained a clause stating that Jews were undesirable as German soldiers and relegating them to the *Ersatzreserve* II [Supplementary Reserve II]. Embittered by this, we sang among ourselves a parody of one of our songs, "The Emperor's Cavalry," which originally went like this:

> *The first regiment is marching*
> *In long columns*
> *Three or two abreast,*
> *And in the rear the captain.*
> *Tarü-tara, tarü-tarei,*
> *We are the emperor's cavalry... .*

Instead of the last line, we sang, "We are substitute reserve."

The crowning example of our attempts to "Germanize" despite the external political developments was our final winter camp during the Christmas and New Year's holidays of 1935–36. Thereafter the group dissolved. Some members emigrated, others probably perished in the Final Solution. My contact with most of them broke off for good after this last gathering. Once more we traveled to Nieder-Klein-Aupa to meet there with Gert, who came from Paris, and a few small groups of the former *Schwarzes Fähnlein* that for more than a year now had also operated illegally. Before we went on this trip our Berlin group had rehearsed a play Dresch had written and which we wanted to present at Nieder-Klein-Aupa. Similar to my short stories that portrayed us as soldiers in a war conducted by Germany, Dresch's play had also as its core a "Declaration of Belief in Germany." During the last scene we all stood in a circle, each boy's arms over the shoulders of his neighbors, and sang, full of emotion:

Holy Fatherland [who are] in danger,
Your sons crowd around you....
Look how all of us
Stand by you, son by son.
You will never perish, [our] country,
Although we shall!

I was surprised by Gert's disgust at our dramatic effusion. My parents, to whom I read some passages before departing for our winter camp, reacted similarly.But none of this held us back. We only sobered up when Gert very carefully prepared us for the return trip home by "playing theater." Pretending to be an SS interrogator, Gert asked each of us in turn what we had done abroad and if we belonged to a *Verein*. When we got to the border the next day, one after the other and not as a group, no such questions were asked. All the guards did was inspect our baggage, which contained primarily used underwear.

That concluded my time in the—at the end illegal—youth movement. It had given me a communal life that, as a Jew, I wouldn't have found anywhere among my non-Jewish peers. It had also been the first time that I was able to determine an—admittedly very restricted—aspect of my life largely by myself. In the *Bund*, and especially among the Mohicans, I made friends and learned to think about the concerns of others and not just my own.

Our trips on weekends or during vacations opened my eyes to the beauty of the landscape, whether around Berlin, in Silesia, or in the Sudetenland. I had also learned how to sleep in the open and protect myself from the cold, how to pitch a tent, and how to light a campfire. But most important for all of us was our close community, the feeling of belonging together as it manifested itself when singing our songs, during nocturnal hikes, or sitting around the campfires at night in the woods. It was a period of juvenile romanticism, frequently accompanied by strong adolescent eroticism, thirst for adventure, and an idealism that looks rather questionable in retrospect. Finally, it gave us, for a very limited time, some distance and diversion from the anti-Semitism not just of the National Socialist regime but, increasingly, of the general population as well.

CHAPTER 4

Gross Breesen Training Farm for Emigrants, 1936–1937

It having been decided at the beginning of 1935 that I wouldn't continue on to the *Abitur* (the high school diploma obtained after passing an examination), the question gradually arose as to which profession I should pursue. This matter should have become all the more urgent to me in September 1935 when the Nuremberg race laws were announced, but the declaration made no particular impression on me; I didn't even mention it in my diary. It was only when our servant girl at the time, who had managed our household after Frieda and Erika departed, was obliged to leave us because she was under forty-five (younger "Aryan" women were no longer allowed to be domestics for Jews) that I began to wake up. My brother Fritz and I now had to help with the washing up after dinner and otherwise lend our mother a hand. Our attempts to hire a male and then a female domestic older than forty-five were pathetic failures, so we had to look for a "non-Aryan," which wasn't so simple. The reality of National Socialist anti-Semitism, which until then I had almost never experienced outside of school, had intruded into our home life in a very concrete manner.

On a Sunday not long after the announcement of the Nuremberg Laws, my father proposed that we take a walk together. We walked down Victoria-Wildenow-Strasse along the botanical gardens and past the villa of the *Reichsbauernführer* Walter Darré, where two SS guards stood outside. In a low voice that trembled with stifled agitation, Papa told me I could no longer remain in Germany. The Nazis had instituted the Nuremberg Laws to take away the Jews' rights and honor. The younger generation to which my brothers and I belonged no longer had a future in our country and thus had to think about emigrating. His generation would in all likelihood have to stick it out in Germany. He told me to think about what profession I wanted to learn in the coming year after I finished school, and he would try to find some practical training for me.

So for the first time I had to think about what I wanted to do with my life. Of course I talked it over with my friends in our group, but the professions they were interested in didn't coincide with my ideas. Vici, for example, wanted to be a printer like his father. Knirps was apprenticed to a plumber. The others wanted to go into the clothing industry or other such practical professions, and some had already started their training. But I had more romantic notions. Partly because of the love of nature that I had acquired in the youth movement, partly because of the books I was reading at the time, especially Ernst Wiecherts's stories and novels, I tended toward something elementary, something related to nature. I was convinced that I loved living with animals, which years later proved to have been an error. So not long after our conversation I told my father that I would like to work in a zoo (according to my diary this must have been in early October 1935). He instructed me to write a letter to the director of the Berlin zoological garden, Dr. Lutz Heck, applying for a training position as a *Wärter* [zookeeper]. Amazingly (in hindsight), I received a personal reply. Dr. Heck informed me that zoo employees were included under the *Arierparagraph* (a law precluding non-Aryans from becoming civil servants), and for that reason he couldn't take me on as a trainee. Considering the political circumstances of the time, Dr. Heck's personal, polite way of writing to a Jew was remarkable. I wish I had saved his letter. My father didn't seem impressed by the zoo director's good manners. "Look, even the monkeys are anti-Semitic," he said.

A few weeks later my father called my attention to a short item in the *CV Zeitung*: the *Reichsvertretung der Juden in Deutschland* [National Representative Agency of Jews in Germany] announced that a Jewish training farm for prospective emigrants was about to be founded. Its purpose was to provide training in agriculture and teaching crafts to non-Zionist boys and girls to prepare them for future group emigration to countries other than Palestine. I sent an application to the *Reichsvertretung*. Before an answer arrived we moved again, for the fifth time in my young life, this time from Lichterfelde to Wilmersdorf and the former apartment of Onkel Arthur and Tante Rosa at Holsteinische Strasse 24. They had meanwhile moved into a smaller apartment to wait for a move abroad, following their children, who had recently settled in Brazil.

On April 1, shortly after I left school with my mediocre final report card, I got a telephone call. A Professor Bondy asked me to come immediately to the main office of the *Reichsbund Jüdischer Frontsoldaten* [RJF, Jewish War Veterans League] at Kurfürstendamm 200. He wanted to talk to me about my application to the Jewish training farm. That was all he said before hanging up. My first reaction was skepticism. One of my friends was probably playing a joke on me. They all knew that I had applied, and one of them had obviously chosen April 1 to send me on a bike trip to Kurfürstendamm. I phoned a few of them, but they all vehemently denied playing an April Fool's joke on me. Still dubious, I rode my bike over to Kurfürstendamm 200. There I met the man who during the coming few years was to form my character more than anyone else before or after, including my parents.

Curt Bondy was two days before his forty-second birthday when I walked into his office for the first time. He was joined by a volunteer assistant and friend, Hans Quentin. Bondy sat at a table covered with files and shook my hand without getting up. I had hardly ever seen such an ugly man! His younger brother Fritz told me later that he'd once

said to Curt: "Man, you're so ugly, you seem downright handsome again." There was some truth to this. Curt Bondy's gray-blue eyes pierced me so that I hardly noticed the rest of his face. He offered me a seat and Hans Quentin handed him a file (containing my application, I assumed). Then the questions started. Most of them I can't remember anymore. But I know that I felt very unsure of myself, especially when Bondy wanted to know how I felt about being Jewish. Since I knew as little about his own position on that subject as I knew anything else about him, I was tempted to describe myself as a conscien-

Professor Curt Bondy at Gross Breesen in 1936.

tious Jew. Instead I told the truth. Without commenting Bondy went on to the next point, and after about fifteen minutes I climbed back on my bike and rode home. Bondy hadn't given me any indication of the status of my application, only that I would receive news soon.

A few days later I got another call informing me, to my great relief, that I had been accepted. I was told to come to Bondy's office at the RJF headquarters every day that he was away. I and another boy would staff the office and wait for Bondy to phone with instructions. Incoming letters were to be put unread in the applicants' files, which we were strictly forbidden to look at (especially if they were our own). So began my first job, albeit unpaid. Every day I sat in the office with one of my future Breesen roommates, either Jochen Feingold or Gerd Tworoger, nicknamed "Dackel" (short for dachshund). We had hardly anything to do. The biggest challenge was just getting into the office, passing through one of those "Berlin rooms" (where the RJF employees, mostly soldiers, worked), without being scolded by one of the RJF board members who were sitting there. On the first day I tiptoed through the room, so as not to disturb anyone. The Jewish war veteran on desk duty that day barked at me, "Don't creep through the room like a cat! You're a German boy. Stand up straight!" The next day someone else was sitting there, and when I stamped over the wooden floorboards in good military posture, I was snapped at again: Did I think I was on a parade ground? A little consideration, please, and so on.

Our job at Kurfürstendamm 200 didn't last long. The *Reichsvertretung* [the Jewish Agency] found an appropriate training farm at the end of April. After difficult negotiations with the district administration, the agency leased Gross Breesen, a former knight's manor in the district of Trebnitz bei Obernigk in Silesia (today western Poland). It still formally belonged to a Herr Rohr, a Polish Jew who had bought the property at the end of the First World War and then settled with his family on other land he owned in Poland. Breesen, as we usually called it, is today named Brzezno and is about thirty kilometers north of Wrocław (formerly Breslau). I described the farm in my diary: "Standing in the middle of rolling terrain with nice groves of trees and a roomy manor—the *Schloss* ["the Castle," as the farm laborers called it], which stood apart from the barns and the extremely primitive housing of the permanent laborers— was very suitable as an institution for agricultural education."

I left Berlin for Gross Breesen on the morning of May 9, 1936, together with another boy, Walter Steinberg, who only stayed at Breesen a very short time. My mother accompanied me to the Zoo train station, and our parting was quick and painless. A new part of my life was beginning, the first time I was leaving home and family, and my preoccupation with the unknown and the new experiences that lay before me outweighed any inclination toward a tearful farewell. Besides, I had already gained some inner distance from my family during my youth movement days, so that, when the train finally pulled out of the station, I dutifully waved until the first curve and then sank into my seat with something like relief. When we arrived in Breslau, we changed to a slow local train that took us to Gellendorf, and there we found ourselves alone at the little depot. Nobody had come to pick us up. Walter, whose job it had been to forewarn the people at Breesen of our arrival, swore to God that he had sent a postcard with our arrival time.

There we were feeling miserable, standing on the empty platform with our suitcases. There was nothing left to do but leave our bags at the baggage check and find out how to get to Gross Breesen on foot. The stationmaster—who also took care of baggage, sold tickets, and probably swept the floor—gave us precise directions in a dialect that sounded very strange to us. Then we set off on foot along the Gellendorfer Landstrasse to Breesen, which was lined with apple trees on both sides. A bit over an hour later we arrived at the estate and were received in a rather unfriendly way by the Professor, as we called Bondy at the beginning. Why hadn't we notified him of our arrival? Where had we left our baggage? Unsatisfied with our answers he assigned me to the room I would share with Jochen and Dackel, the boys I had worked with at Kurfürstendamm 200. Sighing, I got myself a mattress, laid it in a free space on the floor (bunk beds and wardrobes didn't arrive for weeks) and considered my future with mixed feelings.

Jochen, Dackel, and Hans Quentin (Bondy's assistant, who joined us a few days later) all were assigned to the group living in the same room as I was. Together with a small group of Breeseners, Jochen emigrated to Kenya in 1939 as an agricultural worker. There he became a farm manager and eventually the owner of two large agricultural estates. He stayed in the country during the Mau Mau rebellion (though he sent his wife and children to England) and later became agricultural advisor to the government of Jomo Kenyatta. He died a few years ago in England.

Like me, Dackel, who got his nickname in the *Bund Deutsch-Jüdischer Jugend* [German Jewish Youth Association], emigrated in 1939 to the United States, where we both worked at Hyde Farmlands, a farm in Virginia leased for Gross Breeseners. After the war he became the owner of a large transport company in Florida. He died a few years ago of cancer.

Our "model Aryan," Hans Quentin (we always called him Hänschen), was a special case. For years he had been Bondy's assistant in different teaching positions, and this association continued after Bondy, as a Jew, was fired in 1933 from Göttingen, where he was a university lecturer. In the meantime Hänschen had started to study law. Following Bondy's advice that he protect himself as a student under the National Socialist state, he joined the *Sturmabteilung* [SA, the political fighting troops of the Nazi Party], but only pro forma. He never did any duty in the SA. Shortly after Gross Breesen was founded he came to the farm to deliver Bondy's car and was supposed to return home the following day, but he never did. The day of his arrival he was assigned to our room. He talked with us intensely the whole evening, and the next morning he told a perplexed Bondy that he wanted to stay and work at Gross Breesen, if Bondy would allow it.

"Storm Trooper" Quentin stayed more than a year as an intern at the Gross Breesen Jewish training farm for emigrants, living in our room and becoming our friend. He left us to study theology after realizing that under the given political circumstances it wouldn't be appropriate to study law, as he had originally planned. He spent the Second World War on the western front, in Italy, and at the end was a U.S. prisoner of war. When the war was over, having been an SA man, he had to be "de-Nazified" before he could finish his studies. Bondy wrote a letter taking full responsibility for having advised Hans Quentin to join the Storm Troopers in 1933, and Hänschen was able to finish his degree in theology. He became a Protestant minister, married, had two children and five grandchildren, and died in Kassel in December 1995 at the age of eighty-four.

I stayed at Gross Breesen only one-and-a-half years. But in spite of its short duration, my time there influenced me profoundly for the rest of my life. I soon noticed that the Gross Breesen community was very similar to the *Schwarzes Fähnlein* [SF, Black Platoon]. This wasn't surprising, since a high percentage of the agricultural trainees (soon more than one hundred boys and girls) came from the German Jewish youth movement, that is, the *Bund Deutsch-Jüdischer Jugend* [BDJJ, Association of German Jewish Youth] and the *Schwarzes Fähnlein*. Two such friends were Knirps, who had been a Mohican, and Edda, who had belonged to another group I knew well. The latter's real name was Max Neumann, but since he was a redhead we called him Edda, an acronym for *ewiger Dachstuhlbrand* ["roof always on fire]."

The influence of the youth movement revealed itself, for instance, in the composition of our room groupings. Thus, the dozen boys in our room, known collectively as "the Hanniots" [*Hannioten*], almost all came from the BDJJ or the SF. We held our *Heimabende* once a week after work, sang our old youth movement songs, and at Friday dinner wore our "room uniform," which consisted of a plaid shirt and blue shorts. Why were we called "the Hanniots"? Almost all of the groups of roommates were known by the name of their oldest member, who usually had come to Gross Breesen as an intern. In our case this was Hermann Ollendorf of Breslau, who in the youth movement had gotten the nickname "Hannio," a combination of Hanno from Thomas Mann's novel *Buddenbrooks* and Tonio from Mann's novella *Tonio Kröger*.

Strangely, I wasn't aware of the irony of our position in 1936. We trainees of both sexes lived in a stately manor (the "Schluss," dialect for *Schloß* [castle]) bordered by a beautiful park. And in that manor we had all the modern conveniences, like electric lights, central heating, and bathrooms with hot and cold running water. On the other side of the fence lived the "Aryan" permanent farmworkers, called *Instleute*, with their families. Their quarters above the cow and horse barns of the estate were oppressively small and had no electric lights, toilets, or running water. A wooden outhouse stood on a huge pile of manure under the windows of their rooms, but only the adults were allowed to use it; the children and teenagers were sent directly to the manure pile. The water for drinking and washing came from a pump at the lower end of the manure pile, and since the whole estate sloped down considerably from the Castle to the manure pile, you can imagine how hygienic the drinking water was that came out of that pump.

In a number of ways, the estate seemed quite feudal. On Saturday afternoons, for example, the workers stood in line in front of the house of the *Schaffer* [overseer], who held a list of names and bags and baskets full of food. When he called a name, that man or woman stepped forward and received, first, the payment in kind (the bags of food). Then the mustached, basically quite good-natured overseer took out his wallet and paid the rest of the individual's weekly wages. Very rarely did I see an amount change hands that was great enough to require a paper bill.

In other words, the people were paid just as they had been for hundreds of years on the large estates of eastern Germany.

Our relationship with the permanent farmworkers was quite delicate. On the one hand, we often worked with them, for example hoeing out the weeds in the potato and turnip fields, harvesting the crops, or helping the drivers of the horse teams. On the other hand, any kind of fraternity beyond work was strictly forbidden. The permanent farmworkers were "Aryans," we were "non-Aryans," and between us stood, like an invisible wall, the race policies of the National Socialist government. And so we worked next to but not with one another in the fields (all of which had names—Paschäke, der Grosse Fuchsberg, and so on). On the one side were the women farmworkers in their poor working clothes, on the other we young Jewish trainees. The women workers (the men were usually team drivers and didn't do group work with us) were paid for piecework and were almost always ahead of us. We tried to keep pace with them, but we seldom succeeded, especially since we talked with each other a lot, at least during the first few weeks. It didn't help much when the short, plump farm manager Gamroth, also "Aryan," ran behind us and urged us on in his Silesian dialect. When our job was to remove the stones from a field, he threw at us small stones we had overlooked, sometimes hitting one of us. We didn't take him seriously at the beginning, but we reacted immediately when Head Manager Erwin Scheier or the most respected of the interns, "Wastl" Neumeyer of Munich (whose father was a high Bavarian legal official), both Jewish, showed up at our field and let us know what they expected of us.

During the first break, around ten o'clock, the girls from the manor kitchen brought out malt coffee and slices of bread with plum jam. We sat and ate separately from the women farmworkers. Now and then one of them called out to us a sarcastic remark, usually something to do with our lack of experience and our slowness, but that was generally the extent of our contact with the permanent farmworkers, male or female. There was only an occasional exception. For example, one day during the first hay harvest in June 1936, I was sitting with some of the other trainees and one of the permanent farmworkers, named Pilz (Mushroom—this was not a nickname!) in front of the open barn door waiting for the next hay wagon that we had to unload. Suddenly Pilz took off his cap, pointed to his bright red hair, and murmured just loud enough for us to hear, "That's how I used to vote." That was all, but it told me enough. Nothing like that ever happened again.

Our separation from the permanent farmworkers avoided what could have been problems in 1936 and 1937. It wasn't until November 10, 1938, the day after Kristallnacht, that the farmworkers demonstrated their feelings toward the residents of the "Schluss" by wrecking it. Not a hair on any boy's or girl's head was harmed. Today I think the bitterness they showed that day was directed mainly at people "up there" generally, whoever they were, and at the Castle as a symbol of social repression, rather than specifically at the Jewish trainees. At that time the trainees just happened to be the residents of the manor. But I was no longer in Breesen then.

A few years ago, consulting the newly opened "'Special Archives"' in Moscow, I discovered that the secret service [*Sicherheitsdienst*, or SD] of the SS leader [*Reichsführer-SS*] was well informed about Gross Breesen, which is mentioned several times in the documents. It appears likely that the Gestapo, which worked closely with the SD starting in 1937, was also well informed. Naturally, I wonder who delivered information about the staff and trainees of Gross Breesen to the SD and Gestapo. There are no clear clues, not to mention evidence. But in my opinion only two people were likely to have been informers: the farm manager Gamroth and the *Schaffer*. Both were in constant contact with us, and both were intelligent enough to meet the demands of the SD or the Gestapo. Back then it never occurred to me that we might be watched.

In the short time most of us spent at Gross Breesen, a sense of community developed thanks to which many of us who are still living continue to keep in touch, and the human values that Bondy transmitted to us have guided us over the decades. From the youth movement many of us brought a sense of community and a feeling of belonging that, in the completely new circumstances of Gross Breesen, became stronger and stronger. In addition, we brought with us from our time in the *Bund* a romantic idea of nature and animals that our hard daily work, usually anything but romantic, never dimmed. Bondy also came from the youth movement, not the Jewish one but rather the general German youth movement of the prewar period.

Who among the leaders of the *Reichsvertretung* [German Jewish Agency] decided to appoint Bondy as the director of the training farm can no longer be ascertained. But the idea was a stroke of genius. Bondy was an educator as well as a psychologist. He had done a lot of work with young people—including with young prisoners when he was the director of the Hanöfersand prison in Hamburg—and he combined authority with an ability to understand, sympathize with, and even befriend us. Back then we didn't concern ourselves with the fact he was a bachelor. Today I realize that he was one of those homosexuals who suppress their predisposition by devoting themselves to their work, who live through their tasks and don't try to have a real private life. To us he was "Herr Professor," the man we admired and respected for his fairness and obvious sense of responsibility for our training and our future. But sometimes we were also afraid of him, such as when he was dissatisfied with us and gave us a lecture.

Saturday wasn't a workday in the fields for most of us, so that morning everyone except those who had duty in the cow or horse barns would meet on the back porch of the Castle. There Bondy spoke about problems that had come up during the week, then invited discussion. He called these informal talks *Lebenskunden* [Life lessons], and through them he transmitted to us values that most of us held on to for the rest of our lives. Honesty, responsibility, sincerity with ourselves and others, and especially "consciousness-raising" about our own behavior—these were the subjects that we talked about and that he sometimes gave rather pompous titles, like "The Technique of Intellectual Work," "The Individual's Responsibility to the Community," "Speaking and Being Silent," "Work and Recreation," and so on.

I usually sat somewhere on the edge of the group and tried not to attract attention. I never wanted to participate in the discussion; the mere thought of standing up and saying something in front of my fellow trainees made me panic. In my wildest dreams I couldn't have imagined that thirty-six years later I would give lectures to hundreds of students. But I listened carefully and completely uncritically, hanging on every word Bondy said.

At many points the "life lessons" continued what we had learned in the youth movement. Bondy drilled into us that a boy must be loyal, brave, and ready to sacrifice. Above all, he had to put the group's interests before his own, an idea similar to the Third Reich dictum *Gemeinnutz geht vor Eigennutz* ["The common good goes before private concerns"]. Of course Bondy—ever the educator and psychologist—also talked about the relationship of the individual to the community, but it was most important to him that we young people work on ourselves, that we pay conscious and critical attention to our own behavior, to how we reacted to other people and to our work and, if necessary, that we change that behavior.

The words "consciousness-raising" and "sense of responsibility" came to be engraved more and more deeply in our minds, or at least in mine. I didn't recognize until many years later the extent to which this eloquent man instilled in us his own rather elite values, and molded and strengthened our characters. He wanted to create a basis from which we could develop into people with strong principles who could go their way alone and shape their own lives, regardless of the circumstances. Considering the short time his Gross Breesen experiment existed (1936–39), Bondy's education led to remarkable success in most of us. That is what we discovered, in any case, when, half a century after the founding of Gross Breesen, about fifty of us from the United States, South America, Europe, and Australia got together for a reunion in Israel in May 1986.

His pedagogy, however, wasn't without controversial aspects. The rank of sergeant that he attained in the First World War had gotten into his bones. He took discipline very seriously, which was in many ways quite necessary. But occasionally he exaggerated and thus made a fool of himself. For example, every Sunday morning we had "inspection." With the exception of the area the girls occupied, he went from room to room, inspecting the wardrobes and gliding his hand along the heating pipes to check for dust.

Each of us shared a wardrobe with one other roommate; I shared mine with Hermann Neustadt of Breslau who, like me, had been in the Schwarzes Fähnlein. Being very good-looking, he acquired in his SF group the nickname "Prinz" [Prince]. We quickly became good friends and have stayed so for the rest of our lives. The only son of a wealthy stocking manufacturer, Prinz was lovingly spoiled by his parents. After his training at Gross Breesen he emigrated to the United States and served four years in the U.S. Army during the Second World War. He earned a Ph.D. in agriculture and worked overseas, especially in Latin America and Somalia. He never married. When I visited him in San José, Costa Rica, a few years before his death in 1998, he was a wealthy but lonely man.

When we first met, Prinz was lazy and messy. I had to straighten up our wardrobe carefully early every Sunday morning so we didn't fall victim to Bondy's passion for order. I put the underwear, handkerchiefs, shirts, and so on, on our respective shelves in precise piles (except for the socks, which lay nicely in rows of three in front of the underwear) and waited with pounding heart for the arrival of the big man. With an icy face, he started his hunt for dust, going first to the heaters, then the window sills, and finally the wardrobes. Then the sparks flew. If the laundry wasn't piled straight as a ruler, or if dirty laundry hid behind a carefully arranged Potemkin pile of shirts, Bondy swept the entire contents of the wardrobe onto the freshly cleaned floor with a couple of grandiose gestures. The wardrobe I had straightened up always passed inspection, but for some reason almost no other did. When Bondy went out the door without a word and stepped into the next room, where we all were waiting for him, our room looked like a battlefield.

One day—I believe it was sometime in early 1937—Dackel, Jochen, and Hänschen suggested to me that I explain to Bondy the emotional havoc he was wreaking with his Sunday inspections. Hänschen, who had known him the longest and best and was the oldest among us roommates, gave me more precise instructions on one of the following Sundays, after another catastrophic inspection, and so shortly after lunch that day I went to Bondy's room, which was directly across the hall from ours, and rang the bell. Like all the doors in the Castle, it had double doors with a space in between, and next to the outer door Bondy had installed a sort of traffic light that shone green, yellow, or red. On green, one could enter. On yellow, one could enter only if it was urgent. On red, one wasn't allowed to enter.

That Sunday the light was green. Bondy was just about to begin his half-hour afternoon nap: he was lying on his sofa under a blanket and looked at me searchingly. I felt quite unsure of myself, but after he invited me to sit I took a chair next to the sofa and explained why I had come. I said that I was a delegate, stressed how demoralizing his Sunday inspection methods were, and emphasized that the impression on newcomers was especially devastating. Bondy lay there with his eyes closed and said nothing. When I had finished talking and was sitting there quietly, he opened his eyes, stared at the ceiling, and said something like, "Thank you, Töpper, for speaking to me so openly. I will think about it." So I was allowed to leave. He tried for a while to proceed less drastically, but the Sunday inspections remained an annoyance, at least for us. Many years later, when I reminded him of that conversation, he said he had been very impressed that I had spoken to him about that matter. He knew how hard it must have been for me to "bell the cat," so to speak. I could only agree.

Bondy's attitude toward sex in Breesen was interesting and, for many of us adolescents, frustrating. But any scandal—such as, for example, the pregnancy of a fifteen-year-old girl—was to be avoided at all costs. So Bondy's "life lessons" made clear that sex had to wait until marriage, which of course wasn't in the foreseeable future for any of us. During my stay at Breesen there was one uproar because of this matter. In retrospect it seems almost ridiculous, but at the time it shook Gross Breesen to its foundations.

On the evening that sex reared its impudent head, I had returned from the fields and was taking off my dirty boots in the basement to get ready to shower. At that moment a young emissary of the staff came in and told those of us who had just gotten back from work that all the boys were to report immediately to the dining hall without showering or changing clothes, and the girls were to go to another room. Bondy wanted to speak to the boys, and the Head Manager's wife, Frau Scheier, under whose guidance and custody the girls were being trained, was to speak to the girls. When I walked into the dining hall, most of my comrades were sitting silently in their chairs. Bondy, also silent and grim-faced, stood at a lectern and scrutinized us through his glasses. When everyone was finally there, Bondy began to explain to us the reason for this unscheduled meeting. A trainee had made a lewd proposal to one of the girls (she wasn't even attractive, in my eyes), who had reported this to Bondy. The Professor now continued with a twenty-minute "life lesson" out of all proportion to what had happened.

And what did happen? A trainee had suggested to a girl that she sleep with him. Instead of simply telling the boy no, the girl rushed to Bondy, probably to show how important she was, and Bondy immediately made a major affair out of a bagatelle. Remembering this incident still embarrasses me. We all sat there wretched, wishing Frau Scheier would come and call us to dinner. But she was busy telling the girls about the "shameful act" to which one of them might have fallen prey. As I learned later, she did this very briefly, without drama but with visible discomfort. Then she sent the girls to their rooms. We boys, however, received a lecture about the possible consequences for Gross Breesen of the pregnancy of an unmarried, underage trainee, none of which was news to us. He then said that he had thrown the Casanova out at once, sending him home to his parents. (Shortly afterward, the boy emigrated to South America.)

We boys sat in silence, hoping that we could finally go shower. When Bondy, still looking grim, asked if anyone wanted to say anything, I raised my hand, I who wanted nothing other than to flee the stupid situation. Why I raised my hand, I still don't know today. Maybe I wanted to somehow reduce the tension. Later in life I often reacted that way, especially in departmental meetings at the university, when my colleagues were ready to physically attack each other. In any case, I stood up and said that since at the moment no girls were present, I wanted to point out something. On the basis of my recent experience with laundry duty (to which we all were assigned a day or two a month), I wanted to suggest that people should wipe their bottoms better, as it was very embarrassing for me in the presence of Frau Scheier and the girls to see the filthy underpants that had been put in the laundry. After all, we had enough toilet paper. To my relief Bondy, who surely could have reacted differently, nodded his head several times. Töpper was right, he said, and we were to make a greater effort in that regard. Then we were allowed to leave.

Twice I was almost thrown out of Breesen. The first time was probably in spring or summer of 1936, when I had started my six-week training session in the dairy barn. The *Ober* (short for *Oberschweizer* [head dairyman]), whose name I never learned, was a short man who was supposedly henpecked at home. In the barn, however, he was a tyrant. He gave us (about six trainees, sometimes including girls, who could volunteer to do duty in the dairy barn) our orders in his pronounced Silesian accent as he walked through the barn. The barn itself was a relic of past times. Probably built in the eighteenth century, maybe even earlier, when Gross Breesen was still a knight's castle, it was completely outdated and impractical. On top of that it stank of a mixture of cow dung, hay, distiller's wash (the liquid residue from potatoes that were made into alcohol), and soiled straw on which the cows stood or lay. The "Frisian" animals lay in their own filth most of the year. Although they grazed in the meadow in the summer and were curried and combed after every morning milking year-round, most of the filth stayed encrusted in their hair, especially since they lay in the straw every night, summer and winter, and the straw was dirty again every evening. There were no milking machines at Gross Breesen, although these had already been introduced in the United States and in a few other European countries. At Gross Breesen we were supposed to learn to milk by hand.

A trainee who had duty in the dairy barn got up around four in the morning, quickly ate breakfast, and went across the courtyard down to the barn, where the *Ober* assigned him a row of cud-chewing cows. Then the trainee had to milk five, six, or more cows, depending on his skill. Sitting down on a three-legged stool and wiping down the udder as well as possible with a dirty rag, the trainee began carefully to pull on the teats. This usually hurt the cow, and she kicked at the milker with her right rear leg, tipping the bucket over. Since the sound of a bucket kicked by a cow could be heard all over the barn, the *Ober* was suddenly standing next to the poor unfortunate who had caused the "accident," loudly reprimanding him in Silesian dialect.

When the trainee was finally finished in the evening, after having unloaded the heavy and somehow always matted green fodder and fed it to the cows, he could go back to the Castle. There he had to eat separately from the other Breeseners, because in spite of a shower he still stank of the dairy barn. During this phase of training he was a pariah.

When I began my six weeks in the dairy barn, I had just found the first girlfriend of my life, and we loved each other ardently, albeit within the restrictions Bondy had set for us trainees. Kissing was allowed, but what girl wanted to get close to a boy who smelled like a cow barn? After about four weeks of dairy barn duty, I rebelled. One morning shortly before one of the longer breaks, the *Ober* gave me an order and I told him I was first going to take a rest. A quite lively dialogue ensued, which ended with the *Ober* throwing me out of the dairy barn and forbidding me to come back, shouting that I was to report this to the "Prufessor" immediately. Feeling uneasy, I went across the courtyard to Bondy's door, where I got the literal green light to enter. As I vaguely remember, it wasn't an uplifting conversation. When Bondy began to wonder out loud whether it wouldn't be appropriate for me to leave Breesen, since I apparently wasn't able to behave in a disciplined way and follow orders, I gave in and agreed to return to the cow barn. But the *Ober* wouldn't allow it, so I was probably the only Breesen boy who never completed that part of his training. Years later I often helped out on my brother Hans's California dairy farm, where the cows to be milked were driven in from the meadows, cowboy style, by riders on horseback and fed hay outside. But I never again tried to milk a cow myself, not even with a milking machine.

The second time it seemed I might be asked to leave Breesen was in the summer of 1937. All day long we had been turning the hay, and for some reason I was in a bad mood. I was especially annoyed at the length of time it took to put away the pitchforks in the sheds. The boy responsible for collecting the pitchforks was one of my roommates, a short, smart, kind fellow whose name was Ernst Heimann but whom we called

"Pimpf," since that had been his nickname in the youth movement.[3] On the day in question he was taking the pitchforks and putting them on the hooks in the sheds in his characteristically calm way. This was going too slowly for me, and I'd had a hot temper since early childhood, so I threw my pitchfork like a spear, and the prongs pierced the back wall close, much too close, to Pimpf. I hadn't intended to spear my friend with the pitchfork. I hadn't *intended* anything; I was simply taking my frustration out on the pitchfork. In my anger I didn't notice that I had almost killed someone, but everyone else who was there did. The boys standing next to me, whom I had been working with all day long, stared at me horrified, but I just walked away slowly, cursing to myself, and returned to the main house. I was taking off my boots in the basement when someone called to me that I was to go to Professor Bondy *immediately*! One of my fellow trainees had apparently rushed to report my behavior to the highest authority while the gun barrel was still smoking.

I have no doubt repressed my memories of that conversation with Bondy. All I remember is that he was furious and that his voice was ice cold and scathing. He probably made it clear to me that I couldn't permit myself any further outbursts of that kind, or he would send me back to Berlin without hesitation. If I remember correctly, I had to report to him once a week and give an account of my daily behavior. Never again in my life have I allowed frustration to anger me to the point of threatening another person physically.

So Bondy's main tasks were to educate us, supervise our training, and seek emigration possibilities for us. Our professional training, however, lay in the hands of other people, for Bondy had experience in neither agriculture, carpentry, nor mechanics.

Head Manager Erwin Scheier was responsible for our agricultural training. A good-looking man in his mid-thirties, Scheier was surely skilled in his field, to whose theory and practice he carefully introduced us. But he didn't have much appeal as a human being, at least not to me. If he hadn't been born a Jew, he would probably have made a good Nazi. With unconcealed pride he told us that he had volunteered in Berlin in

---

[3] Pimpf and I eventually became good friends, especially after our emigration to the United States. Like me, he fought in the U.S. Army during the war. He then studied law and married a young banker's daughter from Frankfurt am Main, whom he had met during his work for the military government there. For the rest of his life he was a lawyer for the National Labor Relations Board, which mediates conflicts between unions and management.

1918 to take part in attacking the *Marstall* [royal stables] against "the Reds" with a *Freikorps*. He kept his distance from us trainees, like a general from his troops. Even during our Saturday or Sunday walks that I liked so much, when he went across the fields with us and commented on the grain, hay, potatoes, and so on in his somewhat arrogant voice, he wasn't able to get closer to us. He always seemed to be reading aloud to us in a bored voice from our agricultural textbook, Johann Schlipf's *Handbook of Agriculture*. He did his duty, and not one iota more.

Whatever moved Erwin Scheier's wife, Ruth, to marry him will remain her secret. Ruth Scheier's maiden name was Alexander. The Alexanders belonged to the Jewish upper middle class in Berlin. Like her husband, she was good-looking, but, unlike him, she was also warm and understanding, especially to the girls at Gross Breesen, who were educated mainly by her. Under her supervision they learned how to do housework, bake bread, cook, sew, and darn socks, and once a week they (with one boy as a helper) washed the dirty laundry of all the personnel by hand, since washing machines weren't common then and wouldn't have been used at Gross Breesen anyway, as the training in almost all fields was hopelessly outdated. Frau Scheier was also responsible for all the gardening, which was done by the girls mainly but not exclusively. We boys mockingly called work in the garden "small-time agriculture."

Most important of all, Ruth Scheier was the embodiment of all Jewish customs at Gross Breesen. In spite of the fact that almost all the trainees, interns, educators, and administrators were Jewish, it was often hard for her to get their cooperation. Many of us came from families that hardly ever or never practiced their religion. Others had distanced themselves from all religious customs in adolescent rebellion against their parents (I was in this category). In addition, some girls and boys had one non-Jewish ("Aryan") parent and didn't grow up as Jews at all. According to Nazi regulations, these children were nonetheless classified as "non-Aryan." So, except for Hänschen Quentin, everyone who lived in the Castle was "non-Aryan." When Gross Breesen was founded, the *Reichsvertretung* debated whether the people at the new training farm should eat kosher or *treife* [nonkosher] and decided on the latter, which proved to be a wise choice. After all, most of the trainees came from families that didn't eat kosher. Besides that, in 1936 and the following years it would have been very difficult to supply the training farm with kosher food. Several evenings during the week after my arrival in May 1936 we ate raw ham, although it was called, to our amusement, goose breast.

All that changed when Frau Scheier arrived shortly after I did and took on the meal planning. There was no more ham, at least not from the kitchen. (I got Westphalian ham secretly from "Schnauzi" Kirschroth, who came from the Hanover area. Being of Polish nationality, he was deported to Poland in the fall of 1938 and killed a year later when the Germans marched in.) Frau Scheier also took care of Friday evenings, for which we put on our best clothes. The tables were decorated for the occasion, and we always had baked fish. An intern or younger trainee said the blessing over the wine and bread (I remember mainly my friend Pimpf in this role), and after the meal we sang "*Shir Hamalaus*," the "Song of Ascents" which officially introduced the Sabbath. Here Ruth Scheier put her good voice to use, always singing louder than the rest of us. She ignored her husband Erwin, who sat in the back of the hall, provocatively reading the agricultural newspaper. She also ignored the fact, common knowledge in the Castle, that he was having an affair with one of the female interns. And yet she stayed with him until his death in England in the 1970s.

In addition to agriculture and gardening, each of us had to undergo six weeks of training in carpentry. The carpentry workshop, set up in the former servants' quarters, opposite the Castle, was run by the master carpenter, Max Kiwi of Frankfurt an der Oder. His wife made up for what she lacked in height with the force of her lungs. I can still hear the shrill "Max!" that she screamed from the living-room window down to the workshop when she wanted something from him. Their son, Hermann, was a journeyman carpenter. The master carpenter's appointment to work at Breesen probably came at a good time for them, since in 1936 a workshop headed by a Jew in Frankfurt an der Oder couldn't have continued much longer, given the strong anti-Semitism there.

Short but broadly built, Max Kiwi was an excellent carpenter but a small-minded and bad teacher. He and Hermann built wonderful wardrobes and other furniture using electric tools that we "six-week apprentices" weren't allowed to touch. Our tasks were to repair the damaged rungs of the old hay wagons and to make rakes, which didn't require much skill. We carved poles and pegs for the rakes by hand and then put them together. Now and then we also had to do small jobs that required a handsaw or hammer. When we, as apprentices, held the hammer handle in the middle, the master came by and said, "The whole hammer costs money." The most important thing for him was that we *looked* busy. He was incredibly afraid of Bondy, which was completely unjustified. One day when I sat down on the carpenter's bench to catch my breath after having finished a rake or some other task, Kiwi bawled me out, waving his index finger around in front of my nose, saying I should get back to work because "the Professor up there in the Castle looks in here with binoculars to see if we are really working." (Hermann was able to emigrate with us to the United States in 1939, but he had to leave his parents behind; they both died at Auschwitz.)

I only went into the blacksmith's shop once. He came from somewhere in the vicinity of Breesen and—like the permanent farmhands, the *Schaffer*, and the farm manager Gamroth—wasn't Jewish. I only saw him now and then when he was shoeing the horses in the left-hand corner of the courtyard where his little shop was. He stuck in the memory of many of us Breeseners only because on November 10, 1938, the day after Kristallnacht, while the SS men were arresting and dragging out the Jews, he was smashing the windows of the Castle, tipping over wardrobes and cupboards, and taking the Torah roll from the room where services were always held on Friday evenings and Saturdays, throwing it on the dung heap, and chopping it up with an ax.

In spite of its less-than-ideal circumstances, most of us took our training quite seriously, especially the agricultural component. At the beginning we chatted too much and didn't pay attention to our work, but that changed during the first hay harvest. After the permanent farmworkers mowed the hay, we helped load the bales onto the old wagons, took them with the horse teams into the barns, and, finally, unloaded and stowed them in the haylofts over the stalls. It was hard and very dusty work. We were all unskilled novices until then, and those of us who had to move the hay with pitchforks stood in the low, dark lofts surrounded by whirling dust. We could hardly breathe; we were streaming with sweat and constantly in danger of stabbing each other with the pitchforks. Nonetheless, this experience developed in us a spirit of belonging and the will to do good work. These two qualities largely influenced the atmosphere at Gross Breesen and were transferred by us "veterans" to the newcomers, whom we condescendingly called "Ottos." As during my time in the *Bund*, I competed earnestly with the other Breeseners, whether it was working with hay, grain, potatoes, or turnips.

We couldn't know how unbelievably outdated our training was. Not only did we never see a milking machine at Breesen, but the tractor there was old enough to be in a museum. It had to be warmed up around four every morning, summer and winter, so that it could be started at six or seven o'clock. The threshing machine, mechanically driven by a standing "locomotive" fired by coal, was also an antique. The long drive belt that connected the "locomotive" to the threshing machine flew off several times a day, which allowed us to catch our breath but also made the workday longer, since it always took ten or fifteen minutes to get the belt properly in place again.

For pedagogical reasons we weren't allowed to wear gloves while working, which made the late fall potato and turnip harvests, especially, sheer torture. I don't know whether machines existed then that could harvest potatoes and turnips, but at Gross Breesen everything was done by hand, from loading bundles of grain onto the wagons to fertilizing the fields. To accomplish the latter, we spread out the dung that was shoveled down from the wagon as evenly as possible with pitchforks. Thus our adolescent bodies were strengthened daily by working methods that had been used in the Middle Ages. It certainly didn't hurt us. On the contrary, I, at least, who was short and slight, developed muscles that I hadn't known I possessed. I could carry sacks of grain weighing 150 pounds up the ladder to the loft without getting a hernia.

Looking back, it also seems strange how little we learned about the agricultural practices and conditions in the countries to which we hoped to emigrate. After all, Gross Breesen was a training farm for emigrants, and although we didn't know for a long time whether we would resettle in Brazil, Africa, Australia, or the United States, the farm could have at least given us a general overview of the agrarian situation in those places. Instead, Gross Breeseners who farmed in their new countries, some for the rest of their working lives, had to learn almost everything from scratch and had to get used to working with machines. In his theoretical classes on weekends, Scheier taught us quite well which soils in Silesia—and particularly, of course, on the Gross Breesen estate—were right for rye, barley, wheat, potatoes, turnips, and so on, but we never learned about the cultivation of corn, coffee, oranges, rice, and sweet potatoes, or about the grains and fruits native to the countries to which we might be headed.

Nonetheless, we quickly took pride in the challenge of work at Gross Breesen. Besides, our work together in the fields and in the barn greatly contributed to the sense of community essential to what we later referred to as "the Breesen spirit." Our relationship to nature was also strengthened by our work; we began to think and react like farmers. I remember the first summer at Gross Breesen, when for weeks we had no rain and the fields began to suffer. One evening—it must have been in August—I and a few other Hanniots were sitting with Bondy in what we called the "green room" (for the horrible shade of its furnishings), staring out the window into the dark, depressed about the drought. Suddenly lightning flashed, and a few minutes later a thundershower was pounding down. We were so excited that we ran out like crazy people and got soaked. The drought was over, and we, for whom Breesen was only a training ground, and who had no stake in the profit or loss of the estate, were overjoyed that the harvest was saved.

In the Gross Breesen community I slowly matured into an adult. I was by no means seen only positively by my roommates. My frequent fits of anger were first met with humor by my friends, but that soon gave way to annoyance. They also reproached me for being too soft and sentimental and tried to convince me, in various ways, that as a farmer overseas, I couldn't afford to be sentimental. I suffered horribly under this fully justified criticism but found it hard to change myself and master my weaknesses.

Sometime during the hay harvest in the first summer a fawn was run over by one of the mowing machines and badly wounded. One of our senior interns, "Wastl" Neumeyer, brought the little animal to me to be taken care of. I sat in the bay window of our room and tried to feed it from a bottle and nurse its wounds, but they were internal. After Bondy had said good night to us, I sneaked back to the bay window to take care of the fawn. The next day when I returned from work, it was dead. I stood over the body of the little deer, sobbing inconsolably. My roommates and Bondy understood that this loss was sad for me, but my reaction to the death of an animal I'd hardly known for twenty-four hours seemed to them excessive. When I arranged a formal burial in the castle park and shed more tears at the grave, my friends had had enough. They told me to pull myself together and act like a man, not like a child. I have never forgotten this little episode and the rest of my life have tried, if not to hide my feelings in similar situations, at least to keep them under tight control. This has sometimes brought on the reproach that I am cold.

A real reason to be sad came for me and for all the Breeseners at the end of the summer of 1936. On a Sunday in August we Hanniots rode our bicycles to Dyhernfurth to go swimming in the Oder River. It wasn't far, about fifteen kilometers, and the weather was still hot. When we got to the river, those of us who could swim jumped into the water and swam to the other side of the Oder, which wasn't easy because of the strong current. A few who couldn't swim well or only wanted to bathe stayed back. Among those who didn't know how to swim was Herbert Stern, whom we called Stella. Stella was from Nuremberg and had turned seventeen a couple of weeks earlier. We had hardly reached the opposite bank of the river when we heard cries from the other side. Stefan Katz, an especially good friend of mine, called to us that Stella had suddenly disappeared under the water. We jumped back into the river but were driven even further downstream than before. It must have been ten or fifteen minutes before we, completely out of breath, got to the place of the accident. We tried everything we could to find Stella. The best swimmers dived and swam back and forth under the water, but to no avail.

In the meantime one of us had called Bondy from a public telephone, and he soon arrived by car. With him was Dr. Julius Seligsohn of the *Reichsvertretung*, who was visiting Breesen that weekend. (I admired Seligsohn a great deal: he had won a number of medals for his service on the front as a first lieutenant in World War I. This dutiful man and soldier was unfortunately assured of the "thanks of the *Vaterland*." As a leading member of the Reichsvertretung he frequently and courageously entered into conflicts with the National Socialist officials. In 1940, after the deportation of the Jews from Baden, he called on the remaining Jewish community in Berlin to observe a day of fasting and mourning. He was then arrested by the Gestapo and taken to the Sachsenhausen concentration camp, where he died in February 1942.)

Seligsohn and Bondy took over the direction of the search and had us dive repeatedly in the direction of the current. I don't remember who found Stella, but he was lying in a deeper spot within wading distance of the bank. We must have waded or swum past him several times. Under Seligsohn's instructions we attempted to revive him, but it was hopeless, since Stella had remained under water for almost an hour. A doctor who came later said that Stella had suffered such a shock when he slid into the unexpected depression on the river bottom that his heart had failed. We brought Stella back to Breesen, laid his body in the room where we held our Friday night services, and took turns keeping vigil. I know that I cried a lot during the time until his body was taken away for burial. The next day Bondy arranged a short funeral service at which he spoke to us, followed by Seligsohn and Wastl Neumeyer. Then we carried Stella in his coffin across the courtyard to a hearse, which transported him to his hometown for burial. I wrote in my diary at the time: "Stella should be a reminder to us, a reminder of our idea, of our goal.... We should act in the way that he would act. I want to do that. I don't cry anymore, I can laugh again, although it isn't usually real yet.... But I think of him often."

Stella was the first friend who I lost because of death. Only a few months later, in February 1937, another tragedy followed. In many ways this second death was more painful, because I felt I was partly responsible. During the night of February 1–2, 1937, our room leader, Hannio (Hermann Ollendorf) took his own life with an overdose of sleeping pills in a hotel room in Breslau. It hit us like a bolt of lightning. And yet, if we had been more experienced and at least minimally schooled in psychology, my friend Prinz and I would have been suspicious about his behavior and might have prevented his suicide.

Hannio was an intern and therefore older than most of us. He was full of charm, a good-looking young man with curly black hair and a wonderful smile. Sometimes on Sundays—when, except for taking care of the livestock, we didn't work—he would treat some of us Hanniots to a meal at a good restaurant in his native Breslau. Of course we were thrilled. On the evening of February 1, Hannio asked Prinz and me to go for a short walk with him in the park after dinner. He walked silently with us, an arm around each of our shoulders, down the paths of the park. Suddenly, he began to sob, blurting out that on that evening he would leave Breesen forever. He said that he had followed Bondy's instructions and gone to a doctor to be examined, and it had been discovered that he wasn't physically able to emigrate overseas and perform hard farm labor for an extended period. How precise the doctor's diagnosis was, he didn't say, and we didn't ask. We just walked along next to Hannio without talking and struggled to hold back our tears. There was a short farewell, and Prinz and I, without speaking to each other, went to bed completely distraught over the despair of our friend and leader.

Sometime around midnight I was shaken awake. I was lying in my top bunk and saw only Bondy's head next to me. He asked me sharply when I had last seen Hannio and under what circumstances. Half asleep, I told him. In the meantime Prinz had woken up and confirmed the little that I had reported about our walk. I knew that Bondy had been in Breslau that day and hadn't returned by the time we had gone to bed. Without explanation, Bondy ran out of the room, and I fell back asleep almost immediately. The next morning we learned that Hannio had gone to a well-known hotel in Breslau and swallowed an overdose of sleeping pills. Bondy had found him after only four phone calls and gotten him immediately to a hospital, where his stomach was pumped. But Hannio couldn't be saved, and he died the same day. It was the second death among the Hanniots in only a few months, and there was a second burial. I cried again, but this time with a strong feeling of guilt, because I believed, as Prinz did, that we should have recognized Hannio's state and told an adult about it.

What had really happened? Here are some excerpts from my diary, dated February 18, 1937:

"Hannio took his life in the night of the 1st to the 2nd [of February] in a Breslau hotel. It sounds terribly raw and cold, the way I write it here, but I am doing it so as not to write sentimentally, which would be worse. Hannio was physically weak, he was sick, he had a kidney disease and didn't feel he could be a settler. He had, in the end, built his life in Breesen, after many unsuccessful attempts in other professions and communities. That was the inner reason. The immediate cause was that several hundred marks were missing from the canteen cash balance. [Hannio ran the canteen, where we could buy small items once or twice a week.] He was confronted and asked to account for it, and claimed that he didn't know where the money was. They believed him, but the money was still missing. In this mood, and with the feeling that he might not be able to come with us ... and settle, that he would have to leave Gross Breesen because of his physical ailment as well as because of the unfortunate canteen business, because he didn't want to stay back when all the others group by group went over, since he loved Gross Breesen, he took an overdose of sleeping powder ... which he died of at five o'clock on Tuesday, February 2. Hannio was messy and disorganized in the canteen business, but honest. Hannio wasn't a dishonest person, that is certain.... Hannio was my leader ... my friend.... I miss Hannio everywhere. Bondy is leading the group, Jochen is managing the technical organizational part. But we miss Hannio."

That is how I saw it then, two weeks after the suicide of our group leader whom I respected so much. Years later in the United States, I asked Bondy what had actually happened. He looked at me with amazement and asked if I really didn't know why Hannio had taken his life. He told me that Hannio had "borrowed" money from the canteen that he ran—

Hermann Ollendorf ("Hannio") in 1936.

most probably with the intention of paying it back sometime—in order to treat us to a meal at a restaurant in Breslau now and then. During a routine check it had been discovered that funds were missing, Hannio admitted it without hesitation, and Bondy decided immediately to send Hannio away from Breesen. The story that he was too sick to go overseas to a settlement was made up. The adults had kept quiet about this fact at the time, as is apparent from my diary entry.

Fate was to strike again, and once more it hit someone from our Hanniot group. Gustl, as we called him, was a loner who kept his distance from the others. But he was one of our group. He liked to practice acrobatic feats and didn't worry whether they were dangerous or not. On March 13, 1937, about two months after Hannio's death, he tried to do a flip in the air in the hallway, fell on his head, and broke his skull. He died that evening at the Jewish hospital in Breslau. These three sudden deaths in a period of six months were traumatic for us. Most of us were only sixteen or seventeen. Fortunately, we couldn't know that only a few years later more Gross Breeseners would meet death in a much more horrible way, in National Socialist extermination camps.

The three deaths were painful events for each of us, of course, but they also helped to make us into more mature human beings. The intensity of daily life that gave birth to "the spirit of Gross Breesen," which for most of us has lasted a lifetime, is in retrospect still amazing. It only became clear to us many years later that we were living at that time under almost ideal conditions for our maturation. In the short time that Gross Breesen existed as a training farm, we learned to work and to love our work.[4] Under Bondy's direction we learned ethical and cultural values that we probably wouldn't have encountered otherwise then, at least not so intensely. We developed friendships that for many of us were to last a lifetime and that stretched to the many corners of the world to which we were scattered in the end. Besides professional training in agriculture,

---

[4] After the war broke out Gross Breesen became a work camp for a continually diminishing number of "non-Aryans" and was increasingly watched by the Gestapo.

ABOVE: *Gross Breesen castle in 1936.* RIGHT: *Werner Angress at Gross Breesen, wearing the "uniform" of the Hanniots (dark blue shorts and plaid shirt), 1936.*

carpentry, and mechanics, we gained insight into culture: we were encouraged to read good literature and classical music was played by a quartet every evening (accompanied by Bondy on the grand piano, but not with great skill). We read aloud plays like Gotthold Lessing's *Nathan the Wise* in front of a large group of listeners. We also staged plays and listened to Bondy read from the works of Franz Werfel, Stefan Zweig, and other authors. Aside from Grosspapa's efforts in this area during my early childhood, I owe my initiation into German literature and classical music to the short time I was in Breesen.

But there was also intellectual stimulation from outside Gross Breesen. For example, Martin Buber visited for two days to talk to us on the topic of "Love your neighbor, for he is like you." I have to admit that I no longer remember the content of his talk, because Buber spoke over my head. But I well remember the more prosaic aspects of the short man with the deep voice: he was small, but he was a "sitting giant," that is, when he got up from his chair he appeared to be just as tall, or just as short, as when he was sitting down. On one of the days he visited us, some of us wanted to speak with Bondy for a moment. Assuming he was in his room, we knocked. The "traffic light" wasn't on, not green or yellow or red. We knocked again, and then one of us opened the door carefully, looked into the room, and called back to us softly, "Shhh, Herr Buber is sleeping." Whereupon from the green sofa on which the philosopher was lying came a voice: "Martin Buber isn't sleeping, Martin Buber is resting."

Although we hardly thought about it and didn't talk about it, we were aware of the fact that living at Gross Breesen was like living on an island. The Third Reich surrounded us, and when we went to Breslau or home for the very short Christmas vacation, the Nazi state, with its uniforms, flags, and bellowing SA people, was everywhere we looked. But as long as we were at the training farm we had hardly any contact with the brown swamp. We experienced no animosities from our neighbors until November 1938.

The village itself was small. We only rarely had anything to do with its inhabitants, and the little that we saw of them gave us no cause to worry. They were almost all farmers who simply went about their daily tasks. If I remember correctly, the whole eighteen months I was there I never saw anyone from the village in an SA or SS uniform. The mayor, a farmer, was also the postmaster for Gross and Klein Breesen. He was a conscientious man. One evening after the mail had gone out, he appeared at the Castle, walked into Bondy's secretary's office, and handed her an express letter that Bondy had put in the mail: the "Prufessor" had affixed too much postage. Someone had to drive fast to Breslau to get the letter into the night mail.

Although we had no personal contact with the permanent farm-workers at Gross Breesen, sometimes our work took us beyond the boundaries of the training farm, and then we dealt with all sorts of people. But in those situations there were no unpleasant incidents either. Sometimes I accompanied one of our interns with horses and wagon to the local mill to have our grain ground. The miller's wife, a young woman, welcomed us every time with the same greeting: "Get down from the horses and on your knees" (i.e., "Let's get to work!"). After we had unloaded our wagon, she often gave us a piece of cake. When we took the potatoes to the distillery, we were treated by the workers and bosses there no differently than if we had been "Aryans." Business was business, and potatoes were potatoes, and that was that. But everybody in the whole region around Breesen knew who we were. We saw that plainly when we sent our pure-bred bull, a huge, aggressive beast, to a local agricultural competition. The person who had taken our bull there came back and said he had been given to understand that our splendid animal would have won first prize if he hadn't been the bull from Gross Breesen.

We learned what was going on in the world outside of our "island" mainly from Bondy, who reported to us periodically on the political situation. His regular, usually brief evening lectures about the happenings in the world, especially in Germany, kept us pretty well informed. He was very careful about what he told us, but we quickly learned to hear "between the lines," so to speak. One day he gave me the job of helping one of our interns, Friedel Dzubas,[5] burn in the basement furnace books by authors the regime found politically objectionable. Bondy had asked us all beforehand to allow him to look at the books we had brought from home, and he explained to us why some of them had to be burned. And then Friedel and I fed the furnace with books by Arnold Zweig (*Caliban, or Politics and Passion*), Bertoldt Brecht, Heinrich Mann, and many others. While I, an ignoramus, was simply sweating, Friedel, who was several years older, was very angry and cursed vehemently. We must have burned fifty books that day.

But events in the lives of our friends also reminded us repeatedly that the world outside was broken for us. One day a newcomer, Manfred Gottschalk, was assigned to our room. When he walked in I stared at him, fascinated, because I knew his face from somewhere. I bluntly asked him if I had maybe seen his face in Julius Streicher's anti-Semitic propaganda newspaper, *Der Stürmer*. Manfred, visibly disturbed, put his index finger to his lips and asked me very softly why I asked him that. Well, about a year earlier in Lichterfelde, on my way to Herr Schimmelmann's

---

[5] Friedel wasn't Jewish, but he had a Jewish father. Later he became a well-known abstract painter in the United States.

boring religion class, I had become engrossed in reading the free paper in the "*Stürmer* box" on the street corner on my way to school. The accusation it made against the fifteen-year-old Manfred, complete with a large picture, was *Rassenschande*, literally, racial disgrace, the Nazi term for sexual relations between an Aryan and a non-Aryan. He had supposedly seduced a German girl under a stairway and was sent to a concentration camp. The picture and report had made a strong impression on me. Manfred then told me that he'd only kissed the girl, a friend, and that they'd been caught at it. The girl was immediately brought to a doctor to be examined, and her virginity was confirmed. But Manfred was taken to the Sonnenburg concentration camp near Küstrin anyway, where he was kept for almost a year. When he was let out, he applied for training at Gross Breesen and was accepted after a long interview with Bondy, who made him promise not to talk about his experience. Aside from me, no one at Gross Breesen ever learned about it. With an anglicized name, Manfred lived in the United States until his death.

My girlfriend, whose nickname was "Leus," was involved in another *Stürmer* incident. She was from Nuremberg, and her father ran a sawmill in the Bavarian Forest. One day I found Leus in tears in the park. She told me that there was a long article in *Der Stürmer* about her father and his business. I can no longer remember the details of the accusation, but it was another reminder that even on our island, we were never completely free of problems intruding from the external world.

The end of my training at Gross Breesen came unexpectedly and totally against my own wishes. The last weeks that I spent in Germany, not suspecting that I would be leaving the country very shortly, today seem to me like scenes from a bad movie. First I got a skin infection on my chest and was advised by our Breesen doctor, Ilse Lehmann, to go to the Jewish hospital in Breslau. After a few days of collect phone calls, I had put so much pressure on my mother that she allowed me, of course with my father's consent, to come to Berlin for medical treatment. On the evening before the Sabbath, without going through the usual formalities, I snuck out of the Breslau Jewish hospital, which I hated because of its uncleanliness and its inattentive care, threw my little bag over the wall, climbed over, and took the next train to Berlin. I stayed about four weeks, from mid-September to mid-October, and was cured by a prominent board member of the *Verband Nationaldeutscher Juden* [League of German National Jews], who was an authority in his medical specialty.

During this stay in Berlin, a suspicion I'd long had, even before my training at Gross Breesen, was confirmed: my mother was having an affair with one of her Kahlmann cousins, Didi's oldest brother, my uncle Fritz, whom I'd once so admired. I found out that this uncle had been let go from my father's business one or two years after Papa had hired him. During the few weeks I was in Berlin this topic wasn't discussed, but the atmosphere was tense and unpleasant, so I spent as much time as possible out of the house.

In mid-October I was hardly back in Breesen when I received a postcard from my father. It was dated October 19, 1937, and read, "My dear Töpper [Papa had loved my nickname from the beginning], … I am writing to you at this unusual time for a reason. I must speak to you, and ask you to come to Berlin on Saturday [October 23] with a weekend ticket. Monday noon you'll go back to Breesen. Don't ask any questions; just write us immediately when you will be arriving.… . We will talk about it when you're here.… . a big kiss, Papa." I had no idea what this card could mean. So the following Saturday I arrived in Berlin and went right away to Holsteinische Strasse, where I found only Mutti. She appeared more nervous than usual and told me that Papa had decided to leave Germany with the family. The money he had in the bank he planned to smuggle to Amsterdam, against the national currency regulations. Then we would all go to London and from there emigrate somewhere overseas. Papa was in Amsterdam at the moment, she said, but would be back the next day, a Sunday, and then he would talk to me. She and my two brothers were to travel to London the following Friday, October 29, quite legally as tourists with ten marks per person in their pockets. On Saturday I would fly with Papa from Tempelhof Airport to Amsterdam, but only with carry-on baggage. The following Monday the Jewish moving company Silberstein—with the rhyming slogan, *"Zieh aus, zieh ein mit Silberstein"* [Move out, move in with Silberstein]—was to empty our apartment and ship the furnishings to London.

My head was spinning. The thought of having to leave Gross Breesen and my friends so suddenly, to break off my training, maybe never to settle overseas with my friends, was more than I could handle at that moment. Mutti didn't notice my state, since she was very distressed herself because of her imminent separation from Onkel Fritz. For the first time she dropped her mask in front of me, saying that she and Fritz had planned to meet and she had to go to his house right away. She said she would come back later and make supper for the two of us. Then she disappeared, and since my brothers were visiting friends, I was left alone in the apartment. As soon as my mother closed the door behind her, I decided that I wouldn't emigrate illegally with my parents. I found a pad of paper somewhere and wrote my parents a rather confused letter in which I told them that I wasn't going with them but was staying in Breesen. What they planned was a violation of the currency laws and therefore a punishable crime (!!). I intended to emigrate later with my Breesen friends, but under no circumstances would I go with them now. If they tried to force me to emigrate with them, I would take my life. Putting the letter down someplace where they couldn't help seeing it I began to choose about a dozen books from their bookcase that I wanted to take with me. I stuffed them into a suitcase that I found in a closet, went down the back stairs to avoid meeting my mother, and dragged the suitcase to the Hohenzollerndamm subway stop. From there I went to the railway station, where I took the next train via Breslau back to Gellendorf.

I had barely arrived in Breesen again, exhausted from carrying a suitcase heavy with books, when I was told to see Bondy. He gave me a serious and penetrating look and said that my father had called him and told him that I would soon arrive in Breesen in an excited state and that I must talk to him, Bondy, about some important matters. My father told Bondy that he unfortunately couldn't explain the situation over the phone, but that Bondy would find out shortly what it was about. Bondy had promised that he would call my father back. After my report and my repeated claim that my mind was made up and I would stay in Breesen, Bondy only said that he had to go to Berlin the next day, to the *Reichsvertretung*, and that he would then talk to my father personally. In a hopeful mood, I shoved the suitcase under my bed in the Hanniots' room and went to Scheier for my work assignment. I was convinced that I had made the right decision and would now be able to stay in Breesen.

But it didn't happen like that. When Bondy returned from Berlin he called me to his room. Calmly but resolutely he informed me that he had spoken with my father as well as with Fritz Schwarzschild, the accountant for Gross Breesen at the *Reichsvertretung*. It wasn't possible for me to stay at Breesen after my parents had left the country, he said, because sooner or later I would be arrested and used as a hostage and thereby endanger Gross Breesen. He told me I had to do what my father expected of me, that is, go to England with my family and wait there to see how the Breesen plans for overseas took shape. As soon as there were definite prospects for an agricultural settlement somewhere, I would of course be included in the planning. Then I would have to discuss with my parents whether I would settle with the Breesen people or go wherever the family went. Bondy added that my father sent the message that he could understand why I had reacted so emotionally to the idea of leaving Breesen. He promised to consider all Gross Breesen's future settlement plans together with me. After all that had happened, Bondy said, I could hardly expect more generosity from my father. So I was to meet him the next Saturday morning, October 30, at the Zoo station in Berlin. Dackel, who was in Berlin then, would meet my train and give me new clothes to put on. Then I was to meet my father at the station restaurant and the two of us would fly to Amsterdam. Bondy stressed that under no circumstances should I tell anyone in Breesen about my forthcoming emigration.

After this conversation it was time to start taking my leave. In the few days that remained for me, I spent as much time as I could with my girlfriend, Leus, and my friends in the Hanniot group. On Friday evening, before I took the late train from Breslau to Berlin, there was a short official farewell. Bondy said a few words, spoke of a probable reunion someplace, sometime in the future, and then the quartet, with Bondy at the grand piano, played Tchaikovsky's "Italian Capriccio" in my honor, a piece that they knew I especially liked. After that I quickly took my luggage and someone drove me and Leus, who was seeing me off, to the Breslau train station in Bondy's "Adler." Around midnight, after a painful farewell from Leus, I left for Berlin. Thus ended one of the most important phases of my youth.

CHAPTER 5

The Road into Exile, 1937–1939

During the trip to Berlin that night I hardly slept. The bench seats in third class were hard, and the other passengers, some of them Polish, spent most of the trip eating food that they took out of their knapsacks and suitcases and passed around, talking almost without interruption. My mind was on Gross Breesen. I simply couldn't imagine the future, so I probably didn't think about it. Around nine in the morning I arrived at the Zoologischer Garten station, where I had departed for Gross Breesen with a traveling companion in May 1936. Dackel was standing on the platform holding a large package in his hand. Not wasting any words, he took my arm and led me downstairs to the men's restroom, which was huge and incredibly disgusting, and there I changed into a suit with the first long pants I had ever worn. My mother had dropped off these clothes for me at Dackel's parents' house. The clothes I had come in I stuffed into one of my two suitcases. Then we went upstairs to the big entrance hall, and my father arrived shortly thereafter.

After a brief farewell to Dackel, Papa and I took a taxi to Tempelhof airport. We didn't speak much on the way, but he smiled warmly and assured me that he was no longer upset about my behavior of a week earlier. Let bygones be bygones. Mutti and my brothers had gone to London the day before by train and boat, and the two of us were to fly to Amsterdam just before noon that day. He had told the members of our family remaining in Berlin not to come to the airport. There were to be no farewell scenes that might draw the attention of the officials there, especially the Gestapo.

The Tempelhof airport terminal then had only four or five gates. I felt as if I were sleepwalking. My departure from Breesen, spending the whole night more or less awake in the train and now waiting for the first flight of my life—all this overwhelmed me. I trotted behind Papa with my suitcases. He showed our tickets to the two men posted at the gate wearing trench coats and, as I remember, derby hats, the favorite outfit of low-ranking Gestapo officials. He explained we were on our way, via Amsterdam, to England, where I was to receive special agricultural training for several months. He would be returning to Berlin as soon as he had found a place for me to stay. Then we had to open our baggage. Papa only had a small suitcase, appropriate for someone who only meant to take a short trip abroad, and they soon let him go through. But they searched my bags thoroughly. One of the officials asked me what a farm-hand was doing with so many books. I answered that where I was headed (fortunately he didn't ask where that was), there was nothing better to do in the evenings after work than read. The man believed me, and I shut the suitcase with a feeling of relief.

My concern that they might object to the authors of some of my books and then confiscate them proved to be unnecessary. We had hardly gotten past that hurdle when my father cursed under his breath, quite unusual for him. He was looking at a corner of the hall. There stood Grosspapa and the Simonsohns (Uncle Arthur and Aunt Rosa), who had turned up after all. Papa took my arm and approached our relatives slowly. But before we reached them, an announcement over the loudspeakers informed us that the airplane headed for Amsterdam hadn't been able to take off from Dresden because of heavy fog. Passengers bound for Amsterdam could either wait until the next day or take the train in the evening.

Now our three relatives got excited. "Copenhagen ... Paris," they whispered. My father, impatient and anxious, explained that it would appear very suspect if he suddenly tried to change our destination to Denmark or France after declaring that we wanted to go to Amsterdam and then England. No, we would take the night train to Amsterdam. He finally persuaded the three of them to go home, whispering, "For God's sake, no tears!" Grosspapa and the Simonsohns left the airport. I never saw any of them again. Fortunately they all died natural deaths, Grosspapa in Berlin and the Simonsohns in São Paulo.

After their departure Papa was visibly relieved. We got our baggage back, took a taxi to Friedrichstrasse and went into a somewhat shabby-looking café. The situation was very strange. We should have been in an airplane about to land in Amsterdam, but there we sat drinking coffee on

Friedrichstrasse, hardly five minutes from Papa's bank. It was noon, and our train left shortly before midnight. Since we only dared to talk about insignificant things, we sat next to each other hardly speaking. Anyway, my thoughts weren't in Berlin but still at Gross Breesen. In the late afternoon my father suggested going to the movies to see a cops-and-robbers film rated for people over the age of sixteen. Lugging our baggage along, we again took a taxi to the cinema where the film was playing. But even the newsreel before the movie was a disaster: it was called "Papi's Fortieth Birthday," "Papi" being Joseph Goebbels, who had, in fact, turned forty the day before, on October 29, 1937. Now he appeared on the screen with his whole family. (Of course these scenes had been taped earlier: "Juppchen" wasn't the minister for propaganda and public enlightenment for nothing.) This was too much for *my* "Papi." He whispered to me that he was going to the home of his old friend and fellow card-player, Leo Gerson. Gerson, also Jewish, was married to a woman who was not. Papa instructed me to leave as soon as the film was over and take a taxi to the Gersons' to join him. He gave me money for the taxi and left.

I stayed and watched the Goebbels' family idyll, in which Magda, Helga, Helmut, Hilde, and Holde handed bouquets of flowers to the beaming good Doctor. The cops-and-robbers movie took place, ironically, in Amsterdam. When it was over I took a taxi to the Gersons', who lived somewhere in the "better" part of Kreuzberg. I didn't even have time to take off my coat. Papa told me to take a taxi, right away, to the Friedrichstrasse station with Frau Gerson. There I was to go to the sleeping car in which he had reserved a compartment for the two of us, give the conductor two marks, and tell him that my father was staying in Berlin for business reasons and wasn't able to accompany me. So I was going to Amsterdam alone. When I asked him what he planned to do, Papa answered that he didn't know yet. I was to go to the Rosengarten Pension on Beethovenstraat in Amsterdam and tell the owner that he would soon hear from my father.

As I found out, this Rosengarten was Papa's contact who had helped him illegally transfer his money to Holland. It was only later, in London, that I learned how this happened. My father had gone to Amsterdam in the middle of October and had made a deal with Rosengarten, who was to get 10 percent of the money they got out of Germany. When my father asked how it would be done, he was told that on the day we planned to leave Germany (October 30), someone would come to our apartment to pick up the money. The rest was Rosengarten's business. Then, a young German woman my father didn't know appeared at the door with a briefcase. Without introducing herself, she said she had come to pick up the money. Papa had brought the money home from the bank the night before and had hidden it under his mattress, about one hundred thousand bundled-up reichsmarks, his whole fortune. The two of them together packed the bills in the briefcase. My father offered the woman money for a taxi, but she said that taxis can have accidents, and that she would take a streetcar to the station. When she disappeared with the briefcase full of money, Papa told us later, he didn't know if he should laugh or cry.

So Frau Gerson and I took a taxi to the station, and she accompanied me to the train, found my sleeping compartment, and told me goodbye. Then I did everything as Papa had instructed me to do: I told the conductor that my father had to stay in Berlin, gave the man two marks and my passport (valid until March 1940), got undressed, and lay down in the lower bunk of the compartment. I don't think it took me a minute to fall asleep.

And what did Papa do? Frau Gerson and I had hardly left their apartment when Leo Gerson took Papa to the same train station in his car, and Papa took a train to Prague. When it arrived at the Czech border, Papa got out on the wrong side of the train, walked on the tracks to the border (thus avoiding the German border guards), and entered Czechoslovakia, where he told the officials he was a Jewish refugee from Germany. Since he assured them he would immediately travel on to Holland via Austria, Switzerland, and France, a route German refugees called *"der jüdische Südring"* [the Jewish Southern Loop], he wasn't sent back. On the way to Amsterdam he mainly visited customers of his bank who lived in Austria and Switzerland. He knew a lot of them personally, and others, customers he didn't know, were people who had deposited their money at Königsberger and Lichtenhein; these people he informed about what was happening to their bank accounts. Considering the circumstances under which my father had left Germany and the fact that all the foreign bank customers he visited were "non-Aryans," it is highly doubtful that they ever saw their money again. My father never spoke to me about this delicate point, and I, not being at all interested at the time, didn't ask him about it.

Sometime early in the morning—it was still dark outside—my train stopped at Bentheim-Grenze, the last stop before the Dutch border. The light in the compartment went on, and I woke up completely groggy. I found myself staring at three men who had appeared at my bed. One of them was the conductor, and the other two wore trench coats and derbies. Gestapo. One of them held my passport in his hand and studied it intently. "Your last name is Angress." I confirmed this. "Where is your father?" Without hesitating I lied as Papa had instructed me: "In Berlin." Fortunately, they didn't ask about my mother and brothers, who on Friday had gone by train and boat to London, with ten reichsmarks each but a lot of suitcases, "to visit friends." The Gestapo men wanted to know where I was going and why, so I made something up, yawning. I was genuinely tired. Then they left the compartment and whispered together in the hallway. After a couple of minutes, which seemed to me like an eternity, the Gestapo official who was holding my passport handed it to the conductor, and he and his partner disappeared without a word. A few minutes later the train started rolling westward.

I quickly dressed and got my passport from the conductor, who was apparently about to get off. After a short time the train stopped again. We were in Oldenzaal, thus in Holland. A few minutes later an elderly railroad employee in a uniform I didn't recognize came into the compartment and asked for my passport in a friendly manner, speaking German with a Dutch accent. Only then did I realize that Nazi Germany was finally behind me, that I was now traveling in a free country, and that I was in exile.

It wasn't until several weeks later, when my father's (Jewish) secretary, Else Radinowsky, visited my family in London and reported on her perspective of our escape, that I understood how incredibly lucky I'd been on the day I left Germany. It was a miracle that I wasn't arrested and held as a hostage. To explain, I have to go back to Saturday, October 30, and thus back to Berlin. The preceding day my father had informed our Jewish lodger, "Peter," that we were leaving Germany, including the details of our planned flight to Amsterdam. ("Peter"'s real name was Ilsegret Traugott; she'd gotten her nickname in the youth movement, and I had a big crush on her.) He told her she had to move out as quickly as possible, since the moving company was coming on Monday to clear out the apartment and ship all the furnishings to London.

But Peter got frightened. What if it didn't work and she was questioned by the police as a possible accomplice to currency smuggling, as it was called then? As soon as my father left the house Saturday morning, after handing over the money to the young smuggler, Peter called the landlord, who was also Jewish and had an account at Papa's bank. He suggested that Peter call Papa's secretary, Else Radinowsky, and tell her she was to come to our house on Holsteinische Strasse immediately. As soon as Else learned what was going on, she got scared, too. Without first checking at the office to see if my father had left instructions for her there (which he had), she contacted the former bank owner and my father's boss, Leo Königsberger, and asked him to meet her. Before the elderly gentleman arrived, Else assured the landlord and Peter that she and Herr Königsberger would take care of the matter. In addition, she advised Peter to move to a friend's house right away, which Peter did.[6]

All this happened around noon on Saturday. Frau Radinowsky and Herr Königsberger assumed, of course, that my father and I were already in Amsterdam—and thus safe—since the plane was supposed to have taken off around eleven in the morning. And so this very dissimilar pair, Leo Königsberger (just over eighty and the spitting image of President Hindenburg) and the much younger Else, decided to go to the criminal police at Alexanderplatz and report that the director of the K and L bank had illegally left the country with his fortune, as they had just accidentally discovered.

At "the Alex" a Saturday atmosphere reigned. The officers were sitting in the police station playing cards, and they weren't at all interested in Else's report. They were criminal police, they said, and since it wasn't at all clear that the K and L bank director had committed a criminal act, Else and Herr Königsberger should go to the state secret police (the Gestapo), who dealt with such matters. The policemen returned to their game, and Else and Herr Königsberger went to the Gestapo headquarters at Prinz Albrecht Strasse 8. There the men were also playing cards. The Gestapo sent Frau Radinowsky and Herr Königsberger to the customs bureau, which was responsible for violations of currency laws and would undoubtedly take care of the business. The people at the customs bureau proved to be very interested indeed. Else once again said her piece, but she didn't give all the facts, failing to mention that my mother and two brothers had left Germany on Friday, because Peter in her excitement had forgotten to tell her. Nor did she report our destination or the

---

[6] Peter soon afterward went to the United States, married a professor of mathematics there, and still lives today in Binghamton, New York. We see each other now and then. Leo Königsberger died in the concentration camp at Theresienstadt.

flight to Amsterdam. So the customs bureau had the impression that the entire Angress family had run off together on Saturday morning to an unknown destination and was carrying a sum of money forbidden by currency regulations. In the presence of Else and Herr Königsberger, the officials of the customs bureau then sent telegrams to all the important border crossings reading "Family of five named Angress to be arrested." The expenses of these telegrams, several hundred reichsmarks, were billed to the Königsberger and Lichtenhein bank.

I wasn't in London when Else Radinowsky visited the family there in December 1937 and reported these happenings; I learned all this later from Papa. Three things probably saved me from being arrested by the two Gestapo officers at Bentheim-Grenze and jailed as a hostage to get my father to return with the money: 1) the fact that in my sleepy state I didn't act like a boy fleeing with a guilty conscience, 2) the fact that I was alone and not part of a family of five, and 3) the two agents' apparently not very high level of intelligence.[7]

During the trip from the border to Amsterdam I had mixed feelings. Of course I missed my friends at Gross Breesen, my girlfriend, and everything that had become so important to me in the past eighteen months. But my leaving Germany—the country that I still loved immensely in spite of now being deemed there a "racially inferior subhuman [*Untermensch*] and enemy of the people"—was for the moment superseded by my curiosity about traveling abroad and seeing and experiencing new things. The flat Dutch landscape was by no means exciting, but still it captivated me: the canals, windmills, and lots of bridges were all new and fascinating to me. Finally there was my completely uncertain future. Of course every young person has an uncertain future, but under normal circumstances he or she can plan and choose a professional goal. I did have the goal of working as a farmer somewhere overseas, but where that would be I hadn't a clue.

I didn't know, either, what would be awaiting me in Amsterdam. In my pocket I had only the ten reichsmarks allowed by the currency regulations. Following Papa's instructions, I took streetcar number 24 from the *centraalstation* to Pension Rosengarten on Beethovenstraat. (Streetcar 24, I would soon discover, was called "the Orient Express" by German

---

[7] I have reconstructed this story based on three sources: Else Radinowsky's report to my parents in the winter of 1937–38; Else's later recounting in Amsterdam, where she immigrated in 1938 and where I often met her in my parents' apartment; and a conversation with Peter in the United States shortly after the war ended.

Werner Angress, on the day after emigrating to Amsterdam, October 31, 1937.

Jewish refugees, because it went to the southern part of town where many of them lived.) All this posed no problem. The pension was in an apartment building; it was quite dark and full of German Jews who were sitting around, apparently bored. Rosengarten, a heavy man, shook my hand and asked, "Where is Minna?" Uncomprehending, I stared at him. Minna? Yes, he said, your father sent a telegram from Prague that read, "Wire whether Werner and Minna arrived." Then I understood. I told him that my father probably wanted to know if I and the *money* had arrived. Since he didn't want to use the usual word for money, *Marie* ("moola," more or less), he had chosen the word *Minna*, betting that I would understand. So Rosengarten wired Papa that the two of us had arrived. After showing me the room where I could stay until my father got there, he disappeared.

Now at least I knew that Papa had gotten out of Germany, and I knew approximately where he was. Nonetheless, I felt incredibly sad. Here I was sitting in a pension full of people I didn't know and didn't want to know. Suddenly I remembered that as I was leaving Gross Breesen someone had given me an address. It belonged to a Werner Warmbrunn, a former member of *Schwarzes Fähnlein* in Frankfurt am Main. His nickname was "Meui," and he now lived in Amsterdam with his parents and went to school there. I called him from the pension and reached him right away, it being Sunday. He said he would come to the pension, and ten minutes later we were greeting each other somewhat awkwardly. He invited me to go home with him to meet his mother. We had hardly left the pension when he asked if I really wanted to wait for my father in that dreadful atmosphere at Rosengarten's. If not, he could ask his parents to let me stay at their house until my father arrived. And so on October 31, 1937, began a close friendship that has lasted to the present day. We had both been members of the *Schwarzes Fähnlein*; we both later emigrated to the United States (although at different times and under very different circumstances); we both studied European and German history and taught, did research, and published for decades. Even when we lived a great distance from one another and saw each other only rarely, our friendship continued. I still visit him whenever I go to California.

The week I spent waiting for my father, who was traveling through Austria and Switzerland, was a very good week. Meui was in his second-to-last year of a school equivalent to a classical German *Gymnasium* of the time, with courses in Greek, Latin, and French. In the Dutch schools they studied English as well, so he was busy with a lot of homework. But he still took time for me, and we did something together every day after school. The afternoon after I arrived we hitchhiked to Haarlem and went to the Frans Hals museum. In the evening on the way back to Amsterdam, we jumped naked into a canal next to the street and swam around like young dogs. It turned out that Meui shared my feelings for Germany and was probably even more nationalistic than I. Strengthened in this fervor by my new friend, I was to hang on to my blind German patriotism for almost exactly another year.

After a week, Papa arrived in Amsterdam and stayed two days, which we spent together in a hotel. He seemed to be immersed in his own thoughts most of the time and spoke little. The only conversation I remember happened when I let on once how much I missed Gross

Breesen, my friends there, and also Germany. Papa told me then that he had always been a patriot and had volunteered several times to go to the front (which I knew) and had been very disappointed to be classified as g.v. (*garnisonsverwendungsfähig*, only useful on a military base) because of his hearing impairment. But Hitler and his Nazis weren't letting us be Germans, he said, and had humiliated and degraded us to second-class citizens. For that reason Germany was no longer our homeland. "I'll take up a gun again against those crooks [*Verbrecher*] anytime," he said. These words made me think, but they certainly didn't convince me, and as we left together for London, my heart was heavy. Not only had I liked Amsterdam from the beginning, I also didn't want to say goodbye to another friend, this time Meui.

For me going to England meant being completely dependent on my family again, without any concrete prospects for the future and isolated by not knowing the language very well. For the first time I experienced the mixture of feelings common to emigrants at the time: being without a home country, with prospects for the future uncertain and the uncomfortable feeling of being a foreigner everywhere and, as a Jew, not welcome anywhere. Today young people, especially those from Western countries, expect to be able to travel to other countries without problems, often to stay there for a long time or even for good if the opportunity presents itself. All this was simply not part of the world prior to 1945.

Starting in the early 1930s, the world was deeply affected by the international economic crisis. Millions of people everywhere were unemployed, extreme nationalism prevailed, borders were strictly patrolled, and almost everywhere anti-Semitism was widespread. Only wealthy people were accepted in foreign countries—people who could invest money, hire the unemployed, and pay taxes. But most of the German emigrants of the 1930s had no money. This was due to the slowly increasing expropriation of Jewish property beginning in 1933 through anti-Jewish measures like professional restrictions, the forced sale ("Aryanization") of Jewish property, and also by the tax on leaving the Reich, which left Jews only a fraction of their capital if they departed the country legally. That we still had money was thanks to Papa's decision not to pay the tax for leaving and to take his money out of the country illegally. Although one hundred thousand reichsmarks was a considerable sum at that time, life abroad was expensive, and the money we had was meant to be a basis for emigrating further overseas, where my parents could begin new lives.

In London my parents wanted to plan their future, as far as that was possible. So Papa and I boarded a ship on a cold November evening. The trip from Hoek in Holland to Harwich across the English Channel was my first "sea voyage," and I greatly enjoyed it. I had begun to smoke a pipe at Gross Breesen, where it was only allowed outdoors, and after we left the harbor I leaned on the railing and smoked, staring across the water and feeling like the captain of a pirate ship. Papa worried that we would have problems with immigration and customs officials in England, but everything went smoothly. We got stamps on our passports permitting a stay of six months. We were instructed to report to the police registration office on Bow Street in London within a week to register as foreigners. Right away I noticed how miserable my school English was. I understood hardly a word. "Fatzke" had only taught us dumb songs. But my father's English was even worse, and I felt embarrassed for him when he repeatedly called out, "Where is my tash?" (meaning his *Tasche*, or bag).

England was the first station in my exile. My stay there was short but traumatic, mostly depressing, and often chaotic. The England we arrived in was trying to keep peace at all costs and was therefore willing to make almost any concession to the dictators of Germany and Italy. It was the time of appeasement. Like all the nations of the Western world, England was in a deep economic crisis. Unemployment was high, and the prospects for the revival of trade and employment were dim. People weren't pleased to see immigrants from Germany, so they usually ignored us and made it clear that our stay on their island could only be short.

It would be presumptuous of me to claim that I realized all of this clearly at the time. I didn't know much about politics, and nothing at all about English politics. At school we'd only heard what official Nazi doctrine wanted us to believe about non-German politics, and at Gross Breesen, where Bondy had tried to inform us of at least some things, my thoughts were usually somewhere else. Now I was in a strange country and had little contact with its inhabitants. In London I encountered English people on the streets, in shops, and at government offices, but my poor English would have made any profound conversation impossible even if I had become acquainted with anyone. And so I spent my first stay in England under a dismal cloud—literally as well as figuratively: we had arrived in November, and when I woke up in the morning I looked out on a continually depressing, overcast sky. So much smog was created by the smoke from household chimneys that visibility was greatly reduced. London buses were often forced to travel at a very slow speed. In the evenings the conductor had to walk in front of the bus with a burning tar torch.

At first we stayed with our old friends from Hessenallee 3 in Berlin, Walter and Else Gruen, in a small house in Hampstead, where they let us use two rooms. It wasn't much space, and while we were looking for a pension, the atmosphere was tense. In Berlin, Papa and Mutti had tried, without success, to hide the crisis in their marriage and her affair with her cousin, Uncle Fritz. Now that we were emigrants and faced an uncertain future, secrets were even more difficult to keep. The heated discussions in my parents' bedroom were quite audible. The Gruens only shook their heads. My brothers and I at first pretended that it didn't concern us, but of course we couldn't keep that up for long. Finally we talked about the situation together but came to no conclusion about what to do.

A few years earlier I had looked up to Uncle Fritz. He was a tall, good-looking man with a full head of hair (he wasn't bald like Papa), and he had often told us about his experiences in the (First) World War, when he had been a locomotive engineer on the Western front. Years later I learned from Didi that he was a big braggart, even a liar. As my parents' marriage was coming apart in London in the winter of 1937, I vented in my diary how my admiration for Uncle Fritz had turned into an aversion.

I also contributed my part to the tension. One day, when we were still living at the Gruens', I informed my parents in our hosts' presence that I wanted to go overseas with my Gross Breesen friends, although at that time there were still no concrete plans for a settlement. Today I realize that I was acting in the heat of the moment, out of desperation over the family situation. For, if my parents had given me their consent and then received permission to emigrate to some country abroad, would they have gone without me and left me alone in London with my future still uncertain? This is highly improbable, for where would I have stayed in the meantime, and what would I have lived on? Without thinking about these practical questions that day, I informed my parents of my intentions. Before they could answer, Uncle Walter, big old-fashioned Bavarian that he was, yelled at me that it was my damned duty and obligation to stay with my parents and to go with them wherever fate would take them. It wasn't at all clear, however, whether my parents would stay together or not.

What was going on in Mutti's head at that time I don't know; she never talked to me about it later. She apparently had the idea that her cousin Fritz, who was a first-class failure as a breadwinner, would

meet her somewhere in Europe —but where?—and then they would
live together. He wrote her at the address of Grete Kempner, a London
acquaintance of my parents who, after much hesitation, had given in to
my mother's request that she function as a secret post office. I was charged
with delivering Uncle Fritz's letters to my mother, a task I performed
with much gnashing of teeth. I worked unofficially for Grete Kempner,
typing letters for her on the typewriter Mutti had bought for me in Berlin,
learning in the process to type with two fingers, as I still do today. But
even the typewriter became a part of the whole miserable situation for
me. Shortly before we fled Germany, Papa had given my mother money to
buy each of us sons a suit and for me a typewriter as well. As my brothers
promptly reported to me in London, she had used part of that money to
buy Uncle Fritz a suit as a parting gift, and for this reason the typewriter
was of poor quality and hardly lasted a year. So I held that, too, against
my mother and Uncle Fritz.

In my first few weeks in London I tried desperately to get out of this
situation somehow. And I succeeded. After several unsuccessful attempts to
find an affordable place to live, we finally landed with a former Berlin classmate of my mother's. This old friend, who in England went by the name Lo
Hardy, had been an actress in Germany and had had one minor movie role
before the Nazis took over. In London, she now ran a small pension near the
underground station at Lancaster Gate. Lo was charming but totally incom-
petent as a businesswoman. Her guests were all German emigrants, so the
house language was German. Except for us, no one paid regular rent, and
Lo was always in a panic, never knowing how she would pay the servants
or for the meals we ate together every evening at the round dining table.

Shortly after we moved in at Lo Hardy's, I asked my father for
permission to spend Christmas and New Year's in Amsterdam at Meui's.
We had return tickets to Berlin, which we had bought to disguise our
real intentions, and these tickets would soon expire. I wanted to use one
of them for at least part of my trip to Holland, and Papa consented. He
was probably glad to have me out of the house while he and Mutti tried
to straighten out their marriage problems.

My two-and-a-half weeks in Amsterdam were wonderful. London,
my parents' misery, the worries about an uncertain future, all of this I banned
from my mind. On December 23, Meui and I took a bus to Antwerp, and
from there we hitchhiked on to Paris, where we hoped to attend midnight
mass at Notre Dame. In spite of the cold, we wore our youth movement

outfits, the shorts and the jackets we weren't allowed to wear in Germany anymore. The driver of a delivery truck for the Galleries Lafayette department store took pity on us and gave us a ride, although it wasn't allowed, as he told us repeatedly. We found a cheap room in the Latin Quarter at the Hotel Victoria on the Rue des Ecoles. Neither of us had much money. To our regret, Notre Dame wasn't heated that evening and midnight mass didn't take place. But the heat was turned on again on Christmas morning so the bishop of Paris could hold a service. To Meui's annoyance I threw a whole franc in the collection box—given our tight finances, a few centimes would have sufficed. It was the first mass I had ever attended.

We stayed in Paris for four days, did sightseeing in all parts of the city, and even went to Versailles, where the German Empire was founded in 1871 and the infamous peace treaty—the *Diktat*—was signed in 1919. My former *Bund* and group leader Gert Lippmann and his friend Harsch had been living in Paris for a while, and we got together with them. It was a brief and uncomfortable meeting, at least for Gert and me, since I'd had a falling out with him earlier. We decided to go our separate ways in peace. The next time I met him was sixty years later, when he, now a wealthy old man, came to Berlin from Australia with his wife. Harsch, who also found a new homeland in Sydney after the war, I never saw again. He died in the early 1990s.

Meui and I were naive and knew almost nothing about the political situation in France. The Popular Front government of Camille Chautemps, with Léon Blum as the vice-minister president, was under pressure from both the Left and the Right. Without a clue or a care, we wandered around Paris in our shorts, once attracting the unwanted attention of a gentleman who liked boys, and we wondered, late one night walking back to our room, why the bridges over the Seine were full of armed soldiers and why police were carrying piles of the Communist newspaper *L'Humanité* out of a house and throwing them into a waiting truck.

On December 27 we hitchhiked back north again, since we wanted to meet Büh (Gerd Bühler), a former *Schwarzes Fähnlein* comrade, at the main post office in Brussels on December 29. Büh had also gone to Gross Breesen for training, but he was visiting his parents in Cologne over the holidays and so was able to get together with us. He was the only one from Gross Breesen who would die on the battlefield in the Second World War.

Meui and I spent the night in Reims and were given a ride to Laon by an elderly Frenchman with a white beard. When he stopped to drop us off just before Laon, where he was turning off, he got out of the car with us and pointed to a ridge, the Chemin des Dames. There, he told us, many young men had died fighting in the First World War. He raised a warning finger and said that Germany and France must never wage war against each other again. "Don't ever wish for war! *Jamais!*" Then he shook our hands and drove on to his village.

We hitchhiked from Laon on to Brussels and arrived in time for our rendezvous with Büh. Together we spent two days looking around the city, and admired the *Manneken Pis* [Little Man Pee] sculpture at the marketplace where the Spanish Duke of Alba had the Count of Egmont beheaded in 1568. In the evening we went to see Jean Renoir's new movie, *La Grande Illusion*, which I have since rewatched many times. We spent New Year's Eve in the little village of Langemarck, where on November 10, 1914, more than two thousand German volunteer soldiers died because of incomplete training and poor planning by their commanders. Soon after the war ended, Langemarck became a synonym for patriotism, and the mistakes of the supreme command were concealed. But we believed in the Langemarck myth, and it drew us to the place. Before dark we found a Flemish farm where we could spend the night. The owners took us in as if we were their children. We sat together in the kitchen with our hosts and their other guests until midnight, sang songs to each other, and got a short introduction to Esperanto, which they encouraged us to learn so that different nations could understand each other.

The next morning, January 1, 1938, the three of us walked in the bright sunlight to the German military cemetery at Langemarck and for several minutes stared silently at the unending rows of wooden crosses. On one of the graves I found an oak leaf and a white feather, which I took with me and put in my travel diary, where they still are today. The pathetic patriotic thoughts that I confided to my diary on the occasion of that cemetery visit I will kindly spare posterity.

The next few days we spent in Brugges and Ghent, admired the beauty of these old Flemish cities and froze at night, three in a bed, in the unheated youth hostels. It was all like a dream to me, and the thought of soon having to return to England was like a nightmare. Finally we hitchhiked together to Antwerp, said goodbye there to Büh, who had to go back to Germany, and were back in Amsterdam on the evening of January 4. I stayed a few more days as the guest of Meui's parents at Minervalaan, then traveled back to London with a heavy heart.

In London I found my parents' conflict still smoldering, but the question now front and center was where the future would take us. In my absence, two factors had helped defuse the situation. My father's best friend, who had also been our dentist, "Uncle" Georg Silberstein from Moabit (in Berlin), had visited my family over the holidays, at my father's invitation, and had functioned as a mediator and peacemaker. As my brothers reported to me, after my departure it had looked as if our parents' separation was unavoidable. But there were still a number of unanswered questions, especially where each of them wanted to go or could go and whether we three sons wanted to stay with Mutti or with Papa. Hans, just nine years old, had cried and told my parents he wanted to stay with Papa. Fritz had kept out of it all, and I was on the continent. Uncle Georg had since returned to Berlin, having succeeded to a degree in calming the waters.

I had also missed another visitor, Else Radinowsky, who revealed what had happened after Papa's and my departure from Berlin. Although at first the police and the Gestapo had been more interested in their card games than in hunting us down, the next day, the Gestapo had sealed off the apartment on Holsteinische Strasse, and soon afterward publicly auctioned off our furniture and household effects. My uncle and aunt Kurt and Margot Baumgart had gone to the auction and bought some personal items, including several paintings by Grosspapa. The family photo albums weren't included in the auction and disappeared forever. I was angered more, however, by the sale of my books. Today I still go into used bookstores in Berlin in the hope of finding a book with my name in it.

My brothers and I were mostly left to our own devices during this agitation. I now and then typed letters for Frau Kempner in order to earn some money. In the course of this work, with Frau Kempner's encouragement, I was able to help end the correspondence between Mutti and uncle Fritz by burning his most recent letter in the fireplace. I then told my mother that no more mail for her had arrived. She accepted this report and never asked about it again. On this score, my conscience has never troubled me

My occasional typing work notwithstanding, my brothers and I had much more free time than we knew what to do with. Since my father was trying to spend as little as possible of the money he had managed to get out of Germany, our allowance was cut to a shilling a week. (Alas, he was less careful on the London stock exchange and lost part of his money buying Brazilian railroad stocks. It appears that the situation at home and abroad troubled his formerly very levelheaded business sense.)

I, Werner (with the pipe in my mouth) and my brother
Fritz in London, winter 1937.

Almost every day, Fritz, Hans, and I walked for hours around downtown London, aimlessly. We soon got to know Oxford and Regent streets, Piccadilly Circus, Trafalgar Square, Hyde Park Corner, and Marble Arch. We liked to go to Selfridges, the big department store on Oxford Street, and were fascinated by the animal department, which no longer exists, but where then you could buy a lion cub for fifty pounds sterling. Now and then we walked to the Cumberland Hotel at Marble Arch, especially on rainy days, and sat in the lobby all afternoon reading books we had brought along. We were always afraid that they would throw us out, since we obviously didn't belong there, but this never happened. How lost and forlorn we three brothers felt back then I will never forget. The uncertain future, our parents' marital problems, and the English winter with its smog all brought us closer together than we'd ever been, but today none of us likes to think back to those days.

During the four months that we lived there, it was clear to all of us that we wouldn't be staying in England, and not just because our visa was only valid for six months. After all, we surely could have found a way to stay in England, as many German emigrants did. You needed money, good connections, and luck. We had the money, a few connections, and might have found luck as well. But my father didn't want to stay in England. Besides the fact that he had little hope of ever learning English well, the climate didn't suit him. The fog and rain worsened his hearing impairment, he maintained, although today I suspect this was an excuse: in Holland (to which we would return that March) the climate wasn't much better. Someone suggested we investigate emigrating to a South American country, and Papa followed this advice.

He asked me to accompany him on his trips to the different consulates. For days we went from one South American legation to another. Usually they told us curtly that it wasn't possible for us to immigrate to their country. Some of these nations had good trade relations with National Socialist Germany, which they didn't want to spoil by taking in Jewish refugees. Other officials said they could do something for us if we would, as they delicately expressed it, cross their hands with silver, which Papa refused to do. He was also against trying to enter the United States with a so-called "capitalist visa," as many German emigrants were able to do at the time, outside of the annual quota, by showing they had enough money to insure that they wouldn't be a financial burden to the country. In practice this meant that you had to surrender most of the money you brought with you for five years, after which it was given back to you. The money my father had would have sufficed to procure such a privileged entry for us.

But, conservative German businessman that he was, Papa said this was out of the question. The money we would have been able to keep simply wouldn't be enough to live on, although many other German Jewish emigrants who entered the United States under the regular immigration quota system got by in the beginning by taking on any humble work. This was the case for friends of our family, but Papa refused to take such a risk. Finally, we were advised to buy fake certificates of baptism and emigrate as Catholics to Brazil, where the children of Papa's eldest sister already lived and were arranging to have their parents follow them. But my father was Jewish and, as an honest person, wanted a country to take him without his having to lie. All attempts to get him to change his mind failed. Even Mutti's argument, which I supported, that he could simply destroy the fake certificates of baptism once we had settled in Brazil, was useless.

Then at the end of January 1938 luck appeared to smile on us. The consul of Uruguay promised us visas to enter his country under certain conditions: we had to prove that we had enough money not to be a burden on the state, and we all had to have a physical examination. After that we would hear from them. Now, Uruguay was, next to Brazil, *the* South American country that most interested Papa. He had a friend in Montevideo, one of his former card-playing pals from Berlin, who had written him and enthusiastically encouraged him to come to Uruguay, saying it was easy to build up a business there with little money. With the news from the consulate, the whole mood of our family suddenly changed. We made plans and preparations. I tried to get my father to promise to let me go from Uruguay to a Gross Breesen settlement, wherever one would be founded. He promised only that he would think about it later. Then I got a cold sore on my face. It only itched, but it was visible at the physical. In short, this ended all hopes of our going to Uruguay. On February 15 we were refused a visa. Later we found out that a new consul had taken over in the meantime, and that he wouldn't have let us into the country even without my herpes. It wasn't much consolation.

The day after we'd been rejected for Uruguay, my father went to Amsterdam to try to get us residence and work permits for Holland. An acquaintance, also an emigrant at Lo Hardy's pension, a "Consul" Schleyn (I can't remember which small country had conferred his title on him), had advised Papa in London to get in touch with a Moritz Rosenthal in Amsterdam, a former Berlin city councilman and a specialist in expensive women's lingerie. He was looking for a partner with money to help him open a lingerie store in Amsterdam. Rosenthal had been a controversial figure in Berlin. He was implicated in the Sklarek scandal, in which three Jewish brothers had bribed city officials to win a virtual monopoly on supplying clothing for municipal employees (Goebbels's daily paper, *Der Angriff*, used the affair to drum up anti-Semitism prior to the local elections of 1929). But I didn't know all this at the time. Later, when I got to know this man better, I found the negative judgment fully justified.

After Papa's departure at the end of February, I very briefly saw Bondy, who was traveling from Hamburg to New York to promote a Gross Breesen settlement project in Virginia that was apparently in its initial stages. His ship had a few hours' layover in Southampton and I met with him for half an hour on board. Although he didn't have anything concrete to report, it did me good to see him again and talk to him. My spirits brightened noticeably.

At the beginning of March we received instructions from Papa in Amsterdam to come to Holland as fast as possible. So we packed our odds and ends—if I remember correctly, there were almost twenty pieces of baggage, most of which Mutti and my brothers had brought from Berlin—and took a train and boat to Amsterdam, where I was eagerly looking forward to seeing Meui again. The outcome of the first phase of our exile suited me just fine. Now I could wait calmly and see what would develop with an overseas Gross Breesen settlement. None of us were sad to leave London. As much as I later came to love that city, it was then only the site of our family problems and our uncertain future, not to mention bad winter weather. Lo Hardy cried when we left, not because we were that close to her but because we were among her few lodgers who paid their rent on time. A few weeks after our departure, she took her life with an overdose of sleeping pills.

Although the peculiarities of the marital crisis that came into full view in London were specific to my parents, such an experience was far from unusual among German Jewish refugees. The marriages of many other Jews fleeing Germany were subject to turbulent conflicts, and there was often tension between parents and children. Relationships fell victim to the stresses of being uprooted, of facing an uncertain future, and of being a stranger in a new country. Having to leave their homeland, where their parents, grandparents, and great-grandparents were buried, where they had felt they belonged until Hitler put an end to all sense of security, was a radical change that most refugees found difficult to cope with. Personal habits, social status, and the familiar surroundings of (for most) middle-class family life were suddenly swept away. Overnight they became outsiders asking for favors, unwanted immigrants, aliens, and it wasn't always clear which was more burdensome, being German or being Jewish. They often lived for months in insufficient, even primitive housing and longed for their former middle-class living rooms and dining rooms. In the end, most marriages did survive, spouses made their peace, and children who had felt their needs were misunderstood and unmet reconciled with their parents. But all this required time. At least one of the parents had to keep his or her head, take the initiative, and guide the family through the hardships of wandering and of settlement in a new homeland. This role usually fell to the mothers.

Compared to the four months in London, Amsterdam was for all of us a ray of hope. We found a pension on Stadionweg, Huize Langenberg, where we lived until early 1939. (Here my mother lived again when she went underground from September 1943 until the liberation in May 1945, working as a house servant with the papers of a "Reich German" named Kiefer who had been killed in the bombing of Rotterdam.) The Langenbergs were friendly people and we felt at home with them. Mr. Langenberg was a ship's cook on a Dutch steamer, the *Veendam*, that I was to take to the United States at the end of 1939. Mrs. Langenberg was a large, strong woman who, with the help of her also sturdy daughter Jopie, did her work efficiently and with good humor. Since *Mijnheer* Langenberg spent most of the year at sea, *Mevrouw* Langenberg was the real manager of the pension.

The seventeen months I spent in Holland were for me a time of constantly changing impressions, for political as well as personal reasons. In retrospect, I feel as if I am looking at the time through a kaleidoscope. Until the opening of the women's lingerie shop, Mayfair, on Kalverstraat in the summer of 1938, I was largely left to my own devices. I spent a lot of time in the green areas full of wild vegetation on the southern edge of Amsterdam, where it wasn't yet built up. I would sit on the bank of a little drainage ditch with my bare feet in the water, a pipe in my mouth and a book in my hands, reading or daydreaming. In the evening after eating dinner with the family at the pension, I usually met with Meui, who was studying hard for his final exams. These get-togethers, maybe because they were so limited in time, became more and more intense and our friendship closer and closer.

I didn't have much contact with my brothers anymore. Hans went to school, and Fritz was busy helping to prepare the opening of Mayfair. I was still convinced that I would soon go to the United States, especially after Bondy came back with news that a rich Jewish department store owner in Virginia, William B. Thalhimer, had bought a farm for the Gross Breesen settlement project. So I kept my distance from my family at the beginning. They were concentrating on opening the store, but I was thinking about a future in the United States with my Breesen friends.

Of all the cities I have lived in, Amsterdam has remained one of my favorites. The Dutch language sounded harsh to me at first, but I soon felt at home with it. I learned it quickly enough, albeit superficially, because of daily dealings with the people there, especially after I began working in my family's shop. And so I refrained from calling Dutch a "throat disease," as many other immigrants did at the time. I also kept my distance from fellow Germans. Amsterdam-Zuid [South Amsterdam] was full of them, and we ran into each other all the time. The fact that I was one of them didn't keep me from making fun of them, with youthful arrogance mixed with a good dose of my own anti-Semitism. On Beethovenstraat were two cafés, Delicia and Café de Paris, that were frequented by German immigrants. My brothers and I amused ourselves with the rhyme,

> *Die jüdischen Patrizier*
> *die gehen zu Delicia.*
> *Aber die, die obermies,*
> *Geh'n ins Café de Paris.*

[The Jewish patricians
go to Delicia.
But the upper plebs
go to the Café de Paris.]

Since Amsterdam was a biking city, my father bought each of my brothers a used *fiets* [bicycle]. I didn't get one because I was going to America soon. So I constantly borrowed one of my brothers' bikes and explored the city, especially on nights when I wasn't with Meui. As I rode along the canals in the moonlight, the streetlights reflected in the water. Most of all I liked to ride to the harbor, where I climbed onto one of the wooden posts used for tying up ships, lit my pipe, and enjoyed the nocturnal peace and the view of boats and water.

Sometimes I also rode to Jodenbreestraat in the old Jewish section of Amsterdam, where Rembrandt and Spinoza had lived, and where Rembrandt's house still stands today. During these forays I got my first impressions of Orthodox Jews, mostly small shopkeepers, many of them from Eastern Europe. What I hadn't experienced in Berlin's Jewish ghetto I now saw in Amsterdam, namely, Orthodox Jews of all ages, the men in their typical black robes, pushing their carts of fruit and vegetables through the streets of the Zuid on Sunday mornings, singing, in the *niggun* [wordless] synagogue melodies, the prices of their wares: "*Tomaten een dubbeltje de kilo!*" [Tomatoes ten cents a kilo]. My brothers, watching from the window of Huize Langenberg, mischieviously answered with "Oh-oh-mehn [Amen]," also in *niggun*.

I grew up a great deal in 1938, thanks largely to the increasingly alarming European political situation. At first I experienced these events primarily as they might threaten or make more urgent what I most desired: emigration to the United States to join my Gross Breesen friends. But I gradually began to mature into an adult and notice what was going on around me for its own sake, instead of exclusively through the filter of my personal problems. For instance, on February 16, 1938, shortly before we left London, I commented in my diary on the Blomberg-Fritsch crisis (two related scandals involving German officers that enabled Hitler to tighten his control over the Wehrmacht):

Things seem to be seething in Germany. Hitler wants to secure his power by terror and threats, domestically as well as abroad. He seems to have succeeded initially in both arenas. I don't share the view that Hitler has destroyed only Jewry. First of all, he hasn't destroyed it, only chased it abroad. Thereby he has created enemies in the whole world.... . But he has sinned against the German people! He has debased them to the level of rabble, taken away their sense of beauty and goodness, awakening and inciting in them bad instincts. He enslaves and violates the people, and they love him nonetheless. But there's no point in protesting and complaining here in my diary. It can and should be settled in only one way: he should be told this two minutes before being shot, and then—bang! Germany would be free again.

A bit less than a month later, on March 11, Meui and I sat up late into the night listening to news of the annexation of Austria (the *Anschluss*) on the radio. We wondered if England and France wouldn't finally intervene. We hung on the Radio Luxemburg announcer's every word, hoping desperately for news that Hitler might finally be confronted, but nothing happened. That night I wrote a long entry in my diary, concluding, "Hitler is tyrannizing two German countries—who will break the chains?"

Then in September came the Munich Conference, at which Britain and France accepted Hitler's annexation of the Sudetenland, an area in western Czechoslovakia where many ethnic Germans lived. I knew part of this region from my stays in Nieder-Klein-Aupa with the youth movement, and I remembered the unconcealed enmity between the Czech police and border officials and the Germans living there. Back then my sympathies were with the Germans—how could it be any different, given my nationalism? By September 1938 I had changed, in large part because, for the first time, I was reading newspapers and listening to radio stations that weren't controlled by Joseph Goebbels.

On a personal level, 1938 was a time of waiting. Immediately after the purchase of Hyde Farmlands in Virginia, a few of the older trainees from Gross Breesen were able to go there. They had been included in the regular annual immigration quota, having applied early enough to one of the U.S. consulates in Germany and also having affidavits from close relatives already living in the United States. I had been on the list of people wanting to settle in the United States from the beginning. But when I applied at the U.S. consulate in Rotterdam, I got a quota number that wouldn't allow me to emigrate until 1943.

Meanwhile representatives of U.S. Jewish organizations, especially the American Jewish Joint Distribution Committee (JDC), were negotiating in Washington with U.S. immigration officials. Almost all of these organizations employed mainly German refugees. The objective of Mr. Thalhimer and the JDC was to get U.S. officials to let the Breeseners into the country via the non-quota immigration category as future agricultural settlers in Virginia and shareholders in the farm. For this purpose we needed a "Washington letter." With this magical instrument, the U.S. immigration office would notify its consulates in Germany and Holland to let those of us with valid affidavits into the country as farmers at Hyde Farmlands. Looking at my correspondence (mainly with Bondy) that I managed to save through all these decades, I see that almost every week a new ray of hope arrived by surface mail from America—rays of hope but no Washington letter. First, Germany's synagogues had to burn.

My situation was more complicated than that of Breeseners still in Germany, since the U.S. consulate in Rotterdam responded negatively to my various petitions. As long as the Washington letter, which was expected anytime but delayed again and again, hadn't arrived at the Rotterdam consulate, I remained a normal applicant on the normal quota waiting list and would have to wait until 1943. Since I was in constant fear that my friends would go to America and leave me behind in Holland, I wrote many urgent letters to Gross Breesen. I'm still amazed today at Bondy's patience in answering them, consoling me and promising me that I would not be forgotten.

Aside from my anxious correspondence with Bondy and my Breesen friends, I basically had a very pleasant life, even if I didn't always recognize this at the time. In April, Büh visited us again for a week, and since Meui was busy studying for his school exams, Büh and I decided to hitchhike through Holland. Only a few months earlier we had gotten to know Belgium that way, and we knew that we got along well together. Our meager allowances at first made us unsure we could take the trip, but one day during a walk in Amsterdam I found a gulden, just enough money to make our trip seem possible.

And so on the afternoon of April 13 we stood by the side of the road, intending to hitchhike to The Hague. We got as far as Dordrecht. At a police station there we asked about a youth hostel but were told there wasn't any. The police directed us to the Salvation Army, where we slept in a big dormitory with a number of homeless people. The next day we got to Middelburg near Vlissingen, in the southwestern corner of the country, and found a dilapidated restaurant where the owner gave us a dark little garret for a few cents, and we slept well there. After having a look at Middelburg we decided to hitchhike to the east and were soon picked up by a friendly young man on a motorcycle with a sidecar. He dropped us off in Breda, where we got a ride to 's-Hertogenbosch.

In the late afternoon we were standing on the road to Nijmegen-Arnhem-Apeldoorn, hoping to hitch a ride to the northern coast, when two policemen on a motorcycle with a sidecar stopped and asked us in a friendly way where we were going so late in the evening. We told them, and the officers advised us to come to the police station with them, since it was dangerous to hitchhike at this hour. They put Büh and me in the sidecar and took us to the police station, where they gave us something to eat and played checkers with us.

Then suddenly the situation changed. We were led to a cell furnished with two cots, two thin blankets, and a bucket for a toilet. Before they locked the door behind us, they took our belts, shoelaces, passports, and wallets (which were practically empty). In the cells next to ours were drunks who made a racket most of the night. The following morning we were taken to the office of the Dutch border and street police [*marechaussee*]. There a large, unfriendly man, who wore a uniform very similar to that of the SS, reprimanded us for several minutes. We learned from him that we had been "arrested" the evening before, that it was forbidden for us as foreigners to hitchhike on Dutch roads, and that we were to return to Amsterdam by the quickest and most direct route. If we were caught hitchhiking again, we would be put in jail again, and not just for one night. Büh was told to return to Germany as soon as we arrived back in Amsterdam. Only then were our passports, belts, and other belongings returned, and we left looking like two crestfallen poodles.

But our contrite appearance was deceptive. Barely out of sight of the police station, we came to a fork in the road, where the left side went to Amsterdam and the right one to Leeuwarden, from where one could go over the dike of the IJsselmeer to the Jewish *Werkdorp Nieuwesluis* in Wieringen. We took the road to the right. By dark we were in a village near Leeuwarden, more than two hundred kilometers north of 's-Hertogenbosch and its police station. Since we planned to be in Amsterdam at the end of the following day, we even had a clean conscience. I only understood much later how reckless we had been.

We spent the night in a barn, sharing it with a quite friendly young bull, and hitchhiked the next day across the Apsluitsdijk, which separates the IJsselmeer from the Waddenzee. The driver who picked us up took us to the *Werkdorp Nieuwesluis*, which the Dutch had created for young Jewish refugees from Germany and Austria to do agricultural and craft work until their emigration overseas, predominately to Palestine. I had quite a positive impression of the work camp, which greatly reminded me of Gross Breesen. Later on, from Amsterdam, I sent a report on our short stay to Bondy, who shared it with interested Breeseners. Thus began my work as a chronicler, which would take a number of different forms in the following years. When Büh and I arrived in Amsterdam late in the evening of the same day, I told my horrified parents about our adventures "discovering" Holland. I shouldn't have mentioned our night in jail. I had to promise my father I would forgo such mischief in the future. I kept my word for the rest of my time in Holland.

In early summer, Mayfair, my family's women's lingerie shop, opened on Kalverstraat, an elegant little shopping street in the center of Amsterdam. At the same time we moved from the Huize Langenberg into our own apartment at Cliostraat 39. My father asked me to help out in the shop a few hours every day. I complied without enthusiasm. There were two reasons for my reluctance. The first was my duties, which consisted mostly of attaching price tags to women's silk panties, chemises, and stockings, which I found terribly boring. The other reason was the co-owner, Moritz Rosenthal. Papa, as a silent partner, was only responsible for financial matters and sat upstairs with his files. Neither I nor my brothers could stand Rosenthal. He was a moody and severe manager who tormented his personnel. But he was submissive and brownnosing in his dealings with anyone official, as I often had occasion to observe. He was later deported and killed. Ever the businessman, he took along a case of samples of his wares to the Dutch transit camp at Westerbork (on the way to "labor deployment in the East," as it was euphemistically called in Nazi terminology) in order to sell the stuff there.

My time at Mayfair was made at least bearable by the fact I usually worked together with Fritz and a young woman apprentice and by the friendship that was slowly developing between Papa and me, which in fact had already begun in London. I have long forgotten the girl's name, but I remember vividly what she looked like and how we talked together and (softly) sang unflattering songs about our boss. I also remember a poem about Hitler that she taught me:

> *Huichelaar en moordenaar,*
> *Ingemene zwendelaar,*
> *Terging van zijn volk,*
> *Leugenaar, die zijn land verried,*
> *Ellendeling, die bloed vergiet,*
> *Rotzak, waarom sterf jij niet?*

> [Hypocrite and murderer,
> Lowdown swindler,
> Tormenter of your people,
> Liar who betrays his country,
> Wretch who sheds blood,
> Swine, why don't you die?]

For the answer to this question we had to wait seven long years.

My relationship with my father warmed for a strange reason. Having started smoking a pipe at Gross Breesen (despite everything I'd learned in the youth movement about how bourgeois and harmful smoking was), I bought myself a cigar one day in Amsterdam. After smoking it, I had to run to the bathroom. As I emerged pale and trembling, Papa walked by and asked what was the matter. When I told him, he invited me upstairs to his office, where he gave me a short course on how to smoke correctly. He said I shouldn't start with cigars, which are too heavy for beginning smokers. He invited me to come up the next morning at eleven to smoke a cigarillo with him. And that is how it began. Every workday thereafter I appeared in Papa's doorway at eleven and we smoked together. He also talked to me about things that concerned him, showing trust in my discretion. (Mr. Rosenthal was a frequent subject of his remarks.) Thus a bond finally developed between us, one-and-a-half years before we would see each other for the last time.

Besides working in the shop and waiting impatiently for my American visa, I continued to get together with Meui as often as I could. In September 1938 we attended together the celebrations of Queen Wilhelmina's fortieth year on the throne. We watched the parades, and I photographed the queen waving to the crowd as her coach proceeded down Kalverstraat. I wasn't impressed by the Dutch troops, whose rows weren't straight, and many of whom didn't even march in time (my admiration for the German military tradition that had so inspired us in the *Schwarzes Fähnlein* was still quite ingrained). Shortly before dark, Meui and I climbed into his kayak and paddled through the city's canals, which sparkled with reflections of the lights decorating the bridges. How many kilometers we paddled I don't know. We didn't stop until the break of day.

In the fall of 1938 I also lost my first girlfriend, Leus, to one of my Breesen roommates, Dackel. The magnanimity with which I reacted to this loss and which I recorded in my diary makes me uncomfortable when I read it today. Maybe I was able to confide such generous thoughts to my diary because Leus and I had already grown apart. In any case, this personal loss was very soon overshadowed by an event for which all German Jews were completely unprepared: Kristallnacht.

The first news reached us in Holland via the press and radio announcements on November 10. Two days later I learned from a former Gross Breesener who lived in Holland that Bondy and twenty trainees had been arrested at Gross Breesen and taken to a concentration camp (my informant had just read this in the Belgian newspaper *Het Volk*). Then began a time of feverish efforts to help the arrested Breeseners from outside the country.[8] Meui and I contacted the Amsterdam *Comité voor Bijzondere Joodsche Belangen* [Committee for Special Jewish Interests, hereafter Jewish Committee], which had been established by the Jewish

---

[8] For a more detailed account of these events, see Werner T. Angress, *Between Fear & Hope: Jewish Youth in the Third Reich* (Columbia University Press, 1988).

businessman and politician Abraham Asscher with the support of the Dutch government. Even though we didn't yet know to which concentration camp the arrested Breeseners had been sent, we wanted to get written assurance from the committee that they would be able to come to Holland after their discharge. We hoped they could come to the agricultural residence and training camp that Büh and I had visited on our hitchhiking trip at Eastertime, the *Werkdorp Nieuwesluis* in Wieringen.

The scene we encountered when we went to the Jewish Committee was chaotic. Hundreds of people were trying to get into the building, which was already overflowing. Many had tears in their eyes, and others paced back and forth in the square, wringing their hands, desperation written on their faces. All had relatives or friends in Germany who had been arrested and whom they wanted to help get out. For emigrants living in Holland, the Jewish Committee seemed the only institution that could make rescue possible. I can't remember how Meui and I got inside, not to mention how we found the right office. But Meui guided us through the hysterical crowds with careful movements and a calm but resolute voice until we were standing before the office where we wanted to present our petition.

It was the office of two people with whom we were to work together closely from then on, Rudolf Elk and Gertrude van Tijn. Both were members of the board of the *Stichting Joodsche Arbeid* [Foundation for Jewish Labor] that came into being in February 1934 after the founding of the *Werkdorp*. Now they became our negotiation partners in our attempt to get our friends who had been arrested in Germany into the work camp in Wieringen. Meui knocked, opened the door, and we entered without waiting for permission. Unlike me, Meui spoke fluent Dutch, and he presented our request calmly, succinctly, and with impressive resolve. Elk and van Tijn listened attentively. It is clear to me today that this was the first decisive step in freeing Bondy from the Buchenwald concentration camp along with the Breesen boys who'd been arrested with him. All of them planned to emigrate to the United States and already had the necessary affidavits. Without Meui that day, I would have been quite helpless.

The next several days we did everything we could to get support for our plans. Meui dealt with the various Dutch authorities—especially the Jewish Committee but also an elderly Dutch judge, Mr. de Jongh, who knew Bondy and who tried to get him a visa—while I mainly wrote to friends and acquaintances in the United States, asking them for help. Papa gave me time off from work at Mayfair, immediately understanding that I needed time to help my friends. He also gave me money for telegrams. Back then telephoning was much too expensive, and there was no airmail yet for ordinary mortals, since it was very expensive and less regular than surface mail. Besides telegrams, we depended on steamships, mainly French, Dutch, and English ocean liners, of which at least one carried mail across the Atlantic each week. (Of course, we no longer trusted our letters to German ships.) I especially sought help from a friend in New York, Joseph Loewensberg, the older brother of a Gross Breesen intern, Ernst Loewensberg, with whom I had a good relationship and who was already in Virginia. Joseph was well-known among the various Jewish activists in New York, including Ingrid Warburg, the daughter of the Hamburg banker Max Warburg.

So I sat up late at night writing, pleading mainly for money, which was needed by the Jewish Committee in Amsterdam as a financial guarantee for the "Virginia boys" sitting in Buchenwald before they would be let into the *Werkdorp*. It was a vicious cycle: the committee promised to prepare entry permits and send them to Germany for the incarcerated Breeseners, provided they had affidavits and therefore would only stay in Holland for a limited time. But first their living expenses at the *Werkdorp* had to be financially guaranteed, and that could only be obtained through the United States. The sum that the committee demanded for this was relatively small, forty guldens per person per month. But at that time it was difficult to find someone who could or would finance such a guarantee.

The negotiations dragged on and wore us down. I wasn't getting enough sleep and was irritable, which surely didn't help matters. Besides corresponding with New York, for which purpose I had to find out every day when the next ship was departing so the letters could be brought to the post office in time, I phoned Ruth Hadra (Bondy's secretary at Gross Breesen) and Frau Scheier, as well as my old love, Leus, who had been living with her boyfriend's parents in their house in Berlin since Dackel's arrest. I was trying to get a list of all the Breeseners at Buchenwald, and especially the names of those who had affidavits to go to Virginia. Unfortunately, I got no concrete information from any of the three women I contacted, since they were afraid to answer my questions over the phone. I urgently needed the names for the Jewish Committee, which couldn't issue entry permits without them.

Two weeks after Kristallnacht, our efforts began to bear fruit. From New York came assurance that money for financial guarantees would be made available not only for the "Virginia boys" but for all the arrested

Gross Breeseners, provided that it would help get them out of detention sooner. We took this confirmation to the Jewish Committee, which immediately demanded an extended list. Again I tried to get the information from Gross Breesen, again without success. Then suddenly a telegram arrived from Fritz Schwarzschild, who worked at the *Reichsvertretung der Juden in Deutschland* [National Representative Agency of Jews in Germany], telling me to call him. His functions at the *Reichsvertretung* included the financial administration of Gross Breesen. I received from Schwarzschild the information that I'd been trying to get for days, and we talked on the phone almost every day thereafter. In addition to learning the names of all the Gross Breesen boys imprisoned in Buchenwald, I also found out that Head Manager Scheier and the master carpenter Kiwi were being held at Buchenwald too and that something had to be done immediately to get them out. Now I was able to give the Jewish Committee the list of all the arrested Breeseners and at the same time inform Joseph Loewensberg in New York how much money we needed for a financial guarantee. We received a telegram right away confirming that we would get the money.

Why did Schwarzschild get in touch with me, of all people? We had met only briefly during his occasional visits to Gross Breesen. A popular man with a good sense of humor, Fritz Schwarzschild was in his mid-forties and the father of two sons who would later become quite well known in the United States. While visiting a Berlin museum sometime in the 1930s, he had gotten into a conversation with another man while looking at the paintings, and they became friends. This other museum visitor was Herr von Freeden, at that time, if I remember correctly, an undersecretary in the Ministry of the Interior. On November 9, Freeden called Schwarzschild late in the evening and told him to come to the ministry right away. The doorman had instructions to let him in. And so the Jew Fritz Schwarzschild sat in the Ministry of the Interior as Freeden's guest for several days, until the first wave of arrests was over. From his "hiding place" Schwarzschild phoned Frau Scheier and Ruth Hadra at Gross Breesen and thus learned about my and Meui's efforts to get the Breeseners held at Buchenwald to the work camp in Holland by obtaining entry permits for them. After that he got in contact with me. When the war ended in 1945, he immediately sent CARE packages to Herr von Freeden and his family.

In order to get Bondy out of Buchenwald, we'd hoped at first that his younger brother Fritz, who lived in Amsterdam with his wife and child, could arrange for him to come as a close relative. When this proved impossible, Meui turned to the Amsterdam judge who was familiar with Bondy's work with young people in prison. Mr. de Jongh was able to get Bondy a temporary residence permit for Holland, which got him released from Buchenwald. Bondy didn't make use of his Dutch residence permit, however, until early 1939. First he went back to Gross Breesen and tried to find someone to succeed him as director.

The release of our friends from Buchenwald, where so many other Jews perished, was mainly thanks to Schwarzschild and Martin Gerson, the agricultural director of the Gut Winkel Jewish training camp, affiliated with the Zionist movement *Hachscharah*. Gerson had visited Gross Breesen several times. In November 1938 he contacted German government officials not only to get his Gut Winkel trainees out of another concentration camp, but also to get the Breeseners out of Buchenwald. He argued that because of their agricultural training they had good chances of being able to emigrate from Germany soon. Though I never learned the details, I know that Gerson was later murdered at Auschwitz, while Schwarzschild succeeded in emigrating to the United States with his family in 1939.

On December 6, St. Nicolas Day, a telegram from Berlin brought the first good news: with the exception of Bondy, Scheier, and four other Breesen prisoners, all the others had been released. Five days later came a telegram from Bondy saying that he and Scheier were also free. The last Breeseners were released at the beginning of January. From then on, miraculously, everything progressed smoothly. On December 15 the first six boys who'd been accepted to Wieringen arrived in Amsterdam. The whole day long I stood on a platform at the *centraalstation*, freezing and excited as a child. Whenever a train arrived from Germany I ran the length of it looking for familiar faces. Although the boys had traveled together to the border, they weren't all processed together and thus arrived in Amsterdam at different times.

The first one to arrive that day was Hans "Juwa" Rosenthal, who was from our Hanniot group. I was shocked when he appeared before me bald. He said he hadn't worn a cap so that the Dutch would see that he and all the other concentration camp prisoners had had their heads shaved. I had to tell him that no Dutch person would associate a shaved head with a German concentration camp, since members of Dutch fraternities, of which there were many in the city, traditionally had their heads shaved. He put his cap back on.

In the summer of 1939, Juwa succeeded in emigrating to Brazil, where his father had bought land for him in Rolândia in the southern state of Paraná. There he started a coffee plantation he named Nova Breesen, which his widow still manages today. (In Brazil, Juwa and his family were neighbors and friends of the family of former German Vice Chancellor Erich Koch-Weser, who founded the German colony in Rolândia after fleeing Nazism—he was a Protestant, but his mother was Jewish—and bought a large coffee plantation there. His grandson Caio Koch-Weser, who was born in Rolândia, served as Germany's finance minister from 1999 to 2005.) The last Breesener to arrive that day was my friend Prinz. For some reason the Gestapo had held him at the border until evening, but, since punctuality had never been his strong suit, I found his late arrival quite normal that day too.

For a few days all the boys stayed in Amsterdam, where Meui and I found places for them to sleep. Amazingly, most of them were in relatively good physical condition, aside from a few colds. But they were very thin, and at first they reacted to our questions about Buchenwald with steely silence. There were two reasons for this. First, they'd all had to sign a statement when they were released that they had been treated properly and would keep quiet about their stay at Buchenwald. Second, their shock over the past few weeks was so profound that they needed a few days of complete quiet before they finally began to talk about their experiences after Kristallnacht.

I eventually learned how they were arrested at Gross Breesen, locked in the horse stable, and then loaded onto trucks that took them to Breslau. There they walked to the train that took them to Weimar and then to Buchenwald. The beating they got from the SS in the station tunnel in Weimar was the beginning of the systematic brutality that they underwent in the camp for four weeks. They were able to get through that time without permanent physical and psychological damage mainly thanks to the fact they stuck close together as a group, under Bondy's direction. They also helped others in their barracks, especially the weak and the elderly. They obtained extra food for these people whenever possible, which was quite difficult. In addition, they helped the elderly and prisoners with physical problems get to the two filthy community latrines. They could only do this in the daytime, since it was forbidden to leave the barracks at night.

In the beginning, Bondy had to master his own crisis as well, which resulted from shock. I couldn't believe my ears when some of the boys said that on their first night in Buchenwald, Bondy had an attack of weeping that lasted for several minutes. They'd lain near him at the camp in what served as beds: low, narrow wooden platforms several levels high. This incident didn't correspond to their, or my, picture of "the Professor," the director of Gross Breesen. It didn't happen again, and for the remainder of their stay at the camp, Bondy was once more the one in control.

After a few days of rest in Amsterdam, the boys went to the *Werkdorp Nieuwesluis* in Wieringen, where most of them lived and worked for over a year. Twelve more Breeseners for whom the Jewish Committee had procured entry permits ultimately arrived, filling the two barracks set aside for Breeseners at the *Werkdorp*. I would have loved to join them, but it wasn't possible, since the *Werkdorp* then was only for kids who didn't have parents to support them. So for the following six months I stayed in my parents' new apartment at Cliostraat 39 in Amsterdam. My room was on the level slightly below ground, but the windows let in plenty of light. I continued working at Mayfair, but neither my heart nor my thoughts were there. My relationship with Mr. Rosenthal deteriorated, which caused Papa concern. Whenever I could get away on weekends, I hitchhiked to see my friends in Wieringen.

In addition I enjoyed the short visits of friends who were passing through, usually friends from Gross Breesen. Kristallnacht had not only increased the pressure to emigrate soon, it also had increased the willingness of other countries to open their gates a crack, especially for younger people, at least for a while. Almost every week I received from another friend a postcard with the short message that he or she was on the way to England or South America or Australia, and could I find a place for him or her to stay in Amsterdam for a night or so. This wasn't a problem: Meui and I asked our parents or friends of the family to take in these travelers. And so I was often standing at the Amsterdam train station to greet these emigrants. The short time we were together, often getting to know each other even better than before, was like a happy dream. Like a dream, too, the memories of these very short meetings evaporated. In many cases, the one or two days I spent with these people in Amsterdam was the last time I would see them.

Twice I fell in love. The first time was shortly after Kristallnacht. While Meui and I were hectically trying to obtain entry permits for our Breesen friends detained at Buchenwald, I got the news that a creature unknown to me, Hilla, would be passing through Amsterdam and staying two nights, until her ship sailed for Australia. I have forgotten where and how we met. Nor do I remember whether she had been at Gross Breesen after my departure, but at least she had friends there. It was from Hilla that I got the first complete report of what had happened at Gross Breesen on November 10. She also told me that she was engaged to a man whom she only knew superficially and apparently didn't love, but who had obtained an entry permit to Australia for her by financially guaranteeing her as his fiancée. I knew the man only by name and that he had been a leader in the Breslau group of *Schwarzes Fähnlein*. Amid all the confusion of November 1938, Hilla and I discovered very quickly that we liked each other a great deal. She was staying with friends who had just emigrated from Germany, and we had only two evenings, on which we wandered around the city, talking almost constantly, doubtless noticing our feelings for each other, but also aware that we would probably never meet again. And we never did.

The second time I fell in love was with Traut Fleischer, the girlfriend of my friend Jochen Feingold, both of them former Breeseners. Jochen had passed through Amsterdam weeks earlier on the way to Kenya, where Bondy had found him and a few other Breeseners positions as farmworkers. Since he couldn't take Traut with him, she went to London as domestic help, as did many other young Jewish women. She and I already knew each other well, but our two days together in Amsterdam in late March 1939 went far deeper. Entwined, we walked, talked, and silently thought our thoughts. But that was it. The ethics concerning sex at our age that Bondy had instilled in us, as well as the impossibility, for both of us, of betraying our friend Jochen, set limits to our feelings. Nonetheless the hours we spent together were unforgettable. Five years later, in the summer of 1944, when I was a U.S. soldier on a short leave in London and Traut was working there as a nurse, she took twenty-four hours off to be with me and we repeated the experience. She died in 1947 after a routine operation, and I mourned her and our friendship for a long time.

One of the highlights of 1939 was seeing off the Australia group, which set off from Rotterdam on June 10. Over the course of two days, I wrote the following in my diary:

It is Friday, June 9, 1939. I feel like there are only Gross Breeseners in Rotterdam. They arrived this morning, from Germany, Brussels, and Amsterdam. Dackel and I showed up as envoys of the Dutch Breeseners, and this evening Bo[ndy] plans to arrive by plane from Berlin. Fifteen Breeseners, thirteen boys and two girls, are leaving for Australia tomorrow on the Dutch ship *SS Slamat*. Our headquarters is the Hammelburg. This isn't an old citadel from the Geusen wars, it's a pension, whose Jewish owner is feeding our group for one day. The group is staying at three pensions… . In the Hammelburg we are only eating.

Since their arrival at the train station this morning everyone is busy. First all the technical things, like passports, tickets for the ship, and baggage, have to be taken care of. In a dark, narrow hallway in the Hammelburg we squeeze between luggage, coats, and hats. A gentleman from the [Jewish] Committee is standing downstairs impatiently waiting for Dackel and Pitt, who are to accompany him with passports and tickets. It's hard to find things in the confusion. Herko's ticket for the ship has disappeared, never to be found again, and we both look through his things. Dackel, as always in such situations, sweats in his excitement and swears like a Berlin garbageman. Every two minutes the man from the Committee declares categorically that he doesn't have all day and he has to go. In my haste I break … an ashtray that was entrusted to us. Töpper! But finally everyone finds what he is searching for and leaves, [Dackel and Pitt] with their papers and the gentleman in a hurry, and we are directed to our rooms. So we all finally have some peace and quiet. We sit in each of the rooms for a while talking, because the boys and girls temporarily without passports can't leave. They talk about Breesen, about their trip here. I tell them about the departure of the four Wieringen friends—not Breeseners—who are also boarding the ship for Australia, and about the others at Wieringen, about Holland, about myself. While we are talking, the thought sometimes passes through my mind, "Good Lord! Here we are sitting and talking, some of us getting to know each other for the first time, happy to get to know each other or to see each other again, and tomorrow morning they're leaving for the other end of the world, for Australia. We're living in crazy times, because we have to be glad they can emigrate to Australia!"

When everything is taken care of—that is, when the whole business with the papers is in order—we have some free time. Part of the group goes to the movies for the first time in a long while, and the others, among them Dackel and I, go for a walk, have a look at the harbor, talk with each other, and try not to think about the fact that at this time tomorrow they will all be gone.

At ten in the evening we're all at the little KLM pavilion, the office of the Dutch airline, waiting for Bo… . [After he arrives] those who want to talk to him go off with him, and the others of us walk through the city and sit down in a café together for the last time. We don't return to our pensions until midnight. For the group, this will be their last night on European soil.

Now the time has come! We're all standing in front of the *Slamat*, a not very big ship of Rotterdam Lloyd. Suddenly Prinz and Floh have appeared, having hitchhiked here. At about ten o'clock in the morning we all go onboard. For many it is the first big ship they've seen. I haven't been on an ocean steamship either, except for ten minutes on the *Hamburg* [in Southampton in 1938, in order to speak briefly with Bondy]. It feels very strange to walk through a floating house. Almost all the stewards are from Malay or Java. While we're standing in one of the cabins, I suddenly sense something behind me. When I turn around I see it is one of the stewards, who has stepped in noiselessly. Their feet clad only in sandals and their heads wrapped in a sort of turban make a strange, exotic impression. It reminds me of [Ernst] Wiechert's *Geschichte eines Knabben* [*Story of a Boy*] when I see these brown people with their large, dark animal eyes before me. They understand as little English as they do German. It will be strange for the boys to be served by these mute, noiseless people.

The whole ship is full of German and Viennese emigrants. It's sad and somehow depressing to see some of them, already quite old people, going to a country they will never comprehend, whose language they will never learn to speak well, and that is located thousands of miles from the place where they were born. Australia! For these people it really is at the end of the world. It's more reassuring to see the Breeseners going there. They are all confident, and which of us wouldn't be? All of a sudden I'm possessed by the desire to go with them, and not to have to leave the ship. But I know that in a couple of hours the signal will sound that will separate us for a very long time, perhaps forever.

Up on the tourist class promenade deck we all stand together one more time. We don't make any farewell speeches, nor does Bo say anything about what he expects from the group. We are Breeseners and we have confidence in each other... . Standing together up there, we notice that we belong together. In a moment, mountains of farewell letters are written. There is no melancholic atmosphere. Only now and then someone sneaks a look at his watch and mutters, "Damn! ..." As we stand at the railing for the last time, someone in the group says to me, "Just a week ago we were singing, 'And soon it will be / That we will stand by the sea / And think of our distant homeland. / For the little troop / Is busy getting ready / To leave the gray walls. / Nothing holds us back any longer, / And we are looking forward / To traveling east with fluttering sails.'" I only nod. If only you knew how I would love to go with you! "Visitors are requested to leave the ship." There it is, the signal that we'd been waiting for. Now things get serious. We shake hands once again. "Take care!" "You, too!" We slowly leave the ship—Bo, Prinz, Dackel, Floh, and I. The ship hasn't sailed yet. We're standing down below on the quay, and they're standing up there on deck—fifteen Breeseners, our first large cohesive group: Pitt, Herko, Erich, Leo, Klaus, Werner, Spitz, Wachsi, Franz, Erwin, Fritz, Hans, Herbert, Hanni, and Inge. Hardly a one older than seventeen. In Colombo they're meeting Johnny with the other three from Wieringen: Posche, Bosi, and Rudi. One of them has gotten out his accordion and now they're singing songs we sang in the *Bund* and later in Breesen: "The Gray Fog," "Comrades, When Will We Meet Again?" "We won't falter, we won't retreat, we will stand as one." And then: "Who wants to move to Australia, when no one's in command, yeah, in command."

Now the last lines are loosed, and the bridge for first class ... is pulled in. Slowly, ever so slowly, the little tugboat pulls the steamship into the middle of the Maas. Some last calls over here, over there. They sing again, and the sound gradually fades. We've taken out our handkerchiefs and wave them. So they can see it across such a distance, we all wave together in rhythm. Bo commands, "Up! Wave! Down! Up! Wave! Down!" The group, standing at the sternpost, waves back in the same way. They get smaller and smaller, less and less visible. And then we see only the ship going down the Maas slowly but steadily. It is taking our comrades to their new destination. Fifteen Breeseners sail to Australia, and five Breeseners go slowly back into town.

A few weeks later I moved from Amsterdam into one of the two Breesen barracks at Wieringen. I had obtained permission from Gertrude van Tijn of the Jewish Committee to live and work at the *Werkdorp Nieuwesluis* until my departure for the United States. I lived and worked there for a little over four months. Once again I was getting up early, working physically all day long, and getting used to continually changing weather. I enjoyed it thoroughly. But it was different from Gross Breesen in many respects. The great majority of the people at the *Werkdorp* were Zionists, and while I was there an illegal *Alijah* [emigration to Israel] transport went to Palestine on the *SS Dora*, which was chartered by the Jewish Committee, with 467 "passengers," of which seventy-five were from the *Werkdorp*. It took the ship six weeks to get there. But the captain succeeded in avoiding the British patrol boats that were supposed to obstruct all illegal immigration into Palestine, and the boys and girls were put on land, after which they were immediately placed in various *kibbutzim*. Saying farewell to the *Dora* group, I was tempted, for the only time in my life, to become a Zionist and to go to a *kibbutz*. But this impulse disappeared quickly, especially as a few days earlier, in anticipation of the nearing *Alijah*, they had danced the hora loudly and wildly all night long, which I noted very negatively in my diary.

What often disgusted us Breeseners in the *Werkdorp* was the vulgarity of the people there, especially the refugees who had come to Holland from the workers' districts of Vienna. When we worked in groups on the *polders* [fields that had been won from the sea], for example, picking flax, they often told dirty jokes out loud, which we Breeseners, from upper-middle-class families and products of Bondy's training, found very offensive. Nonetheless, the few months I spent in Wieringen were very pleasant for me. I like to think back on the evening walks I took alone or with one of my friends. I considered the familiar physical exertion demanded of us by the grain harvest to be a meaningful challenge, and working together with the others was rewarding, as it had been earlier at Gross Breesen. We enjoyed seeing the herons fly by above us.

Then September came, and with it the outbreak of war. Suddenly we were seeing Dutch fighter planes flying back and forth to the east of us, near the German border. Of course, we wondered what would happen to us if Hitler attacked Holland. On August 24, one day after the signing of the German-Russian nonaggression pact, I wrote in my diary, "I would like to grow older than nineteen, but I think I will sign up. I won't shoot against Germany, but rather, against the end of the world." A few days later, in a somewhat more sober frame of mind, I, together with almost all the other people working at the *Werkdorp*, placed myself at the disposal of the Dutch government as an agricultural worker. We understood that we wouldn't be called to bear arms. Hitler's attack on Holland didn't come until May 10, eight months later, a delay that probably saved my life. My friends in the *Werkdorp*, Breeseners and others, who didn't manage to leave Europe before May 10, 1940, died almost without exception in the Final Solution, most of them at the Mauthausen concentration camp.

After my decision in June to go to the *Werkdorp* and work together with friends, immigration to the United States occupied my thoughts much less than before. The new surroundings, new challenges, and my resolve to work hard and well, all these things took priority for me in the short run. This changed very quickly with the outbreak of the war, when my emigration to Virginia became as important to my father as it was to me. He had already given me his general permission earlier, and now he became quite impatient and paid close attention to my sporadic contacts with the U.S. consulate. During one of my regular visits to Amsterdam

My mother with my brother Hans in Amsterdam, 1938.

he confided to me his concern that sooner or later Hitler would attack Holland. Thus it was important for him to know that I was safe in the United States. If bad turned to worse, the family could perhaps follow me over there.

A few days before my departure, when the Dutch press reported rumors of several German divisions gathering on the border, his worry practically turned to panic. Then, unexpectedly, during the last week of September I was suddenly summoned to the U.S. consulate in Rotterdam. In the meantime I had obtained a new sponsor, who provided me with an affidavit from the American Jewish Joint Distribution Committee in New York. My original sponsor was a cousin of my father's, Sam Trepp, a wonderful person as I was to learn later. He worked as an engineer in the basement of Bergdorf-Goodman, a big New York ladies' clothing store, where he saw to it that the lights and elevators worked and the water pipes didn't drip. His wife, born into the Goodman family, had gotten him a lifetime position. But the affidavit that Sam Trepp had provided for me wasn't good enough for the consulate. I had already been summoned to Rotterdam in July and informed that in addition to Trepp's affidavit I needed twenty-four hundred dollars as a financial guarantee, a sum Papa couldn't raise. Now they had found a new sponsor for me, Lewis L. Strauss, co-owner of the New York bank Kuhn, Loeb, and Company, who in 1953 was appointed chairman of the Atomic Energy Commission by President Eisenhower. An affidavit from this man fortunately corresponded to the expectations of the consulate.

When I went to Rotterdam, Papa accompanied me in case any financial questions should come up that I couldn't answer. That day I stood with trembling knees before the consular official and answered a number of routine questions, including whether I had ever been a Communist, whether I wanted to murder the president of the United States, and whether I had ever served a prison term. This last question I answered only by shaking my head. Büh and I had, after all, spent that night in the 's-Hertogenbosch jail, "as protection against accidents," as the nice Dutch policemen had put it. Fortunately there were no more questions of this sort at the consulate. After all the formalities were taken care of, I was sent back to the *Werkdorp* and told to wait for a summons to a physical examination. That took place on October 3, when I was declared fit as a fiddle and given my visa.

Now it was time to prepare to leave. I returned to Amsterdam to do some shopping and to pack. As a farewell gift my parents gave me a new typewriter, this time a very good one. October 28 was the big day. Meui rented a car to drive me and my parents to Rotterdam. From there I was to take the train to Antwerp where the *SS Veendam* was docked. It would leave the next day for the United States.

The farewell in Amsterdam was short but emotional. None of us knew whether we would ever see each other again. Several friends from the *Werkdorp* had come to Amsterdam and were standing on Cliostraat in front of our apartment to say goodbye to me and to wave as we left. My little brother Hans, then eleven years old, cried uncontrollably, and I too had trouble holding back my tears. Meui then drove my parents and me to Rotterdam, where I once again and for the last time said goodbye at the train station. My baggage had gone a few days earlier and was now on the ship. My parents tried hard to smile as they hugged me. With a pounding heart I got on the train and waved to them from the window. It was the last time I saw my father, standing by the car, waving to me.

CHAPTER 6

United States—Hyde Farmlands, 1939–1941

The crossing to the United States was my first ocean voyage, but it wouldn't be my last. It was late October 1939 and Europe had been at war for almost two months. But Holland was still neutral, and the ship on which I was sailing, the *SS Veendam* of the Holland-America Line, was brightly lit at night so that German U-boats could see the Dutch colors clearly. The ship was overcrowded, mainly with Jewish emigrants from all over Europe, and cabins meant for two people were now occupied by four.

I knew two people on the ship. One was *mijnheer* Langenberg, in whose pension we had lived for several months when we came to Amsterdam from London in the spring of 1938. He was the head cook on the *Veendam*, supervising and coordinating the personnel of three different kitchens. Since he was a busy man, I saw him only occasionally and usually briefly. But the first time we met, shortly after departure, he took the time to give me a tour of the whole ship, from the captain's bridge to the machine room deep below deck. The other person I knew was Bruno, a young man who had been at the *Wieringer Werkdorp*, although we had seldom seen each other there. I had met him on the train from Rotterdam to Antwerp. We were hardly on board the ship when we were joined by another passenger our age, Hans, and the three of us spent most of the voyage together.

The crossing lasted from October 28 to November 10. The weather was stormy for most of the trip, and many of the passengers stayed in their bunks half the day and only occasionally came to meals. We younger ones who didn't get seasick consumed double and triple portions at the almost deserted dining room tables.

Third class, where Bruno and I were lodged, was especially crowded. Hans was in first class and visited us regularly. On the first or second day

I went to see Hans in his cabin and the steward politely but unambiguously threw me out. In a travel journal that I typed daily on my new Remington, I reported on the impressions that the other passengers made on me. It is still embarrassing to me today to read the anti-Semitic tone of my remarks. Two short paragraphs will suffice.

10.30.39 ... It is very very sad how most of the other passengers behave. Loud, undisciplined, and insolent. Almost all of them have forgotten what they experienced, or they learned nothing from it. Sorry for them!

11.5.39 ... A lot of Eastern European Jews are onboard, Galicians, Poles, and Hungarians. They all behave better than the Viennese. But the latter are more adaptable and will probably be more capable in their work once they are over there... . Here on the ship I clearly see how sad and hopeless the Jewish question is! You pity these people because of their past and also because of their future. On the other hand, they are annoying because of their pushiness and sometimes just plain awful behavior. It will always be so.

My harsh criticism of my fellow passengers and their "Jewish behavior" wasn't Jewish self-hatred. I was nineteen years old and still heavily influenced by my upbringing at home and what I had learned at Gross Breesen. I had been repeatedly instructed on how I was to behave as a Jew in public, and how I was *not* to behave. I also had by no means overcome the prejudices against other Jews that I'd had as a fifteen-year-old.

On the whole, the voyage was rather monotonous, to the point that I found the storms and the agitation they provoked on the ship quite stimulating. But on the third day, October 30, an incident occurred that could have prevented my continuing on to the United States, at least for an indefinite time. The night before we had anchored at the Downs, surrounded by several other ships from neutral countries, all of which had to submit to inspection by a British Navy officer. For that purpose we had to anchor before Southampton and wait for the inspecting officer. But the passengers hadn't been informed of this. Around noon those of us on deck saw a longboat from Southampton come up alongside and moor to our ship. Approximately forty more passengers, mostly stranded Americans, as well as a few British Navy officers and two or three official-looking civilians, came on board. The Englishmen stayed quite a long time, and we waited for them to reboard their longboat and let us continue our voyage. But that didn't happen.

Curious to know what was going on, I stood directly behind the rope that had been put up to cordon off the boarding passengers and officials. The first officer of the *Veendam*, my cabin steward, and one of the occupants of my cabin hurried by me twice, while I politely held up the rope to let them through. Some of the British Navy officers stood in front of the first-class lounge, apparently waiting for something. Suddenly Bruno appeared next to me, grabbed my arm, and said that they had been searching the whole ship for me for the past half hour. I was the only person on the passenger manifest who hadn't yet been questioned, so I had to go to the first-class lounge immediately. I hurried to the lounge, where I was interrogated by two British officers and three civil servants. Why was I going to the United States? Why did I have no "J" stamp in my passport like all the other Jews from Nazi Germany? Why had I spent several months in London in 1937 and 1938? Why had I then left England? And why had I been hiding for half an hour today? This last point was the crucial one for them. To make a long story short, they thought I was a non-Jewish German who for some reason unknown to them was on the way to the United States. With obvious impatience they demanded that I answer their questions promptly and truthfully. If I didn't, they would intern me in England as "an enemy alien."

First I tried to prove with the help of my birth certificate that I was a Jew. But birth certificates can be forged, they said. Suddenly I got unexpected support from one of the Dutch stewards who worked in the first-class lounge and by chance was witnessing my interrogation. When one of the British officers questioned me about the *Joodse Werkdorp Wieringerwaard*, where I, according to a stamp in my passport, had spent several months, the steward suddenly interjected that as a former resident of the *Werkdorp* I must be a *jood* [a Jew], as only *joden* [Jews] lived there. I repeated that, far from hiding, I had been on deck the whole time. It wasn't my fault that my cabin steward was so stupid as to run by me twice without seeing me. Greatly annoyed, I managed to express this in my poor English. Finally I was let go in a somewhat more friendly way than I had been received, and after the gentlemen had climbed back into their boat, the *Veendam* was finally able to continue its voyage. My fellow passengers reproached me, half joking, half annoyed, saying it was my fault that we would probably arrive in the United States the following week at least half an hour late.

Contrary to my expectations, the ship docked not in New York Harbor, but at Hoboken, New Jersey. During the landing procedures I sat on one of my suitcases with a pounding heart, not comprehending all the chaos. Again and again I checked to make sure that I had my passport and other papers and that my baggage was with me on deck. Bruno, who was met right away by a relative, said goodbye to me hastily and stormed down the landing bridge. We have never seen each other again. It was the same with Hans. American officials walked around on deck, and several times I asked them when I could finally disembark. I always got the same answer: "Wait until your folks get here." Okay, but who was going to come, and where were they? Then, when I was practically the last person left sitting on deck, an official called to me that I could leave the ship. Down on the pier stood three men, only one of whom I knew: Joe Loewensberg. The other two, who greeted me warmly, were my father's cousin Uncle Samuel Trepp (the man who originally offered me an affidavit) and his son Richard. With their help, the immigration formalities, including the searching of my bags, went without problems, and we were soon on the ferry to Manhattan.

My first impression of the city hasn't changed over the decades. Its boulevards and skyscrapers were impressive but also overwhelming, and its diversity was imposing. "The city that never sleeps" seemed too big even back then, quite apart from its masses of people. In short, contrary to some of my friends, I never fell in love with New York. I have always liked to visit the city, but the thought of living there has never entered my mind.

The six days I spent in New York were filled with new impressions and old friends and acquaintances. Once again I was in a new country, but this time I had the hope of being able to stay and become a citizen. As in London and Amsterdam, I had very little contact with the natives. For the few days that I was to stay in the city, Joe Loewensberg got me lodging near his apartment on the corner of 103rd Street and Broadway. Since the evening of my arrival was also the first anniversary of the Kristallnacht pogrom in Germany, my hosts suggested taking me to a service at a liberal synagogue in Manhattan, but I declined. Instead, on that quite warm Indian summer afternoon I walked with Joe and his girlfriend along Broadway, where I drank the first milkshake of my life and was surrounded by mostly German-speaking people, all immigrants who had settled in that part of Manhattan. That day I even met two *Werkdorp* trainees who had emigrated to the United States shortly before me.

During the rest of the time before I traveled on to Virginia, Joe took me with him to some of his friends' apartments. I knew a number of them by sight from their occasional visits to Gross Breesen or from the youth movement. Now they were all getting accustomed to their new city. Some of them were people I had looked up to when they occasionally came to Gross Breesen. These included Heinz (later Henry) Kellermann, the former leader of the *Bund Deutsch-Jüdischer Jugend* [BDJJ, the German Jewish Youth Association], who joined the U.S. diplomatic service after the war, and Martin Sobotker, who'd also had a leading position in the BDJJ. During my short stay in New York we met a number of times, either at their apartments or at Joe Loewensberg's. I felt quite out of place among these leaders of the German Jewish youth movement who had been at a level inaccessible to me in the past.

Once we visited Fritz Schwarzschild, who had been Gross Breesen's finance officer at the *Reichsvertretung der Juden in Deutschland* [National Representative Agency of Jews in Germany]. He now lived in Manhattan with his wife and two sons and invited me to lunch shortly after my arrival. When I rang his doorbell, I heard loud music coming from the apartment. Schwarzschild opened the door, pushed a chair in my direction, put his index finger to his lips and said merely, *"Tannhäuser."* The opera was playing on the radio, and I had to listen quietly until the act was over. Even in exile Schwarzschild, who helped Jews his whole life, couldn't do without his beloved music by the anti-Semite Richard Wagner.

During the week I stayed in New York, I spent some time at the office of the Jewish Joint Distribution Committee (JDC), where I was asked about my experiences in Holland, especially at the *Werkdorp*, as well as about Curt Bondy's plans. I was also advised on how to apply for U.S. citizenship by submitting the so-called "first papers." A young employee of the JDC who towered over me like a Valkyrie was particularly friendly and helpful, devoting a good deal of her time to giving me advice and introducing me to all sorts of people. Her name was Ingrid Warburg. That Monday, after I had spent a good part of the day in her office, it was surely she who arranged for a (Jewish) reporter from the *Daily Mirror*, Ted Friend, to spend the evening with me and show me New York nightlife. For the first time I had to speak English only, and it wasn't easy. At the JDC I had spoken only German, since all the staff members were German Jewish immigrants. Nonetheless it was an unforgettable evening.

First Ted Friend asked me if I owned a hat. When I said no, he took me into a store and purchased a beret, since I adamantly refused any other headgear. Then he took me up to the observation deck of the Empire State

Building, and I was just as thrilled by the view of New York and parts of New Jersey at night as I was by the fast elevator ride up. After that we went to the Waldorf Astoria Hotel, of whose existence and significance I was just as ignorant as I was about the Empire State Building, Times Square, and the other sights Ted Friend showed me. During the course of the evening he asked me a few questions about Nazi Germany and especially about the Kristallnacht pogrom of the previous November, but my English was so limited that he probably didn't learn much about what interested him. When we arrived at the Waldorf Astoria, he introduced me, a not especially well-dressed nineteen-year-old immigrant who barely spoke English, to the conductor of the orchestra that played for the guests in the dining room. The conductor greeted me as if I were the Shah of Persia. It was all very interesting but also somewhat embarrassing. Later Ted Friend treated me to a movie, *The Women*, by Clare Boothe Luce, that everyone was talking about at the time. I understood almost nothing, since it consisted mainly of dialogue, and my limited English failed me completely at that late hour. Since my guide was on the night shift at his newspaper, we had to part after the film. That very pleasant evening was the first time I spent a few hours with a native of this new country aside from my German-speaking relatives, the Trepps.

Although I enjoyed my six-day stay in New York City, and especially meeting people I knew from my correspondence with them as well as people I didn't know, my thoughts were increasingly down in Virginia, at Hyde Farmlands. I didn't yet know how I would get there, but I was full of anticipation about the trip. The day before leaving for the South, I inquired at the JDC about the best and cheapest way to get there. A young woman asked me how much money I had. When I told her that my father had given me fifty dollars as a going-away present, she smiled and said that I could pay for the trip myself, as it cost only eight dollars to get to Richmond. The next evening, November 15, Joe and his girlfriend took me to Port Authority, the Greyhound bus terminal, to catch the bus to Richmond, where I was to arrive the next morning. We said our heartfelt goodbyes, and I got on board for my first bus trip, traveling alone through a country unfamiliar to me to a destination also strange. I was fascinated by the novelty of it all. In many respects my next year and a half in Virginia was strongly influenced by my youthful lust for adventure.

Shortly after dawn the bus arrived in Richmond. I looked sleepily out the window, amazed that we were passing through a very rundown part of town, the place where the blacks lived, the "ghetto" of Richmond. Once again I found myself in new and strange surroundings. The streets were still empty. I didn't see any people, but I did see quite a large rat that was almost run over by the bus. When we got to the bus station, it was still too early for me to present myself to William B. Thalhimer, since his department store didn't open until nine. I was anxious to meet this man to whom I mainly owed my being in the United States and no longer in Europe. The grandson of a Jewish emigrant from Germany who had come to America in the nineteenth century, Thalhimer had worked closely with the New York Jewish Committee, and especially with the JDC, to lay the groundwork that enabled us to enter the country under the preference quota as shareholders in the farm that he had placed at our disposal.

I had a look at the city of Richmond and at nine o'clock on the dot arrived at the department store, where I told a young saleswoman that I wanted to see Mr. Thalhimer. She stared at me as if I were some kind of creature from a fairy tale, then began to giggle and apparently told one of her colleagues—I understood barely a word of her southern English—that this boy wanted to see the big boss. Pleased that finally someone took my request seriously, I followed my escort onto the elevator and up to the top floor to the office of the owner of the department store. Thalhimer, a short man in his fifties, greeted me in a very friendly manner with the ever-present American smile and introduced me to his secretaries as one of the young refugees on his way to Hyde Farmlands. I liked his informality. He spoke to me alone in his office briefly, announced that he would soon visit the farm, and sent me back to the bus station. There I was to catch the bus to Burkeville, in Nottoway County, where I would be picked up and taken to the farm.

The sun shone brightly as the bus passed through a wooded region, and I imagined excitedly what it would be like to roam these woods. In Burkeville, Ralph, a former Breesen intern I barely knew, met me in a red truck. Since my family had fled Germany in late October 1937, I had lived with the hope of being part of a Gross Breesen settlement somewhere overseas, and now this hope was being fulfilled. I had attained my goal without ever asking myself if I really wanted to spend my whole life as a settler at Hyde Farmlands. I didn't start thinking ahead until a few months later. At the moment I was just happy that I had finally arrived where I believed I belonged.

I was received warmly and soon felt quite at home among the former Gross Breeseners, although in the beginning there was only one who had

Hyde Farmlands, Virginia, the main house (1939 to 1941).

been with me in the Hanniots group. This was Manfred Gottschalk, who was now called "Red" because of his hair, and who, as I described briefly in Chapter 4, had spent almost a year in the concentration camp at Sonnenburg for supposed *Rassenschande* ["racial disgrace"] before he arrived at Gross Breesen. More Hanniots arrived a few months later.

From the beginning I liked my new surroundings. The main house, or mansion, where I lived at first, was built in 1792 and somewhat enlarged in 1906. It was a typical, white-columned Southern house, straight out of *Gone with the Wind*. Much later, the mansion became a bed and breakfast called Hyde Park Farm. In front and in back of the main house were large lawns with trees, and about a hundred yards away stood an old slave house. When I arrived, the former slave house was used to store corn, grain, and feed, but then it was cleared out, cleaned, and furnished as living quarters. Two friends and I moved into it in 1940.

A wide path ran through almost a mile of thick woods to an unpaved public road. At the junction of our path and the road our mailbox stood on a wooden pole. The road was also surrounded by woods and connected to other narrow roads that took traffic east to Crewe and west to Burkeville. The woods were impressive, hilly, mostly virgin forest, and surrounded the farm, which covered about twenty-four hundred acres. Here for the first time I saw wild turkeys, cardinals, hummingbirds, raccoons, and occasionally wildcats. Soon after my arrival I discovered not far from the mansion a clearing in the woods where a brook flowed down from the hills and formed a little waterfall. I liked to go there by myself on summer Sundays when the heat was oppressive. I would take a shower naked under the waterfall and then lay down on a blanket to read.

At the beginning my new life was pleasant, interesting, and sometimes even exciting. Dreams and fantasies that I'd had as a boy growing up in Berlin could be realized here. As a child I'd envied my father for occasionally going hunting on an estate in Brandenburg that belonged to a Jew. Now and then I secretly took out the shotgun that he kept in a cupboard in our apartment and admired it. Now I was able to get a rifle of my own. Shortly after I arrived I bought a Winchester rifle for twelve dollars from Sears & Roebuck.

My first kill was an old billy goat who lived in the middle of the forest in a little ramshackle barn, having been left to fend for himself years ago by the farm's previous owners. Someone had mentioned the animal and said that he was eating our corn, so I felt justified in shooting the troublemaker. After several unsuccessful attempts I finally managed to do it one evening, firing several times at the animal lying before his hut in the dark until he stopped moving. When I proudly reported my heroic deed to my father, I got a shattering answer. Papa said I had behaved unfairly and had violated all the rules of hunting. After that I only hunted on rare occasions. Now and then I shot a rabbit for my German shepherd Bingo, whom I bought in the summer of 1940 for one dollar. And once I shot two birds with one cartridge. But the sight of my victims disgusted me so much that I resolved never again to shoot at birds, even noting this in my diary. After the war I bequeathed the rifle to my youngest brother, Hans.

Horseback riding was another story. Before I came to the United States I had sat only once on a horse, the old nag, Bibi, at Gross Breesen.

Getting ready to go riding: Werner Angress and right, Hermann Neustadt (known as Prinz, which means "Prince" in English).

Shortly after I arrived at Hyde Farmlands I was put on one of the draft horses, a heavy chestnut mare named Babe. Since we had no saddles yet, I soon learned to ride bareback. Usually I rode on Sundays, since the horses were needed for work during the week. But that wasn't enough for me, so now and then late in the evening I convinced two of my friends to get the horses out of the stable and lead them quietly and carefully out of earshot of the house. Then we mounted and rode, sometimes by moonlight, through the hilly woods. We never got lost, because the horses knew the way back to the stable very well. It was a wonderful feeling to ride in the dark, letting the reins hang slack and, knowing we were doing something forbidden, enjoying every minute. Unfortunately we were caught one night sneaking the horses out of the stable, and that put an end to the nighttime rides.

My love for these new surroundings didn't diminish during my year and a half at Hyde Farmlands. The woods, for the most part still virgin, awoke visions from my childhood books by Karl May, although I knew that Winnetou and Old Shatterhand had roamed the Wild West and never Virginia. Even the buzzards circling over the farm as soon as they spied a dead animal lying somewhere in the bushes reminded me of my earlier reading. This was also true of my encounters with snakes. Before coming to the New World I had only seen snakes in the Berlin aquarium. Black snakes—usually quite long, but not poisonous—occasionally found their way into one of the houses where we slept and had to be taken outside. One day when a friend and I were sawing firewood at the woodpile and lifted an old door, we found a poisonous copperhead lying coiled underneath, and we promptly killed it. Today I wouldn't do that anymore!

My opening up to this wild nature, previously unknown to me, in surroundings where I continually made new discoveries among the flora and fauna, was a meaningful experience for me. Wandering around in the woods, showering under the waterfall, riding at night, all these things were the realization of my youthful dreams. Some of my older comrades saw things differently and spoke disapprovingly of my "romantic airs." They even told Bondy about it, who reproached me in a letter for my immature behavior. Surely some of these criticisms were justified, but they didn't affect me. After all, I had just spent five years of my youth, from the age of twelve to seventeen, under Nazi rule, with my daily life, as a Jew, increasingly restricted. I wasn't going to curb my enjoyment of this new freedom.

In mid-January of 1940 I had to see a dentist in Richmond and was advised to use the opportunity to apply for my so-called "first papers" to obtain U.S. citizenship. Again I was taken to town in the red truck, and after my dental treatment, which was paid for by Thalhimer (as were all our medical expenses), I went to City Hall. There I told the official behind the counter of my intention to submit my first papers. As he was helping me fill out the necessary forms, we came upon the question of whether I, the applicant, wanted to change my name. Many German Jewish immigrants did this at the time. I looked with confusion at the official, who was waiting patiently on the other side of the counter. His look also turned puzzled when I finally answered that I only wanted to change my middle name. "You really want to hang onto this first and last name?" I explained that I had grown up Werner and Angress and did want to keep them. But I had never liked the name Karl. "Thomas," and especially "Tom," sounded much more like my new self (I had always greatly admired Mark Twain's *Tom Sawyer*). I thought the initial of my new middle name could also stand for my nickname, "Töpper." "Then Thomas instead of Karl?" the official asked again. When I nodded, he said, "Well, why not, it's a free country." With that, I was on my way to becoming an American citizen in a few years.

At the beginning I wasn't too unhappy with the work, which was mostly new to me. The farm manager Thalhimer had hired, Urban Koenig Franken, whose job it was to give us a crash course in American farming, first sent me to the chicken coop to help Ralph. Franken was from Missouri and had gone to the university there on a football scholarship. He said that if it had depended completely on his academic achievements, he never would have been able to complete his degree. Franken was Catholic—in Virginia in those days, Catholics were a minority that the Protestant majority regarded with great suspicion—and the father of several children, who lived with him and his wife in the main house. He took his job as farm manager very seriously. Not that he knew a lot about it, as quickly became clear. He met with us regularly for work sessions, during which he supposedly taught us agriculture, but mostly he criticized our work. He especially liked to schedule these work sessions on weekends, until our protests were finally heard and we succeeded in obtaining at least one day of rest.

Unfortunately, he wasn't satisfied with supervising our work; he also stuck his nose into our private lives. His favorite expression, when he disapproved of something we did, was, "We don't do that in this country." What seemed to concern him most was our moral behavior. We male Hyde Farmlanders, who thanks to Bondy's education were already quite sexually inhibited, now received strict instructions from Franken on how we were to behave: when we visited a girl in her room (the few girls who came to Hyde Farmlands had single rooms, while we boys each shared a room with two or three other boys), the door had to remain open. And when we wanted to meet girls after sundown, we were only allowed to do so downstairs in the large living room of the main house. Franken thought it his duty to check on us, especially in the evening and on weekends. For example, if a boy was invited over by a girl for coffee on a Sunday afternoon, it wasn't unusual for Franken to stick his head into the room without knocking on the half-open door to make sure we were behaving "morally." This nonsense stopped only at the end of 1940, when we finally convinced Thalhimer to relieve Franken as manager.

Farmworker Werner Angress, Hyde Farmlands, 1940.

After my arrival Franken assigned me to the chicken coop, which I cleaned and where I gathered the eggs. When I arrived in November, the farm had only a small, quite dilapidated henhouse and just enough eggs for our own consumption, not enough to sell. After discussing the matter with Thalhimer, Franken decided to focus on raising chickens for our agricultural income. So we spent the first few months of 1940 building two two-story barns in which the chicks could grow up protected. For the construction we had to make cinderblocks. Some of us were assigned to teams that would produce these cinderblocks with a manually operated machine. One of us shoveled in a mixture of sand, ash, water, and cement, and the other made the blocks by applying pressure. Then the blocks were set out to dry. At the beginning many were destroyed before they could harden when the horses and mules came back to the barn from the pasture and stepped on them. They seemed to enjoy doing this. We began taking turns watching over the newly finished blocks when the horses and mules returned, and we put the animals in their stalls before they could indulge in another round of destruction.

One of my coworkers at the cinder block machine was the future painter Friedel Dzubas. Another group of about six people was kept busy for weeks felling pine trees, peeling off the bark, and building ten henhouses with the trunks, each house big enough for a hundred hens. This work was done under the supervision of Hermann Kiwi, the son of the Gross Breesen carpenter Max Kiwi, who died in Auschwitz a couple of years later. It was heavy labor, and I was thankful that I was assigned to the less exhausting job of producing cinderblocks.

When spring came a few months later, Franken appointed me as "Director of the Department of Small Fruit." My unit included no subordinates, but since I sometimes needed help nonetheless, I occasionally worked with the "Director of the Gardening Department," my good friend Ernst "Pimpf" Heimann, whose division was similarly poorly staffed. When we worked in the garden, he was the director, and when we planted or picked fruit, I was in charge.

As Director of the Department of Small Fruit I spent a great deal of time planting strawberries, weeding, and plucking off the blossoms so that the plants could develop fully in the first year. I even worked two days with a team of mules named Lu and Rowdy. Mules, in my opinion, were no match for horses, and so I treated them badly. It was my job to get rid of the weeds between the rows of strawberry plants with the aid of a cultivator, which the mules pulled. I'm afraid I proved to be a bad driver who screamed at the mules and even beat them with the whip when they now and then wandered too far to the left or to the right. By the second day Lu and Rowdy had had enough of me and my fits of rage. After turning their heads as if they wanted one last look at their tormentor, they trotted across the one and a quarter acres, dragging the cultivator behind them to the road and then back to the barn. There an older farmhand found them standing in front of the closed door. He reprimanded me when I arrived, running after the beasts and cursing. From then on I was deprived of the use of a team. The strawberry plants that were destroyed during this incident I naturally had to replace with new ones, which was a lot of work.

In retrospect, the almost eighteen months I spent at Hyde Farmlands seem less satisfying than the same amount of time I had worked at Gross Breesen a few years earlier. The reasons for this had to do partly with me but also to a great extent with the particular character of our community. In addition to that was the complete strangeness to us of our new homeland, the United States. Oddly, we were once again living on a sort of island. But this time our surroundings, Virginia and beyond, weren't hostile, just unknown. Except for two short trips, one to Washington, D.C., and another to New York City, my acquaintance with the United States was confined to Hyde Farmlands, the nearby small towns of Crewe and Burkeville, and more occasionally Richmond.

The poor English most of us spoke limited our contact with Americans. The older ones among us, all former Breesen interns who had arrived in Virginia months before we had, encouraged us to speak as much English with each other as possible. But we stubbornly stuck to German most of the time. Almost every Sunday, curious and unexpected visitors from Richmond and who-knows-where-else came to have a look at us young refugees from Hitler's Germany, whom they'd read about in the newspaper or heard about from neighbors. Conversations with the visitors were carried on almost exclusively by the older members of our group. We younger ones just listened, nodding now and then, and seldom tried to say anything in English. By no means did we understand everything that was being said. Fear of making mistakes and being laughed at—although highly unlikely, considering the politeness of Americans—kept us from speaking or getting to know our neighbors. It was simply easier and more natural for us to speak German among ourselves. One day the interns thought of a compromise solution: we could continue to speak German with each other, but on Fridays only English was to be spoken. Friday became a very quiet day. At breakfast, and when we were sitting at the big table next to the kitchen in the evening, you would hear only "Please pass the salt" and other such phrases. Eventually I began to study English for an hour now and then in the evening, together with a friend, and also to read books in English, but I made only slow progress.

Thalhimer, too, on his occasional visits to the farm, must have noticed that we younger ones were always very quiet. To our surprise, one day he told us that the following Sunday he was going to send a group of his department store salesgirls to the farm, so that we could talk to some "real American girls." When the girls arrived, accompanied by one of their supervisors acting as a chaperone to protect them from us lonely foreigners, I discovered to my great amazement that the driver of one of the cars in which the group had come was Wolfgang Robinow, the other hidden non-Aryan at Lichterfelder Realgymnasium, who had revealed himself to me during my farewell from school. Since he evidently enjoyed being able to speak German again, he told my friends of our earlier acquaintance and expressed very great surprise at my decision to become a farmworker in this remote place. I soon turned my attention from Wolfgang and my friends to the visiting ladies, some of whom I led around (as we all did) and told about our work in broken English. In the evening, we sat in the big living room of the mansion, where our visitors offered to sing us a song. When the chaperone lady asked us if we had a request, I raised my hand and said "Marching through Georgia." Stony silence, and rightly so. For during the Civil War that song was sung by the Union soldiers after they had burned Atlanta to the ground. What prompted me to suggest that song I no longer know. I must have heard it somewhere, but I had no idea of its historical significance. The chaperone gave me an unfriendly look and proclaimed, "No, we'll sing 'Dixie'!" And then the young girls enthusiastically sang the hymn of the South. Thus ended that curious visit.

Shortly after my arrival on the farm came my first meeting with neighbors. This happened on Thanksgiving Day, an American holiday of which I've always been fond. After a sumptuous turkey feast with all sorts of side dishes, Ernst Loew, one of the former Breesen interns, proposed to me and another newcomer that we go visit a neighboring family on horseback. Our horses were heavy, good-natured chestnuts. After riding through the forest about a half an hour, we reached an unpainted log cabin. The man of the house, who lived there with his wife, two daughters, and elderly father, was the local forest ranger. They lived in very humble conditions. The fact no one in the whole family could read or write wasn't unusual in such a rural setting, Ernst told us. When we got there, we dismounted, tied up our horses, knocked on the door, and were invited to go in. Inside was a large room on whose raw wooden walls hung antlers and a number of hunting rifles, but no pictures or other decoration of any sort. On the beat-up couch sat an old man, the grandfather, chewing tobacco. During the half hour we were there, he skillfully spit past me in a large arc to the fireplace, where a fire burned despite the warm Indian summer. Two girls at about the age of puberty stood in a corner of the room wrapped in sheets; it was obvious that they had been walking around the house naked before we came in. They giggled and whispered to each other while eyeing us, but they didn't talk to us. Only the man of the house and his wife spoke, to Ernst, about the weather, the results of the last hunt, and the number of boys and girls still expected at Hyde Farmlands. Then we said goodbye and rode back.

Another neighbor we visited several times was Mr. Hamlin. He was an unmarried turkey farmer and a devoted Bible reader. The main reason he regularly invited small groups of us to his farm on Sundays was that we were Jews. He had found that out somehow, and from then on he regarded us as the children of God's Chosen People. He stressed as well the fact that our religion was also that of the Savior, Jesus Christ. On my first visit he recounted his trip to Palestine in more detail than I could understand, and he showed us with obvious pride a little jar of sand that he'd brought back to Virginia from the Promised Land. These two examples of visits to our neighbors show just how meager our social contacts with Americans were at that time. For aside from these two neighbors and the Sunday invasions of mostly uninteresting strangers whose curiosity and impertinence were quite embarrassing to us, we remained isolated. Only very rarely did we make new and meaningful acquaintances. We directed our attention mainly to each other, until the whole project came to an end in the spring of 1941.

During the time at the farm I also learned in an unexpected and very confusing way about the racial problems in United States. One day in the summer of 1940 William B. Thalhimer paid us one of his frequent, always unannounced visits. He usually came alone (I never met his wife and sons), but he was sometimes accompanied by one of his employees. When he arrived he had us summoned and then talked to us about whatever was on his mind. On that particular day he introduced us to the fundamentals of Southern racial segregation. He sat there, that friendly man, in a rattan chair in front of the mansion, now and then winking at us as we sat on the lawn in front of him. He was our benefactor, and we probably owed our lives to his generosity. If it so happened, explained Thalhimer in his Southern drawl, that we were driving a truck to Richmond and a "negrah" was hitchhiking on the side of the road, we could give him a ride. But he would have to sit in the back of the truck and not up front next to the driver. When addressing a "negrah"—Thalhimer fortunately never used the word "nigger"—we should call him either by his first name or "Uncle," but never call him Mister or use his last name even if we knew what it was. I was completely baffled. Here we were sitting on the lawn of a mansion in this free country, having left Germany, where we had been humiliated and persecuted as "racially inferior subhumans," and now we were being instructed by our benefactor, a Jewish American himself, on how whites were supposed to treat blacks.

Strangely enough, at the time it never occurred to me that I'd never had to worry about earning my own living. All of our routine expenses—such as food, medical treatment, and gasoline for the truck—were paid for by Thalhimer. The farm's monthly income (mainly from the sale of eggs), which during the two years of Hyde Farmlands' existence never covered our expenses, was managed by one of the older Breesen interns, Henry Cornes, originally Heinz Kahn, whom for short we called "Ha-Ka" ("HK" in German). He gave us our monthly allowance of four dollars. At the time this was of course a lot more money than it sounds like today.

In February 1940, two months after my arrival, a heavy snowstorm cut us off from the outside world for almost a week. Ernst Loew had to ride through the snow to Burkeville every day to buy food, and I was thrilled at this natural event so unexpected in Virginia. Shortly afterward an additional group of Breeseners arrived from Wieringen, among them my friend Prinz. He and I had become friends at Gross Breesen and remained close until his death in 1998. Soon after his arrival he and I moved into the former slave house, which, having been used to store feed, was now home to so many rats that for weeks we caught several every night in traps in the hallway. We lived there from then on in a newly built room with furniture that for the most part we'd made ourselves, as well as an ugly but efficient cylindrical black iron stove and a nice photograph on the wall of a sculpture by German artist Georg Kolbe. A third roommate of ours in the slave house was Georg "Schorsch" Landecker. He was from East Prussia and arrived in Virginia, like Prinz, in February 1940 with the *Werkdorp* group. They had all been prisoners at Buchenwald in November 1938. Schorsch spoke with a pronounced East Prussian accent, which he still hasn't lost today, even in English. After Hyde Farmlands closed, he served several years in the U.S. Army, as did most of us. He later acquired his own dairy not far from Utica, New York, with the help of the generous federal loans that the United States offered to veterans at the end of the war. Today, long since retired and a grandfather, Schorsch and his wife live quite close to the dairy farm that he ran for many years and then finally bought. We too have remained friends and maintain regular contact, thanks to e-mail.

Soon after the *Wieringer Werkdorp* group arrived, it became obvious that our crew of about thirty boys and girls wasn't at all homogeneous. It hadn't been put together as carefully as we had originally thought it would be back at Gross Breesen. This was a result of urgent necessity, after the Kristallnacht pogrom of November 1938 forced all Jews in Germany to emigrate. The Breeseners who were released from Buchenwald, as well as the younger trainees who weren't taken to the concentration camp because of their young age, now had to grab any opportunity to emigrate from Germany, no matter to which country. Bondy, working closely with the *Reichsvertretung* after his release from Buchenwald, had put the names of the individual boys on lists and then submitted the lists to the consulates of the United States, Australia, and the British colony of Kenya. His goal was to gain permission for the boys to immigrate into these countries under the special agricultural quotas. In this process it often happened that friends who had lived together in the same group at Gross Breesen and were expecting to be able to settle together in some overseas country were separated. As a result, Prinz, Red, Dackel, and I were the only members of our Hanniot group who went to Hyde Farmlands. Everybody knew each other, to be sure, but not always very well, especially since almost half of the crew was composed of older interns with whom we'd hardly had close contact at Gross Breesen.

The few girls who joined us during the first several months, I also hadn't known well. Unlike us boys, they didn't receive preference visas, at least not from the U.S. consulates, so they couldn't immigrate under the special quota. A few of them could come to the United States with their parents directly from Germany, if the family had applied early enough for a registration number based on the annual U.S. immigration quotas. Other girls came alone via England, where a number of them had found refuge after Kristallnacht. Most of them had worked in England as domestic servants, some as gardeners, and a few as nurses until they were able to emigrate on a family visa to the United States, where they joined their parents or more distant relatives.

One of these women, Marianne Regensburger, remained a close, lifelong friend of mine until her death in April 2002. For a short time, the few months that she was at Hyde Farmlands, we began to become more than just friends. I fell in love with her. But then she received a scholarship to an American university, and from that point on our paths diverged. Shortly after the end of the war she returned to Germany and worked as a journalist for *Die Neue Zeitung*, a newspaper published by the U.S. occupying forces. After that she got a job in Berlin at the RIAS (*Rundfunk im Amerikanischen Sektor*; Radio Station in the American Sector), and, finally, worked for years as a journalist for the second German television net-

My friend, Marianne Regensburger, came in August 1940 from England to Hyde Farmlands.

work (*Zweites Deutsches Fernsehen*), where she became known mainly for the weekly series *Kennzeichen D* that had to do with relations between the Federal Republic and the German Democratic Republic. Her beat was politics from the beginning to the end. She eventually converted to Protestant Christianity and served on the Berlin board of directors of *Aktion Sühnezeichen* [literally, sign of repentance], an organization that tries to preserve the memory of the Holocaust and is especially geared toward young people.

The Hyde Farmlands group also failed to cohere because the original, tightly knit contingent of Gross Breeseners was "infiltrated" by outsiders, which would soon cause trouble. Since Thalhimer had acquired the farm in order to provide a place in the United States for any Jewish refugees from Germany who had agricultural training, the JDC in New York occasionally sent people whom we knew either barely or not at all. One of these immigrants was Martin Sobotker. He and his wife came to Hyde Farmlands because he saw no chance of earning a living in New York and thought he could become a farmer as a middle-aged man. Although I had met him briefly in New York and had heard his name earlier in the youth movement, I and my friends found him and his wife quite unlikable, and it wasn't long before part of our group was in open conflict with him. Sobotker had probably learned his tactics in the

Bund Deutsch-Jüdischer Jugend, the German Jewish Youth Association, of which he'd been a leader.

The growing number of aggressive newcomers such as Sobotker who had never known the Breesen spirit weakened our sense of community. Some of our Breeseners left us as well. Parents who had gotten a foothold in the United States sent for their child and insisted that he or she find a profession other than farming. Such departures from the farm also led to difficulties with Thalhimer. He felt responsible to the U.S. State Department for insuring that at least those of us who had immigrated under the special agricultural quota as shareholders of Hyde Farmlands stayed on the farm. There were very disagreeable discussions with Thalhimer when Friedel Dzubas, who had gotten married in the meantime, was the first of us shareholders to decide to leave. He and his wife moved to New York City so he could pursue his career as a painter.

Friedel's decision gave us all something to think about. In the spring of 1940 we were already asking ourselves whether Hyde Farmlands had a future for us, and if so, what kind. Would the farm ever make a profit? With so few girls at Hyde Farmlands, would we boys ever find wives? Our opinions on these matters were widely divergent. After initial, rather shallow harmony, this uncertainty led to the formation of two camps with very different goals, and quite unpleasant tensions. A number of former Breesen interns (the older ones among us) worked with Franken to try to get the future of the farm into their own hands. This most of us younger ones found unacceptable. What exactly the goals of the different groups really were I can no longer remember, especially because they were forever changing. I recall only the constant complaining, the scheming, the long discussions every evening. In the end it was all useless. The older group was led by Sobotker, who was supported by a few older former Breesen interns, mainly Ernst Loew. Ernst was the brother of Joe Loewensberg, who lived in New York and who had looked after me when I arrived there. With his connections to the Jewish Committee, Joe helped the Breeseners who were taken to Buchenwald in November 1938 get into the *Wieringer Werkdorp*. These two very different brothers were the sons of a wine merchant from Nieder-Ingelheim. In spite of our differing standpoints at Hyde Farmlands, Ernst and I remained good friends until his death.

Several times I tried to mediate, but always in vain. The second camp, of mostly younger immigrants, was headed by Ernst Cramer. Like Ernst Loew, Ernst Cramer had come to Hyde Farmlands before me. He,

Farmworker Ernst Cramer, Hyde Farmlands, around 1940.

too, was an intern and seven years older than I. We had met only briefly at Gross Breesen, since he had arrived there just before my sudden departure in 1937. We became friends at Hyde Farmlands, though, and remained friends until his death in January 2010, although we followed very different paths, especially politically. As the right hand of the publishing magnate Axel Cäsar Springer (whose company has famously refused to publish campaign advertisements by left-wing parties) and longtime editor-in-chief of the Springer newspaper *Welt am Sonntag*, he became a well-known man in Germany.

So by the summer of 1940 our community was fractured and our future was becoming more problematic by the day. We were soon to find out just how little control we had over what happened to us.

But it wasn't just our little world on a farm in Nottoway County, Virginia, that affected us and determined our daily lives. Our attention was directed keenly toward the situation in Europe. Almost all of us had left relatives and friends there. Some of them even remained in Germany, and their precarious situation was constantly on our minds. I corresponded regularly with my parents and brothers, with my friend Meui, with friends who had stayed at the *Werkdorp* in Holland, and with others who had managed to get to England. Of course we mentioned the war in our letters. But during the first five months after my arrival in the United States we didn't take it very seriously. This was the time of the so-called "phony war," when France thought it was safe behind the Maginot Line, and Holland and Belgium believed their neutrality protected them. All this changed very suddenly in the spring of 1940, when the Germans were able to put the *Luftwaffe* [air force] to intensive use, thanks to the good weather. On April 9 the world was shocked to hear that Germany had attacked the Scandinavian countries. Four weeks later, on May 10, Germany invaded Holland and Belgium.

Feeling sad and helpless, I spent a lot of time in the following days listening to the radio and worrying about my parents and brothers in Amsterdam, about Meui, and about my friends at the *Werkdorp*, but I couldn't help anyone. For three months, no mail came. Finally, at the end of August, I received a carefully worded letter from my parents. I understood from it that, given the circumstances, they were doing all right. But between the lines I could feel their concern. It was a depressing situation. There I was living in the United States at a safe distance from the European site of the war, wasting my time in frustration at our situation at Hyde Farmlands, our uncertain future, and the stupid farm manager Franken, while my parents, brothers, and friends were once again under the Nazi domination they had just recently escaped. From that time on, until the Japanese attack on Pearl Harbor on December 7, 1941, and Hitler's declaration of war on the United States four days later, I stayed in contact with my parents and friends by mail, although there were often gaps in the correspondence.

Of course we also worried about Bondy, who since early 1940 was working closely with the Jewish Committee in Amsterdam and trying to enable more young people to emigrate from Germany, not just those remaining at Gross Breesen. On May 10 he wasn't in Amsterdam, however, but in Brussels. He failed in his attempt to return to Holland because no more trains from Belgium were going there. There were only train connections to the south. So he decided to go to France and wait there for a special U.S. visa for people with university degrees that had been submitted for him in New York. As a German, he was confined to a camp by the French for a few weeks, but then, with the help of a former Gross Breesen intern of Luxembourger nationality, Kurt Herrmann, he managed to get to the United States via Portugal in late summer 1940.

We younger immigrants, especially, had great expectations when Bondy arrived at Hyde Farmlands in late August. The former director of Gross Breesen, who with his charisma and his *Lebenskunden* [life lessons] had more or less singlehandedly created the spirit of Gross Breesen, surely would do the same here at Hyde Farmlands. He would take over the management of the farm project, guiding its future and our own. Finally everything would work right and have meaning. But these hopes were not fulfilled. First of all, the events of the two preceding years had had an influence on Bondy and affected his personality. The four weeks at Buchenwald after Kristallnacht, the forced emigration, first to England as an employee at the Kitchner Camp for German refugees, then to Amsterdam as an employee of the Jewish Committee, and finally his flight to France followed by his internment there, all had left scars on Bondy. His aura that we'd so admired at Gross Breesen hadn't disappeared, but it had grown paler. Perhaps we reacted more critically now because we were older and somewhat more mature. In any case, we soon realized that not even Bondy could do much to improve the atmosphere at Hyde Farmlands.

Professor Curt Bondy, in Hyde Farmlands, autumn 1940.

I don't want to go into further detail about the unpleasant quarrels. Shortly after Bondy arrived, we convinced Thalhimer to let Franken go as manager at the end of 1940. Bondy took over the title of manager of Hyde Farmlands, but he mainly left its daily affairs to Ernst Cramer, now his assistant. So we finally won against the Sobotker-Loew group, but this soon proved to be a Pyrrhic victory. For even as we thought about how our futures would take shape within the framework of the farm project, the project suddenly collapsed. The reasons, in the end, were purely financial. And the decision was made neither by Bondy, nor even by William B. Thalhimer, but rather by the latter's cousin, Morton G. Thalhimer, a real estate agent in Richmond. Morton was in fact the legal owner of Hyde Farmlands, which he had bought in 1939 on his cousin's instructions for William's humanitarian efforts. Since then he had been keeping an Argus-eyed watch over the farm's financial health. In mid-February 1941, as William lay in the hospital seriously ill and was expected to die (he lived for more than another decade), Morton informed us that the existence of Hyde Farmlands had become financially untenable. Raising chickens, our main source of income, could no longer support more than thirty people. In spite of our hard work, which Morton recognized, Hyde Farmlands had remained unprofitable and thus had to be sold.

We would have to leave Hyde Farmlands, and so Morton Thalhimer made us a proposal. He could "sell" us to U.S. Senator Harry Byrd, on whose farm we would make twenty-one dollars a month picking apples, or we could join the U.S. Army for a year, where we would earn the same monthly pay. I and several others chose the latter alternative. In my case, at least, the decision was purely practical, mostly because in the army I would learn more English, which I would need to go to college. Neither patriotism (where could that come from without any knowledge of the country?) nor my youthful hero worship of the military influenced me.

So I look back on my eighteen months at Hyde Farmlands with truly mixed feelings. I have already mentioned my great love for the Southern wilderness of Nottoway County, the feeling of freedom that overpowered me when I went hunting, walking, or horseback riding in the woods or showered under a waterfall. I finally got a driver's license and was glad when a visiting friend occasionally lent me his car for a few hours and I could drive to Burkeville or Crewe either alone or with a friend. But still, the country, its people, its politics, and even its continuing economic crisis remained mostly a closed book to my friends and me. Although the *Richmond Times-Dispatch* was delivered every day, I can't remember making much use of it. I only listened to the news when something was happening in the war in Europe. In retrospect I find it shameful how ignorant I was at the time.

During my last weeks at Hyde Farmlands, as I waited to be called up by the army, I for the first time met a black man. Franken, who to our great amazement had offered to buy Hyde Farmlands after Morton Thalhimer's decision, hired this man and asked me if I would mind joining the new worker in cleaning the eggs for shipment. For several days we worked facing each other in one of the henhouses. After he noticed that I behaved toward him differently than he was used to from whites, and after I, in broken English, told him something of my past, he gained confidence and told me something about his own life. He was an older man, the son or grandson of a slave, and from his very carefully formulated report I got an idea of what it meant for someone like him and his family to live in the southern United States. It made me quietly ashamed to be a white person. Perhaps this brief encounter contributed to the fact that in spite of several years in the U.S. Army, where I met many racist soldiers, I have never felt prejudice toward people of other colors.

As for my personal development, the time I spent at Hyde Farmlands wasn't very happy. All my negative traits from childhood reappeared, although I was no longer a child. The smallest frustration caused fits of rage in me, which increased my inferiority complex. My attitude toward my work was also bad. I was constantly reprimanded by Franken as well as by my older Gross Breesen companions, including Ernst Cramer, as it became apparent that my heart wasn't always in my work. Farming seemed less and less appealing to me as a life's calling. This was also evident in my attitude during the evening work sessions and in my inadequate accomplishment of tasks. I became fully aware that I was developing neither intellectually, socially, nor professionally. My spoken English was poor, although after a while I could understand the language quite well and could read with little trouble. But all of these difficulties had an effect on my relationship with our Hyde Farmlands community and especially with my friends. Certainly, at least in some ways, the time at Hyde Farmlands was also a necessary period of adaptation for me as I entered a third and completely new kind of exile. But this time, too, I was at first unable to gain any clear perspective on my future. This new country, my future homeland that I had chosen myself and where I had lived since late 1939, was still almost completely strange to me in the spring of 1941. The combination of all these circumstances doubtless contributed to my ambivalence about that initial period in the United States, a period which should have been formative for me. The original expectations with which we had looked forward to that new stage of our lives weren't fulfilled, probably because Hyde Farmlands didn't become a second Gross Breesen.

Red Gottschalk and I were the last of our group to leave Hyde Farmlands. We were still waiting to be called up for military service, so, after a cool farewell from Franken, the farm's new owner, we worked for two weeks in Burkeville on the grounds of a sanatorium for blacks with tuberculosis. There we helped build a sand and gravel dike to create an artificial lake. Although it was only April, the sun was burning, and we worked for days, together with a few blacks, with shovels, pickaxes, and wheelbarrows, without ever exchanging a word with our fellow workers. This wasn't what I wanted, but there wasn't any opportunity for conversation. The black men stayed away from us.

This first paid job—we earned a dollar a day—was a strange and completely new experience for us. We were given lodging with a man about thirty years old who a few years earlier had stabbed someone while drunk. The Virginia governor had paroled him to the sanatorium, where he spent his time on handicrafts and hunting bullfrogs, which he set before us for breakfast in the morning. Our unease at the idea of living in the same house with a "murderer" (I slept on a cot next to the bathtub) quickly disappeared, and soon we happily accompanied him on his frog hunts every evening after work.

During those two weeks we had to report one morning to the Nottoway County Army Office to take the intelligence test required for entry into the military. The people at the office seemed very happy that Red and I had volunteered to fight. Today I still have the newspaper clipping in which the local newspaper proudly announced that two *white* men from the county had volunteered for a year of military service. That we were foreigners didn't seem to bother them. Only the color of our skin was important. The test went correspondingly. I was put in an office next to an elderly gentleman in a U.S. Army uniform—I didn't recognize that he was a lieutenant colonel because I wasn't yet familiar with the army ranks. When they gave me a sheet of multiple choice questions, I was completely baffled. I didn't understand a word and had no idea what I was supposed to do. One question asked what happens at the burial of a soldier. Of the four possibilities given, the correct answer was "The bugle is blown." But I didn't yet know the word *bugle*. The good lieutenant colonel noticed my quandary and, looking at me with a grin, cupped his hands in front of his mouth as if he were going to shout, made a tooting sound, then looked at me expectantly. Since my confusion hadn't dissipated, he tapped the correct answer on the page. I nodded, and with similar assistance from him I passed the whole test.

Shortly thereafter the news arrived that we would be inducted into the army on May 7, 1941. So a new phase of my life began, which I noted in my diary thus, after receiving a letter from my childhood friend Irene Meier: "I am afraid of the future, that is quite clear to me. I will overcome this fear or be destroyed by it. There will be no more compromises, Irene wrote me recently. What is coming will be new ... and will advance me further. Next month I will be twenty-one. My life will probably change. I don't know what will become of me. I only know one thing: there is no taking it easy for me, there is no time without fighting, no time without longing." I signed this entry that sounds so melodramatic today with my nickname—Töpper.

CHAPTER 7

Service in the Army and War

My transition from civilian to soldier was anything but dramatic. On the afternoon of May 7, 1941, following instructions in the letter we'd received, Red and I, accompanied by Bondy, went to a drugstore on Richmond's Main Street. There we encountered a number of characters our age, every one of them, like us, carrying a small suitcase and looking bored. When I asked to whom we should report one of the fellows pointed to a corner of the store. There, at a table next to which hung Old Glory, a man in uniform sat studying a list. When I stepped up to his table, he told me to leave him alone and wait until he called me. Eventually he called a dozen of us recruits. We stood quite at ease around the table as the sergeant rose and told us to raise our right arms. He spoke loudly and slowly some kind of formula that we collectively repeated. "You swear?" he demanded. "We swear!" we replied in unison. And that was it. We were now soldiers of the Army of the United States. No marching or trumpets, only the sergeant in his ill-fitting uniform in the corner of a store, and we recruits in civilian clothes holding our little suitcases.

Why "Army of the United States" and not "United States Army"? The latter was the name of the professional army that had been established following the First World War. Numerically speaking it was relatively small and consisted, as I soon found out, predominantly of men who were intellectually somewhat underdeveloped. Most of them had joined because it gave them a regular paycheck and, at the end of their service, a reasonably good pension. In civilian life, they had failed to find jobs that could support them. Now, in 1941, they formed the training and administrative staff in the various army camps to which we, the new recruits, were sent for our military basic training once we had been sworn in. As civilians, whose numbers in the army had rapidly increased on the basis of the Selective Service Act of 1940, we didn't belong to the "Regular U.S. Army" but to the "Army of the United States," which disappeared again once the war was over. Moreover, in order to train us militarily, most of the numerous divisions demobilized after the First World War were now hurriedly reactivated and assigned to the former military training camps, which were overwhelmingly in very poor condition. Finally, besides the draftees and recruits of 1940 and beyond, there were also civilians who for years had served in the U.S. National Guard divisions, joining in part out of a sense of adventure and in part to boost the generally poor income they earned in their civilian jobs during the Depression. The National Guard divisions had been mobilized throughout the country in August 1940, one month before Congress passed the Selective Service Act. During the months that followed they were assigned to the military training camps.

As soon as we had sworn our oath, Red and I took the train with the other recruits to Fort George G. Meade in Maryland, less than an hour from Washington. Fort Meade was also the base for the recently mobilized 29th Virginia National Guard Division. Here, in the beautiful wooded landscape of Maryland began the four-and-a-half years of my military service; and here it also ended, in September 1945.

As was probably true for most of the other recruits as well, the beginning of my military service wasn't easy for me. In my particular case a number of factors added to this. First, my English was very poor. Second, I was thoroughly ignorant of how an American military unit was structured—be it a squad, a platoon, a company, a battalion, a regiment, a division, and so on. And third, I felt terribly lonely, at least initially.

After we had been issued our uniforms and, during the next few days, taken a variety of tests, we were quarantined for two weeks and not permitted to leave the area of our barracks. And initially nearly everything went wrong. As I have rather small feet, it took several days for them to find boots in my size. An intelligence test that all of us had to take I barely managed to pass (not having this time the kind assistance of the old lieutenant colonel). Two points less and I would have been sent "home" (where was this?) as mentally retarded. Neither my English nor my knowledge of mathematics was good enough. Still, I was able to answer some of the questions, while others I simply guessed correctly. Then those of us who had volunteered had to discuss with one of the sergeants in which branch of the military we wanted to serve. The final decision, of course, lay not with us but the sergeant. Mine happened to be a pleasant young man who smiled at me when our interview began. I told him I would prefer to be trained in an armored division (most of us wanted to avoid the tedious drills and maneuvers of the infantry). "Well," he replied, "what would you do if you were driving a heavy truck and the axle broke?" I stammered something about wire and iron rods—and shortly thereafter found myself assigned to Company B of the 116th Infantry Regiment, 29th Virginia National Guard Division. Red was luckier. At Gross Breesen he had driven and maintained the farm's only tractor, so he knew more about heavy vehicles than I did. Since he also spoke better English, he was soon assigned to an armored division. From June 1944 until the end of the war, he was a tank driver in General George Patton's Third Army.

On one of the first days of our quarantine, at a moment when there were no tests, no checkups, and no issuing of clothing, I was sitting on my bed (which I had learned to make according to military regulations), bored to tears. Suddenly two of my barrack mates walked over to me. The taller of them, a man with an ugly and yet very striking face, introduced himself as John G. Barnes; the smaller man was Bob Jackson. Barnes was a civil engineer from Newport News, Virginia; Jackson was a journalist from Washington, D.C. Barnes asked me where I was from, having judged from my faltering English that I was not an American. I replied that I had fled Nazi Germany and in 1939 had come to the United States. Yes, but why had I left Germany? he asked. When I replied that I was a Jew who had no future in Hitler's state, Barnes, without moving an eyebrow, asked whether Hitler might not have good reasons to force the Jews to leave the country. I was stunned and stammered something but was unable to find a coherent response.

Jackson, obviously embarrassed by Barnes's remark, changed the subject, but Barnes also seemed to notice that he had upset me. They both offered to help me learn proper English. They had me read the political section of *The New York Times* every day, and they discussed the most important stories with me every evening.

And with that a friendship began that only ended on D-Day. Although Jackson was soon transferred to the military police, Barnes stayed in Company B and during the time I served in that unit looked out for me as if he were my older brother. After I was transferred out of the company we wrote each other regularly. Never again did I hear from him the slightest hint of anti-Semitism. The last time I wrote to him was on June 4, 1944, sitting on a cot in a hangar of a British airport from where we were to join the Allied invasion the following evening. The letter came back to me several months later, unopened. On the envelope were three scrawled letters: *KIA*, killed in action.

I served as an infantry soldier in this division until the fall of 1942. Like most National Guard divisions, the 29th was a rather mediocre outfit, at least during the time I was with it. The men of Company B, 116th Infantry Regiment, came overwhelmingly from Lynchburg, Virginia. These young men were all white (integration of the U.S. armed forces didn't begin until 1948), and most were poorly educated, having started to work in Lynchburg's textile mills when they were fourteen or fifteen years old. I was very surprised at the time to hear that 10 percent of these kids were unable to write their own names and on payday every month had to sign their receipts with an X. The company commander, Captain Pugh, and nearly all the noncommissioned officers of the company were from Lynchburg and in many instances were related to each other. In civilian life Captain Pugh was a milkman, although he earned additional money as a revenue officer for the State of Virginia, tracking down moonshiners.

Pugh was one of the most incapable officers I encountered during my army service. He was unable to read military maps, so during our numerous maneuvers Company B was always wandering aimlessly through the forests. Eventually, shortly after I had been transferred to our regimental Headquarters Company, Pugh was replaced as company commander by First Lieutenant Ettore Zappacosta of Pennsylvania, a lawyer in civilian life. With this rather small and wiry man, Company B finally was under the command of an efficient, self-confident, and tough officer. He freed it of the prevailing Lynchburg nepotism by replacing nearly every noncommissioned officer in the company with a draftee or recruit. Zappacosta was killed on the morning of D-Day while leading the company onto Omaha Beach.

As I soon found out, soldiering required a lot of adjustments. The first thing one noticed was a complete lack of privacy. In Fort Meade we lived in wooden barracks, two stories high, with two large dormitories that contained one small room for our platoon sergeant and another for his deputy. In the large bathroom, the showers and toilets were all out in the open. I tried to always use the shower and toilet at night after lights out.

As the infantry training required a lot of time and effort, and as the organization for this training was often inefficient, we spent many hours sitting around waiting. When the day's basic training schedule involved a march into open terrain, we were woken up at 4:00 a.m. Crowding into the bathroom, we struggled to find a place at one of the washbasins to shave and brush our teeth. Once dressed we were ready to sit, often for hours, with our baggage and weapons in the lower dormitory, waiting for the trucks that would drive us to the training grounds. I was reminded of a saying popular among German soldiers during the First World War, "Half his life a soldier waits in vain" [*Eine Hälfte seines Lebens wartet der Soldat vergebens*].

When we finally reached our destination we spent many hours "attacking" or "defending," either walking for hours or creeping on our bellies like snakes in order to sneak up on the "enemy." I always enjoyed the sneaking up the best, since for a moment I could pretend again that I was Winnetou or Old Shatterhand. But whatever was on the program during a day of training was always strenuous, especially since the weather in Virginia and southern Maryland was warm from spring to fall and our commanding officer, Colonel Opie (an editor and journalist in civilian life), restricted us to one canteen of water a day as a matter of principle. Once during a daily maneuver I was assigned to direct traffic at a crossroads. The day was unbelievably hot and humid, and by afternoon my canteen hadn't a drop left. Suddenly a cross-country vehicle stopped next to me. In it sat Colonel Opie—a frightfully ugly man, by the way—who ordered me to show him my canteen so he could see how much water was left in it. Well, the canteen was empty. In a condescending voice he told me that I had to get by on one canteen a day. As he ordered his chauffeur to move on I noticed, behind his seat, several cases of Coca-Cola, packed in ice.

By far the most exhausting part of our training was the long practice marches. Around Fort Meade and later in other parts of the South, maneuvers lasted for several weeks as we dragged ourselves across fields or through the woods for fifteen, twenty-five, or thirty miles. That meant fifty minutes' hiking, ten minutes' rest, fifty minutes' hiking, ten minutes' rest—often late into the night. And we did this carrying a full backpack, rifle, ammunition, bayonet, and metal canteen.

Once we'd finished basic training we left Fort Meade and went down to North Carolina for maneuvers. In fact, until August 1943, my army career consisted predominantly of drills and maneuvers. After a while this became terribly boring and I wished again that I'd known what to do if I were driving a heavy truck and the axle broke. There was some relief, however, to the monotony of marching: in North Carolina I dug so many latrines that when Captain Pugh had me promoted to Private First Class shortly thereafter, I asked myself whether I'd earned the honor based on my achievements as a soldier or as a sanitation engineer.

The outcomes of Company B's maneuvers were depressingly predictable: Captain Pugh looked at the map; we got lost; we were captured by the "enemy" (another regiment of our division participating in the maneuvers). After about three hours of marching through the fields and forests, I was shocked by how many of my fellow soldiers sat down by the side of the road and claimed to be incapable of taking another step. Crass malingering, but it worked for them. When enough men were sitting on the embankment, a truck came by to drive them to the march's destination. Those who were too proud for such shenanigans continued dragging ourselves along for miles on end. One time only five of us—the platoon sergeant, his deputy, Barnes, another soldier, and I—reached the final destination on foot.

Despite my frequent boredom, I learned a lot during my sixteen months with the 116th Infantry Regiment. Thanks to Barnes and Jackson's tutoring, I managed within a few weeks to speak English without difficulty. Nobody seemed bothered by the pronounced German accent I have never lost. I could understand what anybody said, make myself understood, and everything I read was in English. I also performed well during basic training. Undoubtedly, my agricultural training at Gross Breesen and Hyde Farmlands had something to do with this. But I also was supported and encouraged by Barnes and Jackson; the platoon leader, Sergeant Wilkins; and his deputy, Sergeant Jennings.

Wilkins was one of the few men from Lynchburg who had been a college student when the division was reactivated. Somewhat older than I, he was tall, intelligent, and had a quick sense of humor. Captain Pugh always treated him with respect because Wilkins obviously came from a higher social class than Pugh or the various relatives he'd had appointed as noncommissioned officers in the company. "Rooster" Jennings earned his nickname from his habit of announcing loudly, proudly, and days in advance his weekend visits to local brothels. Like many of the other men in the company, he had worked in the Lynchburg textile mills, but, unlike many of them, he could read and write. Both sergeants were excellent military instructors. They acquainted us with military tactics, taught us how to shoot, how to fight with the bayonet, how to clean our weapons, how to move into attack in open formation, and similar basic military skills. And they did so without the senseless yelling that today has become customary in most armies of our world. The fact that all of us were civilians in uniform made a great difference and set the tone. To be sure, we were soldiers now and had to execute orders, but we were still treated decently as individual human beings.

Each in his own way, Wilkins and Jennings tried to integrate me, the little outsider, into the company and turn me into a regular American GI. For instance, prior to a night march approximately a year after I had become a soldier, Wilkins told me to fill in for my regular squad leader. Needless to say, I was very proud. Wilkins told me I was responsible for seeing to it that no member of the squad straggled along behind. After a while, however, one of the squad members began to ignore my orders to close ranks. This was Private Mays, a good-looking boy of partly Native American descent with a well-known allergy to exertion of any kind. After several vain attempts to make Mays move up I did something that I have regretted all my life: I kicked him in the behind until he had moved up again to the end of the squad.

On the following day I was called to Sergeant Wilkins's room. The sergeant looked at me very seriously, invited me to sit down, and then said: "Tommy, for the first time since you've been in the army I entrusted you with a command position, and you promptly abused it!" Only then did it dawn on me how badly I had behaved. I promised Sergeant Wilkins that I would never act like that again, apologized to Mays (who, like Wilkins, survived the war), and with that the matter was closed. But I have never forgotten this incident, and in retrospect I'm grateful that for the balance of my life I have never again yielded to the temptation to abuse whatever power I have possessed. The students I taught for thirty-five years at several American universities benefited from this resolve.

Sergeant Jennings took me in hand from the outset and occasionally invited me to fence with him, using sticks instead of the sabers our company lacked. A scar on my right wrist still bears witness to these bouts. One of Jennings's duties was to inspect us during night maneuvers to determine whether we were wide awake and able to raise the alarm if "enemy" forces were sighted. During one of his nightly inspections he found me fast asleep. He read me the riot act, and it was effective. For the balance of my army service I never again fell asleep while on duty.

Like Barnes and Zappacosta, Jennings died on June 6, 1944, during the landing on the beaches of Normandy.

The first big maneuver was finally over in early December 1941. We were moving in trucks from North Carolina back to Fort Meade but stopped for the night at A. P. Hill Military Reservation in Virginia. It was December 7. We settled down around a campfire to chat about where we planned to spend Christmas leave. Suddenly the radio operator of intelligence headquarters joined our group and shouted that the "Japs" had bombed Pearl Harbor. Much of the U.S. fleet there had been destroyed and sunk. "Where is Pearl Harbor?" I asked innocently. My buddies stared at me. There would be no Christmas leave. On the following day, once again in open trucks in icy cold weather on the way to Fort Meade, we learned that Congress had declared war on Japan, as a result of which we would now remain soldiers "for the duration"—until the war was over. Four days later, on December 11, Germany and Italy declared war on the United States. This country had entered the Second World War.

The big question for me now was the fate of my parents and brothers. Would I be able to keep in touch with them? That was especially important for me because I had learned that my father had been arrested in Amsterdam and I was trying, despite my very limited financial resources, to find a way for him to emigrate. My mother had written to me that it might be possible to obtain a visa for Cuba, at least as soon as he was released from prison. We only found out much later that she was completely mistaken in this respect. She and I corresponded regularly until Pearl Harbor, and once in a while I even received a few lines from Papa, who could write to me as long as he was still being held in an Amsterdam jail. But after his trial in Berlin he was sent to the Brandenburg penitentiary and all contact ceased. After December 7, 1941, the letters from my mother and brothers also stopped. I had no news of them until shortly after the end of the war, when I found them again in Amsterdam.

What had happened to my father? As I have said, we had left Germany at his instigation in late October 1937. In the process, Papa had illegally transferred his entire capital, approximately one hundred thousand reichsmarks, to Amsterdam. During the German invasion of Holland on May 10, 1940, my parents and brothers tried to get to England by boat, but they failed and had to return to Amsterdam. During the months that followed the fear of being arrested hung over my father like the sword of Damocles. On April 25, 1941, eleven months after the German occupation began, two officials of the *Devisenschutzkommando* (roughly, Guardians of Currency Transferred Abroad) came to my parents' flat at Cliostraat 39 and demanded to speak to my father. My mother told them that he was away on business and that she didn't know when he would return. But instead of keeping my mother as a hostage or staying in the apartment until my father returned, they told my mother (very politely, as one of my brothers who witnessed this "visit" later told me) to contact my father as soon as possible and that they would return the following day around the same time. With that they departed, thereby giving my father twenty-four hours to get himself and his family to safety by going "underground," as many German Jews in Holland did by staying under false names with Dutch families. As a matter of fact, my parents had been prepared to take such a step. There existed an underground organization run by Dutch citizens—although a few *Reichsdeutsche* [German non-Jews] also belonged to it—that organized the hiding of Jews, German as well as Dutch. My parents had the telephone number to call once they had decided that the time had come.

When my father came home that evening—my mother had informed him by telephone—he lay down in his bed and refused to accept my mother's proposal. As my brother told me later, he lay there apathetically, continually repeating, "I cannot impose this on you!" The next morning at eleven when the two officials reappeared, Papa was waiting for them with a small suitcase in his hand. According to my mother and brothers, the two officials looked at him with utter disbelief. But they of course had no choice in the matter and took him away. It was the beginning of a long road that led him through various prisons—first in Holland, then in Germany. The road ended for him on January 19, 1943, in Auschwitz. In September 1943 my brothers and my mother went into the Dutch underground, each to a different family, and all three of them survived. How I eventually found them I will tell later.

Thus, for the duration of the war I lived in two worlds. On the one hand, I was an American soldier, one among millions being trained for battles in Europe or Asia. On the other hand, I was no typical American GI. I still had no real home in the United States—on paper my domicile was listed as Bondy's address in Richmond. But my home was with my family, and I worried constantly about them, without being able to do anything for them, without even knowing their whereabouts or even whether they were still alive. I tried to keep up contact with my friends, mostly from Gross Breesen, all of whom had had to leave Hyde Farmlands too. As long as I remained stationed on the East Coast, I used whatever leave I was given to meet with one or more of them, and on free weekends I often traveled to Richmond to see Bondy. I also wrote letters nearly every day, above all to Leus and Traut in England, but also to friends who lived in the United States. I was able to keep in touch with Meui in Holland and was very happy when, in 1941, he was able to come to the States, and after that we saw each other from time to time. I felt very much divided and an outsider during my military training. Thus I wrote in my diary on March 2, 1942: "Eleven new corporals, six new sergeants have been appointed. I was not promoted. A German and a Jew and not from Lynchburg, that's too much! I felt terribly down in the dumps."

In contrast to many of my buddies, I kept track of the international situation, especially, of course, after Hitler began to invade other European countries. About these events I made brief entries in my diary. But there were few people with whom I could talk about what was happening in the world (one of them was Barnes). Although we were regularly shown propaganda movies in a series titled *Why We Fight*, some of which were excellent, most of the soldiers watching the films used the time that they were shown to take a nap in the darkness of the theater. The lack of interest so many American soldiers displayed in what was going on overseas was remarkable. After all, each of us knew that sooner or later he would be committed to military action somewhere. At night in the barracks at Fort Meade I also listened to President Franklin D. Roosevelt's fireside chats on the radio. My buddies listened to these, too, because he was our president and commander-in-chief and had our fate in his hands. I can still hear FDR's voice: "My friends ...".

But we found out very little about the situation that the Jews faced in Germany and in the countries Germany occupied. From the very carefully written letters my mother sent me until December 1941 I ascertained that the living conditions for Jews had further deteriorated, in Holland and beyond. But Mutti didn't go into any specifics, as that would have been too dangerous. Now and then I did find out about anti-Semitic measures from newspaper reports. Thus in January 1942 I wrote in my diary that according to the eleventh decree [*Verordnung*] of the *Reichsbürgergesetz* [citizenship law] of November 25, 1941, every Jew leaving Germany would lose his or her German nationality. I only found out much later that I had already been deprived of my citizenship after leaving Germany in October 1937. Thus I stupidly commented that the decree was advantageous to us emigrants because we could no longer be considered "enemy aliens" by the United States.

My ignorance about the threat to Jews in Europe, which I shared with most Americans at that time, was due partly to our having left Fort Meade and the vicinity of large cities such as New York, Philadelphia, Baltimore, and so on. We could only rarely get our hands on serious newspapers such as *The New York Times* or *Washington Post*. On maneuvers and at training camps in the Deep South, good newspapers were hard to find. We were limited to the servicemens' paper, *Stars and Stripes*, which focused nearly exclusively on matters military. But even in *The New York Times* we would have hardly been able to find specifics about Hitler's Final Solution, as the U.S. press gave little credence to the bits of information that leaked through on this subject and treated the "Jewish question" in Europe with great skepticism. Thus for me, too, the occasional references to deportations—not to mention mass extermination—remained mere "rumors." And rumors, especially in wartime, couldn't be trusted since they often were circulated as propaganda. The word "Auschwitz" I heard for the first time in May 1945.

After Hitler declared war on the United States we soon left Fort Meade. Instead of getting Christmas furlough, Company B was transported in mid-December to the Chesapeake Bay to guard the coast and repel any possible German attacks. We were sent initially to, of all places, Berlin, Maryland. But we stayed there only briefly, and within a few days my platoon—the third—was sent by ferry to Chincoteague Island, Virginia, where we arrived on New Year's Eve and stayed for a month. We were one of three National Guard divisions deployed to defend the East Coast of the United States, from the Canadian border to Key West, Florida. Two-man teams were assigned sectors of the coast approximately two miles long, which we patrolled twenty-four hours a day: two hours on duty, four hours of rest, then again two hours on duty, and so on. I shared my sector with Barnes. It was winter and our combat uniforms were much too thin (uniforms suitable for the climate were only slowly being manufactured). Each infantry soldier was issued forty bullets, and every two-man team got one pair of field glasses. The latter had been stored somewhere since the First World War and had lenses that looked like the glass one finds in the windows of a public toilet— white, misty, and opaque. As Sergeant Jennings put it, "Uncle Sam has issued you this and you'll just have to make the best of it." And that was that.

Our weapons also dated from World War I. I still own a smart-looking photo of myself carrying a very venerable rifle and wearing one of the "Tommy helmets" we'd inherited from the British and U.S. forces of 1918. With these arms, forty bullets, and the wild ponies of Chincoteague roaming behind us, we walked up and down the beach, ready to defend the North American continent. Rather than our uniforms or weapons, what most warmed and fortified us for our guard duty was the kindness of the island's civilians, who immediately began looking after us. Day and night, every time we returned from our lengthy patrols, someone was standing there waiting for us—sometimes a man, sometimes a woman, occasionally also teenagers and children—all of them with hot coffee, cookies, and other baked goods.

We were relieved from our assignment on December 21, 1941, and returned initially to "Hotel Fort Meade," as we called it because of its heated barracks. In the meantime the Japanese had besieged Singapore and threatened General MacArthur's troops in the Philippines. In Europe, the Russians were slowly pushing west. Of course we asked ourselves to which of the two theaters we would be sent, and how soon. I hoped strongly that I wasn't sent to the Far East to fight the Japanese. I wanted to fight Hitler and the Nazis; I had no hostile feelings against the Japanese.

After our return we were given ten days' leave. As usual, I spent it with my Gross Breesen friends. When I got back our training continued and gradually got on my nerves. I was fed up with the continual long marches, either sweating like hell or freezing, and with cleaning the barracks until late at night, only to be reprimanded by the inspecting officer because he had found a spot on a window pane. In February 1942 I received a letter that my mother had sent the previous November, shortly before Pearl Harbor. She merely confirmed that they had received the visa for my father—I believe it was for Cuba—that I had bought with the assistance of Fritz Schwarzschild, the former financial advisor [Finanzreferent] for Gross Breesen at the Reichsvertretung der Juden in Deutschland [National Representative Agency of Jews in Germany] who was subsequently employed by a New York travel agency. But aside from the fact that nobody was allowed "to travel abroad," as Mutti put it, my father was by that time imprisoned in Germany.

In March 1942, Ernst Cramer, my friend from Gross Breesen and Hyde Farmlands, was drafted and assigned to the 116th Infantry

Regiment. The following month, my knowledge of German won me a transfer from Company B to the Intelligence Section of the First Battalion's Headquarters Company, and shortly thereafter Ernst was assigned to the same section. There we worked jointly until the late summer of 1942. Besides the customary drills and marches, our duties consisted of studying the German military organization and the German conduct of war in general. When I was promoted to corporal in June 1942 I became Ernst's superior, at least technically speaking, since he was still an ordinary private. This new hierarchy felt strange to me. He was older, and at Gross Breesen, but above all at Hyde Farmlands, I had looked up to him and gotten used to following his directions. But our friendship outweighed this, and we managed to work well together without paying much attention to who held which rank.

I would have liked very much to have stayed in the 29th Infantry Division and eventually to have gone overseas with my new friends. For although I had been transferred to the intelligence section of the First Battalion's Headquarters Company, where I had no friends except for Ernst Cramer, I kept spending a good deal of time back at B Company, visiting with Barnes, Wilkins, Jennings, and the others. I was waiting impatiently for my naturalization papers, which I had applied for quite some time earlier and without which I could not be sent overseas and ultimately into combat (prohibited for aliens). No one could explain this delay to me. Suddenly everything developed very fast. In July 1942 the division was moved from Fort Meade to Camp Blanding, near Jacksonville, Florida. But before we got ourselves on the road in our long columns of trucks and jeeps, Cramer was taken out of the intelligence section and transferred to Minnesota, where he would work with an undefined special unit.

What caused this sudden transfer? Ernst was only told that the order had come from headquarters of the Counterintelligence Corps in Washington. Subsequently we found out that at the time a small group of German undercover agents had disembarked from a German submarine that managed to reach the East Coast. Captured virtually at once, the German agents said that the person with whom they were supposed to establish contact after their landing was named Cramer. This sufficed to send Ernst to the "special unit," which turned out to be a penal company in which he and other "aliens" who had aroused the suspicion of their military superiors did hard labor. In the winter of 1941–42, this consisted mainly of felling trees. In the spring of 1942, an alert army officer found out about Ernst's situation and discovered that the reasons for his transfer were completely unfounded. Ernst was then sent back to the East Coast and ended up, like me, at Camp Ritchie, Maryland, where he trained to become an intelligence officer specializing in psychological warfare. This remained his responsibility for the duration of the war.

The separation from Ernst was a very sad and completely unexpected development for me, especially since the division was moving down to Florida, from which, rumor had it, the next convoy would take the Twenty-Ninth to either Great Britain or Northern Ireland, there to await the Allied invasion of the European mainland. And thus in July we moved south. I rode in one of the several jeeps our intelligence section had at its disposal, which was more agreeable than being crammed into a truck. The further south we moved, the more beautiful the landscape became. As there were no superhighways in the United States at the time, we drove along the two-lane Highway 1, which in southern Georgia passed through the Okefenokee Swamp. On both sides of the road ran deep ditches in which we spotted several poisonous snakes, mainly water moccasins. Scattered throughout the swamp were giant old trees draped with long grey-green Spanish moss. As at Hyde Farmlands, I enjoyed the still-unspoiled Southern landscape and continued to do so during the night marches and brief maneuvers around Camp Blanding.

In mid-September 1942 the Twenty-Ninth was placed on alert and told to prepare to sail for Northern Ireland. To my great disappointment, but not surprise, I couldn't go along with the division because my naturalization papers still hadn't arrived, and no one knew where and why they were held up. As long as I didn't have U.S. citizenship I had to stay in the United States. Thus while the Twenty-Ninth was getting ready to depart I was transferred to the 314th Regiment of the 79th Infantry Division, which then was also stationed at Camp Blanding. Once again I had to say goodbye to friends, above all to Barnes, Jennings, and Wilkins.

The next eleven months following my transfer, from September 1942 until August 1943, proved to be the most unpleasant period I spent in the Army, though at first everything seemed to be working out all right. I was assigned once again to a normal infantry company—no more intelligence section or giving German lessons like I had done during the past months. But there were a number of nice men in my new unit, and the company commander, Captain Rountree of Texas, although demanding of us, was utterly fair and decent with his men, so I soon felt at home.

Since I was now a corporal, Captain Rountree appointed me first as deputy, then as regular squad leader, and during the first two months all went well. The division moved to Camp Forrest in Tennessee, where we continued to go on boring maneuvers and again spent months in the woods, "fighting" against other regiments of our division and freezing our butts off at night in our pup tents. Shortly after we returned to Camp Forrest, Captain Rountree called me into his office. I was surprised to see him look embarrassed. He told me that all soldiers in the division who hadn't yet received their naturalization papers as U.S. citizens were being transferred immediately to an "alien detachment." He hoped that my papers would arrive soon so that I could return to the company.

In this alien detachment I spent the better part of six months. It consisted of fifteen to twenty men, most of them German Jewish immigrants like me. There were also some non-Jews of German descent from Chicago who, as their occasional remarks on German politics soon revealed, sympathized with the Nazis, at least to some extent. But they never engaged us Jews in a political discussion. There were also a few lost souls such as a Czech (whose country Hitler's army had invaded in March of 1939) and several young men from countries also occupied by Germany. What bound us together despite these differences was the fact that we were all soldiers of the 79th Infantry Division whose naturalization papers languished somewhere in the bureaucracy and who thus had become "enemy aliens."

How did we get into such a miserable situation? (After all, I had been an "enemy alien" throughout my time in the 29th Division.) As we found out later, two men were responsible for creating the "alien detachment": the nearly senile colonel who headed the division's intelligence detachment and his ranking master sergeant, a Jew from Brooklyn. The latter had persuaded the former to establish the special detachment, maintaining that we might be German spies even if we claimed to be Jews. Fear of fifth columnists was widespread at the time, both among the Americans and the British. But I have never heard of other units that meted out such humiliating treatment as the 79th Division did to us in 1942 and 1943.

We had to hand in our weapons, were refused any leave, and were quartered separately at the edge of Camp Forrest, in tents instead of barracks. In short, we were treated like outcasts and considered ourselves as such. For months we did chores in our working clothes (we also had to hand in our uniforms), cleaning windows, raking leaves, and similar jobs. As I was the ranking noncommissioned officer in the detachment I supervised the daily cleaning of the officers' club, notably of the toilets. There was no contact whatsoever with other units in the division, including those quartered close to our tents at the edge of Camp Forrest. Occasionally we were verbally abused by drunken soldiers who called us "Nazi pigs" and yelled, "We ought to shoot you bastards!" All attempts to get assistance from staff members of the division failed. I spoke a few times with the division's ranking Protestant chaplain about our situation. He listened to my tale of woe, made a few kind remarks, and promised to help, but he got nowhere either.

One day in the summer of 1943 we were told to our great surprise that we were given ten days' leave. We got our uniforms back and took off at once. I went to Richmond to see Bondy. When I arrived he told me that he had just received a visit from an officer from the Department of War, who, in fact, was sitting in the next room. The man had come to ask Bondy a few questions connected with my naturalization. Would I like to tell him about my unpleasant experiences with the 79th Division? I agreed and Bondy introduced me to the officer, a friendly and polite young captain. When I had finished my report, he appeared shocked and said he had never encountered anything like this. Such segregation was in complete violation of all Army regulations. Promising to report this situation to Washington, he thanked me and left. When I returned to Camp Forrest, our tents were no longer standing. I asked at division headquarters where I was to go now and was told to return to my old company. Captain Rountree welcomed me warmly and intimated how much he regretted and disapproved of my absence of several months. Therewith this miserable phase of my Army service ended, and with it all the related humiliations, obstruction of my military training, and denial of leave.

A few weeks later an unexpected opportunity arose, making it possible for me to leave the 79th Division and turn to a completely new and different area of activity. Shortly before, Captain Rountree had promoted me to the rank of sergeant—the company's communications sergeant, to be precise—charged with transmitting by walkie-talkie the captain's messages and questions to other units participating in exercises. Given my pronounced German accent, a frequent reaction to my efforts was "Here goes that idiot again!" or similar comments. But my future lay elsewhere. One day a message from division headquarters appeared on the company's bulletin board urging all those able to speak another language, especially German or Japanese, to apply for the next training course at the Military Intelligence Training Center (MITC) at Camp Ritchie, in order to become POW interrogators, propagandists, or interpreters. I immediately applied, was accepted within a few days, and, with Captain Rountree's best wishes, departed for Maryland.

My stay at Camp Ritchie was an important experience for me from the start. The camp was beautifully situated in a slightly undulating landscape not far from the Civil War battlefield at Gettysburg, Pennsylvania, and also very close to Camp David, the Maryland mountain retreat of U.S. presidents. A former National Guard camp, it teemed with soldiers in American uniforms, many of whom, like me, spoke English with a pronounced accent; not just German but French, Spanish, Japanese, and more. I was to be trained as an interrogator of German prisoners of war in the Eleventh Class (September–December 1943) of the MITC, which had been founded only a couple of years earlier, and thus I barracked mostly with men whose native tongue was German. People talked and talked, at times in a mixture of languages, which often gave rise to what we considered very funny wordplays. MITC headquarters had placed in each of the barracks an undercover agent to monitor our conversations. We spotted the one assigned to our barracks very fast, as he walked "discreetly" from group to group, not saying a word to anybody but listening intently to our conversations. As we had nothing to hide we simply ignored him, and after a few days he disappeared.

The men in our barracks were nearly exclusively German-Jewish immigrants and, with a few exceptions, very pleasant companions. Three of my barrack mates subsequently became well known. Fred Hechinger, who slept in a bed next to mine, and with whom I soon became friends, after the war became education editor of *The New York Times* and later one of its publishers. Wolf von Eckart, with whom I frequently ate in our mess hall, went on to serve on the staff of Allen Dulles, who from 1942 till 1945 was head of the Office of Strategic Services (OSS), in Bern, Switzerland. After the war, Eckart became a writer and with Sander Gilman published *Bertolt Brecht's Berlin*.

The third person was someone I met fleetingly and in the process came into conflict with. On the day I arrived at Camp Ritchie I was assigned to a temporary barracks where we were to stay until the class began, at which time we would be transferred to quarters deeper inside the base. As I happened to be the senior noncommissioned officer in our little group on the day of our arrival, I was appointed barracks sergeant and became responsible for order and cleanliness. On either the first or second morning I told a fellow newcomer to sweep under his bed. He refused. I warned him that I would have to report this to a superior, but the fellow simply ignored me. I have forgotten what exactly happened next, except that I decided not to report him, as we would stay in these barracks at most another day and I didn't want to begin my stay at Camp Ritchie by reporting a person I didn't even know for disobedience. I told somebody else to sweep under the man's bed and let it go at that. That evening when I went to the movie house on the base, the same man was standing onstage in front of the curtain. Before the lights were turned off he said a few words about the film we were about to see, *Hostages*. In short, my refusenik was Stefan Heym, and the film was based on his bestselling novel of the same title. After the war I read his books with growing enthusiasm, and when he died in Berlin in December 2001 I attended his memorial service. More than a thousand of us listened to the writers Heinz Knobloch and Johannes Mario Simmel eulogize him.

Camp Ritchie wasn't the only base where soldiers trained in military intelligence, but it was the largest and the most important. As I had applied to become an interrogator of prisoners of war, almost all my courses during the three months of the Eleventh Class were devoted to interrogation. There existed two general categories of prisoner interrogation: the overwhelming majority of us, including me, were trained for work in field interrogation detachments (FID), which consisted of two officers and four noncoms. These teams were sent to either Northern Ireland or England, where they were assigned to the various U.S. divisions slated to participate in the upcoming invasion of the Nazi-occupied European mainland. Once these teams were ready for operation at or closely behind the front lines, they were to learn from their German prisoners tactical information such as the strength of the troops facing them, how many losses these troops had lately suffered, where and when they were being fed, and related matters. A few other interrogators were being trained for assignment to the OSS, a precursor of the Central Intelligence Agency. OSS interrogators had to try to extract from high-ranking German prisoners information about Hitler's long-term plans and other strategic information.

So now I was sitting again at a school desk. Although by and large we received good training in the intelligence service, the administration

Buildings in the former Camp Ritchie, as they looked in 2003. This still is taken from "The Ritchie Boys" by Christian Bauer, Tangram Filmstudio, Munich 2004 (DVD & video).

of Camp Ritchie could be inefficient, time-consuming, and even chaotic. I quickly learned that my military intelligence training wouldn't be nearly so secret, or so intelligent, as I had expected. Before our training course began, for instance, we were ordered to move in small groups along the fence surrounding the camp and mark on a map all the spots where gaps might enable enemy agents to infiltrate. The gaps were never closed, but as we now knew where they were, we occasionally used them to sneak out of Camp Ritchie without a pass and go to a nearby restaurant. This fence inspection took place under the supervision of one of the meanest and most unpleasant noncommissioned officers I encountered during my entire time in the army. This sergeant's name was Frank Leavitt, but we knew him only as "Man Mountain Dean," which had been his moniker as a professional wrestler. He was in command whenever we had to leave camp on an official mission. Vastly overweight, he looked like a gorilla and was for a while the bodyguard of General Patton. He detested us "intellectuals," probably as much as we detested him. He loudly and repeatedly informed us that we future interrogators were "girlies," not "real soldiers," and wouldn't survive for long during the coming combat.

Far more shocking to me than this cartoonish master sergeant was the carelessness with which some important operations were handled.

During our training course we were informed under the seal of secrecy that another contingent of trained intelligence personnel was soon to embark for Europe. One of our fellow trainees who expected to be on that next transport to Europe invited his wife for a brief visit and for that purpose rented a room in a nearby private home. The landlady, a pleasant elderly woman, asked our friend's wife whether her husband would be on this next transport overseas. When the wife asked how she knew another transport was ready to leave, the landlady replied that work was going on day and night at the nearby freight station, and the station always got busy before an overseas transport. So much for secret military operations! When we were subsequently warned again and again not to tell anyone about our training or anything that went on at our camp, especially the transports overseas, because this information might then reach German agents, I only shrugged my shoulders in disgust.

We always enjoyed telling newcomers waiting for the next training class that MITC in fact stood for "Military Institute of Total Confusion." And the quality of the courses and the instructors who taught them indeed varied considerably. Most of our training was excellent, as I will try to illustrate. But we also wasted a lot of time. For instance, there was a "quicky" course on Morse code that everyone had to pass in order to get weekend leave. A course on telecommunications was more substantial but not very stimulating either. A lieutenant from the signal corps tried valiantly to instill in us a number of techniques: how to communicate in the field by means of the old-fashioned but still omnipresent telephone cables, how to install the latter, how to wiretap and monitor enemy radios and telephones, and similar technical matters that to me and many others in the class were by and large incomprehensible. But he never lost his patience with us. Once he even sang us a song: "Oh, I'd rather be a pimple on the ass of a whore / than a first lieutenant in the Signal Corps." This, alas, is the only thing I remember from his course.

By far the most important class that we future POW interrogators had to take introduced us to the organizational structure of the German ground troops. The course left out the German Navy and *Luftwaffe* because our training as members of future field interrogation detachments was restricted to the enemy troops we would meet on the ground. The officer who introduced us to this extensive subject matter was Captain Cohn, also a German-Jewish immigrant. Slightly overweight, he always emphasized his military bearing, carrying himself straight as an arrow as he paced our classroom. We had to know who the commanders of the various divisions were, which regiments belonged to which divisions, and so on. Cohn taught us the hierarchy of not only the Wehrmacht but also the Waffen-SS. Thus I learned that a number of SS units consisted overwhelmingly of non-German enlisted men and in part of non-German officers. Among these units were the "First Cossack Cavalry Division of the SS," the "East Turkish *Waffenverband*" [armed unit] of the SS, or the "Indian *Freiwilligenlegion*" [volunteer foreign legion] of the SS, to name but a few. In this course my head was stuffed with dates, names, military formations, rank insignia, and so on. In short, every day I lived with Hitler's military organization and at night I occasionally dreamed of it. At the end of the training course each FID team leader received a copy of the *German Order of Battle*, which gave up-to-date information on the German ground forces. (For obvious reasons, paratroopers weren't allowed to jump with this book, but each officer in charge of an FID team assigned to an airborne unit was handed a copy once he and his men were safely on the ground.)

I can recall no class in which we were taught how to interrogate German POWs. What I do remember are continuous interrogation exercises and at the end of the twelve weeks a final examination. Cohn's class was the heart of our training at Camp Ritchie. On the basis of what we learned in his course, we could impress prisoners with our knowledge of the structure of German ground forces and thus lead our subjects to volunteer crucial tactical information. Casually dropping the name of a prisoner's commanding general could have a psychological effect on him. For these reasons, Cohn repeated, it was our duty to keep up to date and know our enemy.

A few weeks after the Eleventh Class began I finally became a U.S. citizen. On the morning of October 5, 1943, a day when we were scheduled to begin a two-day maneuver for which I had been assigned to lead about ten men through the woods around Camp Ritchie using a compass and a map, I was told to join a small group of fellow "enemy aliens" taking a truck to nearby Hagerstown to get naturalized. In the city hall we were received by a number of officers and noncoms unknown to us. My naturalization was no more ceremonial than my entry into the army had been. We stood around until our names were called, then stepped up one by one to a desk behind which a couple of noncoms sat with our papers in hand. The sergeant who had handled my papers told me that assembling my essential documents had been difficult, since they had been scattered at bases around the United States. He had the impression that this wasn't a coincidence. Did I have any enemies? I mentioned the master sergeant in the intelligence section of the 79th Division to whom I owed a humiliating six months in an "alien detachment." My questioner just shook his head and asked me to repeat the citizenship oath. I did and was handed the papers that finally made me a U.S. citizen.

Half an hour later I and another new citizen, an Orthodox Jewish sergeant, started out for the two-day field exercise, about six hours late. Our troops, who had been put together at random and whom we didn't know, had waited for us impatiently. Our mission was to lead these men with compass and map to ten different locations within forty-eight hours (for us now forty-two). At each location we were handed an envelope with a task (usually a written test) and instructions for reaching our next destination. All this was quite exhausting and challenging, at least for us two sergeants. We stumbled across the countryside in the dark (flashlights were forbidden for this exercise), following our compass in the direction we'd been instructed to take, and at one point finding ourselves in a pasture where a bull greeted us with furious snorts. We finished our exercise just a little later than those who had started six hours earlier, and as a result we were publicly commended the next day. This didn't keep some men in my group from calling me a slave driver, however.

When our final examinations came, we hadn't yet interrogated any "prisoners," although there had of course been constant allusions to interrogation in our courses and we had learned the structure of the enemy's ground troops so we would be able to ask the right questions. The idea behind this absence of practice was probably that you couldn't really teach interrogation. But in the exam we were expected to show how successful we would be in extracting useful tactical information from a "prisoner." Those of us who did well in the exam "interrogations" could expect to be promoted to a higher rank.

On the second or third day of the examinations it was my turn. Unfortunately, as examining officer I got the one all my friends who had preceded me warned me to avoid. Second Lieutenant Bartholomew, a Mormon from Utah, had interrogated POWs during General Eisenhower's North African campaign. In the process he had suffered shell shock, whereupon he was sent back to the States and made an examiner at Camp Ritchie. The day before the examinations started he had given the

Eleventh Class an overview of what he expected of us. First we had to find out to which military unit the "prisoner" belonged, how strong his unit was, where it was located at the moment, and similar tactical information. Lieutenant Bartholomew had clear and simple ideas about how one got answers to these questions. During interrogation prisoners must be forced to stand at attention in front of the interrogator, heels together and hands along the trouser seams. Under no circumstances could they be allowed to sit down, given anything to drink, or offered a cigarette. As soon as they stood at attention they were to be yelled at. This was the only way to do it and, Bartholomew said, the way he'd had such great success interrogating soldiers from Rommel's Afrika Korps in Libya and Tunisia.

I found this a pigheaded and completely misguided approach, and I didn't believe Bartholomew's boasts. Why had he suffered shell shock? I simply couldn't visualize this small man having much success interrogating veterans of the Afrika Korps in the manner he claimed to have used. Nor could I see myself in the role of a yelling interrogator. Small and young-looking as I was at the time, I would only make myself look ridiculous. And after I found out that my fellow soldiers who acted the part of "prisoners" would more or less collapse after about fifteen minutes of interrogation and then would reveal the desired information—regardless of how they had been interrogated—I decided to use a different method than the one Bartholomew expected, one I felt would be more effective. This wasn't a smart move on my part.

When my turn came to be tested I first made every effort to ignore the lieutenant. I placed the little table used for these tests so that Bartholomew sat diagonally behind me. Then I put on the table a bottle of water and a pack of cigarettes that I had borrowed from a friend and waited for my "victim." When the "prisoner" arrived I asked him to grab a chair and sit down behind the table facing me. I offered him water and a cigarette and only then asked him in an ordinary tone of voice a number of questions. As was customary during these tests, the "prisoner" refused to tell me more than his name, rank, and serial number, according to the Geneva Convention. But after about ten minutes of fiddling around and a number of apparently harmless but in reality strategic questions from me, the "prisoner" gave up and told me to which unit he belonged, how high its losses had recently been, and similar pieces of information. With that the interrogation was over. After I had him taken away I turned around and looked at Lieutenant Bartholomew, who sat there and stared at me for a couple of minutes, not saying a word. Then he gave me a dressing-down such as I hadn't experienced since childhood. I was thoroughly incapable of interrogating prisoners of war. I lacked the necessary military bearing and would never be taken seriously by German prisoners of war, and so on. He informed me that he wouldn't give me a passing grade. When I protested that I had after all received the information I had asked for, he merely shook his head with a look of utter disgust and dismissed me. So ended my final examination at Camp Ritchie. In all the other courses I got excellent grades, averaging 90 percent, as my Gross Breesen and Hyde Farmlands friend, Lieutenant Ernst Loew, found out the following day (as an officer he had been granted permission to check my file). But having failed the interrogation test I wasn't promoted to master sergeant, as would have otherwise been the case, but only to staff sergeant, merely one rank higher than I held at the time. I did become a master sergeant subsequently, in the winter of 1944, on the recommendation of Major General James M. Gavin, then commander of the 82nd Airborne Division.

Shortly after the interrogation test I had an experience with a branch of the U.S. espionage services, though which one I never found out. One morning I received orders to report immediately to a master sergeant at Camp Ritchie's main administrative building. After I entered I saw on his desk a copy of a recent bestseller, *Total Espionage*, written by Curt Riess, a German refugee to the United States. The book focused on Nazi spying and, as emerged subsequently, was almost entirely fictitious. The sergeant didn't offer me a seat but simply asked me whether I knew a soldier named X. I did: during one of the short overnight maneuvers at Camp Ritchie he, I, and another soldier had shared a tent. The two men had had a very soft conversation that night, probably assuming I was asleep. X had told the other soldier that the United States would have to be completely and radically restructured once the war was over. Revolutionary cadres would have to be created to represent the people rather than simply the wealthy bourgeoisie, as politicians had done until then. But I didn't tell the sergeant all this. I merely replied that I had come to know X very superficially. When the sergeant asked me for the man's political views I lied, "I have no idea." From the sergeant's questions I understood that we were kept under very thorough surveillance.

X was suspected of being a communist sympathizer, the sergeant continued. He had just applied to an officer training course, but people with his politics couldn't become officers in the Army of the United States. Did I really not know anything about his views? I repeated that I knew nothing about X's politics. Trying to appear naive, I asked the sergeant why communists were barred from becoming officers; after all, the Russians were our allies, weren't they? At that point the "interview" ended. The sergeant ignored my question and dismissed me, but he told me as I left that I was under no circumstances to mention anything of our conversation to X. When I thought of this brief conversation a few years later it struck me that even during the Second World War the U.S. spy services never abandoned their deep-seated suspicion of the Soviet Union. For them, the actual enemy was communism. Hitler and the Nazis were a secondary opponent—one need only remember the FBI's tolerance during the 1930s of the "America First" movement, which the U.S. authorities didn't take seriously until Pearl Harbor and Hitler's declaration of war. Thus even though the Russians were then our allies, any U.S. soldier suspected of sympathizing with their politics was immediately placed under strict surveillance. A few years after the Second World War had ended, when the Cold War broke out and McCarthyism began to tyrannize the United States, I recalled my strange encounter with that sergeant at Camp Ritchie.

When our courses were over word got around that most of us would immediately be sent out on maneuvers again. The thought of yet another maneuver made me furious. I was sick and tired of these miserable scouting games and reacted as I did whenever lower-level commanders made decisions affecting me to which I strongly objected: I went over their heads to the highest officer who would listen to me. At Camp Ritchie this happened to be its commander of the moment (commanders changed continually), Colonel Hochschild. The Hochschilds were respected U.S. industrialists who owned copper mines in South America and had some Jewish ancestry. When I went to see Colonel Hochschild and he asked what I wanted, I said I would like to volunteer for the next transport overseas. After asking me a few brief questions, he promised that he would place me on the list for the next transport, which would leave for England in late 1943 or early 1944. He was true to his word. A few weeks later I found myself with a contingent of interrogators of all ranks at Brooklyn Harbor, New York, ready to board a British troopship within a convoy that would cross the Atlantic. The convoy commander was sailing on our ship. When we asked one of the British sailors what the name of the ship was, he said he couldn't tell us, since this was a strict secret. Shortly after we boarded, however, some of us "passengers" found, under a pile of woolen blankets, a life preserver with the name of the ship written on it. We were on the *H.M.S. Rangitata*, a passenger ship from New Zealand that had been converted into a troop transport.

The crossing took more than two weeks because the convoy could only move as fast as its slowest boat. We Camp Ritchie graduates had to do guard duty, regardless of our (noncommissioned) rank, and also had to be ready to move the ammunition to the ship's antiaircraft guns should we be attacked by German airplanes. My guard duty lasted every morning and every afternoon from 4:00 to 8:00, four boring hours twice a day. The torpedo boats that guarded the convoy discovered German U-boats several times, as we could tell from their flag-waving and the detonations of their depth charges. But traveling at the center of the convoy on the commander's ship, we felt very safe. Our convoy didn't lose a single ship to enemy fire.

We arrived at Liverpool at the end of January 1944. The weather was mild and the people were friendly. At the railway station we saw a giant poster displaying the question: "Is your trip really necessary?" One of our first discoveries was that many functions were carried out by women, including the moving of heavy freight, and not merely at the Liverpool station. Women in England at this point had taken over jobs normally carried out by men because since the fall of 1939 the latter had been fighting the war on the ground, on the sea, and in the air all over Europe and beyond. Wherever you went you were struck by evidence that this country had been at war for several years already. For most of us this was a new atmosphere, for although we too had been at war since Pearl Harbor, the home front in the United States was barely mobilized compared to England in early 1944.

Shortly after our arrival in Liverpool we were sent by train to Birmingham, an ugly industrial city where we sat around for a few days before moving on to headquarters of the interrogation teams in England, in a town called Broadway. Situated a little south of Stratford-upon-Avon and thus in Shakespeare country, Broadway was at the time a very pretty little town. (Alas, it has since developed into a tourist trap with modern hotels.) There we spent the better part of the spring, which in 1944 was beautiful, and waited to be sent to one of the divisions in which we as interrogators of prisoners of war would participate in the invasion of the European mainland and thereby in the fight against Hitler's troops. There wasn't much for us to do while we were waiting, so the commanding officer made us repeatedly clean the house where headquarters was located and he and a few other officers lived.

This officer, Captain Kovacs—he liked to refer to himself as *Rittmeister* [riding master] Kovacs—was a conceited, lazy, and, as we later discovered, gutless character. He made an impressive effort to render life for most interrogators as unpleasant as possible. I was one of the few who found favor in his eyes because I had been trained in the infantry and had been promoted to sergeant in the process. He therefore chose me as his chauffeur whenever he went anywhere in the line of duty, a task I didn't particularly care for but couldn't possibly escape. However, these jeep rides did enable me to observe the preparations for the invasion. Most English highways, which were still rather narrow, were crammed on both sides with British and U.S. military equipment, predominantly military vehicles and heavy weapons such as artillery pieces. This equipment was guarded in turn by men of the British Home Guard, civilians who in their spare time acted as national guardsmen. They did their duty for the most part after work or on weekends, and we tried to evade them whenever possible. At the time there was a little verse about this organization of armed adult boy scouts that appealed to me a lot:

> 'ome Guard 'arry cleaned 'is gun
> pulled the trigger, shot 'is son.
> "Gee," said 'arry, "Ain't that good;
> it does just like they said it would."

I and a small number of fellow interrogators were billeted in a small manor house where Oliver Cromwell was alleged to have spent a night before the Battle of Evesham. The place belonged to a young couple— he was a factory owner—who spent their working weeks in London but returned on weekends to their small chateau. Shortly after we had arrived—I slept with two of my peers in the nursery, in which there was a rocking horse and other toys of various kinds—the young couple invited us for tea and told us with perfectly straight faces that the manor house was occasionally visited by ghosts, among them a monk who liked to go to the nursery where we slept. When we smiled skeptically they replied, "Well, you'll see; but the ghosts aren't dangerous." I must confess that thereafter whenever I returned to that place late in the evening and in the dark had to pass first through an entry hall decorated with the heads of stags and boars and then through a long passageway so low that even I had to bend down passing through it, my heart beat a bit faster than normal. But it seems that the monk had decided not to visit us Yanks.

Behind the manor house was a small cemetery in which the oldest gravestones dated to the late fifteenth and early sixteenth centuries. There I spent a good deal of my time, got a lot of reading done, absorbed the sunshine, and hoped that Kovacs wouldn't find me and ask me to chauffeur him around. We enjoyed the spring all the more knowing that D-Day was fast approaching. What this would mean to each of us, however, remained a question that was never raised. We were young and optimistic, and thus the fight against the Nazis that lay ahead of us belonged to the sphere of adventure.

The few, rather lazy weeks we spent in Broadway passed quickly, and in April we were told that the interrogation teams had been formed that were to be sent to the various divisions taking part in the invasion. To my great surprise I discovered that I had been assigned to one of the four teams being attached to the 82nd Airborne Division, the "All-American" as it had been known since World War I. Who my teammates were I would find out when I reported to headquarters of the division's intelligence section in Leicester. As I had twice turned down the chance to volunteer for jump training prior to going to Camp Ritchie (being an infantry soldier seemed to me risky enough at the time), I found my assignment to an airborne division rather strange. During the jeep ride from Broadway to Leicester, I pondered how I should react to my unexpected placement.

The day after our arrival in Leicester every interrogator had to meet briefly with a Captain Bushman, who was in charge of the four interrogation teams. Bushman was at least two heads taller than I, blond, and looked like a Germanic warrior. He was nonetheless a Jew. After the landing in France—as Bushman was no jumper he went to Normandy with the glider regiment of the Eighty-Second—he occasionally interrogated German prisoners in Yiddish. He was also an enthusiastic singer. We were told that in the fall of 1943, when the Eighty-Second was still in Italy, he had been set up to sing the "Ave Maria" in a church in Naples. But the day before he was to sing, the division was ordered to attack the German troops stationed at Anzio, and his recital was canceled.

My talk with Bushman was rather early in the morning. He

informed me that I was on the team attached to the 508th Parachute Infantry Regiment and that I would meet my teammates later that day. Suddenly he asked me, casually, whether I was a jumper. I first just stared at him and then, after a brief hesitation, replied: "Not yet." My answer hadn't been planned but was a spontaneous reflex, although my prior considerations of what it would mean to be in a parachute regiment without being a jumper myself may have prompted this response. Bushman looked pleased and promised me training that would qualify me as a parachute jumper prior to the invasion. A few days later I was moved, again by jeep, to Nottingham and reported to headquarters company of the 508th. Having thus obligated myself to take jump training and become a paratrooper, I was warmly welcomed and immediately accepted.

The two officers who headed our team were very different types of people. The commander, First Lieutenant Diamond, was a Jew from Vienna who after the war (in the course of which he was severely wounded) became a professor of political science at the University of Indiana. He was friendly and approachable, but as he and several other officers were constantly on some special mission roaming through England in preparation for the invasion, I saw very little of him. His deputy was Second Lieutenant Hauff. Considerably older then the rest of our team, Hauff was a "Volga German" whose family had settled in Russia during Catherine the Great's reign and then had come to the United States sometime prior to the First World War, in which Hauff had served briefly as a sergeant. When that war was over he married a Sioux Indian woman and lived with her on a reservation in North Dakota. He wasn't a paratrooper. From the beginning, Hauff and I didn't hit it off. There was a mutual dislike, though we both made an effort to hide our feelings. He knew I intended to make five practice jumps in order to qualify as a paratrooper but had no such plans for me, which in itself soured our relationship.

My interrogators on the team were initially Corporal Siggi Koesterich, Corporal Fred Guttman, and Sergeant Ernest Greenwald, all three German Jews and the last two qualified paratroopers. The nonjumper, Koesterich, a somewhat older New York businessman who originally came from Frankfurt am Main, stayed with us until the end of the Normandy campaign and treated me as if I were his son. I liked him and his sense of humor.

Freddy Guttman was a friendly and reliable guy. Politically he, like Greenwald, tended toward socialism. As he was the lowest ranking member of our team, it was his job to drive our jeep, and I would ride with him several times on roads that were or had been under enemy artillery fire. This never rattled Freddy, who calmly maneuvered around shell holes and always got us to our destination unscathed.

Ernest Greenwald was a strange bird. I never managed to find out what he did in civilian life. Shortly after Hitler came to power he had crossed into France illegally. He was caught and, now stateless, jailed for several weeks. Then French officials escorted him to the Belgian border, where he was promptly arrested and jailed again. Eventually he managed to emigrate to the United States, where he got married and became a father. He occasionally told us about his adventures during the 1930s and compared life in the French and Belgian jails (the latter he found more humane). I was always surprised that he never appeared to be embittered. One advantage he gained during those restless years was the ability to speak French fluently, a skill from which we, his teammates, were to benefit.

We four got along well from the outset (Guttman, Greenwald, and I served on the same team until the end of the war). This was in part the result of experiences and ideas we shared. All four of us were German Jews who had emigrated to the United States and received similar military training, first in the infantry, then at Camp Ritchie. We also agreed on how to deal with German prisoners of war. Although I didn't go as far as Freddy and Ernest, who said "those poor bastards" had been cajoled by Hitler and his party, and that once the war was over a sound and healthy socialism would create an entirely new Germany, we all rejected on principle any application of force while interrogating prisoners. After all, we argued, we weren't Nazis but "civilized" American soldiers. I twice came very close to violating this principle, as I will relate later on.

Our regiment—and subsequently the entire division—was stationed in Wollaton Park at the edge of Nottingham. On August 22, 1642, where our tents now stood, Charles I had sworn in the "Cavalier Army" he would lead against Oliver Cromwell and the English Parliament, unleashing a civil war during which he was captured and executed. Although I had no idea then that I would become a historian, the stories my friends told me about our present location left a deep impression on me. Here I met my own team (Diamond, Hauff, Koesterich, Guttman, and Greenwald) as well as Captain John A. Breen, commanding officer of the regiment's intelligence section, which was attached to headquarters company.

Captain Breen was a tremendously pleasant person. In civilian life he was an investigator for the U.S. Treasury and the father of several young children. He was often absentminded; occasionally we had to remind him to put his cap on his head rather than stuff it in his briefcase. He was also the only officer who now and then would join us noncoms and privates in going to a nearby pub, The Cocked Hat, where he drank with us, in violation of the rules governing relations between officers and enlisted men. Breen tried again and again to arrange with a nearby airfield for me and several others to receive the parachute training we'd been promised, the same training most of the troopers in our regiment had gotten at Fort Bragg in North Carolina. But weeks passed and either there was no plane at our disposal, or no pilot, or the weather was bad, or not enough candidates were available.

In late May the division was placed on alert. D-Day was apparently very close. Hardly had we received the order to pack our clothing and equipment and wait for transport to the airfield when Hauff called me (Diamond was at division headquarters that morning). He said that I would have to stay with him and the other nonjumpers of the four teams attached to the Eighty-Second. On D-Day or a little later we would move to the coast of France by landing craft. I was so furious that I could barely control myself. As usual, I decided to "go all the way to the top," skipping the regimental commander and going directly to the commander of the division, Lieutenant General Matthew B. Ridgeway. Without giving Hauff a glance, I ran like Jesse Owens to division headquarters and told the master sergeant on duty that I wanted to see the commanding general. The sergeant said Ridgeway was busy and couldn't see me. What was it I wanted from him? Barely able to breathe after my sprint I told the sergeant my reason, whereupon he referred me to Major General James M. Gavin, the assistant division commander. It was to be my first, but hardly my last, encounter with "Slim Jim." The tall general looked down on me kindly while I requested his permission to jump on D-Day although I had never jumped before. Gavin replied that his chauffeur was no trooper either, but he would be jumping because Gavin would need him in France. Why shouldn't I do the same thing? I was to tell my superior officer that I had Gavin's permission to jump and therefore could now go along to the airfield. I raced back, grabbed my luggage, informed the perplexed Hauff about my meeting with General Gavin, and several minutes later sat in one of the buses headed to the airfield.

We spent the following days in a giant hangar of Royal Air Force

Station Saltby. On the hundreds of folding cots in long rows that were for the time being our "home," we played cards with newly printed French "invasion money" that looked like play money. Food was good and plentiful, and every night a movie was shown. In the daytime a military band played for us. In short, it was quite a while since we had been treated so well. I spent most of my time reading books or writing letters in which I couldn't, of course, mention anything about where I was or what I was doing. I also cleaned and oiled my weapons over and over even though they were already perfectly clean. I had been issued a carbine that was probably excellent for hunting rats but little more. I also had bought from a Royal Air Force pilot a German Luger pistol (with ammunition), which we weren't authorized to carry but which I carried anyway. (Later, against rules and regulations that were easily circumvented, I got myself a Thompson submachine gun, or "Tommy gun.")

On the morning of June 4 we were again placed on alert. Rumor had it that the next day would be D-Day. We made our preparations, packed duffel bags that we hoped ultimately would be delivered to us after the invasion, and finally learned what our destination would be: the Cotentin Peninsula in Normandy. Nearly the entire division, including the glider regiment but with one regiment remaining in reserve in England, was to jump between the Douve and Merderet rivers and assemble in Sainte-Mère-Eglise. A blue light would indicate for us the provisional position of headquarters. This, at least, was the plan.

I finally received my long-expected parachute jump training, which lasted approximately fifteen minutes. The jumpmaster of my "stick" (parachuting group), a master sergeant, for some reason called me "Chicken." A jumpmaster's first responsibility was to make sure that all the jumpers leaped from the plane the minute the pilot indicated they should do so. But he was also a "rigger"—also responsible, after the jump, for collecting all the parachutes on the ground and bringing them to a collection point so they could be reused. For this reason each plane carried one rigger. (This well-intended plan, in most cases, did not work at all on D-Day.)

In our giant hangar stood a large wooden box, about seven feet high, onto which the rigger told me to climb. There I had to decide first what to do with my legs when landing, whether to keep them close together or a bit apart. I chose the latter option. Then the rigger told me that I would have to push my steel helmet, which during the jump would move down onto my nose, back onto the top of my head so I could check during the jump whether any of the chute's panels had torn, making a hole that would increase the speed of the drop to a dangerous degree. Should this happen I was to open the reserve chute, which was worn on one's stomach for easy access. Finally the rigger instructed me to grab two of the risers that connect a paratrooper's harness with the shroud lines and pull on them in order to reduce my oscillation. If I did this correctly I would land securely on my two feet. After these instructions he ordered me to jump down from the box. I did so and landed safely on my feet. This was the end of my "training."

As is well known, on June 4 General Eisenhower postponed the invasion by twenty-four hours on account of bad weather. For us this was quite a blow. Our edginess increased, and the improvised supper we got was atrocious. Most of us went to sleep early after watching a movie in the hangar. But when I woke up on the morning of June 5 the sky was clear and we knew that now nothing more could stop the invasion. Sometime in the afternoon we were told to gather outside the hangar because General Gavin wanted to address us before we took off in our respective planes. We sat on the ground in our combat suits, including the jump boots that we cherished especially, as Gavin gave us a brief overview of the area where we were supposed to be dropped and where we would assemble. He told us not to take any prisoners initially, as under the circumstances they would be an unmanageable burden, and then closed with the words "Good luck, and good hunting!" Shocked, I asked Greenwald and Guttman, who were sitting next to me, why we interrogators were going along if no prisoners would be taken, but they reassured me by saying that this situation would only prevail at the very beginning. As it turned out, I would face very different problems.

Toward evening we all gathered outside the hangar and were fed grilled steak. Then we used the ashes from the grills to blacken our faces so it would be harder for the enemy to see us in the dark. Shortly after supper we were informed that Allied troops had taken Rome, which we considered a good omen. And then we stumbled, heavily loaded, to the runways where the planes awaited us. Although the sun had set, I sweated under my load. The parachute on my back had been packed by a rigger, and I could only hope that he had done a good job. In addition I carried a carbine with ammunition; the Luger pistol, likewise with ammunition; the reserve chute at my belly; and underneath the chute my musette bag packed with personal items such as shaving equipment, two books (Kipling's *Barrack*

Room Ballads and, against all regulations, the *German Order of Battle*, which I had packed absentmindedly), extra underwear and socks, and the "iron [emergency] ration," which consisted predominantly of chocolate. Tied to one of my legs was a gas mask, to the other a small hoe for digging foxholes. Finally, I carried above the reserve chute two ordinary hand grenades and in my musette bag a sulfur grenade.

The aircraft we boarded was a C-47, a transport plane for baggage and paratroopers. Directly by the door lay several bulky bundles with light machine guns, mortars, ammunition boxes, mines, and food rations. Each bundle was tied to a separate parachute that, like ours, was hooked up to the static line. The latter was a long wire cable that stretched the entire length of the plane's interior. To it we hooked our chutes so that when we jumped the connection would automatically pull them open. In contrast to the reserve chute, we didn't have to pull a single handle. Before entering the plane I had noticed the name painted on it, *Son of the Beach*, and underneath that a picture of Donald Duck in bathing trunks.

It was shortly before midnight. Each of us had been given a pill to keep us awake. I put mine in my pocket instead of my mouth. It took a while before the Allied air fleet spearheading the invasion of Normandy was organized. We flew in endless circles over the blacked-out countryside beneath us, and while this was going on I slept a little on my rather uncomfortable seat. Suddenly the rigger who had "trained" me the day before and who was now our plane's jumpmaster woke me and ordered me to stand up and hook up to the static line because we were about to fly over the islands of Jersey and Guernsey, which were occupied by the Germans. I dragged myself to the rear of the plane where the open door was, since I would be the first one to leave the plane right after the bundles had been thrown out. Why was I number one? So that, should I decide at the last moment not to jump, all I had to do was step aside. Since I wasn't yet a qualified paratrooper, I couldn't be court-martialed for this.

Escorted by U.S. and British fighter planes, we flew very low over Guernsey and Jersey so as to evade the German anti-aircraft guns located there (they were designed to shoot at high-altitude targets and wouldn't have time to fire and reload at planes flying as low as we were). In the process the hitherto very orderly formation of our air armada got disarranged to such extent that each pilot was suddenly on his own to find his way to the drop zone. After having passed the two islands, the planes climbed again to a height of approximately twenty-five hundred feet and headed for the coast of Normandy. As soon as we reached it we came under fire from the ground. Since I was standing by the open door, behind the bundles and in front of the "stick," I saw the tracer bullets slowly—or so it seemed—fly up at us. It was such a fascinating sight that I was hardly scared. With an iron grip my left hand clutched the leather connection cable of my chute to the static line because the rigger had warned me under no circumstances to switch the grasp of my hand, or else my arm might be torn off when I jumped. Shortly after reaching the coastline the C-47 flying next to us was shot down, and a few minutes later we noticed that our plane, too, had been hit. The little lighting fixture next to the door with which the pilot gave the order to jump had been hit and no longer functioned. This meant that the pilot would have to give the order for us to jump orally to the rigger/jumpmaster, a fact which the latter communicated to us while cursing loudly and incessantly as he ran like a weasel past the standing "stick" to the pilot and back to the rear exit door. There I stood between the bundles and the first trooper of the "stick," staring at the ascending tracer bullets and cursing softly to myself. The trooper just behind me shrugged his shoulders and said, "What do you expect? SNAFU,[9] just as usual." Suddenly the jumpmaster was standing next to me telling me to help him push the bundles out the door. Then he looked at me questioningly and shouted: "Jump, Chicken!" And "Chicken" pushed forward the handle of the cable that connected his parachute to the static line and stepped into space.

I had been instructed to count loudly "one thousand, two thousand, three thousand," and if the main chute hadn't opened by then to pull the handle of the reserve chute. But my chute opened virtually at once, as I could feel by a painful jerk against my groin of the girth straps in which I was hanging. Very much relieved, I pushed my steel helmet, which had slipped and covered my eyes and nose, back to its proper position, checked whether the chute was open with all of its panels intact, and then pulled on two of the risers to cut down on the oscillation and thus arrange for a safer landing. The time was approximately 2:15 a.m. on June 6, 1944. The moon was out but intermittently covered by clouds. I was surprised not to see any other paratroopers in the air, but I didn't waste time on this thought and concentrated instead on the forthcoming landing. It was a wonderful

---

[9] Acronym for "situation normal: all fucked up." This term was coined during the Second World War and has spread into popular culture.

feeling to float so high up in the sky, especially since I didn't have the feeling of dropping. On the contrary, the earth seemed to be coming up to meet me. Nobody fired at me, which made me wonder a little. I didn't know at the time that the pilot had taken unauthorized evasive action and deviated from his given course in order to avoid the German antiaircraft fire. Instead of taking us to the assembly point near Sainte-Mère-Eglise as he had been ordered to do, he had swerved somewhat to the east, headed for the coast, and there gave the order for us to jump, rather than taking us back to England where we might have had a chance to fly to Normandy again, in another plane. Thus the troopers of our plane jumped east of Cherbourg. The last two members of our "stick," Captain Hawkins and Private Ford, landed in the water but close enough that they made it to shore. Except for the three of us, the rest of the troopers were all captured in the course of the following two days. The pilot, who made it back to England despite the damage to his plane, was court-martialed.

As I approached the ground I saw directly beneath me an orchard in which a white horse was running along the fence, neighing loudly. I pulled hard on my two risers in order to land between the trees but not on top of one. The parachute got hung up in one apple tree, which made my landing especially soft, my butt hanging just a few inches above the ground as I landed. As quickly as possible I slipped out of the harness, let the chute hang where it was, and first of all took a leak. Then I placed the reserve chute underneath the apple tree and set off in the direction where I hoped to find the blue light at the assembly point. I assumed that I wasn't far from Sainte-Mère-Eglise, but where exactly this was I didn't know. No other troopers were in sight, but from the little I could see of the landscape around me in the dusky moonlight this didn't seem very surprising. All around me were little orchards, many of them separated from neighboring orchards by hedges rather than barbed-wire fences. As I was climbing over one of those hedgerows I lost my balance and with it my flashlight. The military map that each of us had been issued before boarding the plane was therefore useless until daybreak, so I put it in my pocket. Suddenly I encountered railroad tracks, which I crossed, crawling carefully. Parallel to the tracks ran a highway, and I noticed to my horror that the (light) traffic on it was German. I recognized this from the shape of the soldiers' helmets, which were especially easily identifiable when worn by motorcycle drivers.

I should have expected to see German soldiers, of course, but it was a shock nevertheless. I now needed to make contact with my own, American, troops. I thus waited for a break in the traffic, ran across the road as quickly as possible, and then walked along a narrow path that led into a forest. After about ten minutes' walk along that path I suddenly saw close ahead of me a clearing and at the edge of it the silhouettes of three German soldiers standing in a dugout with a machine gun, which fortunately was aimed toward the open field. I tried to walk by the soldiers very quietly but was discovered by one of the men, who asked loudly who I was and where I was headed. While walking toward the dugout in which the three men stood I took one of my two hand grenades and, getting ready to throw it, replied, "*Unteroffizier auf Patrouille!*" [Corporal on patrol]. This was a mistake. Ordinarily corporals don't go on patrol by themselves, but if they should do so they are *auf Streife* and not *auf Patrouille*. The latter term from the First World War I remembered from reading books by Erich Maria Remarque and Ernst Jünger, but the term *Streife* I didn't know, and Captain Cohn, alas, had failed to acquaint us with it at Camp Ritchie. Despite these mistakes, I had spoken in pure German with a slight Berlin accent, so one of the soldiers shouted: "Hey, come on over here!"

Walking slowly toward them, I pulled the safety out of the hand grenade and threw it in their direction. Now, throwing things, in sports or otherwise, had never been my strong suit, and I'm fairly sure the grenade didn't land in the foxhole. I didn't wait to confirm this, however. Instead I ran as fast as I could with all the baggage I was carrying. A few seconds later I heard the explosion of the grenade and the loud and agitated voices of the three men. I stopped, turned around, and saw in the moonlight, which was strong enough at this point, that one of the men had climbed out of the dugout and was aiming a pistol at me. I jumped into the bushes at the edge of the forest and continued to run along the path in a panic. Then I heard a shot and felt a bullet hit my helmet. The soldier had fired from a distance of approximately thirty meters, and the bullet tore the camouflage net and made a small dent in the helmet. The fellow knew how to shoot!

I finally got off the path, lay down on my belly under some bushes, carbine ready, and waited for my pursuers. But nobody came. When I noticed that the sun was about to rise I carefully crept deeper into the woods and "cleaned up." First I buried the *German Order of Battle* so that it would not fall into enemy hands, and then the chutes for the same reason. Then I also buried the sulfur grenade that had been issued to me, which I had no intention to use against a human being, even if that human being was "the enemy." Finally, I buried the gas mask and hoe because I wanted to carry as little weight as possible and expected to have no need of either. Then I began walking east, in the woods and not on any path. After approximately an hour I reached a small clearing and decided to rest. After eating my chocolate I climbed into a blackberry patch, where I couldn't be seen, and promptly fell asleep. When I woke up around noon I worked my way out of my bristly hideout and climbed a nearby tree to get oriented. But all I could see were other trees, no houses or other sign of humanity. The rest of the day I continued to walk but without leaving the forest. A few times I had to cross roads that ran through the forest, and every time I did I noticed that the traffic was German. Late in the afternoon I came across another path that ran approximately in my direction. Exhausted as I was, I decided to follow it.

Suddenly I heard voices and stepped behind a tree at the edge of the path. Two people were approaching, an old woman and a little girl, both carrying bundles of firewood. Forgetting that my face was smeared with ash, I stepped out from behind the tree and scared them terribly. "*Je suis parachutiste américain*," I said in my school French. "*Quel est le nom du village prochain, et où sont les Boches?*" Trembling from shock and fear, the old woman stammered that the next village was Videcosville, that at the moment we were in the Forêt de Videcosville, and that there were four *Boches* on the other side of the village. She and her granddaughter lived elsewhere but had just passed through the village. I thanked her and rushed on in the direction of Videcosville.

A few minutes later I saw a building, a barn in which a farmer was milking his cows. In contrast to the old woman and the girl, he didn't look shocked when I entered the barn and started talking in my miserable French. He asked whether I was hungry or thirsty, and when I replied that I was both he handed me a cup of milk fresh from one of his cows. As soon as I had drunk it he handed me a glass with some watery looking liquid that, he enlightened me, was *calvados* [Norman apple brandy]. On a nearly empty stomach this was the last thing I needed. But trying to be polite I took two little sips and told him how very tired I was. He led me to a nearby hay barn, where I collapsed in the hay. He confirmed what the old woman had told me, that "*les Boches*" were located at the other end of the village. They could be ignored, he said. After he left I looked at my map. I was very far from Sainte-Mère-Eglise.

A few hours later (it must have been around midnight) I was woken up by a French boy who couldn't have been older than sixteen. Since I never learned his name he remained for me, and subsequently for my fellow paratroopers, simply "the kid." He told me that two more Americans were close by and that he would lead me to them. I followed him, Luger in hand; after all, I had no idea who he was. He led me to a hollow surrounded by a dense hedge in the center of a large field. And sure enough, behind the hedge were two American paratroopers, but from the 101st Airborne, not the 82nd. Both were artillerists. I greeted them and immediately found two carbines aimed at me. My German accent! It took me considerable time to convince them that although I was indeed of German descent, I wasn't a German soldier. One of the two, a Jew from Brooklyn as I soon learned, finally believed me and convinced his buddy that I was okay.

Since as a staff sergeant I was the highest ranking of the three of us, I took over command, arranged for guard duty (staying on guard for the first two hours after I joined them), and assured "the kid," who had been watching the entire proceedings without understanding a thing, that everything was all right now and he could go to sleep.

During the following days, always in close contact with the kid, who helped us find food and additional paratroopers dropped at the wrong place, we moved very cautiously in a southerly direction. The group became larger and larger. By June 10 we numbered about fifty people. Captain Hawkins and Private Ford, the only troopers from the 82nd besides me, had joined us, as had twenty-one artillerists from the 101st Airborne, including two officers. We could only move very cautiously and at night. During the day we hid in the woods, from which we heard the sounds of the German troops retreating toward Cherbourg. During the following five days the morale of our group steadily declined. Being hungry was one of the worst problems. Since I was the only one in the group who spoke some French, I was faced with ever-increasing responsibilities, notably the procurement of food, which was exclusively restricted to bread and milk. These I had to get at farms in our vicinity, mostly late at night and accompanied by a few of our troopers. As I had no idea where any farmhouses were located, "the kid" led me to one or two closest to us, and with his help I negotiated cautiously with the French farmers.

Occasionally we got the food free, but this was rare. For the most part we paid with the invasion money issued to us in England. The French farmers accepted it with obvious skepticism. While Captain Hawkins kept in the background because he, like Private Ford and me, belonged to the 82nd and not the 101st Airborne, I was constantly consulted by the two artillery officers of the 101st, both lieutenants, even though I was merely a staff sergeant. I in turn placed all my trust in the kid, who acted as mediator between me and the French adults with whom we had to deal. (He was accidentally killed a few weeks later by American soldiers, as I was told during a visit to Videcosville shortly after the fall of Cherbourg.) Nobody knew when and how we would be able to get through the constantly retreating German troops to the American lines south of us. Then, quite unexpectedly, the artillery troopers of the 101st insisted that distribution of the small amount of bread and milk that we managed to wheedle or buy from the French farmers be handled by me rather than by their own two officers, whom they no longer trusted. I felt very embarrassed but finally agreed, especially after Captain Hawkins, whose estimate of the situation was usually sound, advised me in his quiet manner to accept this responsibility.

June 15 turned into a disastrous day. The day before we had decided we would split into small groups the following evening and try and make our way to the American lines. Hawkins, Ford, and I wanted to go together. But before the group as a whole broke up we wanted to eat. As soon as dusk fell I joined two troopers from the 101st and we sneaked together to a French farm not very far from our position, alas without the kid, who had disappeared. At the farm we were promised that at 10:00 p.m., when it was still fairly light, somebody would bring bread to our position. We were also promised milk for 9:00 p.m. We had agreed to meet the milk delivery at the edge of the woods alongside a small road that led to the farmhouse. We hid in the tall grass at the edge of the road. (We had paid, of course, ahead of time.) The farmer or one of his employees with whom I had been dealing had whispered to me that the farmhouse also accommodated a German battalion headquarters, and now and then we saw German officers pass by our hideout, some of them carrying briefcases.

When at the arranged time no milk was delivered, we became nervous, and one of my companions suggested we return to our position in the woods. When we arrived there I reported to Captain Hawkins that the milk hadn't been delivered, and as it was then nearly 10:00 p.m. we stared spellbound at the position where the bread was to be placed at any moment. Our slightly hilly patch of woods was surrounded by potato fields, and the bread was to be deposited at the edge of the woods.

Suddenly shots rang out on three sides. The Germans had detected us and were firing antiaircraft guns into the trees above our heads, where the shells exploded and the splinters rained down on us. Some of the shrapnel hit my upper left thigh. We threw our hand grenades over the ridge from behind which the firing came. The attackers briefly retreated, then returned to their positions. Some of our men who had been at the edge of the woods when the attack started began to retreat cautiously into a neighboring potato field. Next to me lay Clifford, a sergeant of the 101st with whom I had become friends. He had been hit in the shoulder by a splinter of the shrapnel that had hit me. When the Germans resumed firing at us and we no longer saw any way out, the two lieutenants of the 101st decided we should surrender.

One of the two officers called to me that I should yell in German that we were ready to surrender. I called back that this would have to be done by one of them, not by me, a staff sergeant whose accent would give away that he had grown up in Germany (and thus was most likely a Jew). Well, how should he make it clear to the Germans that we wanted to surrender? I answered that he should yell "*Kamerad.*" After he had done so the firing ceased. We twenty-six enlisted men and two officers stood up and, without our steel helmets and weapons, walked in single file with our hands behind our heads, out of the woods and into captivity. The rest of our group had managed to crawl through the potato field and thereby escaped capture, if only briefly: after a few days most of them, including Private Ford, showed up in Cherbourg as prisoners of war. Only Captain Hawkins and eight men of the 101st managed to escape that night and reach the American lines. We found out subsequently that the French farmer who was to have delivered us bread and milk had instead delivered us to the Germans.

Now prisoners, we were driven to a nearby field and searched for hidden weapons. The soldiers who had captured us belonged to a *Volksgrenadierregiment* [regiment of reservists] and therefore were either younger or older than the men in other units of the German Army. Despite some caustic remarks (which only I understood), we were on the whole properly treated. They made us lie down on our stomachs so they could search our pockets. The young German lieutenant in charge of the reservists radiated self-importance. He ran all over the field on which we were being searched and warned his men to watch us closely. When he came to me, he grabbed my gas-mask container and, without looking at what was in it, threw it into a blackberry patch, commenting, "You won't need this anymore." Had he inspected the container he would have discovered that instead of a gas mask it contained Kipling's *Barrack Room Ballads*, my bag of toilet articles, and my beloved pipe and tobacco. So all of these I lost.

Then, to my horror, one of my fellow captives called to me and asked me to tell the "Heinie" searching him that the ring he was in the process of swiping was a wedding ring he wanted to keep. I was of course afraid that sooner or later it would emerge that I was of German-Jewish descent and thus asked the man to do without my assistance as it might cost me my life. He understood, nodded—and lost his wedding ring. None of my fellow prisoners revealed my identity to the Germans while we were in captivity. I was searched by a very young German. As he began I said, in French, "*Je suis blessé.*" As a result he searched me very considerately and didn't even appropriate my wrist watch.

After the search was finished we all sat together on the ground, closely pressed to each other, and waited to be picked up. The lieutenant, who soon disappeared, had shouted at us before he departed that we were forbidden to talk. But this was a futile attempt on his part. We spoke with one another in low voices, and our guards paid no attention. Meanwhile night had fallen. Finally, a couple of trucks came for us. As I was trying to climb into one of them I fainted, probably from a combination of hunger and loss of blood. But I soon regained consciousness and listened to the conversation between our two German guards, who seemed surprised that we all looked so young and said we made a rather good impression.

Our captivity lasted twelve days. We spent the first night in a low, narrow barn, without food and without medical care for either Clifford or me. The next morning we were searched again and then taken to a nearby house that served as command post for the unit that had captured us. There we were interrogated, Clifford by a first lieutenant, I by a *Sonderführer* [warrant officer]. Clifford was questioned downstairs, whereas I, with my wounded leg, had to follow the *Sonderführer* up a ladder to the next floor. I quickly got the impression that this small, middle-aged man was a decent person. He invited me to sit down and, in typical school English, proceeded to ask the usual questions: name, what unit I belonged to, where it was at the moment, and so on. I answered that according to the Geneva Convention all I had to tell him was my name, rank, and serial number. That I was serving in the 82nd Airborne Division was clearly indicated by my shoulder patch. But to which regiment of the Eighty-Second I belonged I didn't reveal because one of our regiments was still being kept in England as a reserve unit.

He then asked whether I was of German descent. He suspected this might be true because my first name was Werner. Was I perhaps named after my grandfather? He was completely correct, I replied, adding that Grandfather Werner and other members of the family had emigrated to the United States in the nineteenth century. What city in the United States was I from? I replied, nearly automatically, "Lynchburg, Virginia," a town I had never seen and for which Company B had given me rather mixed feelings. To my horror the *Sonderführer* jumped up from his chair and yelled: "Lynchburg! I know that town!" When had he been there last? I asked, trying to hide my distress. He replied that in 1926, when he was a young commercial traveler, the German company he worked for had sent him there. Greatly relieved, I assured him that Lynchburg had changed considerably since then, to which he responded with a nod.

On that note the interrogation ended and we climbed downstairs again. There the first lieutenant asked the *Sonderführer* whether he had found out anything of importance. The *Sonderführer* said "No" and the first lieutenant grumbled angrily that his prisoner, Clifford, hadn't said anything worthwhile either. Then the lieutenant turned to the two of us and said in excellent English how fortunate we were that his unit had taken us prisoner. In contrast, the units of the American 82nd and 101st airborne divisions behaved like bandits, taking no prisoners and bombing army hospitals. Then he informed us to our surprise that we would now eat breakfast with some men of his unit. Afterward, we would be driven to a hospital situated in the nearby town of Valognes to have our wounds treated. And thus we sat down at the kitchen table with several German noncommissioned officers and were served hot milk and bread.

The situation was rather absurd. There we were, two captured Americans having a peaceful breakfast together with soldiers of Hitler's Wehrmacht. Suddenly a soldier in German uniform entered the kitchen from the yard, thrust his mess kit under our noses, and said something in a language I didn't understand. He was a Russian who, like many of his compatriots, had been taken prisoner by the Germans on the Eastern Front and then had "volunteered" to fight for Nazi Germany (perhaps the most famous example of such volunteerism is Russian General Andrei

Vlasov, who after being captured by the Nazis defected to the German side). The poor guy was begging for something to eat, but one of the German noncoms at our table yelled insults at him and chased him out of the kitchen.

The remaining week and a half of my captivity resembled a circus more than a war. After breakfast, Clifford and I were taken to Valognes in a horse-drawn cart, which an elderly soldier drove with the sureness of a sleepwalker. At the German military hospital there a thoroughly unpleasant Wehrmacht doctor treated our wounds very superficially while complaining to his assistant about the "shitty Americans." When something dropped out of the doctor's pants pocket and neither Clifford nor I bent down to pick it up we were treated to another earful of insults, which we ignored, as we supposedly understood no German. Then we were dismissed. We had barely left the room when an orderly approached us and asked in excellent English if we were hungry. Without waiting for an answer he led us to the hospital kitchen and saw to it that we each got a bowl of soup, which tasted wonderful.

That same afternoon we were transported to Cherbourg and deposited at the Louis Pasteur Hospital, where we stayed for three days. As I was only slightly wounded, I was ordered to assist the German noncom responsible for feeding us. Many troopers who lay in our ward were badly wounded, some with amputated limbs. While from the first day all the patients knew that I understood and spoke German, none gave me away. My German proved useful to all of us: every evening before the lights were turned off I told the patients what news I could relate to them about the military situation around us, news I had picked up from our German guards, who didn't know that I understood every word they said. Thus we learned that the landing at Normandy had been successful and that U.S. troops were advancing on Cherbourg. It was rather obvious that before long we would be free again.

On June 19 we received a superficial checkup, and the following day those of us able to walk were discharged from the hospital and transported to an improvised POW camp. There we met up again with a large number of the troopers with whom we had wandered the Norman countryside between June 7 and June 15, when they had briefly escaped capture by crawling through the potato field. We were housed in what was probably an old barn, our double-decker bunks so teeming with fleas that we preferred to sleep on the ground. Within forty-eight hours the first U.S. artillery shells hit in and around the camp. Our guards left their respective posts and we followed them, looking for cover. During the following days, "guarded" by a German sergeant named Meier, we roamed through Cherbourg without finding a place to stay. The French civilians, for the most part children and teenagers, slipped us food as they ran up and down along our column.

Finally we were assigned quarters at the edge of the city at the entrance of a tunnel that led into a hill. This was now the headquarters of the German 709th Infantry Division, with whose troops we had to share the available accommodations. But after having stayed there for just one night, a number of us prisoners, including me, were taken by truck back to the Louis Pasteur Hospital to move beds and mattresses. In the meantime U.S. artillery shells were dropping everywhere in the city, and as the ring around Cherbourg grew tighter, more German troops moved back into the city every day. When they dropped us off in front of the hospital, manned German antiaircraft guns were posted all around the building.

At about 8:00 p.m., after working all day, we went to the front of the hospital and waited there to be picked up again and driven back to the tunnel at the outskirts of the city. Suddenly a heavy shell exploded in front of the hospital entry where we were standing, killing and wounding several German medics. Five of our men were also wounded and one, an artillerist from the 101st named Sig, was killed. The first though by no means the last friend I lost during the eleven months between D-Day and V-E Day, Sig was a former master sergeant recently demoted to private because in England he had returned from a weekend leave several days late. Throughout the entire period we had spent together after D-Day behind the German lines he had supported me. He had proved especially helpful during the often-delicate dealings in our oddly mixed group of troopers and also in securing food from French farmers. I took off his dog tags and handed them to one of our officers, and before the truck arrived to take us back to the tunnel I helped load him onto another truck that carried him away, together with a number of German corpses. I never learned where he was buried.

The following day, June 24, the Americans were advancing within the city, so the Germans transported us to the northern edge of Cherbourg, at the harbor, and took us to an underground arsenal. There, in a cold bunker three meters below ground, we spent the following twenty-four hours. When we looked out the door—there were no windows—we could see one of the forts located on an island just off Cherbourg. The German commanders and the better part of their troops had withdrawn to this fort to await the final battle. We ourselves were quite satisfied with our present situation. For the first time in nearly two weeks we could shave, albeit with an old razor we found and cold salt water, and also wash a little. Our guards became more congenial, bringing us food and mattresses to sleep on. They assured us in their rather primitive English: "Today you our prisoners, tomorrow we your prisoners," to which we just nodded and smiled. Our *Sonderführer* moved into one of the building's subterranean rooms. When he encountered me he greeted me as if I were an old friend. The next morning, June 25, he invited me to play chess with him. As we sat there facing each other, American shells dropped on the harbor, including on and around our arsenal. As we played, the *Sonderführer* asked me nervously whether the ceiling would hold if it were hit. I replied that it probably would as long as the shell was 105 millimeters. But if the shells were 155 millimeters, I had my doubts. He shook his head and muttered, in English, "Why don't they give up, those idiots?" Although I had never been a good chess player, that game I won.

That same day, as German troops outside our arsenal blew up the docks, their din competing with that of the American shelling, we had to move again, stumbling under our mattresses and blankets. We had hardly left the arsenal when the Germans blew it up. The U.S. guns started firing again, so we dropped our mattresses and ran as fast as we could for the bunker assigned to us as our new "home." There the electricity was out, so we were given candles. The *Sonderführer* looked unhappier by the minute. In the evening, the guards brought us champagne from the general's stock and along with it boxes of cigars. They had treated us decently the entire time but now, with their own captivity approaching, they turned downright solicitous. One of them gave me a small notebook, at my request. Lying on my belly in front of a flickering candle, I started to record my experiences since D-Day.

We stayed in that bunker the entire following day, hoping that the Americans would liberate us before we had to spend another night in captivity. But this didn't happen. Our guards asked us about conditions in U.S. POW camps and said they hoped they were sent to the United States rather than to England. We continued to drink champagne, smoke cigars, and wait to be liberated. Ford and I had already agreed that the first thing we would do once we were freed was find our regiment. Night passed.

The next day, June 27, was my twenty-fourth birthday, and I desperately hoped that on that day I would become a free man again. Unfortunately, I had gotten diarrhea during the night, and as there were no toilets in our bunker, I had to run outside repeatedly. Early in the morning, as I was squatting once again outside the bunker, there was suddenly an unbelievably loud explosion: the Germans were blowing up a nearby building. I barely managed to creep back into the bunker, not even having time to pull up my pants. Outside, the rubble of another building was flying through the air, and we had to wait inside our bunker for another few hours. Then the American artillery fire stopped. Soon church bells began to ring, and we heard the barely intelligible voice of an American apparently driving through Cherbourg addressing the local population by megaphone. As I was to discover later, the voice was that of my friend Ernst Cramer.

Almost exactly at noon, the German generals in Cherbourg decided to surrender to a U.S. officer of the 9th Infantry Division. We watched as that officer walked alone to the fort carrying a white flag. Later we saw the German soldiers, among them many officers, leaving the fort to line up in formation between where we stood and the gate of the fort, ready to be moved to a POW camp. Orderlies dragged the officers' baggage. Among the officers was our *Sonderführer*, also accompanied by his orderly. Ford and some of my other buddies suggested that I now approach him and tell him that I spoke fluent German and, like him, was an interrogator of POWs. I declined this proposal. From beginning to end he had treated us with decency, and I wanted to spare him what undoubtedly would have been a humiliating experience. Instead I walked up to him and expressed my hope—in English—that the Americans would treat him with the same courtesy as he had treated us. We shook hands and parted.

I returned to Ford and we discussed how best to find our division. Soldiers of the 9th Division were now everywhere around us, and we eventually found among them an officer whose task it was to organize the transportation of liberated POWs back to their units. Sometime thereafter Bondy told me that my old Gross Breesen friend Büh, with whom I'd hitchhiked through Holland in the spring of 1939, had been killed while serving in the 9th Infantry Division. He was the only Gross Breesener we lost during the war.

Ford and I of course hadn't the slightest idea where our regiment was. As we found out subsequently, the majority of the jumpers of the

508th Parachute Infantry Regiment had landed in and around Sainte-Mère-Eglise, where within five days after D-Day the regiment reorganized. Then, fighting every day, it moved south and at the beginning of July reached La Haye du Puits–Baupte–Carentan. When Ford and I found our regiment on the evening of June 27 it was close to the village of Vindefontaine. We were warmly greeted by our comrades, who had firmly believed we'd been killed. Siggi Koesterich grabbed me by the shoulders and, forcing me to dance, sang in front of a cheering crowd: "Ha Ha Ha / you and me / in the Airborne Infantry!" A regimental medical officer checked my still-unhealed wound and gave me permission to stay with the regiment instead of being sent to convalesce in England. I felt that I at last had come "home." With the help of my friends I could take a bath in a huge pot of warm water and clean my wound again. I was issued new clothing. The last wasn't so simple, for, as I was officially listed as missing in action, all my clothes and other items that before D-Day I'd packed into a large duffel bag had been "lost" (i.e., stolen).

As soon as we were settled, my buddies in the regimental intelligence section started to make fun of me. "We trained and kicked around Fort Bragg for months on end to qualify as jumpers, and here you come, itsy-bitsy Tom, and make your first jump, your first jump carrying battle gear, your first night jump, your first combat jump, all in one, and now you get fifty dollars extra as jump pay every month." One of them, Mayo Heath, who years later fought in the Korean War, during which he was promoted to lieutenant and shortly thereafter killed in battle, said to me: "Now you've become a paratrooper and as such are superior to the other soldiers in our army. We are something special." Enthusiastic as I had become about my new status, I loved to sing together with my friends the following song, about a trooper during his jump training:

"Is everybody ready?" yelled the sergeant, looking up.
Our hero answered feebly "Yes," and then they hooked him up.
He swiftly jumped into space and counted loud and long.
But he ain't gonna jump no more.
Glory, glory, what a hell of a way to die,
Glory, glory, what a hell of a way to die,
Glory, glory, what a hell of a way to die,
But he ain't gonna jump no more.

During the following two-and-a-half weeks I finally used my training as an interrogator of POWs. The senior officer of our interrogation team, First Lieutenant Diamond, had been severely wounded during the jump, was picked up by the Germans, spent a few days in captivity before being liberated by U.S. troops heading north toward Cherbourg, and was promptly flown to a hospital in England (where I visited him that July).

Thus Lieutenant Hauff, who'd come to Normandy by boat with a group of other nonjumping interrogators, one of whom had been killed while several others were wounded, was now the only officer on our team. My initial meeting with him was rather frigid, and our relations remained so. To get away from him as soon as possible I reported as an interrogator to the intelligence section of the First Battalion. I spent my time there as a "visitor," usually sharing somebody's foxhole at night. I quickly learned to interrogate prisoners immediately after they were captured close to the front line, that is, at the forward command post of the First Battalion, before they were taken behind the lines to one of our improvised POW camps. Only when my regiment, the 508th, was detached from the 82nd Airborne Division in March of 1945 and linked to the division's intelligence section did I change this tactic. But by then the war was nearly over.

Looking back, I'm surprised how much freedom of movement we interrogators enjoyed from June 1944 until the fighting ended in May 1945. Of course, we had to check out formally with our team leader whenever we left the regimental base in order to go "up front." For nearly the entire time, we could choose to which battalion we wanted to go. I preferred the First Battalion because I had a number of friends there, but occasionally I worked with the Second or Third. My teammates did the same because it gave us considerable independence from whatever officer happened to be team leader—and in Normandy it was Hauff.

Shortly after I returned to my regiment from captivity, the regimental intelligence officer, Captain Breen, told me to go to a small woods at the bottom of a hill with a number of troopers assigned to the intelligence section. A group of German soldiers had been sighted there and was apparently ready to surrender. When we arrived there, I walked down the hill while two of Captain Breen's men stayed at the top, with the other troopers behind them. I yelled to the hidden German soldiers that they should surrender. Hands behind their heads, they emerged from the bushes, led by their ranking noncommissioned officer. I told the men, with the exception of the noncom, to move to the top of the hill where my two friends were waiting for them. The noncom I told to stay with me and answer a few questions. I learned from this noncom, a Corporal Kegel, the number of his regiment, where the remaining members of his badly shattered unit probably were, and various other bits of information. Then we started to chat.

He told me that he came from Berlin and was a shoemaker in civilian life. He and his men, he told me, were fed up with the war. It was obviously nearly lost; why get oneself killed at the very end? As we were talking, one of my two companions came running down the hill and shouted to me that a lieutenant none of us knew wanted to shoot our prisoners. I told Kegel to follow me and ran up the hill where in fact a lieutenant stood facing the prisoners, holding a rifle and obviously ready to fire. But he had failed to reckon with Private Dick Stedman. Dick's father was a high-ranking officer; once, in England when the father came to visit, I had seen how Dick spoke to him, standing at attention, hands at his trouser seams. Dick was as big or, as the case may be, as small as I was. The two of us often went together to our favorite Nottingham pub, The Cocked Hat. When we tottered back to camp, each would prop the other up so he didn't fall. One time as we staggered "home" in this way he asked me to sing "Lili Marlene," and I happily and rather loudly obliged. That the Home Guard never apprehended us when we were behaving this way was a minor miracle.

Well, Dick posted himself in front of the prisoners and told the lieutenant that these were the prisoners of Sergeant Angress, who was responsible for them. Nobody else, not even the lieutenant, had the right to interfere and certainly not to execute them. As soon as I reached the top of the hill I told the lieutenant that I was under orders from Captain Breen to bring him the prisoners. The lieutenant gave me a black look and disappeared. I found out subsequently that he wasn't a paratrooper. Thus it is conceivable that, having come to Normandy by boat, he was eager to demonstrate what a hero he was. He was soon killed in action.

A few days later Captain Breen asked me how well I knew Lieutenant Hauff. He found it surprising that Hauff's interrogation reports contained little tactical information useful for our campaign but many detailed descriptions of the military situation in Russia. I explained to the captain that Hauff was of Volga German extraction and very interested in everything concerning Russia. Breen then transferred me for the duration of the Battle of Normandy to the regimental intelligence section that he headed. From then on all prisoners Hauff interrogated were brought to me so I could question them a second time, though without ever letting Hauff know this was happening. And so it went until July 13, when our operation in Normandy ended, a few days after Captain Breen's death.

The captain's absentmindedness was his undoing. In order to "celebrate" the Fourth of July, a major attack by all Allied forces had been planned against the German lines. Captain Breen thus told me to focus my interrogations for the coming days on where the German units facing us had laid mines. To my great delight, we found in the baggage of a captured German sergeant a map that clearly indicated the locations of all minefields in front of us. Enthusiastic about this piece of luck, Captain Breen told us that early the next morning he would personally deliver a copy of the map to every unit in our division. I was to drive him in the jeep. But when I woke up the next morning, I was told that the captain had already left. He had decided to let me sleep and instead had another trooper who was already awake drive him. As I was about to prepare my breakfast, news came that the jeep had hit a mine. The captain was dead, the driver severely wounded. I jumped into the car of the trooper who had brought us this news and rode with him to the spot where Captain Breen's dismembered body lay next to what was left of the jeep. I fought back tears. Even though Breen was an officer and I wasn't, I felt I had lost a friend. And what hurt doubly was the discovery that he had been killed by a mine clearly marked on the map he was carrying in his lap.

A little over a week later, on July 13, the division was relieved and transported back to England. Our regiment had suffered heavy losses. Of the 2,056 troopers of the 508th Parachute Infantry Regiment who had jumped into Normandy on D-Day, 1,161 were wounded and 307 killed. As we walked along Omaha Beach to be shipped back to Great Britain, we saw a number of provisional POW camps. Behind barbed wire German soldiers also waited to be shipped sooner or later to England. I thought of our guards in Cherbourg who had speculated where they as prisoners would be sent after their generals surrendered.

Not long after our troopships landed at Dover we found ourselves again in Nottingham. Our tents were still standing in Wollaton Park, and we felt as if we had returned home. We also knew that our next combat jump would probably come soon, but for the moment we enjoyed the break from fighting. Half of the regiment was given five days' leave at once, and when they returned the other half went on its five-day leave. I was in the first group and went first to Broadway to report to the head-quarters of U.S. interrogators of German POWs.

In Broadway, where I had spent that beautiful spring prior to the invasion, I was received with open arms, which I found a little embarrassing. My two military decorations, the Purple Heart and the Bronze Star for meritorious service, were admired, and I was asked to tell the newcomers from the States, who soon would be assigned to a fighting unit, about D-Day and the subsequent events, including my experiences as an interrogator. This reception was largely the work of the ranking master sergeant, who was the first man to greet me when I arrived at Broadway. To my utter surprise he was my former classmate, Wolfgang Robinow, with whom I had gone to school in Lichterfelde and who on the day I left the Gymnasium had told me in a whisper that he, too, was a "non-Aryan." I had met him again later, equally unexpectedly, at Hyde Farmlands. Today he lives in the Federal Republic of Germany.

The remaining leave I spent in London, a city badly damaged by German V-1 bombs and under blackout at night. Here I wanted above all to meet two friends from Gross Breesen, Leus and Traut. Both had become nurses, and at the time I visited London Traut was also a patient in her hospital. A few days before a V-1 bomb had hit near the hospital, shattering a large window, some of whose shards had hit her face. As a result Traut, who had taken a day off from work, was able to spend the entire day with me in London. We walked and occasionally took a horse-drawn carriage. In the area from Oxford Street to St. Paul's Cathedral, we saw the results of the German bombing raids, from the Blitz to the recent V-bombs. As we grew hungry around noon I suggested to Traut that we eat at the Cumberland Hotel on Marble Arch. In its reception hall my brothers and I, emigrant children without any money, had spent many an afternoon in the winter of 1937, without being hotel guests, ordering any food, or ever being told to leave. Now I could return the staff's kindness by inviting Traut to have lunch with me there.

The guests sitting around us were for the most part Englishmen, including some British soldiers. There were also several American GIs sitting in a corner of the dining hall, men probably stationed in London doing clerical work. We had hardly sat down and given the rather elderly waiter our order when we suddenly saw him walk from table to table, carrying a large sign on which was written "Air Raid Alarm." I asked Traut what we were supposed to do now. She smiled at me and said that

Werner Angress in Broadway, England, 1944.

Englishmen, whether civilians or soldiers, would stay where they were and eat their lunch. The American GIs would in all probability rush to the door, where a sign indicated the direction to the air raid shelter, and rush downstairs as fast as they could. This is exactly what happened. Traut and I remained seated, and I was soon the only American soldier in the place. My fellow countrymen had disappeared. Before long we heard the V-1 explode somewhere far off in the city, whereupon the old waiter, smiling slightly, passed through the room again, this time showing the other side of his sign, which stated "All Clear."

The way the British reacted to the German bombing raids impressed me. During the weeks between my return from Normandy and the beginning of our operation in the Netherlands I never experienced among the British population any trace of panic, regardless of whether I was in Nottingham, London, or other parts of the country where I spent time either on military business or on short leaves. When I once again went to London late in the summer of 1944, the air raid sirens started wailing as soon as I stepped out of the station and into the street. I passed two middle-aged women who were busy sweeping the street in front of their respective houses. One of them looked up into the sky and said, "Another bloody doodlebug [as Londoners called the V-1]; to Hell with Hermann the German [meaning Göring]," and then went on sweeping.

While we waited in Nottingham for our next assignment, I and a newly assigned teammate, Master Sergeant Leo Brodsky, were sent for one week to a POW camp in northern England. (Brodsky had replaced Siggi Koesterich, who as a nonjumper had been transferred to the division's glider regiment. Born in Silesia, Brodsky was an interior designer by profession and made it a point to be "properly" dressed even under combat conditions.) At the POW camp Brodsky and I were supposed to find out the reaction of the German troops to the Normandy invasion, but in such a way that they wouldn't realize what we were after. As soon as we entered the camp, under the suspicious looks of the U.S. guards, I ran into Corporal Kegel, who had surrendered his squad to us in Normandy and then witnessed the near execution of his fellow German soldiers by one of our overzealous lieutenants.

Kegel and I shook hands like old friends. Then we informed the German POWs that we were very interested in their experiences after they were confronted by the Normandy invasion and invited them to send for us if they thought they had something interesting to tell. A considerable number of them indicated that they indeed had something to tell, and Brodsky and I were very busy throughout the week we spent in the camp. As word got around that we were gathering material for a book about the fighting in Normandy, we had to listen to a lot of nonsense while taking notes. But now and then we found out something useful. I remember especially talking with a young Austrian paratrooper. After telling me about a new German weapon that we had never heard of before, he suggested that once peace returned we paratroopers of both sides should pressure the International Olympic Committee to include parachute jumping in the Olympic Games. I promised to give this suggestion some thought and we said goodbye like old friends.

The better part of August and early September 1944 we spent in Nottingham, which now felt nearly like home to us. Again we went to The Cocked Hat, drank beer and ale, and flirted with the girls in the dark. The blackout that affected all of England supported the love lives of both our troopers and the English girls, many of whose boyfriends were fighting for the British Empire somewhere far away. The English soldiers who were still around often didn't care for us at all. Why not? "Because you Yanks are overbearing; you are overpaid; you are oversexed—and you are over here!" Even British children occasionally made fun of us. I still remember a little boy who ran behind us on the street, shouting, "Any gum, chum? Any candy, Andy? Any American cigarettes? Oh, you bloody fucking Yanks!"

Once again we went on brief maneuvers in the countryside around Nottingham, during which we interrogators had to wear German uniforms. If we were "captured" by our American comrades, we had to speak German exclusively. I hated all of this because the British Home Guard continued to make the area unsafe at night.

Needless to say, we speculated a good deal about where we would be assigned the next time. Although the regimental commander, Colonel Lindquist, let it be known that we probably would jump and fight again within the next eight weeks, rumor had it that the division would be moved back to the United States and then be sent to fight the Japanese in Asia. We learned that this rumor was false at the end of August when a parade of honor for General Eisenhower was staged at a large airport in Leicester. At the end of the parade the general thanked us for what we had accomplished in Normandy and told us that very soon we would be needed for further airborne missions. And he made it quite clear that these missions would take place in Europe. Shortly thereafter we learned that all airborne divisions, those of the United States, Great Britain, and other nations (including one from Poland), had been placed under the command of the U.S. General Lewis Brereton and now formed the First Allied Airborne Army. Our division commander, Major General Matthew Ridgeway, was henceforth the commander of its U.S. contingent, the 18th Airborne Corps. Our deputy commander, Brigadier General James Gavin, was now commander of the 82nd Airborne Division and promoted to major general.

When I met General Gavin he was thirty-seven years old, a tall, athletic, and good-looking man. In contrast to most other generals I had met, he treated his subordinates well, dealing with them in a friendly way, as comrades, but without trying to ingratiate himself. As a result, he was very popular with the troopers of his division. In addition to giving him the nickname "Slim Jim," they also called him a "two-star platoon leader," because although he was the divisional commander with two stars, he was frequently all the way up front like the platoon leader of an infantry company. And when he was way up front he always carried an M-1 rifle, although these were generally carried only by soldiers of lower rank and not by officers, let alone by a general.

One evening during the Normandy campaign Captain Breen had instructed me to stay on duty all night long in the tent that served as regimental headquarters. One of my principal duties was to answer the field telephone. In the middle of the night the phone rang and somebody demanded to speak with the regimental commander, General Ridgeway. I didn't know where Ridgeway was but crept out of the tent to look for him. Directly next to the tent's opening lay a sleeping figure. Assuming that this was one of the runners I shook the sleeper and shouted, "Do you know where Ridgeway can be found right now?" When the person I had roused from sleep raised himself I saw that he was still wearing his helmet (we often slept that way, especially when we weren't lying in a slit trench, to protect ourselves from shell splinters). On the front of the helmet were two stars, the rank insignia of a major general. I had woken Gavin. Instead of yelling at me, he merely said, "Son, I haven't the slightest idea where the General happens to be right now." Then he stretched out again and went back to sleep.

Shortly before Christmas 1944, during the Battle of the Bulge, I gave a report on my latest interrogations to Captain Silver, the regimental intelligence officer (and in civilian life a Brooklyn streetcar conductor). I had compiled information about the position and strength of the German troops facing us gathered from the interrogations of several prisoners that day. While I was reading my report out loud I realized that a figure was moving in the back of the room. It was General Gavin. Since at the time the information I'd assembled was of crucial importance, Gavin moved up to where Silver and I were, listened very attentively, and asked me a few additional questions. Then Silver dismissed me and I left. Later Silver told me that my report had impressed Gavin a good deal, especially since it turned out to be correct.

In September 1944, although we didn't know it at the time, the plans for the upcoming mission already existed. At the beginning of the month Allied troops led by British Field Marshal Bernard Montgomery had reached the northern Belgian border, and the plans were to drop three airborne divisions—the U.S. 101st and 82nd and the British First—over the Netherlands. The main objective was to prevent the Germans from destroying the bridges over the lower Rhine River and the Waal River. Furthermore, after the parachute attack the road from Eindhoven to Arnhem had to be captured by the Allies as soon as possible so that motorized British armored forces could move north toward Arnhem. From there, some of the troops were to move on to the Zuiderzee to prevent an entire German army division situated in western Holland from retreating and thereby forcing them to surrender. At the same time, the other half of Montgomery's troops was to move toward the German border in the direction of Brunswick, Hannover, and finally Berlin. Alas, everything turned out differently.

On September 17, a pleasant autumn Sunday, it was finally our turn again. We were informed that we were to be dropped over Nijmegen, where our first mission was to secure the bridge over the Waal. The 101st was to be dropped close to the Belgian border, at Eindhoven, to secure the road running north. The First British Airborne Division was to be dropped at Arnhem. In contrast to what had happened in Normandy on D-Day, the jump on Nijmegen—officially named "Operation Market Garden"—was the dream of every parachute jumper. The 508th Regiment, which since June 1944 had become my "home," was dropped as planned a few kilometers east of Nijmegen and occupied the range of hills close to the German border. I came down on a potato field next to a country road, landing very softly and then seeing around me nothing but familiar faces. In the middle of the field stood a German antiaircraft gun whose crew had decided to surrender rather than fight us. A master sergeant of our regimental staff was the only one hurt during the jump. He had sprained his leg and was now placed in a small handcart pulled by two troopers while he carried on with issuing orders, cursing wildly and loudly. The only one who had the tough luck to land on the roof of a barn was Brodsky. From there he issued instructions to search for a long ladder, which soon was found. The minute he was on the ground he pulled out a handkerchief to clean the dust off his jumping boots as if planning to go to the opera. As he was new to our team it took a few days before he felt at home with us. My initial impression of him as a difficult customer I had already revised during our week together in the English POW camp.

Our interrogation team—Brodsky, Greenwald, Guttman, and I—soon worked closely together. The team had been reorganized after Normandy and remained unchanged nearly to the end of the war. All nonjumpers, including Lieutenant Hauff, were transferred to the division's glider regiment; we never saw any of them again. One of our new team leaders was Lieutenant Nick C. Emanuel, who was born in the Rhineland but as a child had emigrated with his parents to New York City. He was two or three years younger than the rest of us, and by and large we got along with him very well, even though there were occasions when he behaved like a boy in the final throes of puberty, for instance by regaling us with stories about his sex life.

There was, however, a slight altercation between Lieutenant Emanuel and the rest of the team shortly after we had been dropped. Dutch "resistance fighters"—and there were heaps of people who called themselves that after our landing—had brought Emanuel a young Dutch couple and told him the two had been spying for the Germans. Who these "resistance fighters" were we didn't know because none of us was there when the couple was handed over to Emanuel. Without giving any thought to the fact that we had no legal authority to punish Dutchmen even if they had collaborated with Germans, Emanuel suggested shaving their heads so that a swastika of hair remained, then delivering them to the nearest Dutch police station. Brodsky and I told Emanuel that the entire team opposed this idea. A stormy exchange of views followed and ultimately a compromise: Emanuel painted a swastika on the foreheads of the two prisoners and let it go at that. After this initial test of strength, the lieutenant and the team got along with each other rather well.

For the first few days after the jump our team was assigned to stay at a Dutch monastery where the regimental intelligence section was likewise headquartered. The monastery was only a few kilometers from the spot where we had landed. Until just before our arrival it had served as the headquarters of a German military unit. In fact, when we approached and entered the building, weapons at the ready, we found ourselves standing in a dining room, some of whose tables held plates with the remnants of a meal, still warm. In the evening of the same day I climbed up to the monastery's roof garden with several friends and looked down at the city of Nijmegen, where our troops had secured the bridge across the Waal. Throughout the city we saw buildings in flames. The red glow and the sounds of the fighting in and around the city seemed almost romantic. This impression disappeared the following day when I saw our first dead soldiers, but during that first night I was entranced by everything I saw and heard, and I recited for my friends a couple of lines from a poem written during the First World War, "I Have a Rendezvous with Death," by Alan Seeger, a U.S. soldier and poet killed in 1916. The lines were "But I've a rendezvous with Death / At midnight at some flaming town." These two lines were all I was then able to recall. But the way I recited them, trying to impress my fellow soldiers, who were amused, is still very clear in my mind today.

Very soon we learned of the extremely difficult situation in which the British First Airborne Division found itself. The unit had jumped north of us into Arnhem. Unfortunately it had done so just as two German SS divisions were moving through the city. (The tragedy of Arnhem became known to a large audience after the war through the book by Cornelius Ryan, *A Bridge Too Far*.) That something had gone wrong I realized within the first few days after our landing. As I was walking north on a street in Nijmegen a British soldier on a motorcycle braked suddenly in front of me and demanded, "Where is the nearest field hospital?" I didn't know but sent him in the general direction where he would find somebody able to show him the way. Before he left I asked about the military situation in Arnhem. He restarted his motorcycle and shouted: "It's 'ell, Sergeant; it's bloody 'ell." And then he rode off again in search of the hospital, where he hoped to get medicine and dressing material.

Our military operation in Holland, which for us lasted until November 11, 1944, differed significantly from the preceding one in Normandy. During the first week the division, our regiment included, occupied in addition to Nijmegen the territory southeast of the city nearly up to the German border. Mook, Groesbeek, Wyler, and Berg en Dal are names that rise up from memory. So does Bemmel, situated north of Nijmegen, where our regiment was sent a few days after our jump. After the German troops had been repelled we dug ourselves in at Bemmel as if we were in the First World War, not the Second.

Most of our operation in the Netherlands was defensive. There were brief attacks and counterattacks but essentially no major changes. This also meant that we had fewer prisoners to interrogate than we'd had in Normandy. There were some now and then, especially deserters, but as the situation barely changed, the information we obtained from our interrogations was rarely very useful. One time, however, we found out that the *Volksgrenadierregiment* facing us was to be replaced by an SS unit, which signified that there would soon be a major attack on our position. The information helped us prepare for and repulse the attack.

We soon tired of Bemmel and its surroundings. I spent a good deal of time close to the command post of the First Battalion, where a Lieutenant Havens commanded the intelligence section and kept in close contact with the interrogators. Thus I was always ready, day and night, in case a prisoner was taken after all and had to be interrogated before he was dispatched to the nearest POW camp. Furthermore, I had friends in the intelligence section and liked to be with them. Finally, we didn't have to worry that we might encounter a high-ranking officer (they were always stationed quite a distance behind us), which might lead to trouble. On one occasion, however, I failed to avoid such a meeting.

One day when I went from the front line, where I had found a dugout for myself, to a fountain a little behind my dugout to fetch water for shaving, I encountered the deputy regimental commander, Lieutenant Colonel Thomas J. B. Shanley, who was inspecting the frontlines. Shanley was a good, responsible, and courageous officer, but his notorious temper made him more feared than liked by the troops. When I saw him coming my way I gave a friendly nod and said: "Good morning, Sir!" Shanley stopped abruptly, stared at me, and said: "How about a salute, Sergeant?" I responded that we had been told not to salute along the front lines to avoid revealing to the enemy who our officers were and thus making them targets for German snipers. Shanley didn't answer but kept staring at me, waiting for me to salute him. I did, very formally, and each of us went his way, he to the front, I toward the rear.

In the middle of October I escaped death on three consecutive days with a great deal of luck. Of course, while the fighting continued we were always in danger of being killed by a shell or an enemy sniper, regardless of where we happened to be. Guarding against these threats had become routine for most of us, and we had learned very quickly to hit the ground as soon as we heard the familiar sound of German artillery and if at all possible to crawl to the nearest slit trench or foxhole to protect ourselves from shrapnel.

I didn't spend my first night at battalion or company level but, exceptionally, close to the regimental headquarters, where our team was attached to the command post of the intelligence section. As it was getting dark Guttman and I bedded down in a rather narrow slit trench. During the night I was woken up by artillery fire. Around us all hell seemed to have broken loose. We heard the howling sound of enemy shells and then, not far away, the explosions as they hit. I pressed myself against the bottom of our slit trench. Guttman and I spoke to each other now and then to keep each other's spirits up. There was nothing we could do except stay where we were and keep our fingers crossed. We both tried to keep our voices calm, but I at least was shaking from fear. After an eternal ten minutes, the artillery fire stopped, and after a while we fell back asleep. When we got up again at dawn and crawled out from our trench, we found about three feet away an unexploded German shell.

I spent that day at the command post of one of the three battalions of the 508th. There I dug myself a foxhole in which I intended to sleep the night. In general one spent the night in these foxholes uncomfortably, half squatting, but it was safer than a slit trench. During the day, at company level, I had gotten talking with a sergeant I didn't know. He invited me to spend the night in his very sloppily dug and rather shallow slit trench. There we could continue our conversation while drinking whiskey, of which he had managed to find himself a bottle. I declined his offer and retired into my foxhole. During the night there was again enemy artillery fire, but it lasted much less long than the night before and was less heavy. When I returned the following morning to company level, my new friend was dead. A shell had hit his slit trench.

The third incident occurred at the First Battalion level. There, too, I had "my" foxhole. I was especially proud of the fact that it was almost a deep slit trench, long enough to allow nearly comfortable sleep. Situated directly under an apple tree, the foxhole was covered with a few planks onto which I had shoveled sand. Only a very slim entry remained uncovered. My buddies in the first battalion had resolved to have an early supper while the sun was still up and had invited me to join them. They had decided to have grilled rabbits, which originated, like the planks on top of my foxhole, from a nearby farm that had been deserted by its owners. After we had killed and skinned a few rabbits, we started to grill them on a hastily and primitively constructed grill next to my foxhole. Suddenly we heard the sound of German artillery only a few kilometers away. This was a shock because up to then we had been shelled mostly during the night. Two or three of my friends and I raced to our foxholes, of which mine was the closest. I crept as far to the rear of the hole as possible and a few minutes later heard above me a loud explosion, the air pressure of which hurled me against the rear wall of the dugout. For a brief moment I crouched without moving, still under the effect of the explosion. Then I saw that the blanket lying beneath the entrance to the foxhole at the opposite end, which the wooden planks with sand on them didn't cover, was full of holes. My small shaving kit was likewise damaged. I heard the voices of my friends shouting from above: "Are you alright, Tommy?" I was greeted enthusiastically as I climbed out of the hole, my knees still shaking. The shell had exploded as it hit the crown of the tree above my foxhole, and the shell splinters had hailed down like raindrops. I had been protected by the sand-covered planks—but only barely. Since our "grill" hadn't been damaged—a second miracle—our supper was rabbit after all.

About two weeks after the initial jump, British troops located south of us pushed their way through, and we were no longer cut off and alone. For the remainder of the campaign we were therefore under British command, which was no problem either for us or for them. When the first British tanks reached us after dark one evening, I ran down to the road where they had stopped and was stunned to see under each tank a small camping stove burning to heat water. Instead of keeping my big mouth shut, I told one of the tank drivers that German reconnaissance planes could easily spot the British tank columns with their lit stoves. Shouldn't they be turned off? The tank driver looked at me with a mixture of amusement and pity and replied: "Fuck the Jerries, Sergeant, it's teatime."

Thanks to the British reinforcements, which moved on toward Arnhem to relieve their troops, the rest of us, taking turns, were given a few days of rest in Nijmegen. When it was the turn of the regimental intelligence section and along with it our interrogation team, we found quarters at the edge of the city in a small house whose owner put two rooms at our disposal. Of course, whenever we left the house we had to carry our weapons with us, but aside from that we felt as if we were on vacation. We enjoyed the comfort of sleeping in for a few days, being able to take showers, and eating meals sitting around a table instead of at the edge of a foxhole. For the moment, the war seemed distant. But only a few kilometers away the fighting continued, and we regularly heard the explosions of the German artillery. We resolved nonetheless to ignore the war, at least for a few days.

One afternoon during this rest period, the intelligence section was invited by the city council to a dance at a café in the heart of the city. Needless to say, we accepted the invitation with enthusiasm. In the café we encountered a considerable number of young women, for the most part seventeen or eighteen years of age, each of them accompanied by one or even two older ladies. Despite their gratitude to their American liberators, the inhabitants of Nijmegen were by no means going to leave their daughters and granddaughters unchaperoned with the young paratroopers. Once we got to the café I first had to act as an interpreter, helping our troopers break the ice with the Dutch guests. As I had never learned how to dance, I then sat down with my Tommy gun in a corner of the café and watched the goings-on.

After a while one of my friends asked me to calm down one of the young women, who was terribly afraid of her dancing partner, Private First-Class Charles Under Baggage Jr., a full-blooded Sioux who looked as grim and aggressive as if he had just dropped into the café out of a Karl May book. Because he had already drunk a lot of wine and could no longer stand firmly on his legs, he clung so tightly to his dancing partner that she panicked. In short, the situation was rather tricky. I separated the two and the young woman disappeared. Under Baggage, however, insisted on continuing to dance, and I saw no other choice than to be the partner of a thoroughly drunk man until the next break. In the process our respective weapons, which we weren't allowed to put down, constantly got in each other's way. When the music stopped, I steered him into a corner of the café, made him sit down, and left him there. A few minutes later he was asleep. Private Under Baggage didn't survive the war. He and five other troopers, including Lieutenant Emanuel, died on March 14, 1945, during a practice jump.

Looking back, during the eleven months of fighting between June

6, 1944, and May 8, 1945, the campaign in the Netherlands was the least exhausting period. About a week after our jump, we, together with the British to the right and left of us, found ourselves in a war of position. Much as during the First World War, we faced the Germans dug in opposite us in their foxholes, exchanged artillery fire with them, and tried by means of daily patrols to find weak spots in their lines. The German lines were generally manned by *Volksgrenadier* regiments, that is, by reserve infantrymen who in the fall of 1944 weren't fighting for the Führer with a great deal of enthusiasm, at least in my opinion. With a lull in the fighting (though not in the artillery fire), I spent a good deal of time on correspondence. For a while I wrote in a greenhouse full of grapevines. As it rained frequently, I needed a roof over my head to write, and although it was dangerous to sit in a building made of glass because of the incoming rounds, I preferred that risk to trying to write in my foxhole. In this way the greenhouse became my "office" for a while.

My principal correspondent was Curt Bondy in Richmond. This correspondence has survived. Reading through it I am amazed at how intense our exchange of ideas was. Three themes dominated: the unknown fate of my parents and brothers, news from and about other Gross Breeseners in the armed forces, and Germany's future. As the correspondence shows, I was particularly frustrated by the fact that Amsterdam, where I assumed my parents and brothers to be, was physically so close, and yet I couldn't get there (our mission didn't include a massive westward campaign of liberation, which would have led us into Amsterdam). Since I spoke Dutch reasonably well, I asked all Dutch civilians I met what they knew about Amsterdam's situation under German occupation. But since most of the people I asked hadn't been to Amsterdam for a considerable time, I found out very little. For this reason I remained extremely worried about my family until May 1945.

To my great surprise, the correspondence among us former Gross Breeseners continued even though we were scattered around the world. Fortunately, the generally very brief bits of news tended to be positive. There were reports about this or that one having been slightly wounded, but aside from Büh no other Gross Breesener was killed. I regularly received mail from Leus and Traut, who were still nurses in London, and also from Marianne Regensburger, who had begun studying at a university in the United States.

In my contribution to a Gross Breesen circular letter [*Rundbrief*],

I told my friends that as I was writing, American shells were dropping on the German line. And that brought me to a question that a Gross Breesener I didn't know had raised shortly before: What would happen to Germany and the Germans once the war was over? I replied that the U.S. shells dropping on their lines was the beginning of their "reeducation." And I added that "this will require shells, rifle bullets, retreat, the recognition that the 'Führer' was wrong, because a '*Herrenrasse*' [Master Race] does not exist... . They will have to be taught that it does not pay to start wars... . Thereafter, many years of methodical work will be needed, during which selected teachers, Germans and also Americans, will have to make a giant effort to reeducate the future German generation." Emigrants such as us, however, should keep our distance from this task, as our involvement would only create problems. And it would probably be quite some time before such a reeducation program bore fruit.

In the fall I received a letter from Red, a Gross Breesen friend then driving a tank in General Patton's army, saying that he thought the 60 million Germans should simply be killed. Only then, he said, could peace be restored to the world. I replied to Red "indirectly," that is, in a November 6 letter to Bondy. I wrote that at the moment I couldn't stand the "Jerries" any more than Red could, but his proposal was "un-American" as well as short-sighted. To be sure, first we would have to defeat them, destroy their entire war machinery, and place those who had shown themselves to be sadists and murderers before a court of law. But to kill 60 million people was madness. It probably wouldn't be impossible to reeducate the young German generation, those now fifteen to seventeen years old, who had experienced the "glorious" Hitler era as children and remembered of it the turmoil of war, air raids, fear, and hunger. The task might not be easy, but in the end it would be worthwhile.

On November 11, Armistice Day, the division was relieved and the Netherlands campaign was over for us. This time we didn't return to our beloved Nottingham, however, but were sent to Camp Sissonne, a former French artillery base not far north of Reims, capital of the Champagne region. During the German occupation of France this camp had housed Wehrmacht units. The camp consisted of barracks and a few larger buildings such as the dining hall and the respective "clubs" for officers and noncommissioned officers. The walls of the dining hall had been illustrated by the Germans with caricatures of all sorts that were supposed to be funny but weren't.

Here we rested, were reequipped, and waited for the promised Christmas leave, which many of us hoped to spend in Paris—now liberated. The first lucky ones were able to take leave at the end of November, and the rest of us waited eagerly for our turn. While we waited, thanks to Greenwald's fluent French, we drank a lot of good champagne that he bought from the local vineyards. One day Captain Silver invited some of us to celebrate his birthday with him, and that evening we drove to Reims in open jeeps and went to a nightclub, where we were served a strikingly good dinner with excellent wine. Our table stood at the foot of a small stage on which a scantily dressed, very comely young Frenchwoman sang and danced—obviously for us above all. I sat directly at the ramp of the stage and, already inebriated, smiled up at the woman who sang her songs directly above my head. The tune of one of them I can still hum today. Suddenly she bent down to where I sat, pulled a small rose from her bra, and stuck it in my hair. Whatever happened thereafter I no longer remember. When I woke up I was lying on my bunk bed at Camp Sissonne and was the only person in the room. The others were on duty somewhere and it was nearly noon. I was told later that they'd had to carry me out of the restaurant and drop me into one of our jeeps. Captain Silver and my friends didn't let me hear the end of my little Reims interlude for some time.

CHAPTER 8

From the Battle of the Bulge to the End of the War, 1944–1945

The day after my Reims interlude, December 16, began the German military thrust into Belgium known as the Rundstedt or Ardennes Offensive. Its goal was to drive the Allies westward, and if possible into the sea. Within a few hours twelve German divisions, Wehrmacht and Waffen-SS under the high command of General Field Marshall Gerd von Rundstedt, overran three U.S. divisions stationed in the Ardennes, pushing them further southwest. I had just been promoted to the rank of technical sergeant and on December 17 was proudly sewing the new stripes on my uniform when word came that our division had been put on alert. All leaves were cancelled, and the following morning we rode in open trucks in the biting cold from Camp Sissonne to the Belgian Ardennes. Thus began what is known in the United States as the Battle of the Bulge, as well as the most stressful and difficult eight weeks of my career as a soldier.

For our division, fighting in the Ardennes lasted until mid-February. During this period we beat our way through an area south and east of Liège, Belgium, from Werbomont to the German village of Schmidt, a bit south of the Hürtgen Forest and somewhat west of the Roer River. Living for two months in snow and ice wasn't easy for me. As a child in Westend I had hated winter, something my parents could never understand. But then it was always possible for me to go home to our apartment, whereas during the Battle of the Bulge, we spent the better part of our time in the open. The enemy artillery fire was constant. When we had the good fortune to be able to spend the night in a farmhouse or other shelter, we occasionally had a heated room. But most nights we spent outside, digging foxholes in the icy ground, unless we were lucky and found some dug by the retreating German troops. We tried to make ourselves as comfortable as possible in these enemy foxholes, downright appreciative for the unintended assistance. A few fir tree branches served as a mattress on the ground, while above our heads we placed as many pieces of wood as we could find for cover.

One time, as we moved slowly but steadily east and I was dragging my luggage on a sled behind me, we saw a badly wounded trooper lying in the snow at the edge of the road. A medic was giving him first aid when an enemy shell hit close by. Like the rest of the men I immediately hit the ground. When I stood up again, medic and patient both lay dead.

Christmas 1944 found us in an abandoned farmhouse in the village of Haute Bodeux. Our team, together with the regimental intelligence section, spent several days there. Although around us we could hear, as usual, the impact of hostile artillery shells, we tried to make "our house" as pleasant and comfortable as possible. And yet, my memory of this village is sad.

Shortly before we left Camp Sissonne and were transported to Belgium we had received some replacements, among them a number of very young fellows without any combat experience. One of these replacements assigned to the regimental intelligence section was a small, skinny kid named Lewis P. Baco. He came from Pennsylvania, where his father was a coal miner. When Baco had volunteered to be trained as a parachute jumper he hadn't the slightest idea of what this war was about. He had lied about his age, telling the army he was nineteen, when in fact he was seventeen. When we arrived in the Ardennes, Lou, as we called him, volunteered regularly for the reconnaissance patrol, which was run every day by troopers of the regimental intelligence section. After a few days Lou and I became friends and he told me a lot about himself and his family. When I asked him why he kept volunteering for patrol, he replied, "I like to play with the big boys," meaning the German enemy.

On the evening of December 27 we went to sleep fairly early in our Haute Bodeux farmhouse. Some of us, including Lou, me, and the sergeant in charge of the regimental intelligence section, "Pappy" Morgan, preferred to lie down in the hallway upstairs, whereas most of the other soldiers decided to sleep in a large room on the ground floor. Lou, who lay next to me wrapped in a blanket, wished all of us a good night and soon was asleep. He needed his sleep, as he was scheduled to be on guard duty in the downstairs room later that night.

A few hours later we were awakened by a bang that shook the farmhouse. "That hit our building," Pappy said. We rapidly put on our shoes and ran downstairs. As I searched in the dark for the door to the room where our buddies were sleeping and where Lou was on guard, I noticed from the frigid air that there no was longer a door. A shell from a German .88-caliber gun, which we feared more than any other, had entered and exploded in the lower room. The room was devastated, though things could have been much worse. Several of our men who had been sleeping, like us, on the floor, were slightly wounded, but the majority were unhurt. But Lou was dead. He sat in the chair where he had been keeping guard duty. A shell splinter had hit him in the head and he slumped forward, covered with blood. After giving first aid to the wounded, Pappy Morgan and I carried our buddy, wrapped in a shelter half, to the regimental ambulance station, where all bodies were taken so they could be buried. It was the second time a person dear to me was killed. The first had been Captain Breen in Normandy, this time Lou in the Ardennes. Shortly before New Year's I wrote a long poem about Lou and his death. I still have it in my possession.

A few hours later I had to deliver something to regimental headquarters, where I was asked by a young lieutenant I had met only briefly before why I looked so sad. When I told him that a friend of mine had been killed that night, he looked at me and said: "Because things like that happen, you can't have friends in wartime. I, at least, always keep my distance." Though I didn't reply, I thought, "You poor bastard!"

One evening I had to wait at First Battalion headquarters for prisoners of war. We were under attack by a regiment of the Sixth SS Army and thus urgently needed additional information. Nothing was going on at battalion headquarters, and anyway I wanted to be closer to the frontlines, where it was easier to get information from prisoners of war who had just surrendered and usually were still in shock. So I moved up to the battalion's machine gun company. There I found an unoccupied foxhole, which I made my lodging for the night. We were located on top of a hill and the attacking SS came from below. I then witnessed for the first time a German infantry attack by the light of signal rockets. Cheering each other on by shouting, the SS soldiers charged uphill into the carefully aimed machine-gun fire of the Americans. But not every bullet was a hit, and although I saw many bodies lying still on the ground, the SS attack continued. Suddenly two men ran by my foxhole to the rear—our company commander and his "topkick" (master sergeant). Thus we were without leaders. I was just about to run back to battalion headquarters to notify the officers in charge when I heard a lieutenant close to me (he happened to be Jewish) yell, "I take over command" and then issue the necessary orders. The SS attack was defeated. The next morning for about half an hour I crept from one dead SS soldier to the next searching their pockets for pieces of information. The company commander and his topkick none of us ever saw again. I found out later that both were court-martialed and convicted of cowardice under enemy fire.

Despite the cold and the danger, there were also situations that in retrospect make me smile. One evening we were moving eastward, as we did continuously during those weeks. For some unknown reason we stood for a few minutes at an intersection that was iced over and where several troopers of the regimental machine-gun company were posted. While we stood around, waiting to move on, one of the machine gunners sitting in the snow called to me, "Hey, Sergeant, how about some ice cream?" Stupidly I accepted the offer and received a mixture of chocolate powder and snow from the edge of the road, which the man served to me on my mess kit like a waiter. It didn't taste bad, but the result was diarrhea.

Another time, as so often during that part of the war, I sat crouched with some of my buddies from the intelligence section in the snow at the edge of the forest, taking a short break. We hadn't eaten anything all day and were now chewing pieces of old dry bread that we'd pulled from our pockets. We started to tell each other what sort of food was going through our minds: "roast pheasant," "pineapple cake," "veal cutlet," and similar goodies. We acted like children—which some of us still were. Quite a number of them were too young to vote. At twenty-four years old, I felt at times like a grandfather.

Although originally I had been trained as an infantry soldier and during our maneuvers back in the United States used to go on patrol, Captain Silver had forbidden me to join my friends when they went on patrol during the fighting. My job, Silver said, was to interrogate prisoners of war, an important task. Should I be captured or killed while on patrol, I would be difficult to replace. Silver was a very pleasant superior, but when it came to patrol and me he wasn't to be trifled with. One day Corporal Bruce Howard, a good friend of mine from the First Battalion intelligence section, where I felt most at home, suggested that I accompany him and a few additional troopers on a patrol. Our task was to check out a ridge of hills for German positions. I considered the invitation a compliment and let myself be talked into it. At the time Captain Silver was at the regimental command post, quite a bit to the rear, and I assumed that he would never find out about my disobedience. Thus we set off, which meant initially climbing a steep hill covered with snow. As we had learned during one of the interrogations, the hillside was also covered with bombs placed in wooden cases. But because the snow lay thick and heavy, so that we sank nearly to our knees with every step, we assumed that the risk of triggering a mine was relatively small. Each of us stepped carefully into the footsteps of the person before him. The leader, a Jew from Brooklyn, if I remember right, climbed slowly uphill, unfazed by the risky situation and loudly droning a song I had never heard before: "Spread / your legs, / you're breaking my glasses. / Open up and let me in." The idea that this male fantasy he was singing for us might be his last words didn't seem to have occurred to him. Approximately fifteen minutes later we reached the top of the hill, found a paved road, and moved along it until we did in fact discover some German positions. We noted them on our map and were back at our lines a few hours later. Captain Silver never did find out.

Although my evaluator at Camp Ritchie, Lieutenant Bartholomew, had flunked me for not shouting the way he did, this never tempted me to interrogate prisoners of war using his method. From my first interrogations during the Normandy campaign, I had learned that each interrogation was different and each prisoner I talked to an individual, reacting according to his personality. It was thus important to evaluate his character quickly and pose questions accordingly.

Did I hate these prisoners? They were, after all, soldiers in Hitler's armed forces, and one could expect many of them to be Nazis. But despite my occasional contempt for the Germans in general, the answer is no. In fact, like my fellow interrogators, I often pitied the German soldiers I questioned. Most were our age, and they faced us unarmed and defenseless. Repeatedly prisoners asked me in a whisper whether they would be shot. My usual response was, "No. After all, we're not Nazis." Their response was usually a cautious smile, but occasionally a cold look. Sometimes they asked why I spoke German so well, and for this I also had my standard reply: "I am an American of German descent," which was both correct and incorrect.

I never told any of them that I was an émigré and a Jew, though I assume that many guessed I was. Occasionally there was some trouble with German officers shortly after they had been captured (I interrogated them only very rarely because it was a waste of time, especially since they looked down on me because I wasn't an officer). Many of our troopers collected "souvenirs," including medals and decorations worn by captured officers. As soon as one of these "robbed victims" found out that I spoke German and was temporarily responsible for the prisoners taken, I became the target of their fury. Most of the time I reacted by telling them they should be glad they were alive.

All our questioning of POWs was restricted to the tactical level. Our team was one of many field interrogation detachments, and our task was to find out which enemy units were facing us, how strong they were, how long they had been at their present location, which heavy artillery or machine guns were placed where, and so on. The more details we learned, the better our officers on either the regimental level or at division headquarters could adjust to the prevailing situation, be it to prepare for defense or attack.

Although the 1864 Geneva Convention gave prisoners the right to tell us only their name, rank, and serial number, very few made use of this formula. I frequently got the impression that they talked out of fear or in the hope that their cooperation would somehow be rewarded or at least get them protection.

In Normandy, shortly after we were freed, a few U.S. troopers had shown up guarding a small group of prisoners. Except for the noncommissioned officer in command, all of them were Russians, former captives of the Germans who now served "voluntarily" in Hitler's army. We all sat down at the edge of the woods where the battalion was headquartered and I asked a few questions of the noncom, who looked about nineteen years old. To my amazement he suddenly started to cry and didn't stop even when I assured him he had nothing to fear. Finally, still sobbing, he said that he had betrayed his *Führer* because these "damned Russian swine" had forced him to surrender. The Russians grinned but remained silent. Instead of continuing with my interrogation, I consoled the boy, telling him that there were always unforeseen circumstances stronger than the will of an individual, and similar platitudes. In the meantime one of my teammates walked over and sat down behind me. He whispered to me to let the guards take the prisoners away; we wouldn't get any information from them anyway. Then he took me aside and said, "Tommy, you're an interrogator, not a pastor. Please don't forget this!" I never did.

During the Battle of the Bulge, one day while we were staying in Haute Bodeux, I was to interrogate a German master sergeant. This fellow was no longer young, wore several military decorations, and greeted me curtly when he entered my room. I asked him to sit down and said something like, "*Spiess* ["Topkick," or First Sergeant], how is it possible that an experienced old bird like you was taken prisoner by a bunch of green young Yankees?" The man stared at me, began to stutter, and then simply exploded. During his torrent of words I now and then interrupted him with brief tactical questions, all of which he promptly answered. In this manner I learned the identity and approximate strength of his unit, the name of his commanding general, and similar information. As usual at such interrogations I tried to look terribly bored. I occasionally yawned and interrupted the man with brief questions. As one point I said that he was probably unable to read an American military map—or could he? "Of course I can!" he shouted, and within a few minutes I knew where his unit's regimental headquarters was located, where he and his fellow soldiers got their food each day, and where their machine guns were stationed. When I had no more questions I wished him all the best for the time that he would be in captivity, gave him a few cigarettes, and we shook hands firmly. When he was gone, I sat down and listed everything of importance I'd just heard from the *Spiess*. The report then went immediately to the regimental intelligence section.

Late in April, shortly before the end of the war, our team was quartered in a small house near the Elbe River, south of Hamburg. A German prisoner was brought to my room and I was told that this man had surrendered to our troops, most of whom had already crossed the Elbe. After I had gotten whatever information I thought I could obtain from him, I asked him a number of questions about his life and his family. He began to cry. He was sitting opposite me, on a chair, and I on a bed, watching the tears run down his cheeks. After he had quieted down a bit, I asked him whether he cried out of fear of me or of Americans in general. Shaking his head, he told me that he and his parents had been Social Democrats before Hitler took power. Because this was known in his unit, he had been badly treated, never was promoted, and remained an outsider. And now, as a prisoner of war, he was being treated for the first time in a friendly way and as a human being, by "the enemy."

These three examples of tactical interrogations I conducted show me in a positive light. And I can say without boasting that I was a good interrogator, which earned me two promotions in a period of three months. In the fall of 1944, I was made a technical sergeant and in the winter of 1944–45, a master sergeant. There were, however, two incidents while I was an interrogator of which I am certainly not proud. Only through unbelievable luck was I saved from becoming a murderer, at least indirectly. Both interrogations happened during the Battle of the Bulge in the winter of 1944–45.

Sometime late in December or early January, as we advanced slowly eastward in ice and snow, I was serving temporarily with the intelligence section of our regiment's First Battalion, where I had a number of good friends with whom I liked to work. We had stopped advancing late at night, and just as I was trying to find a dry place to sleep in the farmhouse where the battalion's headquarters was then stationed, I was told to report at once to the intelligence officer.

The officer told me that we were apparently entirely surrounded by German troops, that we temporarily had no contact with the remainder of the regiment, and that would have to find out, by whatever means, which enemy troops were close to us, how strong they were, and so on. A small group of prisoners was about to be brought to the command post, and I was to do everything possible to extract from them the required information. Shortly thereafter I was facing three German POWs of low rank. From their *Soldbücher* [pay books], I saw that all three of them had been serving in the Luftwaffe, but as ground troops, not pilots.

The *Soldbücher* didn't say to which infantry unit they had been transferred. This was what I was supposed to find out. We were crowded into the small kitchen of a farmhouse, and around me stood the paratroopers who had brought the prisoners to me. Instead of interrogating the men separately, I asked my questions with all three of them present. I started to yell at them, but they remained silent. A few of the troopers offered to beat them up, an offer I declined. But I told the prisoners I would have them shot if they didn't talk. The troopers grinned, and one of them said they would gladly take care of this for me. I began to feel very uncomfortable. As during most of this campaign, we hadn't slept properly for days, or received sufficient food, and our nerves were edgy to the hilt. Once again I turned to the prisoners and demanded that they answer my questions. I would count to ten: should they continue to keep silent they would have to be shot. I started counting out loud. Just as I was about to reach ten the senior noncom of the three gave me the number of the unit to which they'd recently been transferred. As it turned out, the three prisoners were stragglers looking for their unit and had so far not found it, so the entire business turned into a farce. I had come very close to ordering the executions of three men, for information that turned out to be useless.

During our advance east toward the German border we had taken a large number of prisoners, and I was entrusted with finding a place where they could be held securely overnight until their transport to a POW camp the following day. In the village where we stayed that night—it was either Odrimont or Arbrefontaine—and where our command post was also located that day I found an abandoned house with a huge basement. Into that basement we drove the prisoners, enlisted men as well as officers. After everybody had gone down, I warned them under no circumstances to open the door. I then turned to the sentry assigned to me—a pleasant young man of Swedish descent—and told him that if the prisoners should try to open the cellar door he was to start shooting at it. Then I found a place to lie down and go to sleep. I had hardly dropped off when a friend found me and shook me violently awake. The sentry had to talk to me at once, he said. When I arrived at the entrance to the basement, the door was half open. The sentry, shaking and stuttering in his agitation, told me that one of the German officers had pushed the door open and had said something—in German—that the sentry didn't understand. He had yelled at the officer—in English—threatening to shoot if the door wasn't closed at once. And as the latter failed to obey the sentry's order he had pulled the trigger. However, for some reason the weapon failed to function. No one was shot.

At that moment I realized what I had come very close to doing. Dead tired and nervous as I was that evening, I had failed to think through the instructions that I gave the sentry, and I had failed to inspect the basement before filling it with a large number of prisoners. Furthermore, I had ordered one of our soldiers to shoot into the cellar if the prisoners attempted to open the door—an order I wasn't entitled to give. Finally, I had failed to realize that the prisoners had to stand all night long cramped in a dark basement, without sufficient air when the door was closed. As soon as I realized what I had done, I was once again in command of the situation. I walked down the steps to the cellar door, opened it widely, and faced the officers. They were exhausted and barely able to stand. One of them struggled for breath. Another told me that they had opened the door in defiance of my orders, first, because they couldn't get enough air and, second, because several of the men had diarrhea, making the smell down there unbearable. Men had collapsed and were lying on the floor of the cellar, in danger of being trampled by comrades in the cramped space. I promised to keep the door wide open but instructed the highest-ranking officer not to permit any of his men to step over the threshold. The next morning, when we let the prisoners out, many first had to take care of their diarrhea. Then they lined up in formation and, accompanied by guards, started walking to a prisoner of war camp behind our lines. Once again I had been very lucky.

Ever since the Normandy campaign I had often chosen to attach myself for a few days and nights to those units where I felt most at home while doing my job. For the most part I chose to settle in the territory that lay between the command posts of one of the battalions and the troopers at the front lines in their foxholes. There one was left at peace, did not have to salute, and was able to interrogate prisoners immediately after they had been captured.

Although interrogators of POWs enjoyed more freedom of move-ment than other soldiers, this freedom was considerably restricted during the Battle of the Bulge. The reason for this was alarming: our intelligence service had found out that German soldiers who were able to speak English well had been given American uniforms and orders to infiltrate our lines. They weren't doing this only to gather information but also, if possible, to raid U.S. command posts at night. For this reason the daily password issued every morning was chosen in such a way that generally a German soldier couldn't pronounce it without a German accent. I therefore had been instructed that whenever I needed to move through terrain not held by troopers of our regiment (among whom I was well known), I was only to do so accompanied by a native English speaker. I also was to leave it to whoever accompanied me to demand the password of soldiers we encoun-tered. (In fact, on D-Day I had been instructed not to reply to any American demand for the password, which that night was "whistling thistle.")

On a beautiful sunny day when we were finally able to relax a bit, Bruce Howard and I were strolling about the territory behind the lines. We unexpectedly found ourselves in the terrain of the neighboring regiment. We came upon a small farmhouse where two troopers were dunking dead chickens into a rain barrel so as to be able to pluck them more easily. I yelled to them that with those dead chickens they were contaminating the rainwater in the barrel, the drinking water for the owners of the house. Seconds later Bruce and I found ourselves staring into the barrels of two rifles. "You goddamned Heinies," the troopers yelled at us, and one of them suggested we be shot forthwith. Bruce protested in his pronounced North Carolina accent that we were Americans, not Heinies. The two men looked puzzled. Bruce suggested they take us to one of their superior officers at the nearest command post for proper identification. They agreed, but Bruce and I had to walk in front of the two troopers with our hands over our heads. At the command post, a colonel interrogated us aggressively, but then, on my suggestion, we were allowed to phone Captain Silver over the field telephone. Silver confirmed to the colonel that I was really Master Sergeant Angress, interrogator of prisoners of war and a naturalized American. At that moment we were free men again. Before we went back to our unit I complimented the two young troopers for their vigilance and quick reaction. Both grinned with some embarrassment, but then we all shook hands. Once Bruce and I had returned to our regiment, I had to listen once more to the usual sermon of Captain Silver: "Seek an honest living at home."

As the first signs of spring made themselves felt, our operation in the Ardennes gradually came to an end. One day in early February, in the Hürtgen Forest close to the little town of Brandenberg, I saw the first anemones and snowdrops that had pushed through the soil. The German troops were retreating, although their artillery fire continued to be our "daily bread." On a beautiful sunny day we were told to go to the supply sergeant to pick up lined and waterproof winter boots that had just arrived. After eight weeks of continually wet boots and cold feet we saw this "offer" as a slap in the face, and the great majority of us simply didn't bother. In the meantime I had been promoted to master sergeant, my self-confidence had increased, and I was well known in the regiment. My buddies in the intelligence section often made fun of me by calling me a "Heinie" and asking, "Hey, Tommy, how many German war bonds have you gotten lately?"

On February 18, 1945, our division was relieved by the Ninth Infantry Division close to the little village of Schmidt in the Ruhr Valley. At this point the Battle of the Bulge was over for us. From Schmidt we were taken via Aachen (Aix-la-Chapelle) back to Camp Sissonne in France. The few weeks we spent there gave us a good rest after two months of extremely heavy military action. This included a special diet,

Visiting Notre Dame, Paris, March 1945.

because most of us hadn't been properly fed since mid-December 1944. Our clothing and equipment were repaired or replaced, and we got a short leave that most of us spent in Paris. I also went to Paris, but not on leave. When the senior officer of our interrogation team, at that point Captain Mauthner, who was originally from Vienna, had to go to Paris for a few days on official business, he asked me whether I would like to come along and drive the jeep. I agreed at once, and shortly after our arrival at Camp Sissonne we took off. In Paris I was assigned a room in a hotel where only noncommissioned officers were allowed. Thus I had three whole days to look around the city, which I had last seen in December 1937.

Whether I was inspired by Paris or by the last exhausting weeks in the Ardennes, I don't know, but I decided I should sleep with a woman for the first time in my life. (The fact that this happened so late had a lot to do with Bondy's educational principles.) I went to a brothel that had been recommended to me by fellow noncoms at my hotel. After I arrived, I sat for a while in the "salon" with the *madame* and several ladies "on duty." They were all waiting for some American officers, whereas I was merely a master sergeant. But then my turn finally came. The *madame* introduced me to a woman at least ten years older than I was who took me upstairs to her room. Basically, everything that could go wrong did, and I can still see the woman's kind face when it was all over and she asked, "*La première fois*?" I nodded. She patted my head and I departed, one experience richer. It was not just my "first time," as she had guessed, it was also my last time in a brothel, but I am still grateful to that woman, whose name I never learned but whose patience and humanity I will never forget.

Shortly after I returned from Paris, when my unit was out in the country on another maneuver, I met Marlene Dietrich. We had just lined up for lunch when someone pulled me by my arm and dragged me toward a group of officers. They were talking with a woman in a U.S. uniform. "Here is somebody from Berlin, Miss Dietrich. He speaks German," my kidnapper shouted and pushed me toward her. Even in uniform she looked the way I remembered from her films. She smiled at me and said, in German: "*Mensch*, aren't you too young to be a soldier?" When I told her how old I was, she shook her head. She put a hand on my shoulder and said, again in German: "Now get yourselves to Berlin so I can see my mother again. And do you know, today is a very important day for me. My daughter in New York will be onstage the first time in her life, on Broadway. Keep your fingers crossed for her." Then she turned back to the officers.

Officially she was the guest of our commanding officer, General Gavin, and, at least according to the rumors floating about, she was a bit more than just a guest. Be that as it may, for the following day she was invited to watch us do our semiannual practice jump. For, in order to get our monthly "jump pay"—a fifty-dollar bonus—all paratroopers in the Army had to make at least one jump every six months, in combat or in practice. Unfortunately Marlene Dietrich had been told that the jump was taking place in her honor, which wasn't at all the case.

The following morning we were driven in trucks to an airfield near Camp Sissonne. The evening before, one of our two team leaders, First Lieutenant Nick Emanuel, had suggested that I fly in the same plane with him. I reminded him of the loss we had suffered on D-Day when several interrogators had flown in the same plane and it was shot down. Perhaps it would be better to leave the arrangements as they were. Nick was my superior, but he was also a little younger than I was, so he gave in. As it turned out, this saved my life.

The practice jump posed no problems for me. This time I was number thirteen in the stick, and for the third time in my life I let myself fall out of a flying plane. The chute opened up and I floated to the ground without anyone shooting at us. It really was fun. Once I had hit the ground I got out of my parachute and carefully folded it for the riggers. Suddenly I realized that troopers were running around shouting. Marlene Dietrich was standing nearby, her hands before her eyes, while her secretary took pictures like mad. It was only then that I noticed the C-47 burning in the field where we had landed. Around it lay scattered the lifeless bodies of several troopers. What had happened? One plane had lost a propeller during the flight and had crashed. Fortunately, the paratroopers who had been in that plane had jumped to safety. But the pilot and three other men, allegedly journalists, hadn't been able to jump in time. Furthermore, as the plane descended, it struck and killed seven troopers who had jumped from another plane. Among these men were Lieutenant Nick Emanuel, Private Charles Under Baggage Jr., and five other friends, all members of our regiment's intelligence section.

Marlene Dietrich was weeping. A trooper ran up to her secretary, ripped the camera out of her hands, and yelled that she should take care of Miss Dietrich instead of taking pictures to which she wasn't entitled. As for the rest of us, we had to get back to our maneuver, which the jump was to have initiated. Shocked, sad, and dazed, we moved away in order

Before the practice jump, Camp Sissonne, Reims, France, March 1944.

to continue playing war games. Marlene stayed behind and I never saw her again, except in the movies.

Shortly after this disastrous practice jump a number of things changed, some of which affected me. The 508th Parachute Infantry Regiment, to which our team had been assigned shortly before D-Day, was detached from the 82nd Airborne Division. It stayed in France until the end of the war and was then sent to Frankfurt am Main, where it guarded General Eisenhower's headquarters. Our interrogation team, however, remained with the intelligence section of divisional headquarters and didn't go along with the 508th.

I was unhappy about all this because I had made good friends with a number of troopers in the regiment and was afraid—rightly—that I would never see any of them again. Before packing my things in order to move with the rest of my teammates to divisional headquarters, I said goodbye to my friends in the 508th and also to its commander, Colonel Lindquist, and his second-in-command, Lieutenant Colonel Thomas J. B. Shanley. The latter was a professional soldier, demanded a lot from his subordinates, and liked to personally inspect the troops at the front lines (when I had failed to salute him that day in Holland I got a taste of the kind of officer he was).

Shanley also saw to it that the troops, wherever they were stationed, were regularly fed and otherwise taken care of. In short, he was a highly competent though not necessarily likeable fellow. When I walked up to him to say goodbye I gave him a snappy salute and said I would be remaining with my interrogation team at division headquarters and wouldn't be going along with the 508th. He looked at me for a moment, then stretched out his hand and said, "Angress, you're a good soldier. Keep on doing a good job, and I wish you all the best." I saluted once more and left the command post, most probably with a red face. I hadn't expected a compliment.

A few days later, in early April 1945, we were loaded into trucks and taken to Cologne, which had been occupied by Allied forces some days earlier. The eastern side of the Rhine, including the entire Ruhr region, was still in German hands. Our division had been ordered to keep these German troops moving, largely by artillery fire, and, if possible, to identify their individual units. And so we waited on the west bank of the Rhine for the German commanders to meet and negotiate their surrender with our general staff.

I was back in Germany. Although we had entered German territory earlier, at the end of the Battle of the Bulge, what we then encountered were largely deserted villages. Real contact with German civilians didn't take place until we moved into Cologne. There we established quarters for our interrogation team in a little house at the edge of the city along the road leading to Aix-la-Chapelle (in German, Aachen). Cologne was a pile of rubble. Nearly the entire inner city had been destroyed by Allied bombing. The famous cathedral also had been damaged but fortunately not so severely that it couldn't subsequently be restored.

We spent two-and-a-half weeks in Cologne. Most of the city's inhabitants, except for the children, tried to avoid any contact with us. The Allied troops avoided them, too: all soldiers under the command of General Eisenhower had been given strict orders not to "fraternize" with the Germans. But this didn't prevent us interrogators from having frequent if strictly official contact with civilians. As long as the Rhine separated us from the German troops we weren't going to be interrogating enemy soldiers, so we were often instructed by our superior officers to seek information from civilians.

One of my first impressions, which surprised me, was the spitefulness of neighbors toward each other. Once we had moved into our new "home," we wanted to have a radio. I walked to the neighboring house hoping to find one there. When I told the inhabitants that I wanted to requisition a radio from them for the time we would be in Cologne, they replied that they had never been Nazis and would very much appreciate it if they could keep their radio. However, they said, two houses further down lived a staunch Nazi, and he also had a radio. When I went to that neighbor I was told a similar story. These were trifling things, but they were revealing. Any trace of *Volksgemeinschaft* [community of the people] had disappeared. But the behavior of the population varied widely. A lot of people we met were obviously glad that the war was over—at least for them. Far more common than angry, grim faces were men and women—particularly men—who behaved obsequiously, trying to ingratiate themselves with us. My reaction to this behavior I wrote to Bondy on April 22, 1945:

Berlin could fall at any moment. The German army is no longer holding together. This is good news that I am glad of. But this situation is clouded by little things we encounter every day.... I certainly have had sufficient opportunity to become acquainted with the German mentality—that of the army, of the civilians, of their women and children. I have seen it when I was a prisoner of war, have seen it in turn when they were our prisoners, and I am seeing it under many different circumstances now. My appraisal is really objective, but I am more than ever convinced that the German nation stinks.... To be sure, not all of them are criminals, but the great majority is beneath contempt. Their attitude toward us is miserable. No dignity, no pride, just dog-like submission and licking of the victors' boots. You can't trust anybody. We have experienced nasty examples of deceit and hypocrisy. I have already written to you about people who have suddenly discovered their Jewish ancestors and who now claim that they had opposed the Nazis from the outset (although they had been Party members from 1933 to 1945) and were pro-American (after we showed up here). Bo, none of us would shed a tear if they were to erase the German borderlines from the maps. This state, this nation no longer has any right to exist. Well, enough of this. Looking at Germany's ruins moves me as much as the sight of a dead dog floating down the St. James River.

My reaction was undoubtedly exaggerated, but this is how I felt at the time.

Our occupation of the city was a heavy psychological blow for the inhabitants. Although we didn't corroborate this at the time, I am convinced today that very few people felt they had been liberated. The majority simply felt defeated. Their future now lay in the hands of the Allies. The destruction all around was symbolic of not only Cologne's fate but also that of Hitler's Germany as a whole. Across the ruins of a bombed-out house near the cathedral the British (who had moved into Cologne before we did) had strung up a huge banner that read "Give me four years and you won't recognize Germany. A. Hitler."

Shortly after we arrived I asked two nice-looking kids who lived nearby, a brother and sister about ten to twelve years old, to go from house to house with a small wagon we had "requisitioned" for them and ask the residents to load into the wagon National Socialist books and journals. I asked the children to then deliver all these to us. Obviously delighted with their mission, they worked very well and efficiently for two days. Then they told us that their parents had forbidden them to keep working for the "Amis." We thanked them for their help and for the considerable material they had gathered, then shook hands with them and they left. I never saw the children again.

All Allied troops were forbidden to have any personal contact with the German population. This ban was aimed especially at sexual relationships (inspiring among soldiers the expression "Cohabitation without conversation ain't fraternization"). But many troopers in our division ignored Eisenhower's order against friendly contact when it came to German children. Thus every morning when I walked to the building where enlisted men received their meals I encountered beaming German boys and girls with candy, fruit, and occasionally ice cream in their hands. The GIs, at least those in our division, didn't consider it "fraternization" to give their dessert to the children of the enemy.

Not long after we had occupied Cologne and part of the western bank of the Rhine I was told to help a newly arrived Military Government officer find German specialists capable of restoring the water, light, and gas in the city. I went to a number of apartments and asked the inhabitants whether they knew such experts. Most simply shook their head and shut the door. On occasion the person I asked would try to assist me, but as soon as I said that the person in question couldn't have been a member of the Nazi Party, the conversation ended. When a Catholic clergyman closed his door in my face, I went to the major who had given me the order and told him the responses I was getting. At first the major just looked at me with surprise. Then he said, very angrily, that he had instructed me to find experts who could restore electrical, gas, and water service. The political views of these experts were perfectly immaterial. With that I was dismissed from the job and my contact with Military Government ended.

On April 13, a wonderful spring day, I was walking to the place where the enlisted men received their breakfast when a British soldier on the other side of the street came over to me, seized my hand, and told me how sad he was that President Roosevelt had died. I was thoroughly shaken, as I hadn't yet heard this news. For me, FDR was the person who had made it possible for me to come to the United States (although he had very little to do with it, as I found out after the war), and since I had immigrated he was the only president I had known. For us soldiers, he was also our commander-in-chief. The news spread rapidly and I saw many very sad faces—a phenomenon I witnessed only once more in my life, when John F. Kennedy was shot. There was an official ceremony of mourning at which we were told that our new president and commander-in-chief was Harry S. Truman. Although he had been Roosevelt's vice president since that January, I knew nothing about him except his name.

While we were in Cologne, I was General Gavin's interpreter for ten days. During the Battle of the Bulge I had given a couple of briefings on my day's interrogations while he was present and listening, and I knew that he appreciated my work. One morning I was called to Division Headquarters and told that the general wanted to get an impression of the area and the population along the Rhine. For that he needed somebody who spoke German fluently, and this "somebody" turned out to be me. During the next few days I came to know better than ever the man who had given me permission to jump into Normandy on D-Day and whom I had admired from the beginning. We rode around the region in a jeep driven by his chauffeur. His adjutant and I sat in the back seat. Whenever Gavin wanted to talk to someone he ordered his driver to stop, told me the questions I should ask, and waited for my translation of the replies. One day Gavin and several of his officers went to swim in a pond close to the Rhine. We all stripped naked and went into the water. Gavin and the officers swam on one side of the pond, the driver and I on the other. I nonetheless could follow much of their conversation, which to my surprise touched on literature. The general also spoke with great warmth about his wife and their children, and I am sure he meant everything he said. But this didn't change the fact that during his time in Europe other women occasionally attracted him, such as Marlene Dietrich. Unfortunately, a lot of nonsense has been written about this by, among others, Marlene's daughter, Maria Riva. Gavin was a man women tended to fall in love with, and he responded in kind.

Early one morning while we were in Cologne I was sent to division headquarters with an official paper and was to wait there for a reply. Headquarters was located in a villa, and in the living room where I was to wait stood a bookcase filled with German books. I picked out one, stretched out on the carpeted floor, and started to read. I heard a door open behind me, a door leading to the room where the general was sleeping. Through that door stepped a good-looking woman in a bathrobe, who, with a "Sorry to disturb you, Sergeant," stepped lightly over my body and disappeared, probably into the bathroom. This polite lady who had stepped out of General Gavin's bedroom was Martha Gellhorn, Ernest Hemingway's third wife, though at the time the two already had been divorced or were in the process of getting a divorce. She was then a war correspondent for *Collier's Weekly*. All this information about her identity I got from a fellow interrogator at Division Headquarters.

We left Cologne on April 29, 1945, and traveled in our trucks northeast toward the Elbe River. Predominantly British troops had already driven the Germans back to the Elbe and beyond, and thus our drive east proceeded peacefully. I had fallen sick, however: my throat was aching and I had a fever and as a result was dropped at a U.S. field hospital in the Lüneburg-Boizenburg-Bleckede triangle, southwest of Hamburg. There I received, around the clock, shots of a recently introduced antibiotic called penicillin. Every few hours I was awakened and had to turn alternately the right or left side of my behind to the orderly in charge, who then gave me an injection. Within twenty-four hours my fever was gone and I was dismissed from the field hospital, even though I could barely talk and my throat kept aching for days to come.

Our troops had already crossed the Elbe on April 30, and the German soldiers surrendered after a very brief show of resistance. When a couple of days later I also approached the Elbe, planning to drive my jeep to Ludwigslust, Mecklenburg, where division headquarters was going to be, Field Marshal Montgomery and generals Ridgeway, Dempsey, and other high-ranking British officers were standing at the ramp of the pontoon bridge, grinning at me as I was about to cross the river in a long line of military vehicles. As a precaution I had left the roof of the jeep up to conceal the German soldier, who by law should have been in a prisoner of war camp, but instead was sitting in the back of my jeep. Thus the big shots only saw our very pregnant German shepherd, who sat next to me on the right front seat and gazed with obvious contentment into the future.

But who was my German passenger? He was a noncommissioned officer of the Wehrmacht who on April 30 had surrendered to us with his group of German infantry soldiers without having fired a shot. The interrogator on our team who questioned him was impressed by his fury as he spoke of the Nazi regime. Thus we decided on the spur of the moment to violate all rules by not sending him off to a POW camp but instead taking him along with us, especially after he had told us that he was a good cook. This, as we found out, was indeed true. "Ludwig," as we called him—it wasn't his actual name—was in civilian life a member of the Hamburg fire department, was married, and had children. When he assured us that he had never been a member of the Nazi Party, we took his word for it and brought him along to Ludwigslust, where division headquarters was set up in the palace of the grand duke, while our team and Ludwig made ourselves comfortable in the house of the local *Ortsgruppenleiter* [local party chief].

The 82nd was one of the few American divisions that crossed the Elbe shortly before the end of the war, and during the first days of May it took roughly 150,000 German prisoners of war, for the most part members of the 21st Army. Its commanding general, Kurt von Tippelskirch, together with his staff, surrendered to General Gavin on May 3 in the Ludwigslust palace. Although the war ended officially on May 8, for us it ended a few days earlier. Our team remained attached to division headquarters, but since we no longer had to interrogate prisoners of war, and since the few roads leading west were crowded with German civilians trying to cross the Elbe before the Russians caught up with them, our team was told to create some order. We tried to direct the troops of the 21st Army likewise toward the Elbe, but the roads were so jammed with civilians that there was no room for the retreating German soldiers.

We told the German troops, who were generally under the command of their master sergeants (officers were held separately under "automatic arrest"), to move into the neighboring woods for the time being, and once in the woods to set up their own provisional prisoner camps. We simply didn't have enough troops to set up the camps for them. We saw to it that they were given enough barbed wire and that a daily meal was delivered to them. The camp was then guarded by our troopers with a machine gun at each of the four corners. For me it was strange to witness this massive collapse of entire German regiments. For us former refugees who had experienced the "Seizure of Power" in January 1933, and for years after (until we emigrated) had been constantly humiliated and threatened, the end of Hitler's war was a gift indeed.

On one of those days in early May, we learned of Hitler's death. Together with a fellow interrogator, Woolf, called "Woolfy," I was standing by a country road on which fleeing German civilians and groups of what was left of the 21st Army moved toward the Elbe, when a passing comrade called to us that Hitler had committed suicide. Close behind us stood a truck loaded with food, cigars, and, above all, alcoholic beverages that we had confiscated that morning from passing German troops. Thus we grabbed a bottle of Aquavit and toasted the dead Führer with the words: "Long may he rot!"

It was on this day that we discovered Camp Wöbbelin, a branch camp [Außenlager] of the Neuengamme concentration camp. Since early 1945 Wöbbelin had served as a transit camp for prisoners evacuated from concentration camps further east and then driven west on death marches. When it became known that the Americans had crossed the Elbe and were on their way to Ludwigslust, the SS guards and *Kapos* (privileged prisoners who acted as low-level functionaries within the camps) took off, leaving the half-starved prisoners to their own devices. Most of these prisoners were too weak to leave the camp without aid. The day after their captors fled, however, three of them succeeded in dragging themselves to Ludwigslust, a few miles away. There they were noticed by some of our troopers when they smashed the window of a clothing store in order to put some civilian clothing on their skeletal bodies in place of the striped camp uniforms they wore. In this manner we heard about Wöbbelin, and shortly after finding the three men, our division sent soldiers to the camp. I drove a jeep there with two of our officers as passengers.

At that time I hadn't heard of the "Final Solution," had never heard the name Auschwitz, and, although I had known since 1933 that concentration camps such as Dachau, Buchenwald, and Sachsenhausen existed, I had remained unaware of the fact that in the course of the war extermination camps had been constructed that served only one purpose—to kill human beings quickly and efficiently by the thousands. For the two officers and me, it was the first German concentration camp we had ever seen. Even before we entered it, an awful smell reached us. Once inside its gates we saw starved and half-starved human beings lying outside a few barracks on ground littered with excrement and rotten remains of food. The smell was so terrible that shortly after entering the camp my two accompanying officers rushed to the fence and vomited.

In the washhouse dead bodies had been stacked like firewood, but sloppily, with many lying on the ground on top of or next to each other, a number of them already in a state of putrefaction. Not far from the washhouse a large pit that had once been a stone quarry was filled with water and quicklime. Into it the corpses of prisoners had been thrown to decompose. The stacked bodies in the washhouse would have ended up there as well if the guards hadn't fled the camp.

The sight of what we encountered made me feel perfectly helpless. Everywhere corpses lay next to still-living prisoners, men whose bodies were reduced to skeletons, who could no longer walk, and whose chances of survival were nil, despite the efforts of doctors and medical attendants, whom General Gavin immediately dispatched to the camp. On his orders, German soldiers, now prisoners themselves, had to fish bodies that hadn't yet completely decomposed from the lime pit so they could be buried. In contrast to the victims of the extermination camps, however, the dead in Wöbbelin hadn't been systematically and routinely murdered. Wöbbelin was a transit camp; a work camp, not an extermination camp. The prisoners originally came from nearly all the European countries Hitler's armies had occupied and were now used for forced labor. A fraction of them were Jews who had survived one or even several extermination camps before coming to Wöbbelin. The prisoners who died at Wöbbelin during the last three months of the war did so because they didn't get enough food and because they were mistreated by the guards and the *Kapos*, many of whom were criminals.

After our visit to the camp, I drove my two badly shocked officers back to Ludwigslust and returned by myself to the village of Wöbbelin to talk with some of its inhabitants. When I asked whether they knew about the camp, which could hardly have been overlooked, I received evasive answers. One person said that he preferred to take a detour rather than to pass by it. Another said that he hadn't been concerned with what might have been going on there. After all, one had enough worries already, and so on. I also insisted on looking in the kitchens of the people I talked to and found no empty pantries. The inhabitants of Wöbbelin hadn't been starving.

Several days later, on May 7, two hundred of the dead were officially buried in the palace garden of the Grand Duke of Mecklenburg in Ludwigslust. I wasn't involved in the preparations for the funeral. A number of adult inhabitants of Ludwigslust, especially those who during the past twelve years had held some official position or had been members of the National Socialist Party, were told to dig the graves. It had been arranged that the entire adult population of Ludwigslust was to walk between the two rows of graves, thereby paying their respects to the victims, each of whom lay wrapped in a white sheet next to his or her grave. A number of captured German officers had been instructed to participate as well. We interrogators were responsible for their appearance and participation. The officers stood with us behind one row of still empty graves, watching silently with ice cold looks. When Ludwigslust's new mayor (the former one had killed himself and his family when he was told that the Americans were approaching) started speaking into a microphone, an officer standing directly behind me lit a cigarette. I told him to stop smoking at once; this was a funeral. He looked down at me and replied that I had no right to give him an order, as I was a mere master sergeant. I repeated my order, but he didn't react. Thereupon I pulled out my pistol and told him very quietly that I would shoot him unless he put out his cigarette immediately. He gave me a hateful look but threw the cigarette down. The other German officers simply stared into the distance.

Soon after this I had another unpleasant experience. One morning somebody told me that a few young women had walked into town from the Ravensbrück concentration camp—of which I had never heard before—all of them sick and in need of care and a place to stay. Accompanied by Woolfy, I walked through town until I found the young women, who appeared to be completely exhausted. Looking around, we saw a roomy villa, walked up to it, and rang the bell. The door was opened by a large and opulent-looking Red Cross nurse who at once wanted to close the door on us. I had, however, already put my foot into the opening. When I told her that we wanted a room for a number of sick women who had just arrived from the Ravensbrück concentration camp, she replied that the house wasn't a hotel. Then she tried again to close the door on us. For the second time within a few days, I pulled out my pistol. I asked her whether she had missed the news that Germany had lost the war and told her I wanted to speak with the owner of the house at once. The owner, having noticed what was going on at his front door, walked downstairs quickly, told the Red Cross nurse gruffly to disappear, and listened to what we wanted. He offered us a nice room for the women and promised to contact a neighbor who was a physician to take care of them. He kept his word.

TOP: *The public funeral of 200 forced laborers from the concentration camp (KZ) Wobbelin at the Schlosspark in Ludwigslust, Mecklenburg, May 7, 1945. The population of Ludwigslust was forced to file past the graves in the Schlosspark.* BOTTOM: *Officers of the 82nd Airborne division at the funeral.*

Shortly after the war officially ended, I asked General Gavin for a few days' leave and the use of a jeep. I wanted to drive to Amsterdam to see whether I could find my family. The general told me that the commanding officer of our team, Lieutenant Becker, had just approached him with a similar request. Becker wanted to go to Rotterdam to look for his sister. Gavin suggested that Becker and I drive to Holland together. Becker, who after Nick Emanuel's death had been appointed his successor, was in his forties. He was not Jewish but had fled his native Austria because he was a Social Democrat. Although he wasn't a paratrooper, we had gotten along well from the start, so I was truly glad to drive to the Netherlands with him. On the instructions of General Gavin, division headquarters gave us a brief official note that I still have today. It said that Lieutenant Becker and Master Sergeant Angress had been instructed to drive to the Netherlands to conduct "official Airborne activities." Once the mission was completed we would return to Ludwigslust. There was no firm date set for our return, nor were any limitations listed for our trip. This was typical of both Gavin's generosity and the confidence he had in us.

As soon as I had received the general's permission, I asked all my friends to give me their latest issue of the cigarettes we all got once a week, and also their "iron rations," for Becker and me and any relatives we found in Holland. It was already well known that the winter of 1944–45 had been a hunger winter for the Dutch and that even in the spring many people didn't have enough to eat. The cigarettes were currency; with them one could buy and pay for anything available. And thus Becker and I left Ludwigslust on Saturday, May 12, in a jeep packed with food and cigarettes. We drove west on the autobahns and, although the many destroyed bridges slowed us down considerably, we nonetheless arrived in Amsterdam by dusk. When Becker asked me where we should look for a place to sleep, I suggested the very elegant Amstel Hotel, which I had heard of but never seen from the inside. We drove there and were assigned a room each—free of charge. We were by no means alone. Canadian army officers whose units had liberated Amsterdam had also discovered the hotel and settled there. Warm water wasn't yet available, but we were given clean sheets, and that by itself made the Amstel luxurious.

The following morning—it was Sunday and Mother's Day—Becker and I planned how we should proceed. He suggested that first I should try to find my family, after which he would drive the jeep to Rotterdam to search for his sister. Thus we left the hotel around 9:00 a.m. and drove to the apartment at Cliostraat 39 in Amsterdam *Zuid* (South Amsterdam), where my parents had lived when I went to the United States and where I had seen them and my brothers for the last time. After I rang the bell a tall, sleepy-looking man in a dressing gown opened the door, stared at me, and asked me in Dutch if I was *mijnheer* Angress. When I nodded, he told me in broken English that the day before my mother had come to his place and had asked him to forward any mail he might receive from her son in the United States to her new Rubensstraat address, where she had been living for a few days. It was nearby. He invited us in for breakfast, but we declined with thanks and at once drove to Rubensstraat.

When we found my mother, she sobbed like a child, and I worked very hard to calm her down. Her appearance frightened me. She had changed from a woman normally weighing between 130 and 140 pounds into a virtual skeleton. She weighed ninety pounds and was so weak she could barely walk. Nevertheless, she immediately introduced me to her neighbors, who had also just reemerged from the underground hiding places in which they had lived for many months. One was a Mr. Rabau, a former member of the Jewish Council, the other was Alice Schwarz Mulisch, the mother of the writer Harry Mulisch, who then was virtually unknown but now is considered one of the greatest postwar Dutch authors. Then I got busy unloading the iron rations from our jeep. I warned my mother and her neighbors to eat slowly and in small doses. Mr. Rabau offered me "salad" that was in fact grass picked from the front yard. I politely declined. After Becker departed with the jeep for Rotterdam, my mother told me that a couple of days ago she had been informed that my brother Fritz was living around the corner. She suggested that we go look for him.

How had Fritz been doing? Thanks to my mother's resourcefulness he had been able, after my father's arrest, to get a job working for the Jewish Council. He had to work in the main building, the Central Office for Jewish Emigration, most of the time. His Gestapo superior, *Oberscharführer* [Technical Sergeant] Stube, needed him there. The work he was doing was sad and, in retrospect, rather disreputable. One of the duties he carried out, every night with other young Jews working for the Jewish Council, and thus also for the SS, was to accompany Jews the SS had rounded up to the Hollandse Schouwburg, a theater in Amsterdam that served as the major collection point for people about to be deported to work camps in the East [*Arbeitseinsatz im Osten*]. Once at the

Schouwburg my brother and his colleagues were responsible for keeping the deportees quiet and preventing them from causing any trouble before they were sent first to Camp Westerbork and from there to Auschwitz, Treblinka, and other extermination camps. But Fritz's work at the Jewish Council and his contact with the SS also saved our mother's life, his own, and that of our brother Hans.

In September 1943 a young Jewish coworker told Fritz very quietly that that evening all the remaining Jews in Amsterdam, including Fritz and his fellow workers, were to be rounded up without exception and deported. The young man had found this out that afternoon when he happened to pass the half-open door of *Hauptsturmführer* [Captain] Ferdinand Hugo aus der Fünten, the local commander of the German Security Police. He overheard Fünten, the person largely responsible for handling the "Solution of the Jewish Question" in the Netherlands, giving the relevant instructions to several high-ranking SS officers. Having received this information from his friend, Fritz went to Stube's office and asked whether he could go home a little early that evening as he wasn't feeling well. Stube granted the request with a wide grin, and Fritz hurried home, informed our mother and our brother Hans, and within a few hours all three had gone underground, each in a different place. This of course was only possible with the aid of the well-organized Dutch underground movement, with which our mother had been in contact for a long time already.

After he went underground, Fritz lived briefly with at least ten different Dutch families and twice was nearly turned over to the Germans by members of the Dutch far-right Mussert group. Fortunately he succeeded in buying himself off with the little money he had, and once with his wristwatch. Finally he found a "permanent home" close to Rubensstraat with a family that ran a pharmacy and took him in as if he were their son. The couple has since died, but Fritz remains friends with their children to this day.

When Mutti and I approached, Fritz was standing at the second-floor window of the pharmacy house, dressed in a suit and tie, watching the girls pass by outside. When I called him from below and he saw me, he nearly fell out of the window. We then went back to my mother's room, where suddenly and unexpectedly our youngest brother, Hans, showed up, bringing a bunch of crumpled flowers because it was Mother's Day. He was also very surprised to see me in Amsterdam so shortly after the end of the war, and as an American soldier at that.

LEFT: *Reunited with Mutti and my brothers on May 13, 1945 in Amsterdam. Fritz is on the left, Hans on the right.* BELOW: *Hans, Fritz, Mutti, and me (Werner), in Amsterdam on May 13, 1945.*

I spent two more days in Amsterdam before Becker returned. He hadn't found his sister in Rotterdam. She had been living in a part of town that was virtually leveled by the Luftwaffe in 1940.

Before Becker and I went back to Ludwigslust, my mother found a temporary place to stay with a very helpful and kind Dutch family. I promised to keep in constant touch with her and to help her as much as possible. I handed Hans all the packs of cigarettes I still possessed and as much money as I could spare—as an iron ration, so to speak, for him, our mother, and Fritz. Then I took him with me to the Amstel Hotel, where we talked about the future of our family. Although Hans was only seventeen and the youngest member of our family, I had full confidence in him and his reliability. Then we drove the jeep through the filthy streets to the home of Anton and Alida Kooij, a working-class couple that had taken him in when he had to go underground in September 1943. Both Anton and Alida had been active members of the Dutch underground and were subsequently honored for it in Holland, the United States, and Israel. In 1950 the Kooijs, assisted by Hans, emigrated to the United States. Today their three children are all successful U.S. citizens. We have never lost touch with them.

But what had happened to Papa? This, of course, had been one of my first questions. Mutti told me that in the late fall of 1942 he had been released from the Brandenburg penitentiary and from there was transported to Auschwitz. She had received this news in a letter sent from Berlin by her sister, Aunt Margot (who was married to an "Aryan"), shortly before Mutti and my brothers went underground. That Auschwitz was a concentration camp I had meanwhile heard. But that it was also a slave labor and extermination camp none of us knew in May of 1945, nor did we know that there had been a "Final Solution." Thus when I found my family, we still hoped that Papa might have survived Auschwitz and sooner or later would return to Holland. Mutti turned to the Red Cross but got no reply.

When we finally heard from the Red Cross much later that Papa was no longer alive, we had given up hope anyway. In the 1990s, acquaintances of mine found a file on my father in the Berlin *Landesarchiv* and copied it for me. He had been convicted of violating the currency law (by taking his money out of the country) and sentenced to the penitentiary. The file reveals that after his release from Brandenburg he was sent to Auschwitz and died there on January 19, 1943. Another document from the Auschwitz *Standesamt* [registry office] adds that "the Jew Angress" died of heart failure.

When Becker and I got back to Ludwigslust, a substantial job was waiting for me—my last one as a soldier—which after having been forced to flee Germany as a "racially inferior subhuman" was for me kind of a symbolic triumph. In a small patch of woods not far from the town of Ludwigslust the British Second Army, under whose command our division then found itself, had built a prison camp for approximately two thousand men of the Waffen-SS. I was given the task of going to that camp with three additional interrogators attached to the Eighty-Second and finding out which prisoners were "sheep" and which were "goats." In other words, we were to learn whether the individuals had joined the Waffen-SS voluntarily when they were called up for military duty or whether they had simply been assigned to the Waffen-SS when the army units in which they served were dissolved as a result of combat losses. Those who had volunteered were "goats"; those who had been assigned were "sheep." The goats were to remain in their present camp until they could be transported to the Baltic Sea island of Fehmarn, where the British wanted to find out which of them had committed war crimes. The sheep were to be transferred to one of the provisional prison camps for Wehrmacht soldiers.

Our team of four interrogators spent several days in that camp, which was fenced with barbed wire and guarded by troopers with machine guns. I led the team, as the senior noncom, and it was the last time I interrogated prisoners of war. I had drafted a harmless-looking, businesslike questionnaire that every SS man had to fill out. Thereafter the prisoners were briefly interrogated individually, except for the officers, who were under "automatic arrest" and thus "goats" anyway. Every prisoner had to present to us his military passbook [Soldbuch] which along with his pay records on pages 4 and 17 listed every unit in which the soldier had served since he had entered military service and for how long. We interrogators sat on tree stumps while an SS-Sturmbannführer [sergeant major] ensured that every prisoner reported to one of us and had his Soldbuch and completed questionnaire ready to present to us. (The sergeant major didn't know that he had been classified as a "goat." He had served as a guard in various German concentration camps even before the war had broken out and had then volunteered for the Waffen-SS.) Needless to say, we didn't tell anyone the nature and purpose of our task.

From the questionnaires we learned that nearly half the camp's prisoners had either been assigned individually to the Waffen-SS as late

Werner Angress, in Ludwigslust, early May 1945.

as the winter of 1944–45 (and a few even later than that) or had been transferred from their former units (Wehrmacht, Luftwaffe, etc.) to the Waffen-SS, among them a considerable number of boys seventeen and eighteen years old.

On one of these days as we questioned the individual prisoners I was facing an SS man whose identification indicated that his hometown was Blankenburg in the Harz. Since I had visited Blankenburg several times as a child (my nanny, Didi, had been born there and her mother still lived there), I asked the man whether the blacksmith Faupel was still shoeing the town's horses. The SS-man stared at me and stammered: "Youuu know Faupel?" Whereupon I replied: "We know more than you could ever imagine." This was of course nonsense, but at that moment I got a lot of amusement out of the situation.

Shortly before we finished our mission at the camp I was approached by a very young SS man. He had been conscripted into the SS early in 1945 and wanted to know whether he and some of his comrades could volunteer to fight with the Americans against the Japanese. At first I was amazed, but then I replied that he and his friends should be grateful that they had survived Hitler's war. And what had the Japanese done to him?

They were, after all, Germany's allies. Hadn't he and his friends seen enough violence and bloodshed? With that I left the camp because our working day was over. The next day he again walked up to me and this time asked whether I could tell what I had said to him to his friends also. So I sat with a dozen young SS men on the ground in the forest and gave them a brief lecture about their notion of fighting the Japanese. When I was through I read understanding on most of their faces.

After we completed our interrogations we had to have the "sheep" transferred to a Wehrmacht POW camp. We stood with our lists at the entrance gate of the SS camp and I called out the names of those who were to be transferred. As soon as the person in question reported to me and presented his identification, he was permitted to leave through the gate to be transported to the camp. Those prisoners who weren't transferred were, aside from the officers, men who had served in the SS-*Totenkopfverbände* [Death's Head units), SS-*Verfügungstruppen* [special reserve units] or SS-*Wachtmannschaften* [concentration camp guard units]. Those staying behind also included non-Germans who had volunteered to serve in the Waffen-SS. They were predominantly Lithuanians, Dutch, and Belgians, as well as others from countries that had been occupied by Germany. Once the transfer was finished I saw that the two groups were nearly equal in number—about one thousand "sheep" and one thousand "goats."

Dead tired but also elated by the thought that my military service was ending and that through it I had been able to contribute something of importance, I left the camp with my three companions and we went back to our quarters. The SS men who stayed behind stared at us grimly. They finally understood why we had been in their camp for nearly a week. And there was also a little sequel to our mission. As I checked the filled-out questionnaires once more, sorting through them late at night before returning them to the divisional intelligence section, I suddenly discovered that I had made a mistake. The questionnaire of a very young SS man who should have been among those transferred to a Wehrmacht camp was in the wrong pile, that of the "goats." He was in the wrong camp. It was already dark, but I decided to get the kid out at once and have him sent to the right camp. I notified the guard whose machine gun was closest to the entrance gate that I would have to go into the camp once more. If I fired my pistol and called to him that I was in danger of being attacked, he should open fire with his machine gun at once. Then he let me into the camp and I woke up the first SS man I saw, sending him off to search for the "lost sheep." This young man appeared after approximately fifteen minutes and said reproachfully: "You've forgotten me!" I replied that obviously I hadn't forgotten him. We left the camp without incident.

During that beautiful spring and summer of 1945, the end of my service in the Army of the United States was gradually approaching. We established contact with the Russians, who met several times with our high-ranking officers in the Ludwigslust palace for drinking sessions while at the same time showing their impatience with us for not yet having retreated westward across the Elbe. During this period we received exciting news from the United States: the War Department had published a chart allowing every soldier to figure out exactly how many credit points he had earned during his service. The decisive factors were length of service, rank attained, and number of decorations acquired for bravery or for being wounded in action. If one's total number of points was higher than eighty-five, one could immediately initiate one's honorable discharge from the service.

I had a little more than ninety points and immediately went to divisional intelligence headquarters, where I told the noncom on duty that I wanted to go home as soon as possible. But there was a bit of a problem. A few days earlier I had been notified that I was being processed for promotion to officers' rank by means of a field commission, a process that required no additional training but was based entirely on merit accumulated during combat. For this I would need two different medical checkups, but our medical service at the moment lacked the necessary instruments. Thus I asked the noncom on duty to scratch my name from the list of those scheduled for field commissions and put me instead on the list of troopers to be sent back to the States for their honorable discharge. I have never regretted this decision. I felt no desire to spend years as an officer in an army occupying the ruins of this country that had once been my home. Second, I hoped to be admitted to a college soon after my return to the States so that I could prepare myself for a profession, although what kind of a profession I didn't know.

Shortly thereafter we found out that the division was about to be transferred to Berlin to take charge of what would become the American sector. We "veterans" looking forward to our journey home and subsequent discharge from the service were to be sent to France to await our transfer back to the United States by boat. Before this could happen, however, we had to take care of "Ludwig," our cook and Hamburg fireman. Our entire time in Ludwigslust he had looked after us, done the cooking, washed our clothes, and kept our house perfectly clean. At dinner he also liked to tell funny stories about Hamburg in the dialect of that city. Now we drew up an "official" certificate stating that he was being sent home to Hamburg "legally" by our division. The stamp with which we made our certificate look official we had temporarily "requisitioned" from our friends in the CIC (Counterintelligence Corps), who like us were attached to the 82nd Airborne. Next we found him a good bicycle, which had belonged to a Waffen-SS prisoner, and civilian clothes from the house we occupied while in Ludwigslust. Then we said goodbye and he biked back to his family in Hamburg. Around Christmas time in Richmond, I received a brief letter from him that I still have today. In it he said that the time with us in Ludwigslust had been the only pleasant experience he'd had during his long wartime service in the German Army.

At the end of June those of us on our way back to the United States returned briefly to Camp Sissonne and from there were taken to Epinal, a small town in the Vosges Mountains. There we were separated from the 82nd Airborne, which was then moving to occupy the American sector of Berlin. My new "military home" was the 17th Airborne, but for administrative purposes only, because that division was still in the United States, had never come to Europe, and merely had a few officers stationed in Epinal to take care of us returnees. While waiting to be processed I decided to take a short leave of absence to visit my family in the Netherlands once more. My brothers had found work and my mother a room with Dutch friends. I gave them more money and promised I would do everything in my power to bring them to the United States. In August, after several boring and inactive weeks, first in Epinal, then in Vittel, we were transported by freight train to Marseille to wait for the boat that would take us back to the United States. Once more we were living in tents, but these were standing on the hills overlooking Marseille and the Mediterranean, a very lovely landscape.

Without my knowing it, on the heights of Marseille the seed of my subsequent career was planted. One day a sergeant from the CIC section of our former division, Thomas C. Davis, who like me was on his way back to the United States to be discharged, asked me what sort of future I visualized for myself. A devout Christian Scientist, Davis had come to like me because, in contrast to the other troopers, I didn't use profanity (another result of Bondy's education, but, alas, not a virtue I would maintain). I replied that I wanted to go to college but still didn't know where, or what I wanted to study. One possibility would be psychology (Bondy was a socioeducational psychologist). However, I told Davis, I wasn't at all certain that an American college or university would accept me as a student because I hadn't graduated high school in Nazi Germany (I left without the proper diploma, the *Abitur*). None of the three universities I had heard of—Harvard, Yale, and Princeton—would be interested in me. Davis then informed me about the G.I. Bill of Rights, which the U.S. Congress had just passed. It entitled war veterans to higher education at the government's expense. This was news to me. Davis then told me that he would contact the school from which he had graduated, Wesleyan University in Middletown, Connecticut, and ask for brochures about their offerings. These arrived before we were shipped back and Davis tried, with very little success, to show me how one could plan one's studies. He promised me that as soon as possible after our discharge he would come to Richmond, where I planned to live, and take me to Wesleyan so I could meet with the school's admissions officer.

We boarded ship sometime in August and moved through the Straits of Gibraltar into the Atlantic and on to Boston, where our arrival was greeted by the sirens of all the boats in the harbor. I was soon back in Maryland at Fort George G. Meade, where my military service had begun four-and-a-half-years before and where it now ended. My career as a soldier lay behind me. What was my reaction to this turning point in my life? On the one hand, I was of course glad that the war and with it the Hitler era had come to an end. On the other hand, I had no idea what my future would look like. With some nostalgia I left behind my military equipment, except for the uniform, and silently said goodbye to the Army of the United States, and of course especially to the 508th Parachute Infantry Regiment in which I had found refuge, a home, and in a way a family. Moreover, this period had finally made a man of me, had given me self-confidence, self-respect, and a sense of a bond to the United States, my new home.

With my discharge papers in hand I took the first Greyhound bus to Richmond. There I was warmly greeted by Bondy, who then showed me the room he had rented for me. He suggested that I apply for admission to the college in Richmond where he was teaching, a branch of the College of William and Mary in Williamsburg, Virginia. I declined because during my frequent leaves to visit Bondy prior to being sent overseas I hadn't gained a good impression of that school. I remembered, for instance, a conversation I'd had with a very kind professor of Anglo-American literature who had never heard of Tolstoy or of *War and Peace*. At the end of September, shortly after I arrived in Richmond, I received a letter from Davis announcing that he was coming to take me to Wesleyan. A few days later he showed up and we drove to New England.

Professor Curt Bondy, in Richmond, Virginia, 1950.

Considering how ignorant I was of the American university system, Davis could have easily taken me to a third-rate institution and I would have followed his advice and never known the difference. As it turned out, Wesleyan was—and remains—one of the most reputable colleges in the United States. Although it is not, strictly speaking, a university, this is what it has called itself since its founding in the mid-nineteenth century. Fortunately, I was accepted. The admissions officer—who a few years later became dean of the law school at Columbia University—was of German descent, although not a refugee like me. I told him quite frankly what a poor academic record I'd had at the Lichterfelder Realgymnasium, and why. But that was nine years before, I told him, and I was confident that in the meantime I had sufficiently matured to work successfully toward an academic career.

A week later I was admitted, although with the stipulation that if my grades weren't good enough at the end of the first semester I would have to leave Wesleyan. Well, at the end of the first semester I was in the top 10 percent of my class, and when I graduated in 1949 with a bachelor of arts degree I did so *magna cum laude*. A few months later I went to the University of California at Berkeley, where I got my Ph.D. in September of 1953. This was eight years after my talk with Davis on the heights overlooking Marseille. Thus began my lifelong occupation as a university professor of European and German history, and as a husband and father. My youth, however, lay behind me.

Epilogue

With the beginning of my studies in the late fall of 1945, the story of my youth ends. It was an eventful period that I am glad today to have survived. When I started to study at Wesleyan I thought at first that I wanted to become a psychologist like Bondy. But two classes in that field of study were enough to change my mind. Largely influenced by a number of outstanding historians and political scientists at Wesleyan—including Sigmund Neumann, Carl E. Schorske, Herbert C. F. Bell, and Norman O. Brown, to name only those most important for me—I started to concentrate on history. Stimulated as I was by them and their classes, I asked myself again and again why the age in which I had grown up had been so chaotic, even brutal. Why had there been two world wars in three decades? And how was it possible that a nation such as Germany, the "country of poets and thinkers," could throw itself into Hitler's arms and allow him to govern it for twelve years? My decision to study history was based on very personal experiences.

I chose to continue my study of history at Berkeley not only because Sig Neumann had advised me to work there with Raymond J. Sontag but also to be closer to my two brothers, who had been living in California since 1947. During my first year at Berkeley I wrote my master's thesis, "The Annexation of Austria in the Spring of 1938," under Sontag's guidance. I then moved on to a Ph.D. dissertation on aspects of communism during the early years of the Weimar Republic, which I completed in 1953. After receiving my doctorate I spent the following year, 1954–55, as a special fellow at Wesleyan. In 1955 I returned to Berkeley, where I had been invited to fill in for a colleague who was leaving the university for one year.

This one year of replacement turned into eight. Just as Gross Breesen under the leadership of Curt Bondy had formed me for a year and a half during my puberty, the time I spent at Berkeley as an assistant professor paved my way into the academic world. Here I began to teach and to publish, wrote my first book, *Stillborn Revolution*, and won a number of lifelong friends among the faculty. But when the Department of History had to make up its collective mind in the fall of 1961 whether to promote me from assistant to associate professor and thus give me tenure, I lost by a few votes. To my surprise this caused some protest among the student body, and I still have letters that some of my students wrote to local newspapers.

After the department had made its decision I still had a year at Berkeley, and I used this time to look for another job. I had the necessary interviews that December at the annual meeting of the American Historical Association, the "slave market," as job seekers referred to it. I was lucky. During the three days of the meeting I had three interviews and received two offers, undoubtedly helped by the fact that Princeton University Press had accepted my book, *Stillborn Revolution*, for publication. I decided to accept the offer from the State University of New York, Stony Brook, a recently created campus on Long Island. There I spent the next twenty-five years of my life.

Although I liked teaching at Stony Brook and today am still in touch with a number of my former colleagues there, my farewell from the university in 1988, when I retired at the age of sixty-eight, was much less emotional than my departure from Berkeley a quarter-century earlier. Not long thereafter I moved back to Berlin, Germany, a move that surprised and even shocked some of my friends in the United States. But during the early 1980s I had started to visit Berlin regularly, usually spending three months of the year with friends there, and in the process also had come to know the Federal Republic generally. To my growing bewilderment, I encountered a population very different from the one I had grown up with, a generation that no longer had anything to do with National Socialism. The streets were no longer dominated by people wearing uniforms. Instead, the young people, at least, wore jeans often slightly torn at the knees, T-shirts with strange advertisements on the chest, and boots or tennis shoes. Some wore rings through their noses, ears, or other parts of their bodies.

The general tone of communication had also changed. The news on

TV and the radio was no longer propaganda declaimed in a loud, hoarse, militaristic voice. Instead, it was offered in the way I had become used to in the United States, that is, unemotionally and factually. When I read about politics in the newspapers I could see to my relief that, at least in the Federal Republic of Germany, the state was run by a democratic government and that this democratic government, in contrast to that of the Weimar Republic, was fully accepted by the majority of the population. This realization—reinforced in 1989 when the Wall fell—was largely responsible for my regular visits to Berlin, which I enjoyed and which also influenced my decision to stay at least for a while in the city of my birth. "At least for a while" has become nearly twenty years!

My circle of friends in Berlin has grown larger and larger. Since a number of them were teachers at local schools, I was asked, more and more often as the years went by, to tell classes about my childhood and early youth in Berlin, and what it had meant as a Jew to go to an ordinary school during the early Nazi period. With time, I began talking about what it had meant to be "different" from my "Aryan" classmates during those years. Initially these talks were restricted to Berlin, but as time passed I received invitations to speak in other West German cities—in the Rhineland, Westphalia, Hamburg, Schleswig-Holstein, Munich, and other parts of the country.

Life in Berlin has become so fulfilling because of my friendships and my activities as a *Zeitzeuge* (literally, witness of one's time). My family and many friends, however, live in the United States, and in order to stay in touch with them I have traveled to America every year, occasionally more than once, and often for quite extended stays. I was married three times and have four children from my first two marriages: two sons from my first, two girls from my second.

Percy, the eldest, who turned fifty-five in December 2009, writes movie scripts for Hollywood with his wife, Livia Linden. They have two children. The oldest, Antonia, was born on October 3, 1990, on the "Day of German Unity," so that I felt compelled to phone the parents and ask them under no circumstances to name the girl "Unity." Today, Antonia and I correspond by e-mail. Her brother, Raphael, two-and-a-half-years younger than she, is as intelligent and likable as his sister.

Dan, my younger son, was born in 1957, is married to Laurie and runs a nationwide medical testing firm. They likewise have two children, Isabela and River. The former was born on November 9, 1996, another

In the front row, left to right: David MacWilliams, husband of Nadine Angress; Nadine Angress; the author, Werner T. Angress; and Miriam Angress. Behind Miriam, right to left, are her husband, Stephen Messer; Mili Rapp (my second wife); and Percy Angress. In the background, left to right: Raphael Linden; Livia Linden; Antonia Angress; Isabela Angress; Laurie Angress; River Angress (peeking out from behind his grandfather's head); Dan Angress.

anniversary that is difficult for a historian of German history to digest (the proclamation of the German Republic, Hitler's attempted Beer Hall Putsch, Kristallnacht, and the East German government's decision to let its citizens travel freely all occurred on November 9; in 1918, 1923, 1938, and 1989, respectively). Miriam, my eldest daughter [born 1965], married to Stephen Messer and an associate editor at Duke University Press in Durham, North Carolina, also writes poetry and plays and is, of my four children, the most artistically inclined. When she was in high school and college she frequently performed onstage—playing the principal character in *Anne Frank*, among other roles—and also sang and played the violin. Finally, my youngest child, Nadine, married to Dave MacWilliams, was born on April 20, 1968. They had a son, Brady, in October 2006. She works for an investment firm. Whenever anyone mumbles regrets that my youngest child was born on Hitler's birthday—and this happens often—I respond that this has been my revenge. For if Hitler had had his way, neither Nadine nor her brothers and sister would have ever seen the light of day!

My children and grandchildren as a group continue a tradition in my family that goes back two centuries. Like their forebears, they have married (or lived with) partners because they loved them, not because of their partners' religious or racial origins. In this they follow an example first set at the beginning of the nineteenth century by my maternal great-great-grandfather. My children, of whom three are married to non-Jews, chose these partners without their religion playing any role at all. And they did so without having any idea that this never-spoken "family tradition" existed.

Today, as my life is drawing to an end, I can look back and say that I have been very fortunate. This was particularly noticeable during the first three decades of my life. This period shaped me, turning me into the kind of Mensch, or human being, that I still am today. I owe who I am to different people who were close to me and who influenced me not just during my youth but also during the rest of my long life. I cannot name them all here, but I want to mention at least Didi, my parents, Curt Bondy, and also, at a later stage, my wives and my children, who have been adults now for quite some time. All of them, those now dead and those still living, I want to thank here with love.

Diary covering jump on Normandy (June 6, 1944)
through time in Prisoner of War camp (June 15–27, 1944)

INTRODUCTORY COMMENTS
(June 1, 1994)

The diary that follows this brief introduction I wrote
clandestinely while I was a prisoner of the Germans from June 15
until June 27, 1944. I have followed the original, handwritten
text except for some additional comments, and a few corrections,
including punctuation, to prevent possible misunderstandings of
the text. Comments and corrections are in brackets. When I wrote
the diary my English, especially in its written form, was rather
deficient. In fact, for all practical purposes I had learned
English only after I entered the army on May 7, 1941, having come
to the United States in November 1939 and for the next year and a
half having lived and worked on a farm in Virginia where we spoke
most of the time only German among ourselves. But despite the
often clumsy diction and the occasionally downright funny
Germanisms I decided to follow the original text as much as
possible.
However, there also exists a typed transcript dating from August
1944. When after Normandy the 82nd Division returned to England in
July 1944 to get ready for its next mission --which turned out to
be the Nijmwegen/Arnheim campaign--I was given a few days leave,
one day of which I spent at the headquarters of the American
interrogators at Broadway, near Stratford on Avon. There I was
asked to give a public talk about my experiences in combat, which
I did. After my talk the commanding officer suggested that I
dictate the contents of the diary, which I had taken along with me
and had mentioned in passing, to a member of his staff, and I did
so. But in the process of typing it this person--undoubtedly with
the best of intentions--made stylistic and other corrections and
also added some information which was not in the original
manuscript but which I had volunteered orally while dictating to
him the contents of the diary. When a copy of this typed version
of my --now edited-- diary was handed to me, it was marked, in red
ink, "SECRET" at the top and bottom of each page. As I did not
like the idea of having in my possession a document I had written
myself marked "Secret," I cut off the top and bottom margins , and
this is the way this particular copy still looks today.

DIARY OF STAFF SERGEANT WERNER T: ANGRESS, 33043440
508th Parachute Infantry Regt., 82 Airborne Division

6 June 44:

Jumped at 0215 at railroad south of Quettehou. Flak had knocked
out the light system in our plane; the pilot gave verbal orders to
jump. I was No.1 man and followed the bundle at [sic!:out of] the
door. Landed softly underneath an apple tree. MG fire behind me.
Cut myself loose, gathered my stuff and tried to assemble on the
stick. I did not find anybody and did not know at the time where I
was. I took off west, thought the DZ [dropping zone] to be in this
direction. After 10 minutes I lost my flashlight. After 15 minutes
I was halted by a German M.G. outpost. Answered in German, pulled
the pin of one grenade, stepped closer (on order of the sentry),

threw and scrammed. [Turning back] I saw the explosion, but one of
them jumped up and fired at me with his pistol. Hit me on the
helmet and made a dent into it. I took cover and waited for him,
but he did not come. I disposed of my MI papers and went on.
Walked till daylight and then hid out. Slept and went on at noon.
At 2000 I came to a village. I asked some Frenchman where I was. I
was in Vidcauville. I ate and slept in a barn. The French woke me
up that night, led me to two more troopers. 101st boys . We slept
in a hedgerow.

7 June 44:

Stayed in bushes all day. Took up communications with other
troopers through the French. Information was uncertain as to beach
landings. At night 3 more troopers joined us. We posted guards and
went to sleep. I assumed command.

8 June 44:

French kids brought us the news that more troopers were around. We
decided to join them at night and to move south in order to make
our lines. We had to change plans because of some uncertain woman
[politically suspect, according to the French] that located us. .
We waited till dark for 2 more troopers but they did not come.

9 June 44:

With French guides we moved off at 0300 towards St. Martin
d'Audeville. Picked up 4 more troopers on the way. Arrived at
hillside, a fair position. We could hear artillery all around
(German). Contacted French Chef de resistance. He did not know of
a beachhead up here, was rather noncommitting [sic!:noncommittal].
Promised, though, to help us. Kids came in the afternoon and told
me that one captain and 11 troopers were around. I went with them
and found the boys. We all ganged up in a new position,. got us a
new 50 cal M.G. at night from one of our bundles which the French
showed us; put it up. [Local] bakery was hit by Navy shelling. No
bread!

10 June 44:

Capt. H[awkins] and [Private] F[ord] joined us in the morning, and
about 21 men and 2 lieutenants came as well, brought our strength
up to 50. One M1 in the crowd, two 03's, otherwise carbines. I
forgot to mention that Sig [former 1st Sergeant from the 377 FA
Bn., 101st Div.], got a top secret German artillery code which I
translated. Sig and 2 others tried to get it through the lines
yesterday but failed to do so. They returned. We stayed all day.
Germans all around. A French blond kid [16 years old] and a
French marine [former French sailor?] told us we were betrayed and
had to move. Kid, F.[ord] and I reconnoitered first, then I led
the men over at midnight.

11 June 44:

All day in new bivouac. [German] gun positions all around. Men are
nervous and hungry. Nothing to eat or drink. We have outposts all
around, see the Germans move. They seem to move north-west.

12 June 44:

No food. Morale bad. Too damned many Germans around our place. We
cannot move around and our nerves are on edge. Officers undecided.
I am for change of place at least. Some men want to take off to
the lines. So far we don't know exactly where the lines are. I try
to comfort a little, suggest move [back] to hillside. All agree.
Blond kid brings food at night. Some disturbance occurred at noon
when one [French] kid reported that 30 troopers were led by our
positions as PW's by 6 Germans. The officers decided not to act. I
think it was right. It would not have helped any. French kids were
kind of pissed off. I explained with some success. At night we
assembled and quietly moved over to the hillside. I led on. We
abandoned M.gun.

13 June 44:

Men's morale better. Front seems close. Plans for making the line
take place. We wait for word from the French as to [the position
of] our lines and maybe a guide. Blond boy has my field glasses,
reconnoiters situation [south of St. Martin]. In the morning we
caught 5 Jerries, all Russians. I interrogate by means of a
dictionary, Sig asks in Polish. We find out the Bn. strength,
their approximate lines. Claim that five bns. hold line, 3
Russian, 2 German. We ask them whether they would lead us through
line. They agree. But I don't trust them.- Blond boy comes at
night with plans, information and a little food. Promises to come
back tomorrow. I get milk and meat in a farm house. Little, but
better than nothing. We distribute the food equally. One of our
boys missing since yesterday. We are 49 men now.

14 June 44:

Hungry again. All day only two buckets of milk for 49 people. Men
get restless. Artillery (American) shells gun positions around us.
Men are bad-tempered and weak and hungry. Captain H. suggests
that he, F. and myself make lines at night to get help. I [being
the only one able to speak French], don't want to leave the boys
now. Think we all ought to try it, in [small] groups, after we
have [the promised] information from French. But no Frenchmen show
up. German activity strong. Heavy fighting south of our positions.
Officers suggest to get rid of the PW's. I talk to Sig. We
disagreed, told that to the officers. After some talks we all
decide to let them live for our own protection [in case of
capture] and for ethical reasons. Finally [sic] What is meant
is: after all], we are Americans.
Tense day. Only milk and one bottle of cognac, no food. We go to
bed in nightmare spirit. Tomorrow we shall have to act. Sig,
Noonan and I go out on food patrol but without success. No sheep
close enough and Jerries in between. I go to sleep in low spirits.

15 June 44:

Men tired, hungry. Hunt for food all day. No success. Only 1
bucket of milk, 1 bottle of cognac. The French are getting scared;
too many Germans around. More promised for tonight. Morale lowest
since we started out. We decide to leave this night, come Hell or
High water. We are weak as shit. I go down at 2000 with 2 men to
secure food. Wait [for our French friends] without luck till 2200.

338 | WITNESS TO THE STORM

Many Germans pass by my hideout. No food. When I reporet to
Captain H., the first shot falls. The Germans have found our
positions and attack. MG's, rifles, hand grenades, 20mm AA guns. I
am wounded in the leg by a hand grenade but throw 2 back, so does
Lt. G.. The Germans withdraw temporarily, come back. [We wounded
their machinegunner]. Some of our men on the edge of of the woods
withdraw slowly. Cliff has a piece of the same grenade that hit me
in his shoulder, is being patched up while under fire. The Jerries
come back, give us cross fire [in pencil: 20 mm AA, mortar] and we
hear them call to get the guns turned around. Then Lt. G. and the
other Lt. decide to surrender 26 men and 2 officers. We give up.
It is 2240 and still light, the rest get away. We are searched,
stripped, insulted. No treatment for Cliff or me. No food.
Transport by truck to somewhere close to Valognes. I pass out for
a few minutes, but made it all right after that. They put us into
a barn. I fall asleep.

16 June 44:

They search us again in the morning and interrogate Cliff and me
without success. A *Sonderführer* wants to know when I jumped. I am
so sorry. They [will] bring us two to Valognes [hospital] where we
are [to be] patched up. Valognes is shot to hell. We are in a one-
horse-cart with hay on. A tough ride. Before, we had our first
decent food since 5 days, warm milk and bread. We eat again in the
Valognes hospital where we find lots of Americans and an American
doctor. The same afternoon they transfer us to the Louis-Pasteur-
Hospital at Cherbourg. 150 wounded Yanks on mattresses, open
wounds, 1 doctor and 6 medics. It looks rather like a mess. I
don't speak German as far as the Jerries are concerned.

17 June 44:

Hospital takes form. Doc Adams organizes, makes casts for the
worst cases. We build beds, double deckers. Treatmen good so far.
Jerry seems to know what the score is. Food "German." Too little
and too late, and too bad tasting. My wound gets the first good
dressing.

18 June 44:

All day hospital. The Germans blow [up] the docks, time it with
artillery fire to cover it up. Every time they blow something up
they let their guns go off. A Frenchman told me that the peninsula
has been cut at Carentan. The Jerries are in the trap-and they get
polite. They turned over one ward to Doc Adams, let him do all he
wants to do. Some cases are pitiful. Our boys are badly cut up.
All kinds of wounds and fractures. And insufficient supplies and
medical aid. 2 boys lost their leg today: gangrene.-All beds are
up.

19 June 44:

I was made mess sergeant. A nasty job with German rations.
Distribution is tough, cooperation not too hot. My KP's are doing
a swell job, but their rewards are usually curse words and
insults. We grit our teeth and work on. Our men are patients and
we have to overlook a lot. My leg heals all right. It is a clean
wound, no complications. Luck, I guess.- In the evening a German

doctor goes through, checks the wounds and marks down the names of the light[ly] wounded. My name is among those. I guess we'll move out to a P.W. camp.

20 June 44:

After breakfast they call the roll of the names taken yesterday. We get ready to move out to a P.W. camp. They load us in[to] a truck and move us. Within 10 minutes they are lost. We backtrack and drive along a road when our planes come over, strafing. The guards get frantic, jump off the truck and take cover under the door entrances of the houses. We ask them whether we could dismount (Vrondel [?] is our interpreter) but they refuse. We hope for the best and wait. Luckily, nothing happens. We drive on. The planes did not cover our road. At the P.W. camp we meet old friends, the rest of the bunch from the hillside with exception of Capt. H [awkins] and about 8 men, and our *Sonderfuhrer* and lieutenant who came up from Valognes. We start shooting the bull, exchange our stories. Sig is there, grinning and all right. And Ford. In spite of the situation we are glad to see each other. Jim is with them too. The guards are decent 4 F's, full of Saxonian [sic!] dialect. We have a barrack to ourselves and beds with many fleas in. I cannot sleep at night but scratch, scratch, scratch.

21 June 44:

After breakfast we get our first shock. Our artillery starts shelling, the shells landing 300 yards from the camp. We scram for cover. So do the guards. Half of our men run to the road, take cover in a ditch. The rest duck into a little ditch inside the camp. The *Herr Sonderfuhrer* and lieutenant take off, the guards abandon their posts, leaving their weapons behind, and that is it. One of our lieutenants starts negotiating about moving to a safe place. The Germans call Division. Yes, we are to move. Where? To a cave. We move out. All the wounded limp behind. It looks terrific. The cave is taken by French civilians. I talk to them, get some dope about the situation and more P.W. camps up on Cape Hayne [or:Hague]. But this place does not suit our guards, so we have to move again. The new place is taken by a German engineer outfit. So, back to the first cave it goes. There we bed down, but after I am just fairly comfortable we get orders to move back to the camp. We cuss, but it does not help. I sleep in the flea circus for a 2nd night. We sleep, though, for we are tired from marching around.

22 June 44:

We move out in the morning. The wounded are to come with the kitchen. We march through Cherbourg-- 3 hours. I observe a lot of confusion, lots of destruction, and damned good camouflage. Every 2nd car we meet sports a red cross. The town seems to consist of the Medical Corps only. We get shelled again on the road. The French give us cigarettes and cookies, give us the V for Victory sign. Our guards bicycle beside us. After 3 hours we finally arrive in [sic] a farmhouse, move into a barn. I see lots of Jerries around, Infantry. I don't like it. My dislike gets a basis [sic!] when I learn that we are close to a rear CP. After half an hour we have our first dive-bomber attack. They pinpoint-bomb, and we just sit and watch the ceiling. A house 250 yards to the right,

where some German officers are eating, gets hit and burns. So do
the officers. In spite of the danger we welcome the planes. The
Jerries get kind of restless. After the first wave of planes comes
a second. They strafe and dive-bomb. We cannot stick our nose out
of the door. Finally they decide to move us again and we wind up
in a Division CP (709th, I think), in a tunnel. We live by candle
light, and the Jerries live with us. Our troopers sit down in
their staff cars, but a German captain chases them out, raising
hell. We get a meal and go to bed, dead tired.

23 June 44:

In the morning they asked us for 30 volunteers to go to Cherbourg
into the hospital and move mattresses and build beds. I go with
them. Our artillery falls heavy. The town is smoking, the Germans
look disturbed. I am detailed with Sig and 3 more boys to go to an
underground arsenal to get mattresses. On the way we meet German
troops move from one side of the town to another [sic!:the other],
carrying personal stuff and their arms. Everything looks
disorganized, disturbed. We sweat out our artillery. In the tunnel
are troops, French civilians and "Organisation Todt" men. Outside
fall the shells, inside sit the troops, drinking cognac and
cursing the war. One [German] sergeant falls in his platoon with
orders to go to the front, which constitutes by now the outskirts
around the town. Their faces look sad and discouraged. No superman
stuff. After 15 minutes the platoon is ready to move out, but
suddenly a shell bursts right in front of the entrance of the
tunnel, and the platoon dismisses itself to the rear end of the
tunnel. We laugh and get dirty looks. We still laugh.
We work all afternoon. Some close calls on the roads, but we seem
to be lucky. At 2000 we are through. All of us move to the
hospital entrance, stand around in the hall. We want to go back to
our cave. The Jerries have their guns posted all around the
hospital- and then they complain that our artillery is shooting at
the hospital. Suddenly a shell bursts right in front of the
entrance. The concussion throws us around, I hear yells and cries
and moaning. It is dark and dusty. The walls shake. Boom, a second
shell, further down the road. The panic is terrible. French,
Americans, Germans scramble into the hospital. The [American]
troopers are the first ones to get their nerves back. We carry in
the wounded. 5 of us got it, 4 pretty bad. The "Dago" moans and
cries. One kid has a piece of shrapnel in his head. All of us who
are all right help to get the wounded to the shelter. No light. I
holler for candles in all 3 languages. Doc Adams answers. He takes
charge, and things quieten down. The Jerries look like mad, stare,
are not to be used for anything. The Yanks help to carry in their
wounded, and the French [do so as well]. Then one Frenchman grabs
my arm, tells me that out in the street is a dead American. I go
back through the hospital. The entrance hall looks wild. I see
that a stone wall against splinters saved our lives. Out there
lies Sig. His head and breast are bloody. He is dead. He was with
us from the beginning. I take his tags [dog tags] and report to
Doc Adams. We take care of Sig- the Skipper, Doc and myself. A
French chaplain takes his belongings. Later on we load him and the
dead Jerries on a truck. We have to hurry because the shells are
still falling. The boys look bad. Nervous and tired. But they keep
their chins up. Compared with the Jerries we are the victors, they
the prisoners. We go back as soon as the first pause sets in. The
ride home is a nightmare, but we make it. We lost a good buddy and

[a] hell of a good trooper. It was a bad day. We go to sleep, but most of us stay awake for a long time.— Get more PW's from 4th and 79th [U.S. infantry divisions].

24 June 44:

We stay in the cave most of the day, sleeping. Outside the shells are falling. We don't care anymore. We hope to see our troops soon. In the afternoon come orders to move. We form [ranks], move off into Cherbourg. The town is burning. The Germans look at us, holler:" Tomorrow we shall be your prisoners!" We know. They walk us to the arsenal, right at the Fort [Fort Homet?]. After lots of confusion they finally find a bunker for us, with many rooms, running salt water, light. A Dutch outfit must have been in there before. Many Dutch names on the wall, and the name "Holland." We make ourselves at home and clean up, shave, eat the rations the guards give us. The treatment gets better and better. They want us to be their friends when the Yanks come. The Jerries blow the docks. We sleep well, on mattresses, 10 feet underground.

25 June 44:

Spend the morning in the bunker. The *Sonderführer*, our boss and interrogator, also showed up again yesterday, challenges me to play chess with him. He does not know that I am an American interrogator or that I speak German. I concentrate hard and beat him, my first chess game I have won for months. I get a kick out of it. He feels so defeated anyway. He grabs my hand and shakes it. They believe in etiquette and a stiff upper lip, the German officers. [The main reason why I won was due to the heavy American artillery bombardment that kept shaking the bunker and that worried the *Sonderführer*. He kept asking me whether I thought that the ceiling would hold if it were hit. My reply was that, yes, as long as only 105 caliber shells were fired, the ceiling would hold; but if they started firing 155's, it would not hold. He kept on watching the ceiling while I watched the chess board. This addition made from memory on June 1, 1994].
In the afternoon we move again, out to a bunker at the Fort. They blow up the buildings around us, and our old bunker. We move in groups, carry our mattresses and blankets. Suddenly the shells fall again, and one building to our left blows up. The Jerries don't care who is around. We drop our mattresses and take off. The road looks like a blown up hospital, full of litter and mattresses. Ford and I decide to walk slow[ly] again and look around. The Jerries seem to have disappeared, but their equipment is everywhere. We move into our new bunker, right besides the Fort. The German guards are nervous, ready to give up. They talk among each other, say that 3 E-boats with officers left last night to sneak through to France [thus, a part of France still in German hands on that date], that one was sunk. The general claims that he has orders from Berlin to hold to the last man. Nobody wants to be the last man. They throw everything into the lines they have, even *Marine* soldiers [navy personnel]. We hear small arms fire all day and night right outside the harbor. Shells and bombs are dropping in the town. The harbor installations are burning. It's a grand sight in spite of the situation. We go to sleep, hoping that tomorrow the Yanks will be here.

26 June 44:

We sweat it out. Firing goes on all night and day. Small arms and shelling. We wait in the bunker, drink the general's champagne which the guards snatched and smoke his cigars. No more electricity. We have candles burning. Now and then a dock blows up. We wait for the Yanks to come in. The Fort is hidden by black smoke from burning oil. The *Sonderführer* was around, wringing his hands, calling now and then:" Oh, why don't they give up?!" The guards are nearly as eager to surrender as we are to see our troops. They ask us in detail about our PW camps. Vrondel wants to make the general surrender by handing him a fairy tale. He fails, though. We go to bed, still prisoners, but with the hope in our hearts that tomorrow it will be over. Tomorrow is my birthday, and I want to be a free man again.

27 June 44:

At night I have the G-I's. When I attend to urgent business early in the morning everything seems quiet. Church bells ring, and a radio seems to broadcast in the distance, even though we cannot understand it. Then all at once a tremdous explosion, a burst of smoke, stones and debris. 150 yards from us the Germans blow up a building. I leave my pants down, try to make the bunker. A stone hits me at the arm. I barely make it. Inside everybody is on his feet, trying to get in[to] his shoes. But it quietens down soon. All morning we wait. The rumors are flying thick and wild. There is supposed to be a surrender at 12 [noon]. We wait. The Jerries start throwing away their stuff. Ford and I pack our stuff, reconnoiter the German quarters. Some boys have already pistols promised. I guess we are too late. At 20 minutes to 12 an American officer with a white flag enters the Fort. We can see him. Lt. S. [later] told me the story: he and V. walked out of the bunker and followed the American officers. Inside the Fort all guns were already blown up. The German officer in charge (I don't know who it was) refused to surrender. Then a colonel of the [American] 9th Division came in. His men rounded up the German e[nlisted] m[en] and he ordered the Germans through an interpreter to surrender. The Germans refused. The colonel said he would send in his men with fixed bayonets. Then the Jerries surrendered. Cherbourg's last Fort fell after a short argument at 1210.
We run out of the bunker to welcome the first doughboy from the 9th. We nearly miss him. The German guards line up outside after waving us "*Auf Wiedersehen!*" and are marched off. The *Sonderführer* is in charge. He looks sad and glad at the same time. Most of them are glad it's over. We grab German weapons and supplies, then leave our prison-arsenal. Destruction all around. Dead Germans, dead cows, helmets, cars, bicycles. Ford gets himself a bike and an alarm clock plus a bottle of champagne. I have a bottle of wine. We wait for transportation back to our units. It is time to say good-bye. We were a mixed bunch of men, troopers from both the 82nd and 101st, and men from the 4th and 79th. We have gone through quite a lot together. We say good-bye to each other and we are sorry to part. Most of them were damned good buddies. The trucks take us through Cherbourg and south toward the Douve river. In the evening I rejoin my outfit, glad to be home again.

APPENDIX 2

Travel Authorization into Holland by
Major General Gavin, November 21, 1944

HEADQUARTERS 82D AIRBORNE DIVISION
Office of the Division Commander

APO #469, U. S. Army,
11   May   1945.

SUBJECT: Travel orders

TO   : Enlisted man concerned.

1. M SGT WERNER T ANGRESS 33043440 IPW Team 43 will proceed from this Headquarters on or about 12 May 1945 to THE HAGUE HOLLAND on temporary duty in connection with airborne activities and upon completion thereof will return to his proper station.

2. TDN. Travel by government motor vehicle will be utilized.

3. Authority: Paragraph 13 Corps Directive Number 12 Headquarters XVIII Corps (Airborne) dated 21 November 1944.

BY COMMAND OF MAJOR GENERAL GAVIN:

HENRY McDERMOTT,
Capt., A. G. D.,
Asst. Adj. Gen.

Article from the *Richmond Times-Dispatch*, June 4, 1945

Richmond Times-Dispatch, Monday, June 4, 1945   5

Richmond Sergeant Writes Dr. Curt Bondy Of Mass Burial of Internees in Germany

Writing of the funeral of 200 concentration camp internees who were buried in the middle of a German town, Master Sergeant Werner T. Angress, of Richmond, tells of the German population and army officers who were forced to file through the lines of dead by the Americans in a letter received by Dr. Curt Bondy, professor of psychology at the Richmond Professional Institute, from "somewhere in Germany."

Sergeant Angress, who recently received the Bronz Star for meritorious service in Normandy, volunteered to jump with the 508th Parachute Infantry on D-Day as a prisoner of war interrogator. His citation states, "At all times Sergeant Angress carried out his work in a superior manner and was highly aggressive, showing a high degree of initiative in gaining information from prisoners of war that proved valuable to the tactical operations of the organization."

One of the 26 boys who came to this country as refugees from Germany five years ago, Sergeant Angress volunteered for military service in the American army the following year. Twenty-two of the 26, of which Dr. Bondy was in charge, are now in the armed forces. Upon coming to this country the group of young refugees lived on a farm, Hyde Farmlands, near Burkeville, Virginia, purchased for them by a Richmond man.

Sergeant Angress's account of the funeral which took place May 7 in the public square at a German town follows:

"Today we buried the dead that we found in the concentration camp right outside of our town. We buried them in the public square of the town, right opposite the castle of the Granddue, and the whole population as well as the captured German generals and higher ranking officers had to attend.

"But before I go into details I would like to tell you a few words about the concentration camp. We found it outside of the town, along side the road, in a wood clearing. It is just a small camp, with about 10 buildings behind the usual barbed wire, and it housed from 200 to 300 slave laborers. The sight was the most horrible one I have ever seen. The place was filthy and smelled of decay, of dead bodies and foul turnips; dead bodies and foul turnips were gnawed on turnips were lying around on the barrack floors, in addition to the filth and dead bodies of the inmates. You found them all over the place; piled up, head to feet; in the latrine, in the so-called wash room, in the barrack corners. Two hundred of them lay there, unburied, simply starved to death. Their limbs, partly fallen off their bodies already, were as thin as sticks. It was a repulsing, sickening sight. Their bodies were shrunk, only bones and skin And over a thousand more bodies were being dug out of mass graves by the German population right then, while I was up there. But six kilometers away were people living in a town as good as you can imagine, a bit rationed but not suffering, in nice houses, with dogs and cats that had to be fed and with good clothes to wear. I found several survivors in the camp yet, and talked with them. They still wore their striped suits, they looked more dead than alive, and their faces regardless of age, looked old. They showed me tattoo numbers which were tattooed on their arms; they told me of their suffering. And even if they had not done so the sight out there talked louder than these people could. I don't want to tell you any more. It is one dirtspot in the history of Germany which will never be washed off.

Mayor Makes Speech

"The burial ceremony was rather impressive. The population was assembled and had to file through the lines of dead which were placed beside their individual graves. The faces were uncovered, the rest of their bodies, was wrapped in white sheets which had to be furnished by the population. We soldiers stood alongside the graves behind the white crosses. Men, women and children walked through, their heads bare, their faces sad or sullen. Some of them refused to go. We made them go. Then all of them went back to their places opposite the cemetery and the mayor of the town made a little speech. He said that it was up to the people of X to wash off this undoing and that all decent people and Christians were shocked and sorry. He looked pathetic in his white hair and his black top hat, talking into the loudspeaker which was held by one of our officers. After that the dead were lowered into their graves, while the band played funeral music. I forgot to mention the group of German officers led by five generals, who stood in front of the population at rigid attention, with faces of stone, and stared into nothing. I would have liked to know what they thought. Their faces betrayed nothing. In front of them, facing the row of graves, stood our two generals and their staff.

"When the bodies were lowered, the chaplains said prayers for the Protestant, Catholic and Jewish victims, and one chaplain read a speech in German and English, telling once more the story and explaining why these people were buried in the middle of the town. He said that it was the crime of every German, actually committed by cruel guards, or indifferently tolerated by the people. He warned the people never to allow again any party or any man to arise and do things like that. He appealed to the human decency to atone for these crimes.

"Our national anthem followed. We saluted, and so did the German officers while the tune was played. Then the bugles sounded taps.

"That was the end of the ceremony. Thus were buried 200 human beings, Dutch, French, Poles, Russians and Jews, buried by their former oppressors, and by the liberating Americans, who had come too late for them, in the middle of a German town."

CPSIA information can be obtained
at www.ICGtesting.com
Printed in the USA
BVHW080955010419
544227BV00019B/796/P